Praise for Tiya Miles's *The Dawn of Detroit*

"Beautifully written and rigorously researched. . . . Throughout this riveting text, personal and family stories illustrate and advance a narrative that rewrites our understanding of slavery in the making of the United States."

—2018 Frederick Douglass Book Prize Jury

"A book that will reorient the focus of early slavery in North America westward to include Detroit as central to any understanding of the tangled relations of French, English, Euro-Americans, Indians, and Africans on the frontier from the 18th to early 19th century. A necessary work of powerful, probing scholarship."

—*Publisher Weekly* (starred review)

"Miles's account of the founding and rise of Detroit is an outstanding contribution that seeks to integrate the entirety of U.S. history, admirable and ugly, to offer a more holistic understanding of the country."

—*Booklist* (starred review)

"If many Americans imagine slavery essentially as a system in which black men toiled on cotton plantations, Miles upends that stereotype several times over."

—*The New York Times Book Review*

"New, groundbreaking history . . . that does for Detroit what the Works Progress Administration and the Federal Writers' Project slave narratives did for other regions."

—*The Washington Post*

"Tiya Miles is among the best when it comes to blending artful storytelling with an unwavering sense of social justice."

—Martha S. Jones in the *Chronicle of Higher Education*

"A book likely to stand at the head of further research into the problem of Native and African-American slavery in the north country."

—*Kirkus Reviews*

"'There is currently no historical marker acknowledging slavery in Detroit—revealing that people were bought, sold, and held as property . . . ' Tiya Miles tell us in her rich account, detailing Native American and African American slavery in that city and the surrounding countryside. *The Dawn of Detroit* is a brilliant telling of chattel bondage's long and twisted history and the evolution of race relations in the . . . City on the Straits."

—Ira Berlin, Distinguished University Professor, University of Maryland, and author of *Many Thousands Gone: The First Two Centuries of Slavery in North America*

Awards and Prizes

2018 Frederick Douglass Book Prize Co-winner

2018 Hurston/Wright
Legacy Award (Nonfiction) Winner

2018 American Book Award Winner

2018 Harriet Tubman Prize Finalist

2018 Merle Curti Social History Award Winner

2018 James A. Rawley Prize Co-winner

Winner of the James Bradford Biography Prize

2018 John Hope Franklin Prize Finalist

Longlisted for the 2018 Cundill History Prize

A *New York Times* Editors' Choice Selection

A *Booklist* Editors' Choice Selection

A Michigan Notable Book

Tiya Miles is the recipient of a 2011 MacArthur Foundation "genius grant" and is a professor of history and Radcliffe Alumnae Professor at Harvard University. She lives in Cambridge, Massachusetts.

Also by Tiya Miles

Ties That Bind: The Story of an Afro-Cherokee Family in Slavery and Freedom

The House on Diamond Hill: A Cherokee Plantation Story

The Cherokee Rose: A Novel of Gardens and Ghosts

Tales from the Haunted South: Dark Tourism and Memories of Slavery from the Civil War Era

THE DAWN OF DETROIT

A CHRONICLE OF SLAVERY AND FREEDOM IN THE CITY OF THE STRAITS

Tiya Miles

NEW YORK
LONDON

First published in the United States by The New Press, New York, 2017
This paperback edition published by The New Press, 2019
Distributed by Two Rivers Distribution

ISBN 978-1-62097-481-0 (pbk)

LIBRARY OF CONGRESS CATALOGING-IN-PUBLICATION DATA

Names: Miles, Tiya, 1970- author.
Title: The dawn of Detroit : a chronicle of slavery and freedom in the city of the straits / Tiya Miles.
Description: New York : The New Press, 2017. | Includes bibliographical references and index.
Identifiers: LCCN 2017018381 (print) | LCCN 2017031043 (ebook) | ISBN 9781620972328 (e-book) | ISBN 9781620972311 (hc : alk. paper)
Subjects: LCSH: Detroit (Mich.)--History--18th century. | Detroit (Mich.)--History--19th century. | Detroit (Mich.)--Race relations. | Slavery--Michigan.
Classification: LCC F574.D457 (ebook) | LCC F574.D457 M55 2017 (print) | DDC 977.4/3401--dc23
LC record available at https://lccn .loc .gov/2017018381

The New Press publishes books that promote and enrich public discussion and understanding of the issues vital to our democracy and to a more equitable world. These books are made possible by the enthusiasm of our readers; the support of a committed group of donors, large and small; the collaboration of our many partners in the independent media and the not-for-profit sector; booksellers, who often hand-sell New Press books; librarians; and above all by our authors.

www.thenewpress.com

Book design and composition by Bookbright Media
This book was set in Palatino and Engravers' Oldstyle

Printed in the United States of America

For the renegades closest to my heart: Sylvan David Gone, Erik Miles, Seante Lackey, and Fred Johnson; and in loving memory of Adrian Gaskins

Hence then, commences the history of Detroit, and with it, the history of the Peninsula of Michigan. . . . No place in the United States presents such a series of events, interesting in themselves, and permanently affecting. . . . Five times its flag has changed, three different sovereignties have claimed its allegiance, and since it has been held by the United States, the government has been thrice transferred; twice it has been besieged by the Indians, once captured in war, once burned to the ground. Identified as we are with its future fate, we may indulge the hope, that its chapter of accidents has closed, and that its advancement will be hereafter uninterrupted.

—*Governor Lewis Cass, State Historical Society of Michigan Inaugural Address, 1828*

The story of the new world is horror, the story of America a crime.

—*Jodi A. Byrd,* The Transit of Empire: Indigenous Critiques of Colonialism, *2011*

Contents

THE DAWN OF DETROIT

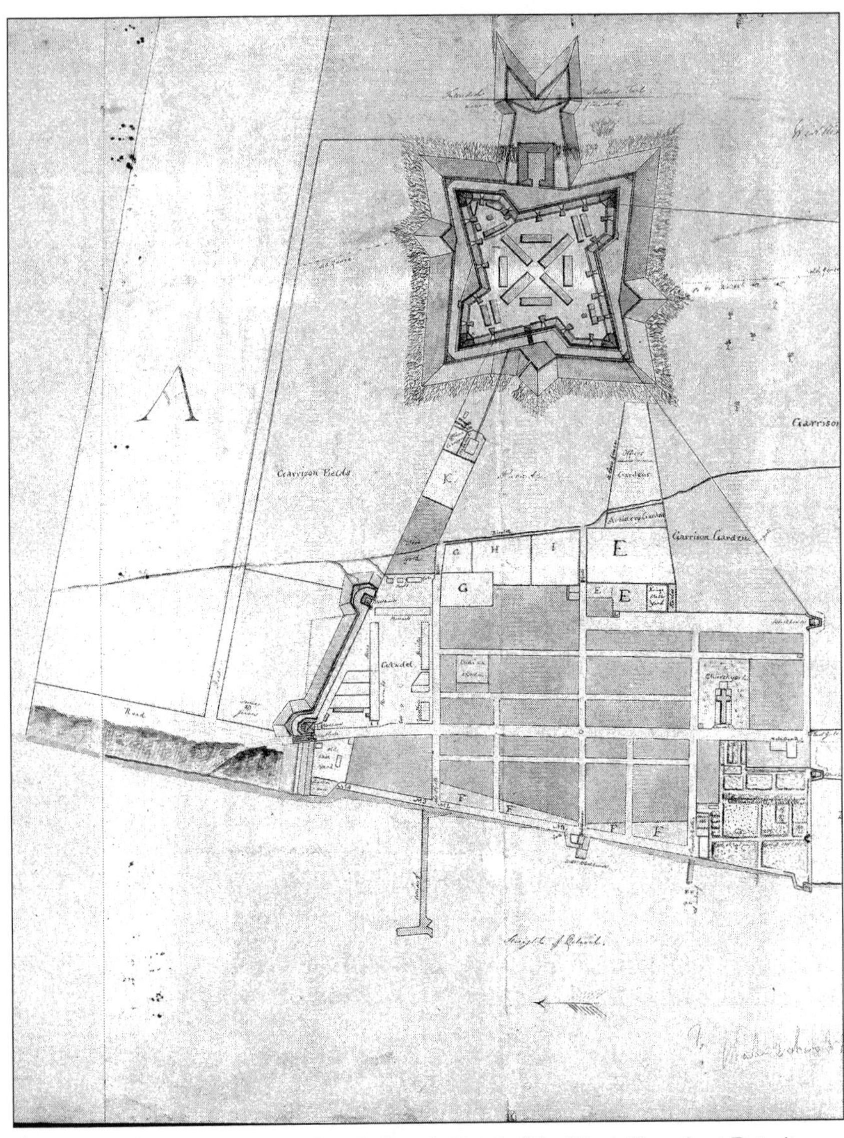

Captain D.W. (David William) Smith, *Rough Sketch of the King's Domain at Detroit*, 1790. Courtesy of the Clements Library, University of Michigan. This rare, hand-drawn map of Detroit in the British period was identified and authenticated in 2016. Clements Library associate director and curator of maps Brian Leigh Dunnigan has pointed out that key features distinct to this map include the depiction of private landholder "encroachments" within the town walls. Landholders identified by Dunnigan thus far include the prominent slaveholders William Macomb (letter A), John Askin (letter D), and Captain Henry Bird (letter E). The map also shows the rivulet, Savoy Creek, flowing behind the settlement and the abatis, intertwined tree branches used as a defensive barrier, around the fort at the rear. Smith, the creator of the map, expressed support for slavery.

Introduction: The Coast of the Strait

It has risen from the ashes. We hope for better things.

—Seal of the City of Detroit, 1827

Detroit is a city of ash, the charred remains of a burning. For centuries the fire has raged, consuming lives, igniting passions, churning up the land and animals, swallowing humans whole. The burn that Detroiters feel—that the nation uncomfortably intuits as it looks upon the beleaguered city as a symbol of progress and of defeat—traces back through distant time, to the global desire to make lands into resources, the drive to turn people into things, the quest for imperial dominance, and the tolerance for ill-gotten gain. We attach a series of words—coded and clean—to the residue left behind by that fire: racial tension, white flight, industrial decline, financial collapse, political corruption, economic development, even gentrification and renaissance. But the challenges faced by the residents of this city, and increasingly by residents of all of our industrial urban places, are not neat or new. Deep histories flow beneath present inequalities, silent as underground freshwater streams. The racial and class divisions that set groups against one another are old, aquatic creatures. We sometimes sense this. We sometimes feel the nearness of history—the imprint of people acting and events unfolding in the past. Beneath the popular culture chatter that calls Detroit a "ruin," grotesquely suggesting some natural process of decay at work, we can dip our fingers into the water and touch the outlines of an alternate, historical dimension. In this dimension, the firestorm that engulfed Detroit was not the result of inevitable decline brought on by invisible market shifts akin to the force of gravity. In this dimension, Detroit is not the scene of natural disaster, but rather the scene of a crime—a crime committed by individuals, merchant-cabals, government officials, and empires foaming at the mouth for more. This book reconstructs that crime, tracing it to the intertwined theft of bodies (both human and animal) and territories (both lands and waters) that we call slavery and settlement. The perpetrators are not always evil, the victims not always noble, and, at times, they join forces for reasons admirable or lamentable. This is the human relational muck of how a great city—how a great nation—came to be, pushed from the guts of an all-consuming capitalism.

Detroit was born of the forced captivity of indigenous and African people and the taking of land occupied by Native people. Captivity and capture built and maintained the town, forged Detroit's chin-up character as a place of risk and wild opportunity. Detroit was formed not only by the labor of enslaved people on indigenous lands, but also, and as importantly, by what those enslaved people came to signify for the identity of the city. It was ultimately through the dauntless acts of fugitive slaves, and the changing ideas about slavery held by free residents of the working and political classes, that Detroiters began to perceive themselves as distinctly American. Black and red people traversing the river between the United States and Canada compelled Detroiters to confront their long-standing, multinational practices of slaveholding. The presence of renegade bondspeople from British Canada tested Michigan's limits on the legalization of slavery and led Detroit dockworkers, hatmakers, and sailors of European descent to threaten their own lawmakers if they returned runaway slaves. By the end of the War of 1812, the second war for U.S. independence, Detroit was an American metropolis that slavery had made.[1]

This is a chronicle of Detroit, an alternative origin story that privileges people in bondage, many of whom launched gripping pursuits of dignity, autonomy, and liberty. To tell the history of the dawn of Detroit with a focus on the experience of enslaved people reveals yet another chapter in the larger narrative of a national truth: America was a place ridden by slavery, where chains stretched as wide as the midnight sky, trapping diverse peoples in an ironclad hold that took generations and bloodshed to break. Even in Detroit, in the North, and in Canada—places that we like to imagine as free—slavery was sanctioned by law and carried out according to custom. And where there was slavery, there were efforts to wrest away indigenous territory, the lands from which elites could draw wealth by means of exploited slave labor. Slavery and colonialism were bundled together in Detroit as in the rest of North America, creating a complex ecosystem of exploitation and resistance. The Ojibwe historian Michael Witgen has succinctly observed about the Great Lakes region: "The two primary sources of wealth for Europeans who came to North America during the seventeenth and eighteenth centuries had been the profits made from this vast inland trade, and land." He need only have added "slaves" in order to complete this catalogue. Productive plots, beaver pelts, black and red bodies—all were viewed as natural resources ripe for commodification.[2]

Remapping Detroit

Please rip your mental map in half and turn it upside down—the one that sees Detroit in Michigan, Michigan in the Midwest, the Midwest as fly-over country in the United States of America. That is a modern map, developed long after Detroit was settled by Euro-Americans and the grinding process of westward expansion gave some Americans a new West from which to turn back and view a "Middle West" and an "Old Northwest." In the 1600s, *Bkejwanong* (an Anishinaabe place name) was a hunting ground and transitional village site for the many indigenous groups who peopled the lake country, expertly moving across this wetland terrain to suit their subsistence needs from season to season. At the end of that century, French explorers associated this spot with another name, Détroit, or "strait," a narrow channel joining two bodies of water. It was the French who built the first permanent European post here—to foster the lucrative trade in fur-bearing animal skins. Detroit was therefore seen for over a century by Europeans and Americans alike as a Francophone place, as a subordinate and marginal "dependency" of French Canada to the north, and then of British Canada following a French military defeat. It would take two wars between Great Britain and the fledgling United States before the American claim on Detroit, and on the loyalty of Detroiters, was actualized. When Detroit became American in 1783 (or 1796, or 1815—the date was always in motion and a French elite maintained economic and social influence well into the 1830s), it was located in the "West," a frontier post not yet matched by Chicago (in the Anishinaabe language, *Chigagou,* "the wild-garlic place"), let alone cities on the horizon of that mangled mental map. A linchpin port town in the Great Lakes by the mid-1700s, Detroit is the second oldest French settlement in what is now the United States, with roots dating back before New Orleans and St. Louis.[3]

The strait that inspired Detroit's first European name stretches thirty-two miles in length and shelters twenty-one islands. This waterway, now the Detroit River, was the hinge that joined the Lower and Upper Great Lakes, a "junction of the continent's major watersheds" that served as a hub of ancient indigenous travel and trade.[4] Centuries later, these massive lakes so central to the continent would form the heart of America's Old Northwest Territory. Water was the earth's blood pumping to and from that heart, making all life and the growth of human societies possible. *Le détroit* joined Lake Erie to the south with Lake Huron to the north by way of the relatively delicate Lake St. Clair. Narrowing above Lake Erie and again below Lake Huron, the strait could duplicate itself, being first one channel, and then two. This waterway, fanciful in configuration, linked the Great Lakes freshwater chain, which merged with the St. Lawrence River, then spilled into the Atlantic Ocean that bound four continents together. North America, South America, Europe, and Africa joined in an embrace at once enigmatic, abusive, and consequential, reverberating inland by way of the rivers and lakes, a fluid "transit of empire."[5]

The swaths of land rimming the Detroit River teemed with plants and wildlife at the moment French explorers arrived in the late seventeenth century. Father Louis Hennepin, a Recollet priest who traveled with René-Robert La Salle on the ship *Griffon* in 1679, called the river a "most agreeable and charming Streight," overflowing with deer, bears, turkey hens, and swans.[6] When Frenchmen journeyed there in the decades that followed, they encountered indigenous people who already knew the place and its bounty, principally Hurons (who came to be known as Wyandots in this region) and Ottawas. The Detroit River zone was chosen ground for Native hunters, including local Algonquian speakers and Iroquoian speakers from the northeast. Hurons, originally from Georgian Bay of Lake Huron, traveled frequently through the area from villages southeast of Lake Michigan and near the straits of Mackinaw. As intimates of the place, they called the Detroit riverbank "the Coast of the Strait."[7] This evocative Huron phrasing brings to mind not only the thin waterway connecting "inland seas," but also land: the marshes, meadows, fields, and forests abutting that river. The strait formed a shoreline from which a signature city would spring. This was a place where the ground met the waters, as much riverscape as landscape. The indigenous phrase "Coast of the Strait" captures the sense that Detroit took shape on organic borders, edges between one kind of environment and another. Social and political life there would come to mirror that aspect of nature, taking on the quixotic qualities of a coastline surrounded by land. Here, where waters and lands made enduring and unpredictable contact, a diverse collection of individuals settled and built their lives. They would become River People who lived, in the words of Midwestern poet Richard Quinney, "on the border, on the edge of things."[8] The edge is not the most comfortable space for habitation, as the Chicana feminist theorist Gloria Anzaldúa explained when she characterized zones like this as "borderlands." In her classic treatise on the U.S.-Mexico border, Anzaldúa called the borderlands (*borderlands/la frontera*): "This thin edge of barb wire." For her, and for many others such as Detroit River People, spaces of merger shaped by conflict are difficult places to reside and, at the same time, are "home."[9] They were a motley bunch, the human inhabitants that would gradually populate the fertile strip along the Detroit River and give it the character of a bustling fur trade town. Hailing from points near and far—indigenous North America, French Canada, Great Britain, Africa, and what would eventually become the United States—with ranging ethnic and national backgrounds and competing cultural sensibilities, Detroit's residents perfectly reflected the quality of the place where they dwelled. These inhabitants lived on the Coast of the Strait, on the edges of each other's cultures, on the line between warring empires, on the border between bondage and freedom. Most of Detroit's early residents arrived at the strait as free individuals, but a significant number of them were held as slaves. Working with, and just as often against, one another, free and enslaved Detroiters built a distinctive community that has faced down time despite its trials.

While the history of colonial and early Detroit has been told from many perspectives and is now a growing area of historical inquiry, published studies tend to render invisible or inconsequential the existence, struggles, and contributions of enslaved people in the city. In contrast to the existing historical literature, and as a hoped-for contribution to it, this book chronicles the rise, fall, and dawn of Detroit while centering the experiences of those who were held in bondage there from the mid-1700s to the early 1800s. In the mercantile settlement that would eventually become an American urban behemoth, hundreds of people—Native Americans, African Americans, men, women, and children—were kept captive, stripped of autonomy, and forced to labor for others. The composite story of their lives across five decades and under three imperial governments illustrates the extraordinary and all-too-ordinary character of Detroit, reveals the role of enslaved people as key actors in the history of the city, and illuminates a defining theme, and indeed paradox, of American history: the breadth and elasticity of slavery and the epic, ongoing quest for liberty.[10]

Native Americans, African Americans, and Euro-Americans were differently positioned in this quest. The Coast of the Strait was a place where their varied fights to realize freedom played out in stark comparative relief, from the colonial conflict known as Pontiac's War in 1763, to the American Revolution from 1775 to 1783, to the War of 1812 in which the young United States sought to reaffirm its political separation from Great Britain. Like the American revolutionaries who called themselves Patriots, enslaved people in Detroit exhibited a deep-seated drive for independence. They verbally and physically challenged their owners and, in the ultimate blow to the system of bondage, fled across the Detroit River to secure their freedom in another country. Native communities living near Detroit likewise adopted a rebellious stance against authoritarian imposition, laying siege to the city and competing with colonial authorities in the battle to retain autonomy in the region. Often these various freedom dreams clashed, but sometimes they coincided, when indigenous groups sided with the Redcoats or Patriots to better their own position, or when enslaved blacks took advantage of wartime chaos to launch escape attempts.[11] Red, black, and white American freedom bids, three streams of purpose and passion in the late eighteenth and early nineteenth centuries, merged at the turbulent site of Detroit just as the waters did.

Cadillac's Town

Surrounded by rich, moist soils and deciduous woodlands, a community, a town, and even an empire, could be anchored at *le détroit*. Such a town could extend its economic reach across the western interior, accessing a vast array of indigenous trade alliances and moving prized materials from the Great Lakes hinterlands into the lucrative markets of North America's eastern colonies and western Europe's populous cities. These materials consisted in the main of treated and untreated animal skins and items crafted from peltry, like textured beaver hats of the kind we can imagine on the head of a mature Benjamin Franklin. The eighteenth century was the height of the international fur trade, which locked European colonial powers in fierce competition for indigenous trading partners: Indian men who had the skills to hunt the animals that were driving a fashion frenzy among the transatlantic cosmopolitan set. The vessels that launched from a site such as Detroit carrying away beaver, fox, and deer parts would return from the East with capital in the form of credits and payments, as well as with sundry practical wares like cloth, guns, and kettles. The town that stood at the western edge of so abundant a trading system would grow fat and important over time, raising its own status beyond that of outpost and stretching the imperial girth of its mother country, France.

This was the vision imagined by the officer and "opportunist" Antoine Laumet de La Mothe, Sieur de Cadillac, when he founded Fort Pontchartrain du Detroit in 1701.[12] Cadillac sought to expand the reach of the French Empire, then situated in the northerly region known as New France (now Canada), to block a growing exchange between Anishinaabe and Iroquois traders at the British post of Albany and thereby hem in the trading activity of British rivals, and to benefit personally from the results. He bet that by building a fort along the Detroit River, what was then a far western point for European colonists, the French Crown could hold back a British advance, buffer economic partnerships that French traders had cultivated with Ottawa, Huron, Ojibwe, and Potawatomi hunters, and gain still more trading partners to the west. "Dream[ing] of the personal riches that would accrue to him by making Detroit the preeminent post for a vastly extended trading network," Cadillac proposed a trial settlement at the strait that would entice indigenous groups to move nearby, hence ensuring immediate access to the animal pelts brought in from their hunts.[13] Native men were "procurement specialists" of these sought-after furs, and the women of their villages were expert at tanning and drying.[14] By keeping Native trade partners close at hand, Cadillac aimed to dominate the region's market in furs, thereby shoring up French supremacy in the eastern Great Lakes and stretching French influence farther west.

From the 1600s through the mid-1800s, the fur trade economy was an Atlantic world phenomenon that linked European and American continental societies by a common ocean and drive for profit. The European rage for apparel fashioned from beaver skins, "a scarce luxury product" then available only in the so-called New World, was augmented by a more mundane use for leather goods made from the thicker hides of species like deer and bison, including "shoes, belts, clothing, bags, book covers, housing, straps, fasteners, and floor coverings."[15] Although there were rises and dips, periods of growth and recession, in the fur trade over the centuries, the historian Claudio Saunt has estimated that in the last thirty-five years of the eighteenth century alone, nearly "six million beaver pelts were exported from North America."[16] The bodies of local animals became sought-after commodities and sources of startling profit, akin to oil in the twentieth century if only people could wear it (and we do, in the synthetic materials that make up much of our thin, breathable, water-resistant yoga and outdoor apparel, not to mention those millennial stretch-style "skinny" jeans).[17]

Skins fueled European expansion into the interior of the continent, becoming, as the historian Anne Hyde has put it, "an industry that dominated commerce in North America and provided the underpinning for its first capitalist boom." That commerce had drawn whole villages and tribes into ferocious combat over position and primacy, including a series of bloody conflicts between Haudenosaunee (Iroquois Confederacy) people and French-allied Anishinaabe (Ottawa, Ojibwe, and Potawatomi) people, as well as Hurons, in the mid- and late 1600s. These wars ended in a costly victory for the French alliance in the form of the Great Peace Treaty of Montreal in 1701.[18] In a contest between European empires dedicated to a modern capitalist ideology and longing to control the natural riches of North America, principally the animal pelts and hides of the trade, Cadillac vowed to deliver France the upper hand and schemed all the while to increase his own wealth and local authority.[19] The French minister of marine, Jérome Phélypeaux, Comte de Pontchartrain, championed Cadillac's cause, leading reluctant officials in Quebec to grant him settlement rights.

Aware that the cost for prime positioning within the fur trade had meant warfare and bloodshed in the all-too-recent past, Cadillac nevertheless did precisely what he had plotted. He established a fort along the strait that joined the Great Lakes together as one mammoth commercial waterway. Westerly enough to connect French traders with untapped sources of furs in the interior, and far enough to the south to provide a longer agricultural growing season than could be had in Montreal or Quebec, or in the older French Great Lakes posts of Michilimackinac and Sault Ste. Marie, Cadillac's preferred location seemed ideal for a settlement with staying power in the French *pays d'en haut*, "Upper Country" or "High Country." From this strategic strait, he hoped to control one of the most powerful resources in the development of human civilization: water. Together with the interconnected major rivers that flowed across this central region—the Missouri, the Mississippi, the Red River, and the St. Lawrence—this tucked-away strait formed approximately "eighteen thousand miles of Inland navigation."[20]

Cadillac sited his military fort where the gleaming skyscrapers of downtown Detroit still tower today, favoring a spot on a slight incline at what he believed was the narrowest stretch of the river. The rise provided good sight lines and higher ground for the essential protection of the military post, while the river provided a ready thoroughfare for the transport of goods as well as people. A proximate stream flowing parallel to the river dipped below this incline, forming a natural barrier to the rear.[21] Cadillac's settlement on the ridged slope at the strait was special from the beginning. He had the self-advantageous insight to invite disparate Native groups to settle new villages on the outskirts of his fort, which some did in the hopes of bypassing tedious trading treks to Montreal.[22] Cadillac also exhibited the unusual commitment to sustain long-term residency for not just lone French Canadian men but also their families, through extensive agriculture. Unlike other commandants of French forts and trading posts in the Great Lakes woods, Cadillac brought a sizeable contingent of one hundred people along, including farmers and artisans as well as military personnel. Enslaved people were likely among this group that settled Detroit and planted a crop of winter wheat that first season. By the fall of 1702, French wives of the leading officers had begun to arrive, making Detroit a settlement where families would grow in the houses abutting the wheat fields.[23] The settlers established "ribbon farms," vertical homesteads of just four hundred to five hundred feet in width that opened onto the banks of the river and backed into fragrant orchards and dense forestland.[24] These ribbon farms, poetically named because of their thin, elongated shape, would, a few decades later in the 1730s, cradle French Canadian style homes inspired by those in the north of France.[25] Dwellings featured wood plank or shingle-sided exterior walls, sloped thatch cottage-style roofs, massive chimneys made of stones, and distinctive glass windows of petite geometrical panes. Residents cultivated the fertile land around their homes, planting orchards of peach, apple, and most notably pear trees, which would come to signify the French botanical heritage of the settlement.[26] The look of this charming, rustic village behind its protective walls was that of a European "fortress town."[27]

In time, the population increased at the fort that came to be known as Detroit, a truncated version of its formal designation, Fort Pontchartrain du Detroit. As the settlement grew beyond its walls, it encompassed farms along both sides of the river to take full advantage of that magical liquid highway. The town grew long and slender, following the water's edge and shaping Detroit's early footprint into what we might now call sprawl. The settlement came to engulf the bight of the river, or bend in the coastline, stretching eastward to westward just as the river flowed. And as social relations became more strained in a vise grip of proximity and exploitation, the people there would soon come to feel in their own skins the second meaning of the word bight: a loop in a taut rope.

In 1710, Cadillac was appointed governor of Louisiana, which would become the site, in 1718, of another famed French colonial settlement: New Orleans. The commandant had made a timely exit. After Cadillac's departure, his town on the Coast of the Strait remained, made up of diverse inhabitants who dwelled together in unsettling intimacy:

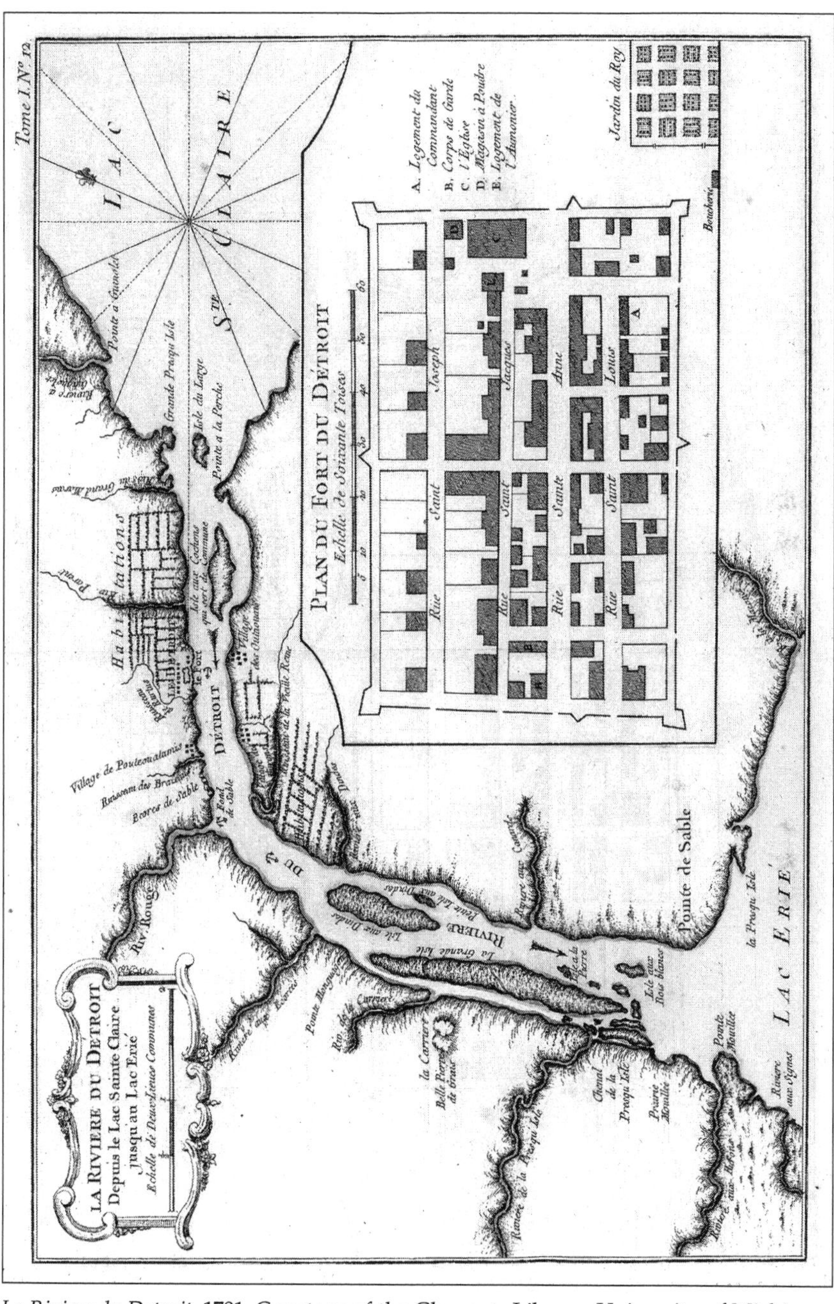

La Riviere du Detroit, 1701. Courtesy of the Clements Library, University of Michigan.

indigenous people of the Huron, Ottawa, Potawatomi, Ojibwe, and Miami societies, French people from New France and old France, the children of Indian and French unions, and enslaved people of indigenous descent. The forced diversity and social hierarchy of Detroit made it a tinderbox. In 1712–13, a conflict called the Fox War broke out between Native villages near the fort. Cadillac had asked more than one thousand members of the Fox, Kickapoo, and Mascouten tribes from the west to move to Detroit in 1710, just before he relocated to New Orleans. A rivalry developed between hunters from these new groups and previous Native residents already established near Detroit. Indigenous men vying for the primacy of their own bands began killing each other in the woods of their hunting grounds. The tension escalated into group attacks that the French authorities did little to settle, leading to the death or captivity of hundreds of Fox and Mascouten people, many of whom would remain in Detroit as slaves.[28]

The racial, cultural, and national multiplicity of Detroit would only increase over the following hundred years to include British residents of English, Scottish, and Irish heritage, African Americans held in bondage, and white Americans from various points east and south. The Coast of the Strait was a place of overlapping borders—natural, cultural, and political—where peoples of various backgrounds struggled to make their lives in a context of growing economic disparity and political volatility. The most vulnerable of those people are also the most invisible in traditional historical treatments of Detroit and the greater Midwest. They are those whose presence was compelled rather than freely chosen, the enslaved who were integral to the town that would one day become the Motor City.

Remnants of Slavery

At the post of early Detroit, free white residents were fiercely resourceful. They invented effective ways to live in an isolated riverine environment, and they plundered natural resources in order to profit beyond their needs. Unfree people were just as creative, as subjects of their own lives and as objects of chattel slavery. Participants in the innovative process of supporting life in a difficult place out of the raw materials around them, they were at the same time viewed as a kind of natural resource themselves. Like the hunted beaver, enslaved people could be trapped and traded, their best parts—intellect, feeling, strength, and versatility—extracted to further what was then a model mercantile experiment. Straining to live worthwhile lives and contributing to the cultural mosaic that characterized this rough-hewn trading post town, enslaved residents of Detroit shared close quarters with those who exploited them like animals. Their owners ran the gamut of society: merchants, traders, gentleman farmers, political leaders, belles of the balls, and even priests.[29]

Piecing together a composite picture of enslaved people's experience in Detroit has depended on scant documentation. Unlike many locales in the American South (and even some places in the Midwest, such as Indiana), Michigan has yielded no full-length slave narratives or WPA slave interviews recorded by employees of the Federal Writers' Project. Even narratives of African Americans who escaped to Ontario in the 1850s do not include fugitives who had been enslaved in Detroit.[30] In a few rare instances, the cloaked thoughts of unfree people filter through formulaic documents like criminal proceedings and dictated wills. But for the most part, we must read the minds of those who were enslaved by identifying and interpreting their actions—by closely examining the things they did—in the light of their circumstances. Although there is a nearly nonexistent record of Detroit bondspeople's direct words, several Detroit slaveholders wrote about their human possessions in matter-of-fact language captured in letters and financial account books. Due to Detroit's character as a swashbuckling fur trade settlement that tolerated a loose legal and political infrastructure for close to a century, and due to a devastating fire in 1805 that destroyed businesses and private homes, even slaveholder records from the town are limited. Perhaps because of the slim nature of the Detroit slavery archive, very few scholarly works, and no full-length books, had yet been written about this subject. (For a discussion of the related historical literature, please see the essay at the end of this book.) But not having at our disposal the sources that make for a fuller history does not mean we should ignore the enslaved in Detroit. Their lives had meaning to them, to their families, and to the region, and can, when illuminated even by the refracted light of limited sources, have meaning for caretakers of the city today. The odds have been against some Detroiters from the dawn of the city's founding, and yet they still fought and fled, created alliances and evaluated circumstances, crashed across international borders and challenged entrenched racial biases. We owe it to them, and ourselves, to bear close witness to their triumphs as well as their trials.

Primary sources for this book consist, in the main, of the wills, letters, and account ledgers of Detroit slaveholder-merchants such as William Macomb, John Askin, and James May. Legal cases in the Michigan Territory Supreme Court involving slave freedom suits and attempts to recapture runaway slaves, together with the papers of prominent Detroit attorneys like Elijah Brush and Solomon Sibley, also provide crucial material. The registry of Ste. Anne's Catholic Church, the only religious institution in Detroit for decades, as well as diaries of Protestant Moravian missionaries who settled in the area, contribute ritual and observational details about enslaved people's daily and religious lives. Census lists, receipts, and bills of sale partially fill the many gaps inherent in this historical reconstruction.

The scattered nature of the archival record on slavery in Detroit resists the wish that we might have for a comprehensive story that includes beginnings, middles, and endings for each individual and family that will emerge on these pages. Rather, the fragmentary state of the Detroit slavery archive reflects the rough, unpredictable nature of enslaved people's experiences. So instead of pushing for story in some coherent and seamless sense, I have striven to offer what I see as a quilted chronicle: a chronological but oftentimes broken account of important events that stitches together historical interpretation, context, and causes, while patching in intuitive descriptions of people moving through a fraught place. What we can come to understand through this patchwork project is that Detroit was both common and uncommon as a site of American slavery. Detroit was a place built not on tobacco, sugar, or cotton but on the skins of animals often prepared and transported by slaves. Its geographical centrality in the fur trade circuit during the heyday of the industry made Detroit unusual even in a broader context of slavery as it was practiced in the Midwest. Most slaveholding settlements in the areas of Indiana, Illinois, Wisconsin, and Minnesota applied stolen labor to military officers' personal services at various forts, domestic duties, wheat production (Indiana and Illinois), mining (Illinois and Wisconsin), and resort hotels for vacationing southerners (Minnesota).[31] In contrast, Detroit's enslaved, while certainly employed to cushion daily life for others through domestic pursuits and in small-scale agriculture, were critical among the labor force that greased the wheels of trade. A close look at life in Detroit therefore draws together two aspects of the U.S. past that are often narrated separately: the fur trade of the great West (often imagined as involving whites and Indians) and chattel slavery (often imagined as involving whites and blacks). Trading in the pelts of beavers and trading in the bodies of persons became contiguous endeavors in Detroit, forming an intersecting market in skins that takes on the cast of the macabre. While black men's backs and legs served as the locomotives that moved these furs across vast distances, indigenous women's bodies were plundered for sexual riches, much like the land was stripped of beaver and other fur-bearing mammals. The theft of unfree people in Detroit, of their knowledge, skills, and corpuses, made the city we know today possible. But out of the shadows of exploitation, enslaved people rose to accomplish a set of rare, phenomenal feats: they ran away consistently, testing new laws of the territory; they contributed to the growth of a subversive Afro-Native community that came to be known as "Negrotown"; they formed an armed fighting force that paraded the streets of Detroit while conflicted officials looked on with worry. In spirit, and surely in flesh for some, they were the ancestors of modern-day Detroit.

Inspired by passionate public discussions about Detroit's past spurred by commemorations of the Underground Railroad, the sesquicentennial of the Civil War, and the bicentennial of the War of 1812, I took up this research project in the summer of 2011 with the aid of a small team of student researchers. I had the privilege of following these public conversations and sometimes contributing to them in spaces such as the Detroit Historical Museum, Wayne State University, the University of Detroit Mercy, the University of Michigan, the Michigan Local History Conference, Underground Railroad tours in the city, and the River Raisin National Battlefield Park. No doubt, the intensity of dialogue among residents and scholars from Detroit and beyond took some sense of urgency from media accounts that repeatedly described Detroit as a symbol of ruin and collapse.[32] But History may have a constructive rebuttal for this demoralizing rhetoric. One of Detroit's prominent slaveholders once called the city "ruined," and yet, from the vantage point of Detroit's most vulnerable residents in his time—enslaved men and women—disarray meant the opportunity for reinvention.

Contradictions of the Coast

A "strait" is a channel of water and also a state of difficulty. Native American and African American slaves in Detroit experienced dual and dire straits. The life they knew along the Detroit River was hard and rife with risk. Most of them had been snatched away from their families of origin in indigenous lake country and the plains, French Canada, New York, Kentucky, or Virginia, and were then sold and shared among members of the area merchant class. Tasked with the essential work of making a distant settlement habitable and even comfortable for their needy owners, slaves cleared land and built dwellings, chopped wood and tended livestock, grew food and prepared meals, and did the onerous heavy cleaning required in a location seasonally soggy with river mud and marshlands.[33] Many of them were compelled to perform intense and dangerous labor as sexual servants or as crewmembers on boats that plied the rough, local waterways. Some slaves in the Detroit area, forced to do work out of doors without proper protection, succumbed to the harsh winter weather of the blustery lakes. An unknown number dwelled in an emotional cloud of anxiety, fearing physical restraint, injury on the waters, separation from loved ones, and violent punishment.

But at the same time that enslaved people in Detroit confronted certain hardship, they lived in a place that afforded them a degree of constructive mobility that was not without significance. Detroit was on the far periphery of European settlement. In some senses the town was like an island in an archipelago, separated from other colonial cities by long stretches of water but connected to imperial networks through trade. Surrounded by indigenous villages and hunting grounds, Detroit had no immediate support from either European colonial or American territorial infrastructures. It possessed what legal historian Lea VanderVelde has described as "frontier characteristics," which meant the town was perpetually engaged in "building itself up, inventing first generation solutions in the absence of long-standing institutional foundations." Far from being strong enough to comprehensively enforce the subjugation of enslaved people, Detroit depended on the cooperation of captives in the city. The tiny free white population of this borderland town always felt itself vulnerable to Indian, British, or American attacks, which meant the settlement needed combined efforts for defense from residents across the class hierarchy. Members of the Detroit elite marginalized, exploited, and punished their slaves, but only to a point. References to whippings and beatings are few in local slaveholders' records. The callous separation of family members, emotional coercion, physical restraint, and imprisonment appear more frequently as mechanisms of control. On an inland coast in a frontier town that stood at the far reaches of European, and later American, centers of finance and government, enslaved people could, to a certain extent, negotiate their immediate circumstances.[34] They seized the opportunity to broaden the scope of their personal actions, to push out the walls of their containment, to adjust relations of power, and, sometimes, to escape. In a lightly populated northern area bordered by Native towns and a navigable river, enslaved men and women found leverage that they applied to the goal of gaining freedom.

Detroit, the experience of enslaved people shows, was a compelling and confounding place in the history of American slavery. Besides being sited near multiple indigenous villages and at a great distance from established white towns, Detroit was shaped by diverse cultural influences, including indigenous practices and the religious mores of the Catholic Church. And just as significantly, Detroit was positioned on a pivotal waterway that, after the Revolutionary War, comprised an international border between the United States and British Canada, guaranteeing freedom for slaves who managed to cross in either direction. In this culturally heterogeneous frontier-borderland environment, slavery evolved as a palimpsest, with subsets of the population enacting and challenging slavery in different ways, and with new cultural practices of human bondage inscribed on top of old. The history of Detroit reveals long-term Indian bondage originating in Native American captive-taking practices that the French adopted and elaborated, as well as African bondage derived from French, British, and American norms. Three categories of enslaved people therefore lived in Detroit: those possessed by the French and their Indian allies, those owned by British officers and businessmen, and those held during the period of American occupation and settlement prior to Michigan statehood. Beyond demonstrating that Detroit was a distinctive site of American slavery due to its geographical, multiracial, and international makeup, this book illustrates the way in which early America was nowhere a place that guaranteed the enjoyment of freedom for peoples of color. Even in the Old Northwest, on the border with Canada, America was a land where freedom necessitated a hammering out blow by blow, and moment by moment, like molten iron in the blacksmith's forge. In this way—in the torpid forging of freedom and long denial of corporeal security and meaningful citizenship for former slaves—the fort town of Detroit was all too common.

The five chapters in this book unfold chronologically. Chapter 1 describes the practice and experience of slavery in the era of Pontiac's siege of Detroit in the 1760s, detailing how slavery came to the settlement with the French and their Native allies and how the practice persisted and changed under British jurisdiction following the French and Indian War. Chapter 2 traces the activities of a circle of British slaveholders in the period of the American Revolution in order to offer glimpses into the world of their slaves, whose numbers reached a high point and shifted demographically during and following the War for Independence. Chapter 3 uncovers the fiction of a free Northwest Territory by detailing the ways that slaveholders evaded the ambivalent antislavery clause of the Northwest Ordinance as well as the ways that enslaved people used the new federal legislation to their advantage. Chapter 4 explores the initial period of American authority in Detroit's history, after the British finally relinquished key military posts in the Great Lakes. It traces the pace and scope of Americanization in the town and evaluates the effect of this political shift, as well as the impact of the great fire of 1805, on the enslaved. It also details a series of cases in the Michigan Territorial Court in 1807, a year that saw a surge in slave freedom suits and formal attempts by owners to recapture runaways. Peter and Hannah Denison, a black couple suing for their children's freedom, launched the first such case that year, setting a precedent for the limits of slavery in Michigan law and establishing a route of escape to Canada that others would follow as an Underground Railroad network developed decades later. Chapter 5 traces the formation of a unique fighting band of runaway slaves known as the "Negro Militia." After an international maritime incident, the Chesapeake-Leopard Affair, raised American fears of an Indian attack backed by the British, Michigan Territorial Governor William Hull authorized the formation of a defensive force made up of Canadian ex-slaves led by Peter Denison. This chapter concludes with an overview of the War of 1812 and speculates on the role of Detroit's black militiamen in the conflict. The conclusion of the book follows the surprising adult life of the eldest daughter of Peter and Hannah Denison, Elizabeth Denison Forth, and reflects on the history of slavery in Detroit in relation to public memory. A final essay briefly positions the book and its arguments within various streams of historical and academic conversation.

The City of the Straits, yet another name for the venerable Detroit, brims with untold stories of crisis and courage, of bold bids and daunting defeats. Although the people once held as slaves have disappeared from public consciousness and have no marker to their memory on the streets of that metropolis, their stories lend meaning and urgency to our understanding of the city's past. By bringing hundreds of captive people into the light of our awareness, people who were expected to fade into the dim recesses of history, I hope to show the struggles, the strivings, and maybe even the soul of Detroit, a place like no other.

Slavery has a deep history on the Coast of the Strait, and echoes of that era sound beneath the surface even now. In 2012, a man named Sedrick Mitchell was convicted and sentenced for holding women captive in the city of Detroit. For months he had secreted away two African American girls in a nondescript house on the east side of town. Mitchell demeaned and physically assaulted the fourteen- and fifteen-year-old girls, forcing them to perform certain acts against their will. His case and others have been investigated by the Michigan attorney general's Human Trafficking Unit. Still, sufferers of modern-day slavery in Detroit, and hundreds of missing and murdered aboriginal women in neighboring Canada, continue to await liberation and justice. It seems that the old streets of Detroit are still drawing traffickers, who rely on the unwieldy size of the 139-square-mile city, its decreasing population, its proximity to major highways and bridges, and its status as America's most active border for international trade to ensure ease of passage and anonymity for dreadful deeds.[35] Centuries ago, slaveholders used the same waters of this river to hike their profit margins, forcing enslaved people to ply the vessels carrying goods processed by still more slaves. But bondsmen and women turned this waterway to their advantage and hijacked the river as a route to liberation. Emancipatory action in our time, too, might be waterborne—ferried by the physical waters that embed social power, fed by the underground stream that is history. On the borderlands of bottom-line globalization, capitalistic expansion, and postindustrial flux, recognizing the historical links between land-seizers and body-snatchers, and exposing the tools and techniques of bondage as well as liberation, are incremental but purposeful ways to make room for visions that see the earth and all of its creatures free.

1

The Straits of Slavery (1760–1770)

How can we make these barbarians, Christians, if we do not first make them men? How make them men, if we do not humanize them? . . . How can we conquer them and make them subjects of the king if they have neither docility, nor religion, nor friendly commerce? All of this is easily accomplished by the means spoken of in my memoir, and by perfecting the establishment at Detroit.

—*Cadillac to M. de Pontchartrain, 1702*

Hundreds of ten-foot-high hardwood planks encompassed Fort Pontchartrain du Detroit, just as the French commandant had originally envisioned it in 1701. Antoine Laumet de La Mothe le Sieur de Cadillac had specified oak as a strong material from which to construct the defensive walls of the post. Fashioned from the solid cores of sheltering trees that grew plentifully in the forestland of the southern Great Lakes, Cadillac's stakes still rose to sharp points above eye level and bored into the rich earth three feet deep. The French fort that had just seen its sixtieth birthday was not only picketed but also manned. Sentries guarded the gates of this old-world village, monitoring the comings and goings of outsiders.[1] A water gate shuttered the river; a rear gate faced down the forest; side gates capped either end of the main road called Ste. Anne's. These fortified barriers were meant to secure the vulnerable populace of a small and fledgling trading town. Here, within a 372-by-600-foot expanse tucked beside an ambling river, streets such as Rue Ste. Anne, Rue St. Louis, and

Rue St. Jacques were packed to bursting with buildings: private homes, merchant houses, a bakery, a church, a guardhouse, a storehouse, military barracks, and military commanders' stations.[2] On Ste. Anne's Street, the major thoroughfare running east and west, perched Ste. Anne's Church with its newly erected belfry, dating, the rugged residents would tell any properly admitted guest, to 1755. Saint Anne, blessed mother of the Virgin Mary, was a favorite saint in Quebec, Canada, and a spiritual match for this riverine coastline, as she was believed to be a protector of sailors and safeguard from storms. Rocking up to the churchyard like so many wooden boats with sails were neat rows of family homes with steep, triangular rooflines. The King's Gardens, a parcel of land set aside for commanding officers, grew near the water southeast of the fort. Below the unwieldy incline of the southern wall, windmills spun beside the river, their oblong fans producing power to grind the wheat so carefully cultivated to sustain the survival of the remote, western settlement.[3]

Past the fortified town that sat on the northwestern edge of the river, elongated "ribbon farms" unfurled along the banks. Indigenous villages curled like strings of gleaming glass beads beyond them, on the north side as well as across the water to the south. A Potawatomi village to the west of the fort marked the border of settlement on the north bank of the river, where present-day Michigan is located. An Ottawa village could be sighted just across the river in the area of present-day Ontario, Canada. Farther west on the southern side, a Huron village was neighbor to an Ottawa settlement, and below the Hurons, French farmers had established another stretch of homes at a bend of the river known as *la petite cote*, "the little coast." The portion of Windsor, Ontario, as we know it today, that shares the coastline with Detroit and is often viewed as a northern destination on the Underground Railroad of the pre–Civil War era, actually lies south of Detroit city. But in the 1760s, there was no Michigan and no United States; there was no Ontario and no international border that drew a stark political line between two nations, or marked a bloody line of desire and loss between two states of being: slavery and freedom. There was, instead, a wooden fort surrounding a French Catholic town that had recently fallen to the British in a costly, protracted imperial war.

To the rear of the fort called Detroit marshlands spread into a dense thicket of forestland used by Native peoples as hunting grounds. To the front of the fort a wooded swath buffered the rich bank of the river, below which sundry boats regularly approached to trade in goods. These waterborne vessels delivered textiles, household supplies, and metal weaponry, and carried away animal pelts headed for distant markets, as well as the flour, oats, and meat that Detroit regularly supplied to the smaller population of Fort Michilimackinac, located at the straits of Lakes Michigan and Huron, nearly three hundred miles to the north. The town on the bluff and its satellite settlements embraced the strait of Detroit, a waterway toward which all life here oriented. For this was a river that flowed into the rippling Great Lakes and, through them, the St. Lawrence River, the Atlantic Ocean, and the greater world. When Cadillac selected this site for his fort in 1701, he described the Detroit waterway as a channel made wondrous by versatility. The river could be accessed for trade and sealed off for defense, depending upon the circumstances. "The situation is agreeable," Cadillac wrote about his chosen spot, "it is none the less important because it opens and closes the door of passage to the most distant nations which are situated upon the borders of the vast seas of sweet water. None but enemies of the truth could be enemies to this establishment so necessary to the increase of the glory of the king."[4]

Fort Detroit was at once a strategic military stronghold and a pivotal commercial trading post set in the hinterlands of the *pays d'en haut*, a French term for Upper Country. Besides the French farms and Indian villages that spun around the picketed town like spokes on an elongated carriage wheel, Fort Detroit was positioned in an interior spot far from any European urban center. Montreal and Quebec, the bustling cities of colonial New France (the province to which the post at Detroit had previously been attached) were 560 and 723 long and tedious miles to the north and east. Although Great Britain had won the war and now claimed this post, the British colonies of the Atlantic seaboard had no effective influence here. Even New York, a principal city with which Detroit did business on an annual basis as the trading boats made their slow circuits in warmer months, was a full seven hundred miles away.[5]

The fur trade formed the economic core of this chiefly mercantile community, with the preponderance of its residents engaged in the business. As an inland hub of the trade, Detroit hosted the people and attracted

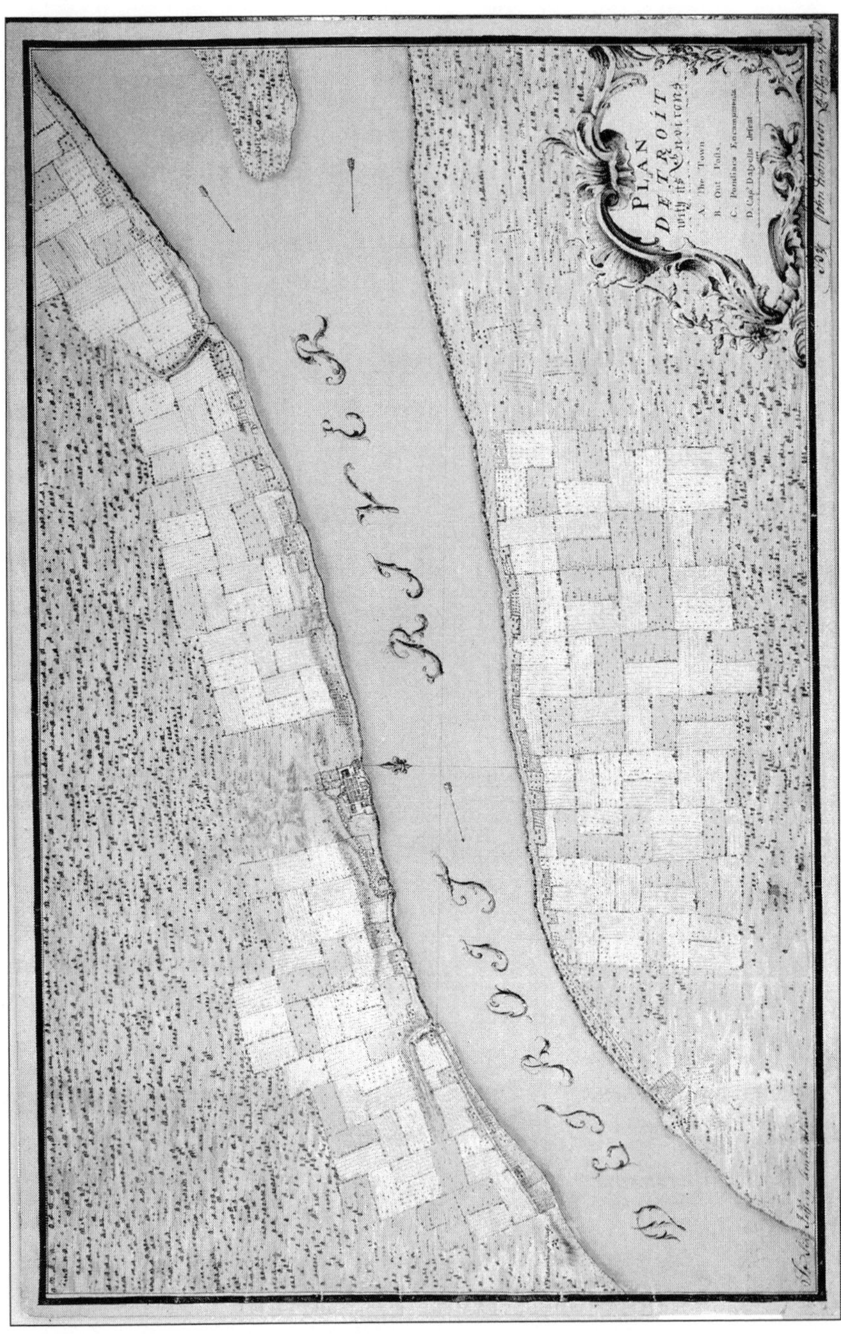

John Montresor, *Plan of Detroit*, 1764. Courtesy of the Clements Library, University of Michigan.

the activities that kept enterprise alive and thriving. Resident merchants received goods from crewmen from the east, procured furs from indigenous hunters in local villages, imported a portion of those furs through the services of French *voyageurs* (rowers and traders), employed free and enslaved laborers to process and pack those furs, and then exported the products to eastern and Atlantic markets by way of combined free and slave labor power. Intimately attached to the cities of the east through the flow of this global trade, Detroit was at the same time a world apart: small, rustic, and surrounded by Native hunting grounds, villages, trails, and preexisting trade networks.

Various classes of French men and women, as well as inhabitants of mixed Native and French descent, peopled the riverside town's dirt-packed roads. On the streets of Detroit in the latter half of the 1700s, a newcomer, perhaps a trader relocating from British New York who had arrived in early summer after the lakes had thawed, would have noticed the elided tones of the French language, along with Algonquian and Iroquoian dialects and a smattering of the English tongue. He would note the formal style of local merchants, the highest class of folks in town, who dressed to signify their position. For even in the so-called backcountry, these wealthier residents kept in step with trends of the cosmopolitan Atlantic. The men wore their hair powdered in white and paired brocaded waistcoats with breeches that buckled at the knees. Their wives donned long gowns wrapped with shawls and accented by strands of hair delicately piled atop the head. Merchant-class women in Euro-Native mixed-race families would have been similarly appareled as they stood on the shop floors with their husbands, co-managing the affairs of the fur trade.

The harvest produced by family farms, especially wheat and orchard crops, fed the town and brought returns in local exchange. So farmers would have been present in this streetscape too, doing business within the fort, although their homes were mainly situated outside the enclosure walls. French farmers and craftsmen in the town would have worn shirts in brilliant shades, trousers with belts or sashes, and Indian-style moccasins. The women in these families that worked so intensively with their hands out of doors would have dressed in knee-length gowns, petticoats to the ankles, and straw hats for sun protection.[6] Farming women, like merchant women, applied themselves both inside and outside. They kept house, tended kitchen gardens, prepared food, made household items, and raised children in a settlement with no schools. Prominent merchants were often also farmers, commanding large tracts of land derived from Cadillac's early claims or acquired, unlawfully, in purchases from indigenous groups. The New Yorker would surely have noticed, too, Father Bonaventure, the local priest draped in stern black robes. Charged with the moral well-being of residents in a town with only one church, the father kept the community's sacred rituals: marriages, baptisms, funeral services, regular masses, and holiday celebrations in honor of the saints.[7]

Any one of these members of Detroit society, from longtime French merchants, farmers, and priests to newcomers from Great Britain, could be the owner of another Detroit resident, that is, the owner of a slave. This would have come as no surprise to a sharp-eyed merchant from New York, as that colony was becoming a primary location from which Detroit slaves were sourced. Black people arrived via boat and on foot through the trading networks that also circulated animal pelts. The connection between slaves and skins in Detroit and other Great Lakes markets was so close, so uncanny, that a French Canadian attorney general had once proposed manipulating slaves' need for clothing as a means to process furs for market.

It was Ruette d'Auteuil who seized upon the notion, in 1689, that the African slaves imported to New France could wear beaver fur as apparel, thereby transforming the rough but valuable animal skins into a prized variety of processed fur. Softened and tempered by long-term wear in which contact with the natural oils of human skin rubbed out the roughest hairs, leaving behind the soft underfur that felted so well into headwear, "coat beaver" or "fat beaver," as it was sometimes called, commanded luxury prices. Ruette d'Auteuil figured that black slaves could be put to work at building "all sorts of manufactures" in French colonial North America while dressed in the prickly skins of another captured species. The black men's bodies would finish the furs while at the same time erecting the infrastructure of the colony, producing extra surplus value by way of the sweat of their stolen labors.[8] While this plan was never enacted in New France, in part because of the easy availability of Indian slaves, the vision behind it reveals an eerie alignment between the fur trade and the slave trade, capturing the ideological intersection of these two seemingly separate exploitative enterprises. The beaver and the black man, both, were reduced to natural resources in the eyes of capitalist body brokers.

We tend to associate slavery with cotton in the commercial crop heyday of the southern "cotton kingdom," but in this northern interior space, slavery was yoked to the fur industry. The cycles and routes of the fur trade, as well as its vessels—Indian canoes, French batteaux, and British schooners—were the cycles, routes, and vehicles of the slave trade in the place we now call Michigan. If the outlines of a triangular trade can be sketched in these thick, forested lands, it existed between upstate New York, southern Michigan, and the northern straits of Mackinac. Along the Detroit River and at trading posts linked by Lakes Erie, Ontario, and Huron, merchants bought and sold peltry as well as people, shaping a *skin* trade of dual nature. The dark underside of fur trade imperialism was not only the rise in conflict among various Native groups and the near destruction of beaver and the lush riverine habitat that the meticulous animal maintained, but also the consumption of human beings in an insatiable for-profit enterprise.

Bound for Detroit

Detroit's strategic location between Lakes Erie and Huron, as well as between the eastern port cities and western Indian nations (such as the Foxes, Dakotas, and Lakotas), made it a prize in the eyes of European imperialists. The ongoing purpose of the fort was to secure and control a flow of goods between indigenous hunters, white traders, and global markets that would shore up the economic primacy of the European empire that claimed it, formerly France, and, at this moment in our chronicle, Britain. When, between 1757 and 1760, France and Great Britain waged a war over the fates of their North American colonies, Detroit was one of the most valuable chips in play. France lost this Seven Years' War (or French and Indian War, as the British called it), forcing French King Louis XV to relinquish all of that country's posts in the Great Lakes region. The once wide-ranging French-claimed territory in North America, a "corridor" stemming from the St. Lawrence River Valley of Canada, through the Upper Great Lakes and southern Illinois country, southwestward into the Missouri River region of Louisiana, was rudely sliced in two. The English took swift command of the Great Lakes posts, including Fort Pontchartrain du Detroit, though the limits to their actual authority were extreme in a country surrounded by Indians. After a small cadre of British commanders trekked from the East to settle inside the old French fort, they purchased dwelling places from local residents, some of whom relocated to homesteads beyond the walls.[9]

French villagers who remained at Detroit were permitted to keep their property after first swearing allegiance to the new Crown that dominated the region. This property could include unfree blacks and Indians. As spelled out in Article 47 of the Capitulation of Montreal following the war: "The Negroes and Panis [Indians] of both sexes shall remain in their quality of slaves in the possession of the French and Canadians to whom they belong; they shall be free to keep them in their service in the colony or to sell them; and they may also continue to bring them up in the Roman Religion."[10] With the promise of French property protections firmly in place and the residents placated, if still wary, the British endeavored to turn Detroit into a central command post for their military operations in the Indians' west.

At Detroit, civilian government had no foothold. In this militaristic and mercantile town, British officers held sway in a tenuous truce with wealthy French merchants, whose economic and social influence was long-standing and deep-seated. In 1760, Detroit was a village on edge, a place on *the* edge—of empires and interest groups. Dangerous and unpredictable, a space of extreme risk and ample opportunity, Detroit drew people—and conflict—like a magnet. White, red, or black; enslaved, indentured, or free, new people were bound for Detroit in the aftermath of the French and Indian War, and when they arrived, they twined their fates with that of the city.

Even under formal British jurisdiction, Detroit remained French and Indian in character. Within the walls of the fort and alongside the sloping shoreline, nearly one thousand people went about their daily lives, keeping hundreds of homes and farms in as good a working order as could be expected in a place where supplies might arrive or might not, depending upon the season and the flowing or frozen state of the river. When the populations of nearby Native villages are included in the count, greater

Detroit residents numbered around two thousand.[11] These *habitants* were French in the main, as well as mixed-race French and Indian, with a substantial number of Native people regularly visiting the fort from their villages just beyond town. French-speaking people of African descent resided at the fort in small numbers, but very few were free. Detroit residents traded furs and sundry goods with one another, attended mass, rites of passage, and celebrations at Ste. Anne's Catholic Church, ran exuberant foot races, and threw festive dances and sledding parties in an atmosphere characterized by a lively communal life.

But while the fur trade flourished, bringing wealth and social stability to European colonists in Detroit, enslaved women toiled behind those festive scenes, keeping the homes and gardens of others, processing and preparing food, caring for their mistresses' children, making clothing and household linens, cleaning private and public spaces, and providing sexual services according to the demands of their masters. Enslaved men in Detroit were likewise taxed by arduous labor, plying the boats that kept the system of long-distance trade running across the formidable lakes, hauling goods, applying the skills of various crafts, building structures and containers, and working the land obtained by their owners.

Free French and mixed-race *habitants*, soon joined by British soldiers and a smattering of British merchants, enjoyed a position of relative safety afforded by town walls and armed patrols. Most French residents made peace with the new political reality, accepting British authority and clinging fast to the things that produced and secured their wealth: healthy trade relationships with Native people, land, and slaves. The picketed walls of Fort Detroit shielded these privileged residents from the threat of attack that could originate from any direction in an era of ongoing imperial warfare: from Indian villages close to the fort, Native communities far afield, or even the vanquished French military that had receded to the jointly occupied French and Indian Illinois territory. But for those individuals who were not free, the palisade may have symbolized physical confinement within the fort and containment within the status of "slave," even as it promised protection from unknown threats outside the common walls.

Detroit counted 33 slaves among 483 residents in the year 1750.[12] By

1760, that number had increased to 62 slaves as the arriving British officers brought their black bondspeople along with them.[13]

This Great, Disastrous Catastrophe

Perhaps James Sterling should have known what trouble loomed. He was, after all, a merchant doing steady trade with the Indians who would soon conspire to attack the fort at Detroit. Born in Ireland, Sterling had lived in North America since the 1750s, serving in Pennsylvania during the French and Indian War and working as a commissary at various British forts. He had relocated to Detroit in 1761 to stand as the western agent of a trading firm with the very long name of Livingston, Rutherford, Duncan, Coventry & Syme. Charged with overseeing the movement of goods between traders in New York and traders in the west, Sterling was not keen at first on his relocation from the populous east.[14] In the fall of 1762 he disdainfully described his new town as "this place of Exile (as I may justly term it)." But business proved good for Sterling, an ambitious bachelor with an eye out for the main chance even in exile. He developed a steady exchange with nearby Native hunters and added a degree of Indian language facility to his proficiency in English and French.[15]

Sterling's correspondence made clear that his thriving business depended on the work of enslaved blacks, especially black men whose muscles became the mode of movement for trade goods. In 1760, in advance of setting up shop in Detroit, Sterling attempted to acquire black slaves from merchants Phyn and Ellice in upstate New York. A letter from the company's owners informed Sterling: "we have tried all in our power to procure the wenches and negro lads, but it's impossible to get any near your terms. No green Negroes are now brought into this Province. We can purchase negroes from eighty pounds to ninety pounds, and wenches from sixty pounds to seventy pounds. If such will be acceptable, advise, and you shall have them in the spring."[16] Sterling's inquiry about the availability of slaves in advance of founding his shop in Detroit reveals his conviction that blacks in bondage were necessary to his western venture. And at the same time that Sterling sought black slaves from New York, upstate New Yorkers were holding black as well as Indian slaves. Isabella Graham, the spouse of a British military doctor stationed at Fort Niagara, wrote in 1769 that her husband "bought me an Indian girl and has since purchased another." This meant that Isabella Graham had "another one to cloak," she wearily yet proudly explained to her parents in a letter. Graham therefore increased her clothing wish-list to include several items of "coarse" material "for each of them" and sent the list to her parents in Britain by way of a ship bound for Detroit. Lamenting the isolation promised by the impending winter weather, Graham's spirits lifted at the thought of "sending one of the Savages thru the roads to York in winter" to collect her return correspondence.[17]

Back in Detroit, over the course of five years, James Sterling mentions several black slaves in his unpaid employ or in the employ of his trading partners. In 1761, Sterling is pleased with a new and important purchase, writing to a ship captain and business associate: "I have bought a Negro here for whom I am to give £75—he speaks French, English and a little Indian language here, seems to be a good lad and I believe will suit very well." In the same missive, Sterling noted to the captain that "your Negro man Charles" was accompanying a group to Niagara. Sterling allowed to another associate, Mr. Collbeck, that the "negro Jack" could be kept in Niagara "during the winter to take care of [Collbeck's] oxen."[18] When a slave of Sterling's ran away, Sterling was concerned that he had been "taken up by a Frenchman." Relieved to later recover his human property, Sterling had the man "secured" by force.[19]

James Sterling used black men like railroad cars in a pre-industrial transit system that connected sellers, buyers, and goods, and he did not hesitate to protect his investment in this human infrastructure of the fur trade. These men of African descent would carry furs to the east in warm weather, winter over with Sterling's partners who used their labor while the waterways were impassable, and then return to Detroit with goods for Sterling's shop in the springtime. Sometimes the "goods" that black men helped to move might include other enslaved people. Like the beaver bodies they transported, these men were viewed by slaver-traders as little more than fur-bearing animals.

With his talented unpaid laborers transporting wares across the waters and creating goodwill in the business circles that benefited from the borrowed use of their labor in the cold season, Sterling was able to focus on the nitty-gritty details of commercial transactions on the ground in

Detroit. And so he should have intuited, perhaps, that conflict was brewing in the summer of 1762, when many of his Native trading partners began to ask for weapons. That season, Sterling took orders for "Three Thousand Weight of the best & hardest Corn'd Powder" and "all the Scalping Knives" that his distant business associates could acquire.[20] Sterling was unable to get his hands on that much weaponry; neither did he record any sense of foreboding at the sheer volume of the requests. But one year later, Sterling would find himself in the thick of a battle that had been brewing since the British assumption of control in the Upper Country in 1760. Fighting beside trained officers of the British military, he would command the Detroit militia in Pontiac's impending war.[21]

Pontiac's Rebellion, also known as Pontiac's Conspiracy and Pontiac's War, is one of the most dramatic and, indeed, celebrated, moments in the annals of Detroit history. It is so famous an event that in addition to the numerous books that have been written about it, pageants have been performed around it, and places (Pontiac, Michigan) as well as things (the Pontiac car and Pontiac Silverdome Stadium) named for its intrepid leader.[22] Pontiac, the son of an Ottawa man and Ojibwe woman, was a skilled orator and warrior who sought to inspire an all-out war against the British Empire, which had spread its reach into his Great Lakes homeland. A French collaborator who had sided with that country in the French and Indian War, Pontiac aimed to gather Ottawa, Ojibwe, Huron, Seneca, Delaware, Shawnee, Miami, and French combatants—some of whom had had group rivalries in the past—to wage war against the British and undercut their newly won military and hence commercial victory in the region. Spurred by the vision of Delaware prophet Neolin, who pictured a world free of white influence in which Native sacred power could be restored, Pontiac planned his attack for months, gathering and sometimes pressuring Indian allies to join him.[23]

For Pontiac, frustration at the shift from French to British rule swelled into irreconcilable anger. Native people in the northern regions had learned to coexist with the French, who had set about cultivating relationships since their earliest explorations.[24] The French object in North America had traditionally been to derive wealth through the manipulation of trade as well as to convert the Indians in order to strengthen the Catholic Church. Unlike the British, who came to establish Protestant towns in New England and profit-making plantations in the South, all of which required massive tracts of land, the French focus had been on controlling trade and extracting natural resources (principally fish and beaver).[25] This meant that French colonists did not arrive in the Upper Country with an eye toward developing sizeable family-friendly settlements. The first French forays into the Great Lakes were made by military men, Recollet and Jesuit missionaries, and traders. Detroit was in some ways an exception to the French rule in its attention to keeping family units intact (bringing officers with their wives) and practicing settled agriculture, though even Detroit was a far cry from the land-intensive intrusion of a Boston or Jamestown. Entering the North American scene with a relatively light but nonetheless self-serving footprint, the French needed to quickly build strong alliances with Native people who knew the environment and geopolitical status quo. Over several generations of the French colonial presence, some French residents and various groups of Indians had formed mutually intelligible aims, bicultural families, and shared habits of life. But the British were a different breed. Not only did they hold Native people at a greater social distance than had the French, but they also approached Indian diplomacy in markedly contrasting ways.[26]

While French explorers, voyageurs, and traders had smartly adopted indigenous customs, intermarried with Native women, and bestowed Indian trading partners and their communities with generous gifts to establish goodwill and grease the wheels of trade, the British took a different tack. British commanders at Detroit gave far fewer gifts to the Indians, thus refusing to engage in a cultural ritual of good faith and social connection that undergirded economic alliances. British military commanders also refused to regularly meet with Native leaders, treating them with a level of disrespect that was unprecedented in the former French territory. Finally, British officials blocked the dispersal of rum to Indians and reduced the trade value of beaver skins. Frustrated with the dismissive treatment of British leaders and propelled forward in his view by Neolin's vision of a return to ancestral ways, Pontiac went on the attack, seeking to put the British down and to help restore French rule at the Great Lakes European posts.[27]

At a series of conferences with leaders of various tribes, Pontiac made his case against the British, whom he deemed "liars" and "dogs clothed in red."[28] Together with his allies, Pontiac adopted a bold plan: he would orchestrate a reconnaissance mission in which he and his fellows would perform a disingenuous "peace-pipe" dance for British officers inside Fort Detroit; meanwhile, others in the scouting party would surreptitiously assess the number of enemy soldiers and guns. He also called for warriors to attack British citizens wherever they found them, to strike the settlers randomly in so many places that they would be overwhelmed. Pontiac's own part in this great battle would be to lead a contingent of warriors in an assault on Detroit. His goal: to isolate the British commanders inside the fort, cut off their food supply, compel them to surrender, and push them back across the Allegheny Mountains to their former eastern posts.[29] Pontiac expected that the French military would abet his multipronged assault, leading to a victory that would ultimately return to the French territories lost in the Seven Years' War and return to the Native tribes more agreeable trading partners.

Pontiac and his supporters planned their attack for early May of 1763, but the British commander in the fort, Major Henry Gladwin, had received a warning about the plot from a disaffected Ottawa leader. The British subsequently increased their sentries and gathered their arms, forcing Pontiac to regroup on what he had intended to be the first day of the siege. His men bided their time for a few days and then split ranks, executing a surprise attack on a family farm behind the fort as well as on residents of Hog Island (present-day Belle Isle), the Detroit River islet treated as common land where the French had allowed their pigs to graze.[30] Leaving a trail of bodies behind on Hog Island and taking three white children captive, Pontiac and his allies pummeled the fort walls with gunfire.

It was the ninth of May. Springtime, a most beautiful season in the Great Lakes, had morphed into a time of crisis, as the fearsome smell of gunpowder in the air mixed with the heady scent of pear and apple tree blossoms. Unable to penetrate the wooden pickets of the fort, Pontiac's six or seven hundred warriors patrolled the riverbank to the east and the woods behind the settlement, seeking to block the delivery of provisions and reinforcements that would come to Detroit from the northward fur trade post of Michilimackinac or from British Canada via the river.

Merchants, farmers, and those they held as slaves cowered behind the wooden gates as Native forces penned them in, laying siege to the town.[31]

The assault on Detroit continued unabated. At the end of a failed peace meeting in the home of a French *habitant* on May 10, Pontiac took hostage two leading British officers, Donald Campbell and George McDougall. He threatened to hold them unless Major Gladwin surrendered the fort, relinquished all arms and ammunition, and departed for the east. When Gladwin refused, Pontiac softened his offer, saying the British could take their property with them but insisting that they leave behind a certain "Negroe boy" who served as a "Valet de Chambre" to a British officer. This unnamed African American boy would be retained for Pontiac's exclusive use.[32] Pontiac's request for a slave, as reported in the journal of Detroit merchant John Porteous, a New York trader who would soon come to work for James Sterling, as well as in the journal of Lieutenant James McDonald, who was stationed at Detroit, is a telling moment in the midst of this battle that bespeaks the entrenchment of human bondage among Europeans as well as Native people in the region. Pontiac's desire for a black boy in particular indicated that young black male slaves carried a special kind of status in the Upper Country. Though bondspeople of African descent had been circulating in the urban areas of New France since the 1600s and trickling into the rural Great Lakes by the middle 1700s, they were harder to come by than Native slaves and twice as expensive.[33] Pontiac likely saw the boy not only as a practical asset but also as a symbol of his personal leadership status. This boy would have been war booty for the Ottawa leader, a valuable prize and a visible trophy. Gladwin did not relent, however.

Meanwhile, inside the walls of the fort, British officers used slaves at their disposal to strengthen their hand. On the first day of the siege an enslaved "*Panis*" (Native) man formed part of a scouting party to assess whether a ship could make it past Pontiac's warriors on the river. All in the party, except for the man and a resident teenaged boy, were killed by their enemies. The unnamed Indian slave was captured by Native warriors, to be held again as a captive or traded to others. Later in June, another enslaved Native man reported to Major Gladwin that he had sighted a supply boat drawing near on the Detroit River.[34] This information was essential for the sustenance of those within the fort. These two indigenous men are among the few enslaved Detroiters mentioned in primary accounts of the siege, but dozens of other unfree people in the town were also witnesses and victims. While Pontiac's contingent was unable to bring Detroit to its knees, neither was Gladwin able to free Detroit from the onslaught. A stalemate followed. As the prolonged assault continued, an unfree man belonging to one of the town's largest slaveholders, Mr. Beaubien, was suspected of joining Pontiac's warriors and faced arrest by the British.

By June, nearly 850 warriors were amassed beyond the walls of the fort at Detroit. Across the Great Lakes, Ottawa, Ojibwe, and Huron warriors were bringing down other British forts like so many dominoes. The fort at Sandusky, Ohio, fell, along with the fort at Miami, Ohio, and the fort up north at Michilimackinac.[35] As word of the defeated forts traveled back to Detroit, the anxiety of the people trapped inside surely increased. Now it was summer on the strait, humid and stifling. The fortified town of Detroit sizzled inside its pickets, steaming as river water rose into vapor, adding to the thickness of tension in the air. Those trapped within the fort expected to be fallen upon at any moment by the Indians outside, even as their commander, Major Gladwin, refused to give in to Pontiac's demands. The walls of the fort had been built to keep danger out, but for weeks in the spring and summer of 1763, these barricades locked danger in, containing even those Detroiters who were accustomed to their freedoms.

Pontiac's major obstacle as the siege continued was his inability to breach the defensive schooner that Gladwin had planted on the river right alongside the town. Neither could Pontiac realize the once possible aim of starving the British into submission, as they had used the purported peace meeting in the home of a French resident as cover for collecting all of the edibles in the fort and amassed a store that could last them for weeks. The British soldiers had also cleared away trees and brush around the town, reducing cover for the Native fighters that shot their weapons into the pickets. The French military support that Pontiac hoped for never arrived, since the French commander in Illinois hesitated to violate the Treaty of Paris signed between his nation and Great Britain.[36]

Pontiac's allied fighters withered in number as the conflict waged on with no decisive victory at Detroit. Just weeks into the siege, bands of Potawatomi and Huron warriors sought meetings with Gladwin and agreed to his terms to end their part in the conflict, damaging the strength of Pontiac's Indian alliance beyond repair. By July of 1763 merchant-militiaman James Sterling could disclose to his business partner in New York that "the Seige [sic] continues here as formerly, tho' we are not so much harassed as at the beginning, having burn'd & destroy'd all the houses, Fences, gardens & c. that were within [800] yards of the fort; not only so, but our garrison is much stronger than it was & the Enemy weaker at present, tho' there are vast numbers of the Northern Nations expected every day."[37]

The gathered force of allied warriors, though great, was unable to overcome Fort Detroit's defenses and soon received word from the French at Illinois encouraging them to retreat. In October of 1763, Pontiac lifted the siege.[38] That same month, James Sterling's mind turned toward vengeance. He wrote to his brother: "we will repay the white and black savages for their rascally behavior." By "white savages," Sterling referred to the small minority of French residents at Detroit who had lent active support to the warriors; by "black savages" he meant the Indians themselves, reiterating a longtime English cultural belief in the association between blackness and evil, and hinting, perhaps, at an elision between the racial categories "red" and "black" in the mind of a man whose society owned members of both groups as slaves.[39]

Sterling's anger, wrapped in ethnocentric language, was warranted from his perspective. The war had taken a great toll on the British, lasting nearly a year and a half and costing "the lives of an estimated two thousand Anglo-American settlers and four hundred British soldiers."[40] Out of thirteen British posts attacked between 1763 and 1765, only four remained standing at the end of Pontiac's War. Detroit, a gem in the crown of the British West, was one of them.[41] Pontiac, for his part, was dissatisfied despite the damage he and his allies had managed to inflict on the British. After all, the British were still there. For the next two years, and to the consternation of the British, Pontiac traveled to various Native gatherings spreading his discontent and voicing the notion that war might be rekindled.

British military leaders agreed with James Sterling that vengeance should be theirs and that Indian warriors must be crushed. Major

General Thomas Gage, commander of the British forces in North America at the time, ordered retaliatory assaults on tribes allied with Pontiac, even though the Huron leader, Teata, the Ottawa leader, Manitou, and the Ojibwe leader, Wasson, sought a peace with the British.[42] After pressing surrender through military action, Colonel John Bradstreet, commander of one of the two retaliatory British armies, entered into a series of informal peace treaties with Native groups in Ohio and then in Detroit. Finally, at a meeting in Detroit in July of 1765, Pontiac himself formally relented. Yet the British would not soon forget his actions. The ultimately failed assault that a nineteenth-century Ottawa writer would later call "this great, disastrous catastrophe" had taken many lives on both sides and convinced the British that they would never be fully secure as long as they trod on indigenous ground.[43] The response of British colonial officials, such as Superintendent of Northern Indian Affairs Sir William Johnson, was to cook up plans to "Settle and Enlarge our Frontier and in time become an over Match for them [the Indians] in the interior part of the country."[44] With rebellion quelled, at least for the time being, Johnson hoped to populate and expand their North American empire. Multiplying the number of British settlers until the indigenous residents were outnumbered, Johnson felt, would be the only means of forestalling future threats.

As Pontiac's Rebellion stuttered to a messy end, scores of enslaved people were still being forcibly held in Detroit.[45] They were the property of French Canadians who had built the settlement, of mixed-race French and indigenous families who controlled a large portion of the fur trade, and, increasingly, of British soldiers who had arrived after 1760 to administer the post. They were also, rarely, the property of Native traders who lived inside the fort.[46] Detroit survived, with most of its residents free to run their own affairs under the aegis of the ruling British power, while others—a black and Indian enslaved minority—were just as trapped as they had been before the siege began.

But if Pontiac and his allied forces had ousted the British and returned French authority to western posts, would enslaved people have fared any better than they ultimately did beneath the Union Jack? By the time of Pontiac's Rebellion, 1,500 enslaved people were living and working in the territory of New France.[47] The evidence of two hundred years of slavery in Quebec indicates that little would have improved for them had Pontiac succeeded. Like the British, the French in Canada kept, used, and sometimes abused slaves of African and indigenous ancestry. To unfree people—Indians as well as blacks—the French were enemies and captors.

Captives in Canada

The history of slavery in New France, or present-day Canada, has only been confronted in the past half century.[48] Canada imagines itself—and is imagined by Americans—as a safe zone for blacks who fled there to escape lifelong bondage via the secret network known as the Underground Railroad. But contrary to this belief, New France was a society with slaves for close to two hundred years. French Canadian merchants, government officials, tradesmen, and farmers incorporated slavery into the workings of everyday life, depended upon the labor of slaves, and legalized their reduction of people to property.

The first African-born person held as a slave had arrived in the St. Lawrence River Valley in 1628 or 1629. A French trader based in Quebec purchased this young boy, likely from Madagascar or Guinea, from an English pirate.[49] Nearly a century passed before more captive Africans began to trickle into the colony. Meanwhile, indigenous captives, mostly women and children, were slowly falling into the hands of the French, who received them as gifts from indigenous allies. By the 1670s, French Canadians were not only accepting slaves as presents but were purchasing Indian slaves outright on their own initiative. Members of various and often distant tribes—the Kansa, Iowa, Arkansas, Natchez, Shawnee, Cahokia, Sioux, Assiniboine, Pani, Pawnee, Fish, Ojibwe, Fox, Menominee, Mascouten, Potawatomi, Ottawa, Iroquois, Mohican, Inuit, and other groups—spanning from the Mississippi River Valley to the south, to the Missouri River at the northern plains, found themselves owned by Frenchmen via capture or sale by members of other indigenous groups.[50]

Despite their practice of slavery, the French did not see indigenous people as a separate caste of human being marked for bondage due to racial difference. In this way, their ownership of Native slaves differed initially from their ownership of African slaves, whom they viewed as occupying a fixed inferior status that was racially derived.[51] Neither were the French indiscriminate about the Indians they were willing to hold. They had formed close economic and political ties with some Native groups, such as the Hurons and Ottawas, and did not wish to jeopardize these relationships. But boundaries blur in the avaricious traffic in human bodies. Although French colonists intended to acquire slaves from Indian groups with whom they were in conflict (enemies) or with whom they had no connection (strangers), the number of tribes named in the long list above reveals that people from allied groups were also taken.[52] Indigenous slaves could be challenging to hold, however, because they were often located fairly near home territory to which they might escape. This was far from the case for the smaller number of African slaves who had been transported thousands of miles from their homeland to labor in North America. With the colonies of New England serving as a persuasive example of the ways that African slave labor could be successfully employed in cold northern climes, more French Canadians began to seek access to black bodies just as eagerly as they had harvested beaver carcasses.

In 1688, leading officials in New France, including the governor, requested the king's permission to import African-descended slaves. Permission was granted and, in 1701, augmented by an authorization by Louis XIV for New France colonists "to own slaves . . . in full proprietorship."[53] Although no slave ship actually landed in New France at the auspices of the king due to a concern about the financial viability of Africans surviving the frigid weather, a limited number of black slaves could be obtained from French territory in the Caribbean islands and, later, Louisiana, or from the British colonies as spoils of war or smuggling. In the two hundred years between 1632 and 1834, 1,443 enslaved blacks appear in French records. Indigenous slaves outnumbered blacks almost two to one in New France, reaching an estimated total of 2,700 over the time period that French Canadians owned people. Of 4,185 total slaves in the territory (some with unmarked racial categorization), 874 resided in the Great Lakes area of the present-day American Upper Midwest.[54]

French slavery was governed by a set of rules called the Code Noir, which strove to align the practices of owning human beings with the ethics of Catholicism, France's state religion. Adopted in 1685 in the French

Caribbean colonies where lucrative sugar plantations dominated, the Code Noir was adapted for use in Louisiana in 1724 and applied loosely to the northern colony of New France.[55] The Code Noir allowed masters to physically punish slaves but discouraged excessive brutality.[56] It discouraged owners from separating families through sale and legislated free Sundays for slaves to honor the Sabbath. In the Great Lakes, as in the Caribbean and Louisiana, slaveholders did not completely abide by the tenets of the Code Noir, which was not uniformly enforced, especially in distant settlements.[57] But French slaveholders, who often took their Catholic faith seriously, were aware of the expectations inscribed within the code. Many had their slaves baptized. Enslaved people could be married in the church and have those unions legitimized as sacrosanct; the church also recognized "natural marriages," or informal intimate unions, between slaves.[58] The children of slaves were baptized under the auspices of their parents' owners and assigned godparents within the church. The French practice of slavery therefore provided a small measure of legal protection for families and a vehicle for social inclusion in the form of religious participation.

Colonists in New France used the unusual term "Panis" to designate Indian slaves, a word that may have several derivations. Many Indian slaves were not originally from the Great Lakes region but instead had been captured farther west, beyond the Missouri River. Members of the western Pawnee nation made up a notable number of Indian captives around the lakes, as this group was a target of slave raids carried out by Missouri and Little Osage bands in order to produce captives to sell to French traders. In addition, Ottawas may have captured and integrated Pawnee people. The late nineteenth-century Ottawa interpreter and writer Andrew Blackbird described his own family background as being rooted in the plains. His ancestors had been taken captive by Ottawa warriors who raided as far west as the Rocky Mountains, and then had been incorporated into the tribe through adoption and intermarriage. Blackbird described these distant ancestors, known to the Ottawas as "the Undergrounds," because they built "their habitations in the ground by making holes large enough for dwelling purposes." Pawnees of the Great Plains loosely fit this description, as they lived in earth lodges built into the high bluffs of riverbeds. For these reasons, a term that sounded close to the name of the Pawnee tribe—"Panis"—came to stand in for Indian slaves as a category and a caste. What is more, a number of smaller Indian groups whose members were vulnerable to capture by Illinois raiding parties had tribal names beginning with the letters "Pan," supporting the theory put forward by historian Brett Rushforth that the partial names of a series of tribes who suffered great losses to slave raids led to the composite word "Panis."[59]

Wide use of the term "Panis" in the eighteenth century resulted in the belief that the Indians called "Panis" represented a single nation.[60] While we now know that the people designated as "Panis" came from a range of ethnic and tribal backgrounds, we can see, in the historical use of this flattening term, that those individuals did have something fundamental in common. They had each been reduced to a state of nonpersonhood in the eyes of their captors. Native people from various tribes reclassified as generic "Panis" now shared a key characteristic with people of African descent who were viewed by the French as natural slaves: unlike other Indians, "Panis" could be deprived of their right to freedom. Central to the significance of the catchall term "Panis," then, was the implicit notion that an Indian slave was no longer a recognized member of a specific tribe or nation. From the perspective of slaveholders, she or he had been stripped of national belonging; she or he had become a no one. The surviving records of early Detroit emphasize this erasure of group connection, as slaves denoted as "Panis" very rarely had a tribal signifier added to records that list them.[61] Although many French colonists had close relations with free Native people and even, for a time, sought to acculturate Indians into French identities, they could nonetheless turn certain Indians into possessions with a crude linguistic act of recategorization. "Panis" came to signify a Native person detribalized, a Native person who, due to a lapse of the kind of protection that came with a recognized national status, could be treated like an African slave, the basest category of "person" in the increasingly capitalist, increasingly race-conscious transatlantic and inter-lake modern world. The magic word "Panis" transformed a Native subject into an objectified slave, a mode of linguistic transit akin to captured Africans crossing the Middle Passage.

All the Panis and Negroes

On April 13, 1709, New France's leading civil official, Intendant Jacques Raudot, issued a proclamation defining the status of slaves in that territory. "All the Panis and Negroes," Raudot announced, "who have been bought, and who shall be bought hereafter, shall be fully owned as property by those who have purchased them as their slaves." Revealing the underlying reason for this declaration, Raudot further asserted that slaves: "are needed by the inhabitants of this country for agriculture and other enterprises."[62] In making this bare statement that was read aloud to the populations of three major cities—Quebec City, Trois-Rivières, and Montreal—Raudot clarified for all residents of New France that unfree people in that territory, both black and Indian, could be held as slaves. Slaveholders in New France need not be concerned about the legality or the morality of their actions because slaves here were property in the very same way as slaves held by masters on the plantations of the French West Indies.[63] As Intendant Raudot stressed to the populace, inducing slaves to run away was a criminal offense in New France; this category of people—people defined as things—had no natural right to liberty.

As in New York on the British side of Lake Ontario, slavery in New France took hold mostly in urban areas.[64] The labor required from these captive people would be domestic, commercial, and, to a certain extent, agricultural, but the scale of large farms and plantations common to the American South, and the constant field work required in that region, would not take root in the cooler climes of the St. Lawrence River, Great Lakes, and strait of Detroit. Here in this northern, water-bound, trade-oriented terrain, slaves would operate boats, package and cart goods across land and water, work at skilled tasks in shops and manufactures, organize and clean homes, make clothing and wash laundry, grow, gather and prepare foodstuffs, cook and serve meals, and tend to the brutally intimate demands of their owners. The gendered breakdown of these labors is both predictable and surprising. Men toted trade goods and worked as ship crewmen. Women worked in domestic and private spheres. And although direct evidence is evasive due to the fragmented nature of slaveholder records in Detroit, it is likely that enslaved Native women were sent to local shop-based factories to process animal skins by scraping, waterproofing, and tanning hides, since transforming furs into useful items was a skill they would have acquired in their communities of birth. Just as likely, enslaved Native women were tasked with turning those finished hides into consumer goods, especially the "frontier" style deerskin moccasins that became fashionable for white residents of Detroit as well as northeastern cities by the mid-1700s. In the Great Lakes, moccasin-making had long been the craft of women, and just as slaveholders in South Carolina took advantage of West Africans' rice growing knowledge to further elite economic interests, slaveholders in Detroit would have sought to channel indigenous women's knowledge. Many of the soft leather shoes that became an "imperial fashion" worn by French Canadian voyageurs and well-heeled Boston ladies alike probably passed through the hands of unnamed Native craftswomen held as slaves in Detroit, the center of moccasin manufacture.[65] Enslaved men and women were essential to the economic viability of this fur trade town, as well as to the maintenance of free residents' homes, farms, and families. Escape from bondage was therefore prohibited and punished. If captive residents of greater French Canada tried to run and were unfortunate enough to be apprehended, they could be branded on the shoulder with the image of a *fleur de lys*, the delicate floral motif that served as the symbol of imperial France.[66]

Ships crossing the Atlantic carried African slaves to New France in limited numbers. In this part of the world considered remote to Europeans, overland trails and inland lakes served as major channels for the delivery of unfree people as pillaged indigenous communities became the most regular source of slaves for northerly French colonists through the mid-eighteenth century. These human beings, often described as bits of "flesh" even by the Native Great Lakes and eastern woodlands people who captured and traded them, were exchanged in a number of ways that carried multiple meanings.[67] Native groups, who had long histories of taking war captives themselves, gave away captives as gifts to French trading partners or respected political leaders. They also offered slaves to "cover" or appease the deaths of loved ones in the families of valued associates. French colonists could buy slaves in trades with Indians who had acquired them through warfare, previous transactions, or, increasingly, as the European demand for slave labor grew, through slave raids.

French as well as mixed-race French-Indian families could and did pass down their slaves as property to the next generation, begetting inherited wealth and advantage.

Members of numerous Great Lakes Native societies—Ottawas, Ojibwes, Potawatomies, Miamis, Foxes, and Hurons—all engaged in captive-taking practices that bled into forms of slavery. The seizure of members of other groups, the abuse of those captives, and their forced assimilation into the captor community is a documented feature of most indigenous societies on the continent. These actions on the part of Native people are further evidence that slavery was a global force, and that viewing some human beings as less than full persons was a transcultural phenomenon and widely shared human failing. At the same time that Native societies participated in a worldwide, inhumane practice of stealing lives, their captive taking included elements that differed substantially from the form of Atlantic slavery in the Caribbean and North America visited mainly upon Africans. In the eastern and Great Lakes regions, Indian people who seized captives in raids or wars with other tribes usually took one of three courses of action: ending the life of the captive through ritualized torture and murder, adopting the captive into the household of a tribal member that had lost a loved one, or trading that captive to slave-hungry Europeans.

Becoming a captive within a Native community meant losing one's life or former subjectivity; it meant murder or forcible incorporation. Being adopted, surely the outcome preferable to death for many captives, was not an easy process, however. Captive people were often forced to do heavier labor than biological family members, facing intense scrutiny and supervision. Captives could be beaten and harshly treated, and women and girls were regularly compelled to serve in the place of a wife, performing domestic and sexual duties. The captive-taking practices of Dakotas, Anishinaabeg (Ojibwes, Ottawas, Potawatomies), Foxes, Sauks, Miamis, Illinois, Crees, and other groups, in fact, favored foreign indigenous women and girls who could be integrated into families and produce new kin.[68] Women captives were thus valued as domestic laborers, sexual consorts, and bearers of children. Since most captives retained in raids were women and children, the trauma of sexual coercion and violence was integral to their experience.

Captive people in indigenous societies were often themselves from groups that took captives in a similar fashion, and so, while gravely disadvantaged and vulnerable, they knew what was expected of them. The better they fit into their adoptive family, the more bearable things were likely to be and the swifter they would be accepted by their new tribe. Full social inclusion was possible—at a cost. Captives were required to shed previous familial and tribal ties and become members of a different community in order to have renewed lives. In contrast to black or Atlantic slavery in which slaves were kept at a social distance from their owners and intimate relations between masters and slaves, though frequent, were viewed as violations of a strict racial and class order, Native people roped captives into the family circles of captors, "toward full, if forced, assimilation."[69] Surely the psychological adjustments of compulsory assimilation were shadowed by mourning and an abiding sense of loss. Slaves in Native societies were people ripped from their families of origin and forced to fit into foreign families in order to save their own lives.

The situation was even less certain for Indian people taken captive and then traded to Frenchmen. The French, who had been enmeshed in trade relationships with Native people for more than a century, brought multiple streams of experience together in their approach to owning slaves in New France. They possessed a long history of race-based, exclusionary African slavery in the Caribbean context (where indigenous slaves were held as well, but in significantly reduced numbers due to massive deaths from disease and hard labor); they had observed the foreign practice of incorporative slavery in Native North America, and they had forged a pattern of marrying into Indian families throughout their colonial history on the continent. Each of these strands of experience made an imprint on the layered forms of slavery the French would adopt in the Upper Country. They continued holding black slaves as a racialized group viewed as inferior and unworthy of incorporation into French families and society. They attained Native slaves from Indian allies and, in the manner of those allies, allowed for a degree of social incorporation, especially through religious ritual. And they took unfree indigenous women as sexual consorts and domestic helpmeets. While French colonists owned both black and Native people as slaves, they did so with an implicit, subtle difference. Black slaves in New France were associated with black slaves in the Caribbean, a denigrated, separate class. Native slaves in New France were part of a population that theoretically could be, and in some cases had been, economic partners, political allies, cultural brokers, and people accepted as kin. If black slaves were held at a social distance by French colonists in the North, Indian slaves were held with a dangerous degree of intimacy.

A European man with an Indian wife was a common sight in fur trade settlements of the colonial period. These couples comprised the roots of the large mixed-race families that played dominant roles in the trade well into the nineteenth century.[70] By the mid-1700s, Frenchmen and Indian women in the Great Lakes had set in motion a pattern of forming intimate unions or marriages "in the custom of the country," as the French termed it. These unions took place in accordance with the rituals and traditions of local indigenous groups and with the consent of Native families. Often marriages formed to further trade occurred at the behest of influential Indian men—political leaders and successful hunters who sought strategic matches for their daughters that would benefit their families and bands. These marriages provided traders with critical kin relationships and links to Native communities that strengthened, and in many cases, made possible, the business of trade. Besides gaining direct lines of access to pelts procured by Indian hunters, European traders benefited greatly from their Indian wives' varied skills as translators, cultural negotiators, and keepers of homes. The union of Native-white couples also provided indigenous people with greater access to European goods and communication networks.[71]

The majority of these mixed, customary marriages took place between Frenchmen and Native women, but British men also adopted the practice as they penetrated the North American interior. Some white men maintained more than one Indian wife and family, mirroring and perhaps taking advantage of indigenous polygamy practices; others had both a "country" wife in a Native village and a white wife, viewed as more appropriate by European officials, in a colonial town or at the post.[72] Nevertheless, many of these cross-cultural marriages seem to have been consensual and resulted in close bonds between wives, husbands, children, and extended kinship circles. After a generation of Europeans and Native people traded and intermarried, white men shifted toward marrying mixed-race women, the daughters of those first intermarriages who were viewed as being more acculturated to "civilized" European ways of life. Despite implicit cultural biases, both white settlers and indigenous communities had something to gain from these publicly sanctioned interracial partnerships. Even though some French officials frowned on the practice from afar (and many British officials condemned it), local priests, military commanders, and political leaders supported these marriages as a means of stabilizing French-Indian relationships, of controlling illicit sexual liaisons, and of assimilating Native people into French spiritual and cultural practices.

At the ground level of cross-cultural colonial encounter, white men in the *pays d'en haut* continually and openly sought out well-positioned indigenous women as domestic and intimate partners.[73] But not all Indian women were destined to be wives in formalized relationships. As slave raiding increased over time and white men gained greater access to indigenous women captives who did not come from local, high-status families, these men sought unfree sex partners outside the bounds of customary trade marriages. The long history of interracial sexual intimacy in colonial New France, the symbolic association of indigenous women's bodies with the land and its resources, and the force of lust unconstrained by community norms of mutual obligation all contributed to European men's eroticized objectification of Native women. Just as they had entered a new land and extracted its living bounty, these men began to feel that they possessed an unbridled right to the bodies of Indian women, with or without the consent of Native families or the women themselves.[74]

In New Orleans, the younger, southern sister city to Detroit, the desire of Frenchmen for Indian women was so great as to be alarming. One colonist wrote in his memoir that French Canadian men seeking "sex" would troll "among the Indian nations and satisfy their passions with the daughters of these Indians." As governor of Louisiana in the second decade of the 1700s, Detroit founder Antoine de La Mothe Cadillac raised strong concerns about illicit sexual relations stemming from the presence of enslaved Native women in the homes of Frenchmen. He and the Reverend Henri Roulleaux La Vente worried that these women were being abused in a "scandalous Concubinage," after which fathers sold away their own children. Cadillac's recommended but untenable solution was to remove temptation by selling these Indian women to the Caribbean islands or encouraging French owners to marry their Indian slaves.[75] The problem of French liaisons with unfree indigenous women continued nonetheless, coming to constitute the majority of interracial sexual relationships.[76]

Given their long history of sexual entanglement with Native women, Frenchmen were primed to adopt the indigenous habit of claiming captive women as substitute wives. When French explorers, traders, and colonial officials fused their own cultural practice of slaveholding with local indigenous ones, they continued this pattern of use for female slaves. They also applied the indigenous practice of incorporating slave women as marginal kin, especially through religion. It was not uncommon for French owners, both men and women, to serve as godparents to slaves in the Catholic faith. Frenchmen often accepted the infants of enslaved Panis women—possibly their own sons or daughters—as godchildren.[77] In the French context, the Native custom of adopting captives into families had echoes in the religious ritual of masters serving as godparents to their enslaved spiritual kin. However, unlike indigenous processes of adoption that incorporated the children of captive women as actual kin with rights to freedom and full belonging, French slaveholders were willing to hold and sell the children of Native sex partners as slaves.

Sexual relationships between white men and Indian women, whether those women were enslaved or free, represented complex forms of bondage and intimacy that trapped many Native women in situations of captivity. Although Indian women owned as "concubines" experienced a degree of incorporation into French social networks, they were still essentially a class of people who could be bought and sold. Their children, like the children of black women in North America, inherited their unfree position. As the historian Kathleen DuVal has captured in her summary of this circumstance, "enslaved Indian women had more in common with their African counterparts than with free Indian women living among their own people."[78] In the American territory claimed by France, unfree black and indigenous women shared a similar subjugated status and the expectation of lifelong servitude that they would pass on to their progeny.

Indigenous women redefined by the French as "Panis," a word that would effectively become the equivalent of "Negro," had been stolen from their home communities, sold to Europeans, and unredeemed by manumission or formal marriage. Their fate was linked to the imperial struggle over authority in the Great Lakes being waged among European empires and indigenous societies, but their fate was not the same as that of free Native people in intact tribal units who could ably negotiate the cultural "middle ground" with European interlopers.[79] Intermarriages and intimacies between Frenchmen and Native women existed on a spectrum that blurred into sexual slavery, and it is often difficult, in evaluating existing records, to distinguish among these various relationships. Due to their ambiguous position in relation to Native groups and the pattern of French-Indian intermarriage, indigenous women may well be the most invisible population in the history of American and Canadian slavery.

Lives of Bondage

Detroit was a Catholic town dominated by a Catholic faith that saw no other religious influence until 1800, when a lone Protestant missionary arrived from distant New England.[80] A petite cathedral built of wood and topped by a narrow belfry with a silver gilded bell, Ste. Anne's Catholic Church fronted the street named for it, facing the river near the fort's eastern gate and adjoining a burial ground where Catholics and people of Protestant heritage were interred together. This had been the first building erected in Cadillac's Fort Pontchartrain du Detroit, and it had burned or been torn down and then rebuilt four times by the 1760s.[81] Detroit's oldest institution, one that had outlasted even the French military, Ste. Anne's served as a moral and social center, bringing people together across class status, racial groups, tribal affiliations, and nations of origin. Native people from Huron, Iroquois, Miami, Ottawa, Potawatomi, Sauk, Sauteur (Ojibwe), and Sioux communities participated in church services over the years. In the decades of British rule following Pontiac's Rebellion, even British merchants with Protestant backgrounds attended Ste. Anne's and had their slaves baptized there. For members of Detroit society seeking spiritual and interpersonal connection, this church was the core of community life.[82]

Enslaved people in Detroit were counted among the number who moved through the physical and social space of Ste. Anne's, as their inclusion in spiritual community was a feature of bondage among the French. French slaveholders in the colonies were expected to raise their slaves in the teachings of the Catholic Church, to baptize their bondspeople and care for their souls. Slaveholders served as the godparents of their slaves or the slaves of family members and associates. And rarely, an enslaved person acted as godparent to another slave. Unfree people, like free people, attended church services and joined in the communal life of the parish. Slaveholding families tended to own just a few slaves who resided in or near the homes of their owners. Enslaved people within Detroit households therefore came to know their owners, as well as one another, intimately. Each household was tied to others through the church. Ste. Anne's connected separate domestic spaces within and beyond the walls of the fort, linking otherwise isolated enslaved people across the Detroit River archipelago. Within the yard and walls of the church, enslaved members of various households saw one another regularly, affording the chance to exchange a glance, touch a work-worn elbow, and share the personal stories of their days. And so it is in the Ste. Anne's Church register, a record book kept by priests in the second oldest diocese in the present-day United States, that the shrouded lives of people in bondage during the era of Pontiac's War emerge.

Several of Detroit's French middle-class and wealthy households contained one to two enslaved people, mostly of American indigenous ancestry and very rarely African. Ste. Anne's register mentions the births, deaths, and baptisms of eighty-two slaves in the decade of the 1760s. The largest category of these—thirty-two—are "Panis" girls and women. Eighteen are "Panis" boys and men. Fourteen are "Panis" with gender unrecorded. Three "Black" slaves are listed, along with two "Mulatto" slaves. Several enslaved people are not identified by race and sex in this record, making precise total counts difficult. One fact is clear, however: most enslaved people present in Ste. Anne's Church in this decade, and indeed prior to the year 1800, were women. The greater part of these captive women were indigenous.

At Ste. Anne's in the 1760s, most free congregants were French, one was British (the trader James Sterling), and three were Native people

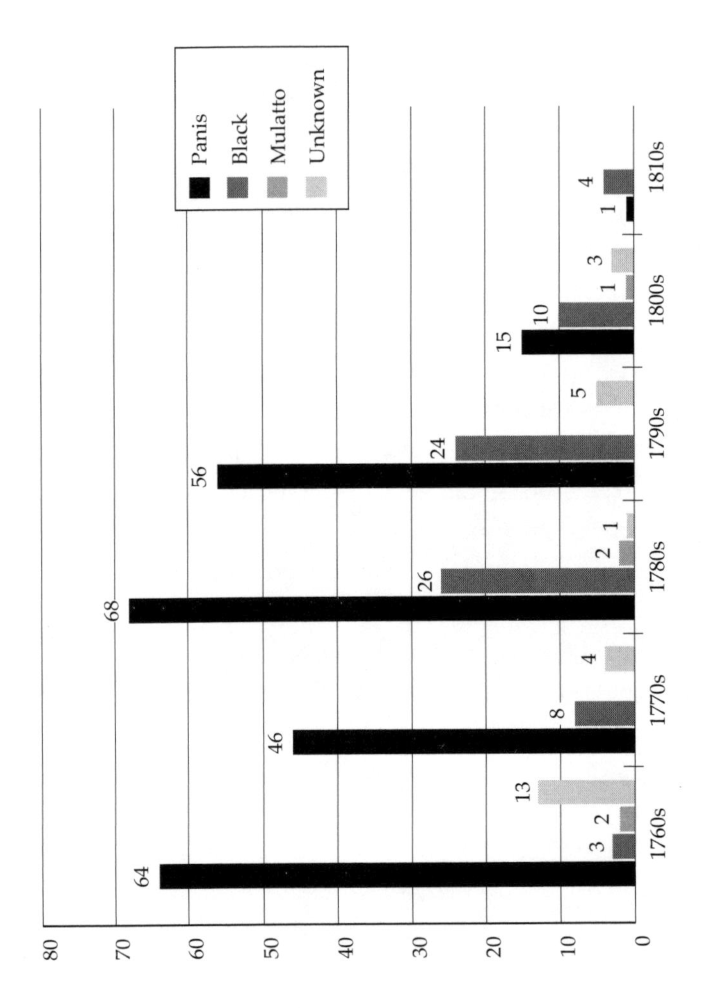

Ste. Anne Church Slavery Data, Race by Decade. Compiled by Michelle Cassidy. Ste. Anne's Church Registers, 1704–1842, Archdiocese of Detroit, available at the Bentley Historical Library, University of Michigan. Courtesy of Ste. Anne Parish (Detroit), Sacramental Parish Register (Marriage, Birth, and Death Records, 1704–1842), Archdiocese of Detroit.

	Panis			Black			Mulatto			Unidentified		
Year	**Female**	**Male**	**Uniden-tified**	**Female**	**Male**	**Uniden-tified**	**Female**	**Male**	**Uniden-tified**	**Female**	**Male**	**Uniden-tified**
1760s	32	18	14	1	1	1	-	1	1	9	4	-
1770s	21	17	8	4	4	-	-	-	-	-	1	3
1780s	39	25	4	13	11	2	1	1	-	-	1	-
1790s	25	31	-	15	9	-	-	-	-	1	-	4
1800s	4	9	2	1	8	1	-	1	-	1	1	1
1810s	1	-	-	2	2	-	-	-	-	-	-	-
Total	122	100	28	36	35	4	1	3	1	11	7	8

Ste. Anne Church Slavery Data: Race and Gender by Decade. Compiled by Michelle Cassidy. Ste. Anne's Church Registers, 1704–1842, Archdiocese of Detroit, available at the Bentley Historical Library, University of Michigan. Courtesy of Ste. Anne Parish (Detroit), Sacramental Parish Register (Marriage, Birth, and Death Records, 1704–1842), Archdiocese of Detroit.

listed by name and tribe (Huron, Métis, Sauteuse).[83] The French Campau (also spelled Campeau) family, whose members appear frequently in Ste. Anne records, typifies the lifestyle of early Detroit elites. The Campau line traces back to seventeenth-century Montreal, where they were, according to French Canadian historian Marcel Trudel, among the "leading" holders of human property, evidencing "an extravagant taste for slaveownership."[84] The Campaus put down roots in Detroit in the early 1700s, when two brothers, Michael and Jacques, moved to the fort, received land grants from Cadillac, and sired an extended clan whose members became influential in Detroit society as landowners, militiamen, and civic leaders. Their progeny would, generations later, co-found the *Detroit Free Press* newspaper, the Bank of Michigan, and Farmers and Mechanics Bank, amassing a fortune worth millions. Jacques Campau lived in a house on Ste. Anne Street, acquired land, and became a successful farmer. His son, Jacques Campau II, gained and sold still more land around the Detroit River.[85] The Campaus may have brought enslaved people with them when they first arrived, or they may have accessed human property through contacts back in Montreal after settlement. At the age of twenty-eight, Jacques Campau owned one slave according to the 1762 French census of Detroit. Louis Campau owned three slaves that year; Simon Campau owned one; Claude Campau owned no slaves but had two paid employees. All of these men were described as economically "comfortable" in the estimation of the census taker, the French notary for the town, Robert Navarre. Three members of the Campau family (Baptiste, Michel, and Charles) who had no slaves were listed as "poor," suggesting, as would be expected, that slave ownership correlated with rising wealth.[86] The two largest slaveholders on the 1762 census each had five slaves: Zacharias Chicoste is listed as "rich"; Claude Jean Gouen is categorized as "comfortable."

Ste. Anne's Church records also reveal the Campaus' active ownership of Indian slaves. In 1761 Louis Campau had his slave, Joseph Marie, child of the enslaved Susanne, baptized. In 1763 Simon Campau had his Panis slave Marie Louise baptized with Alexis Campau serving as godfather. When the enslaved infant Cacille (or Cecille) was born in 1763 to Marie Louise, a Panis slave owned by Chauvin Pere, her godparents were Nicolas Campeau and Cacille Campeau, the slave child's namesake. Large slaveholders relative to other Detroiters at the time, Cicotte and Gouin appear frequently in the church register upon the births, baptisms, or burials of their Panis slaves. Not a single child born of a Panis woman is listed as free in the record.

The registry kept by the priests at Ste. Anne's Church in a sprawling French cursive is visually intricate but lacks texture regarding the experience of enslaved people. Nonetheless, a most striking and moving aspect of an otherwise spare record is the litany of deaths of Indian slaves in their infancy or childhood, often described as "small" or "young" "Panis." The story of one enslaved woman in the priests' notations also demands to be told but resists full reconstruction because of the starkness of the record. She was an unnamed "Panis slave" doubly confined in the state of slavery and a cell of the military prison in the winter before Pontiac's siege. The reason for her incarceration went unstated, but it was within the walls of the prison house that she gave birth to a baby, Marie Joseph, with the aid of a midwife. The enslaved infant was baptized "with condition" in January of 1763. The baby had apparently been intended to go to *"Monsieur Goduel Major commandant pour le roy de Detroit"*—the commander of the fort—but was given instead to the master gunsmith. This change in the plan of who would gain ownership rights to the infant raises questions about paternity as well as clandestine deals between men of influence. It also begs questions about the unnamed mother's imprisonment, her reaction to her and her child's lamentable situation, and her fate after release, if indeed she survived the ordeal. Had this woman been confined because she fought her owner or someone else who had taken advantage of her lack of power? Had she attempted to run away in the weeks before giving birth, realizing that her child would inherit her unfree condition? Certainly other enslaved women in the coming decades in Detroit would take such drastic measures in order to gain a slice of freedom from authoritarianism and abuse. Although we cannot identify the precise conditions of this particular indigenous woman's life, we can try to imagine the bleakness of her circumstances and the possibility that she rebelled against them.[87]

The French Canadian Campaus, the Cicottes, the Gouins, and the master gunsmith who acquired the jailed woman's infant represented some of Detroit's earliest settlers and first slaveholders. Indeed, those categories overlapped, as colonial Detroit seems never to have been a place free from slavery. The British merchants and military men who came to Detroit in the wake of the French and Indian War also owned slaves. With greater access to African-descended bondspeople from the Atlantic coastal markets, British newcomers were more likely than French locals to have black people among their holdings. A chief example is James Sterling, the transplanted merchant from New York who first saw Detroit as a place of exile but soon learned that intermarriage combined with black slave labor was a recipe for success in that place.

In 1762, the "hurry of Business" had kept James Sterling from "having so much pleasure" in the company of the "fair sex," and he was "obliged to content [him]self with that of a Copper Hue," a reference to relations with Native women, likely enslaved. A few years later, his outlook had brightened.[88] In 1765, he reported his marriage to Marie Angelique Cuillerier, a daughter of the slaveholder-trader Antoine Beaubien. For Sterling, this was an excellent match. A reportedly lovely and spirited young French woman who could lightly converse and gracefully dance with equal finesse, Angelique had charmed the first contingent of British officers who arrived in Detroit in 1761. But it was the sharp-eyed Irish merchant seeking his fortune in Detroit who won her hand (as well as her considerable dowry) and used that bond to further his business ventures. Sterling described his bride as "a very prudent woman and a fine scholar" who had "been raised to trade from her infancy and is generally allowed to be the best interpreter of the different Indian languages at this place." Continuing in his rhapsody, Sterling enthused: "Her family is in great esteem amongst the Indians. . . . We shall carry on trade much better and with a great deal less expense than formerly, my wife serving as interpreter and she and I myself as clerks." Besides being multilingual and skilled in the ways of trade, Angelique Cuillerier was a member of a well-connected family with close links to local Native people. She was able to bring unusual Indian items, such as fox fur muffs and beaver blankets, into the channels that her husband used for the trade of foodstuffs and other supplies. Her father, according to Sterling, was trusted by the Indians who had led the attack in Pontiac's War and would likely have been positioned as a French commander in Detroit had the rebellion against the British triumphed. And for Angelique's family, an intimate bond with a subject of Great Britain ensured their staying power after the French defeat. This was a match made in imperial fur trade heaven, where patriotic divides could fade in the face of economic opportunities.[89]

Between their dual nationalities, similar experience in business, access to different sources for goods, and shared zeal for trade (a fact borne out in Angelique's independent control of items in her possession and use of her husband's networks to distribute them), James Sterling and Angelique Cuillerier were the perfect mid-eighteenth-century Detroit power couple. And for each of them, black slaves made up an essential part of this winning package.[90] Sterling is the only person noted as owning black slaves in the Ste. Anne register in the 1760s; he is also one of few British residents listed at all in this early decade of church records. Sterling's human property included a black child named Marie, daughter of the black enslaved couple Babet and Emanue. On the occasion of this child's baptism, her owner was described as "Sieur Sterlin Bourgois commercent of the town." Sterling also owned Antoine, a child born to a black slave, Fébe, in 1768 (with no father named). After Pontiac's War, Sterling continued to procure and distribute black men for his use and the use of his business partners. In fact, he stated a preference for black men over white men who might be employed to do the same work of carrying heavy animal pelts over challenging portages (the miles to be crossed on dry land between waterways on a journey). In a series of letters in 1764 and 1765, Sterling complained about the poor performance of a white worker, Charles Morrison, writing that Morrison was not as good as "negroes" in transporting merchandise (in this case, a massive "eighty-five packs of peltry").[91]

For her part in this successful slaveholding union, Angelique Cuillerier was the child of a slaveholder who probably enjoyed the services of Indian slaves before her marriage to James Sterling. She also secured "a negro wench for her own use" from John Duncan, a business partner of her husband. Angelique paid for this black woman with "the price of the peltry," a trade to Duncan, skins for skin. A black woman held in bondage would have been more than a source of domestic labor for a French elite woman like Angelique. Similarly to the black boy that Pontiac sought in the heat of conflict, such a woman symbolized the status of her owner. A living, breathing ornament that highlighted her mistress's access to exotic, costly things, a black woman in 1760s Detroit was worth her weight in furs.[92] For black slaves were still much more difficult to acquire than Indian ones in the Great Lakes, and females of African descent were the rarest kind of human being transformed into commodities in the settlement on the strait.

Beyond serving as luxury goods for a few European elites, black women could find themselves enslaved in Detroit as a means of keeping black men in line. While French, and to some extent British, men set aside Indian women for their own self-serving sexual purposes, these slaveholders sometimes maneuvered to pair black women with black men. In one recorded example of this kind of strategic purchase of African American women, the explicitly stated reason was to placate black men being held in bondage. James Sterling reveals as much when he writes in 1764 that he has gotten hold of "2 young Negro wenches for the two big negroes whom I have employ'd . . . with the Engineer for the winter. The French are afraid to buy them without wenches for fear they should run away. Yet I have been offered a good deal more than what they cost."[93] Sterling's words indicate not only the high value placed on black women, but also his attempt to allay the fears of French clients by providing sex partners for black male slaves who might otherwise abscond. His stated intention to artificially manufacture couples suggests the existence of more than one sexual market for bondswomen in Detroit. Indigenous women were paired with white men as sexual and domestic servants, and black women were paired with black men as sexual consorts to quell resistance.

Sterling's cynical action here has an element in common with the breeding practices of southern slaveholders who forced black women to lie with black men in order to increase the size of an enslaved population. But rather than explicitly trying to produce greater numbers of slaves through compelled procreation, Sterling is seeking to produce complacency through the formation of black pair bonds. This nuanced exploitation of black women's sexual labor in Detroit is difficult to pinpoint and verify, but trace evidence in the records of merchants like Sterling leaves a trail to follow. The letter book of Schenectady, New York–based merchants provides another example pointing to the constructed coupling of black women and men. The Phyn and Ellice Company often took purchase orders from merchants and residents in Detroit, including several for slaves. In June of 1771, the pair informed Detroit merchant John

Porteous: "We have contracted with a New England Gentleman . . . for some green Negroes to be dilver[ed] here. . . . When your wench will be forwarded together with Negro Boy in case she may sometime hereafter choose a Husband we apprehend he will be useful to you or advantageous at the Sloop or you can despose [sic] of him as you find best the price £50 each."[94] In this case, Phyn and Ellice were providing Porteous with the woman slave he had requested (again, an indication of the market for black women) and throwing a young black man in with the deal, assuming that the man would make a fitting sex partner for the woman, prove useful in boat work, and barring either outcome, be resalable in Detroit.

Although the merchants who doubled as slave traders paired black men and women for practical reasons that served their own profit motives, by forcibly arranging enslaved blacks into couples, Detroit elites provided for the formation of black nuclear families. Sometimes enslaved men and women formed ties that endured and entered the state of formal marriage recognized by the Catholic Church. Most of these enslaved couples were composed of black husbands and wives; the few interracial marriages were between black men and Native women. The pattern of these rare Afro-Indian couplings among slaves stemmed from demographic realities: larger numbers of Indian women than Indian men in the enslaved population and increasing numbers of black men in the area due to British merchants' active procurement of them. The children of these couples were labeled as "Panis" or "Negro" in church records, both terms being synonymous with "slave."

This fate of inherited slavery for mixed-race children with Indian mothers and black fathers departs from much of what we know about how indigeneity functioned for Afro-Native people in early America. In the American Northeast and the South in the late eighteenth and nineteenth centuries, having a Native American mother could be a means to freedom for black people of mixed ancestry. This is because the enslavement of Native Americans was outlawed in northeastern as well as southern colonies and states by individual laws passed between the middle and late 1700s. Holding an Indian person as a slave became illegal in most locations in the east. This did not mean that Native people previously enslaved there were not still secretly held on farms and plantations.

Certainly they were, and many of these hidden American Indian bondspeople would fade into the recesses of historical consciousness. It did mean, though, that people trying to buy or sell indigenous slaves could come under scrutiny and see their claims challenged in the courts. In many cases, when enslaved individuals with Indian mothers and black fathers brought suit for their freedom in American courts, they prevailed on legal grounds tied to an assumption of the indigenous rights to liberty inheritable through the maternal line.[95] Just as black women were seen as producing slave children nearly as a matter of course, Native American women were seen as producing free children.

But Detroit presented a starkly different context. Here in the western borderlands, Indian slavery was the norm, and the practice of owning Native slaves was sanctioned by governing authorities—the French and then British Crowns—as well as by the Church. Having a Native American mother guaranteed nothing to a mixed-race slave, except the likelihood of lifelong bondage. The situation of Marie-Marguerite, an enslaved Native woman, is a case in point. Marie-Marguerite was owned in Detroit by a mixed-race (French and Miami) woman, Marie Suzanne Richard. Marie Suzanne Richard had retained her slaves as part of her inherited estate after her husband's death in a French legal context that permitted women to own and inherit property with fewer restrictions than in British North America. Marie-Marguerite married Charles, a black man also owned by Richard. When the two had a daughter, Catherine, in 1752, the priest recorded the baby's race as "negresse," making clear that this child was to be considered a slave and drawing a visible line of differentiation between this unfree infant and her owner.[96] This instance also shows, like the example of Angelique Sterling, that white men were not the only slaveholders in Detroit. French, mixed-race, and Native women owned slaves as well. In another case, a Miami woman, Tacumwah, who coupled with a British and then a French man in Detroit, had acquired slaves by trading rum. The Frenchman with whom she lived in the early 1770s was a Beaubien, the same family to which Angelique Sterling belonged and that owned the slave arrested by the British for suspected betrayal during Pontiac's War.[97]

Whether held by white or Native owners, children born to enslaved Indian mothers and black fathers were in the extreme minority in Detroit and other French colonial towns. Even fewer enslaved families with both a Native father and mother existed here, and only one such family was listed in the Ste. Anne register in Detroit: Babet, Piere, and their child Catherine, Panis slaves of Charles Cicotte.[98] This marriage pattern, or lack thereof, for indigenous women strongly suggests that white male owners were claiming sexual rights to their slaves, leaving little room for Indian women to marry enslaved men even in a society that sanctioned such unions.[99] Frenchmen, and the British men who moved into town after them, wanted Indian women, sometimes as free wives, but more often as unfree sexual consorts. This may be why Mr. Collbeck, a British trading partner of Detroit merchant James Sterling, liked to keep the Indian women near his home in Niagara, New York, "frequently drunk."[100] The particular value that Native women were perceived as possessing, a value of erotic and sexual potential long instantiated in the social and cultural expectations of fur trade society, coincided with their value as household laborers. In the 1760s and beyond, uncountable infants born to enslaved Native women had been conceived by white men in Detroit. Most of these babies went unclaimed by their fathers and were listed in the Ste. Anne's registry along with their mother's name, their mother's status as "Panis," and the notation that they were the progeny of an "unknown father." For sixty-nine "Panis" babies born in Detroit, the father was listed as "unknown" or not mentioned at all.[101]

There were, of course, exceptions to the scenario in which the child of an enslaved Indian mother was also consigned to slavery. A small number of French slave-owners in colonial settlements are recorded as formally freeing Indian women in order to marry them, women with whom these men had shared beds and conceived children.[102] The majority of Frenchmen did not bother with this formality, however, and did not bestow on their enslaved consorts the legal protections of freedom. With the turnover from French to British control, British military officers and merchants joined the slaveholding ranks in Detroit, though the cultural prohibition against sexual relations across racial lines was stronger in British colonial society than in the French settlements. Still, Englishmen pursued sexual relations with Native women, too, continuing a pattern that was all too familiar in their adopted region. The best-documented example is that of John Askin, who had braved a trip to Detroit to deliver provisions during Pontiac's siege and would later return to become one of Detroit's most prominent merchants and leather-good manufacturers.[103]

The young John Askin had arrived in North America in 1758, hailing from a family of shopkeepers in Ireland. After building a business in Albany, New York, that chiefly provided supplies to the British army, Askin moved to the northwest fur trade post of Michilimackinac in search of new opportunities in the Upper Great Lakes. In Michilimackinac, most likely in the 1760s, he acquired a Native slave woman named Mannette from a Mr. Bourrass. Mannette was probably Ottawa from a nearby village, and her cultural knowledge and social connections along with her linguistic versatility were beneficial to Askin's trading enterprise. Askin's access to rum smoothed his relations with Native traders as did his intimate ties with this unfree Indian woman. He had three children with Mannette: John Jr., Catherine, and Madelaine, born in 1762 and 1764. Askin claimed, cared for, and educated his children with Mannette. In 1766 he freed the children's mother in a manumission letter in which he promised to "set at liberty and give full freedom unto my Panesse slave named Mannette."[104] Askin vowed, further, that "She is a free woman at full liberty and Mistress of herself to dispose of herself as good Seemeth unto her."[105]

Apparently, what seemed good to Mannette was cutting ties with her former owner, John Askin, even if that meant leaving their little ones behind. The children remained with Askin and his French wife from Detroit, Archange Askin, who raised them in a household served by Indian and black bondspeople. John Askin Jr. would become a trader and Catherine Askin would marry Samuel Robertson, a British employee of the Phyn and Ellice Company, whose job was to captain boats carrying furs, supplies, and, likely, slaves, in the New York–Western circuit.[106] The children of an enslaved mother, they were now part of a mixed-race class that participated in slavery. But after Mannette's manumission, there is no trace of this Ottawa mother in Askin's correspondence; she fades into the shadows of colonial history like so many other Indian women held as slaves across the Great Lakes.

Askin's act of emancipation is a rare recorded example of such largesse among British slaveholders in Detroit. Later, John Askin would hold several more Native women as slaves and one Native woman as his ward. These women may have been vulnerable to sexual advances in a household in which their owner had bedded an Indian slave in the past. While there is no indication in the existing documents that John Askin engaged in relations with any of these women, records often fail us in the search for the experiences of slaves in Detroit. There is one thing we can know for certain: most stories of the women owned by John Askin, like most stories of slaves held in Detroit between Pontiac's Rebellion and the American Revolutionary War, did not end like Mannette's, with "full freedom."

A Dim Force

In the 1760s, Detroit was an isolated place where people lived in a concentrated area, depending upon a local exchange of goods and services for their survival. A dim force drove the growth of this linchpin port town in the Great Lakes. Slavery was integral to the workings of the settlement.[107] Leading French and British families owned one or two slaves, usually of indigenous descent and acquired mainly through Native brokers in exchange for utilitarian items such as guns, ammunition, and blankets. Enslaved people could be found laboring in every capacity in the town—in bedrooms, in kitchens, in wheat fields, and in manufactures. And importantly, enslaved men crafted the storage containers, manned the boats, and transported the bundles that comprised the town's chief economic activity—the fur trade.

More invisible in the historical literature than even these unfree men whose labors supported the frenzy for fur, were unfree women. Most enslaved people in Detroit, as notated in the Ste. Anne's Church register, were indigenous and female. Both the practice of marrying Indian wives according to local customs and the habit of using Indian slaves for sex informed the unspoken view among male slaveholders in Detroit that indigenous women were fit for sexual-domestic roles. Free Native women with a recognized tribal or national designation, and the protections that came with this political identity, were accorded social regard in this French-Indian dominant community. Panis women, by contrast, those stripped away from their families and tribes of origin, were just as vulnerable to sale and abuse as slaves of African descent. Because Indian women could be found in a spectrum of arrangements with white men in Detroit, the lines between free Indian wife, long-term Panis concubine, and casual Panis sex slave blur in the historical record.[108] In popular understandings of Midwestern history, Native women who were owned by Frenchmen have faded into the background behind more positive narratives of Native women who were married to them. But unfree indigenous women lived and struggled in Detroit, too, making up the largest portion of the enslaved population.

In the era of Pontiac's War, slavery in Detroit was a multidimensional, multicultural, multiracial, and malleable tradition. Traders, merchants, farmers, and priests could own people of color in this fortified French-Indian-British town where colonial laws governing slavery were inapplicable, unenforced, or undeveloped. Due to the relatively short life spans of enslaved people in New France (with an average death occurring before the twentieth birthday) most bondspeople in this period were young and Indian; a handful were black.[109] These individuals were compelled, by the theft of their freedom, to meet the fundamental demands of privileged residents in the Detroit River region—residents who sought slaves for mobility (the movement of goods), for intimacy (the satisfaction of sexual desires), for domesticity (the maintenance of households), and for luxury (the pleasures attached to owning prestige goods). On this razor-thin edge of settled life along the strait of Detroit, scores of Indians and a smattering of Africans were held as captives by fur trade elites, and also held captive, along with their owners, by forces that were changing the course of North American history.

2

The War for Liberty (1774–1783)

> If that Post be reduced we shall be quiet in future on our frontiers.
>
> —*Thomas Jefferson to George Rogers Clark about Detroit, 1780*

What was going through Ann Wyley's mind when she entered and burgled the furrier shop of two of Detroit's most successful merchants? Certainly not that she and her accomplice, the Frenchman Jean Baptiste Contencineau, would escape unpunished if caught for theft.[1] Like most British businessmen in the bustling frontier maritime town, James Abbott and Thomas Finchley, targets of the break-in, dealt in furs and imported goods. Their job was to procure skins from local hunters or middlemen and ship those pelts to purchasers in the East in exchange for supplies; they then sold or distributed manufactured items to customers and American Indian trade partners. The pair operated a shop located near a host of others along the northern bank of the Detroit River, the liquid-gold main street of colonial Fort Detroit.[2] And in addition to co-owning the store itself, Abbott and Finchley co-owned Ann Wyley, an enslaved woman of African descent. Abbott was an Irishman by birth whose arrival in 1768 had been timed to take advantage of opportunities afforded by the British assumption of former French posts. Finchley, his business partner, is a more reclusive figure in the records of early Detroit, who appears only infrequently in conjunction with shorthand notations about the pair's firm. Both men were slaveholders, as were other members of the newly arrived British merchant elite. Between Pontiac's Rebellion and the American Revolutionary War, these men joined their French and Euro-Indian mixed-race counterparts in the capitalist enterprise of the Great Lakes skin trade, acquiring the pelts of beasts and bodies of humans to build wealth and influence. Between the waning years of the French period and the rise of the British period, the ratio of indigenous to black slaves tilted only slightly. An approximate count of the Ste. Anne's parish records indicates sixty-four Natives to five blacks in the 1760s and forty-six Natives to eight blacks in the 1770s. It would take a revolution and shifting political balance of power for numbers of enslaved blacks to substantially increase in a town defined as part of the American Northwest Territory.[3]

Ann Wyley was among few blacks, enslaved or free, living in Detroit in the early 1770s. How the firm of Abbott & Finchley came to count her among its assets is unknown. Equally mysterious are the precise details of what took place on the night the storehouse was robbed, as the fragmented testimony of participants varied at the time, and the testimony of Ann Wyley, portrayed as the instigator by her co-conspirator, was not preserved in the record. In the spring and summer of 1774, a series of petty thefts had been taking place inside the walls of the fort, wrangling the frayed nerves and thinning the pocketbooks of resident merchants. Ann Wyley, "a negro slave" of Abbott & Finchley, Jean Contencineau, "a Canadian of humble station" in the employ of Abbott & Finchley, and Charles Landry, another laborer at the firm who worked alongside Jean packing peltry, were all suspected as perpetrators in "a system of small pilfering that had been going on for some time."[4] The most dramatic of these crimes—the burglary at Abbott & Finchley's store apparently facilitated by an act of arson—was the final straw, the bold incident that led to a government crackdown, Ann Wyley's jailing, and Jean Contencineau's death. The violation of property rights within the heavily guarded fort unnerved the moneyed class in Detroit, and "a feeling prevailed that there could be no security until such worthless characters were adequately punished."[5]

In this heist that set the wheels of Detroit's barebones justice system in motion, "eight pounds of beaver skins, two otter skins, and some raccoon skins, to the value of four pounds sterling" along with a handful of domestic items and "little knives" had been stolen. Of the spoils, Ann Wyley had come away with "a purse containing six guineas, the property of James Abbot . . . which purse were found on [her] person," as well as "a handkerchief, containing two pair of women's shoes and a piece of flannel."[6]

Was Wyley making a statement of political import through her illegal action? Did she wish to adorn herself with the feminine items now in her possession, to embellish the rough apparel provided by her owners that likely marked her inferior status as a slave?[7] Did she think she could improve her material condition by taking the goods and selling them on the illicit market? Or was there a deeply emotional element motivating her actions? Perhaps Ann had bonded with or felt indebted to her accomplice, Contencineau, who worked in the shop as a "servant," and might have been indentured (bound for a period of years) to Abbott & Finchley's firm.[8] Perhaps Ann longed to strike a blow against her owners where she knew it would hurt the most—their commercial enterprise, the other valuable "things" they owned.

Whatever her reasons for taking the risk, Wyley, along with her accomplice, faced dire consequences for her actions. Arrested by the authorities, the duo faced indictment for "subtilly, privily [and] craftily . . . steal[ing], tak[ing], and convey[ing] away" the "goods and chattels of the said Abbot and Finchley" as well as "attempting to set fire to the house of the said Abbot and Finchley." Confined to the barracks where prisoners were kept in the fort, the unlikely pair awaited trial for nearly two years, an expanse of time during which Wyley stood at the mercy of her military jailers, much like the unnamed "Panis" slave woman who was similarly imprisoned there for reasons unknown in 1763.

In the spring of 1776 Ann Wyley and Jean Contencineau finally had their day in court, but the proceedings of that court were far from regular. The passage of the Quebec Act in 1774 had established the boundaries of British Canada and included Michigan within the legal jurisdiction of Quebec.[9] Officials in Quebec then appointed military and civil leaders to run the distant posts. In 1775, Henry Hamilton, a captain in the British army described as "overbearing and supercilious," became lieutenant governor of Detroit. As the town's chief civil leader, Hamilton worked closely with Philip Dejean, Detroit's notary and justice of the peace since 1767, who was suspected of being "a bankrupt merchant from Montreal . . . that came west to better his fortune by leaving his debts and creditors behind."[10] Dejean's mandate was never clearly defined by British officials in Quebec; nor were the legal rights of Detroiters in relation to local governance.[11] But there was a sense among residents that Dejean's nebulous authority did not grant him the right to judge serious offenses or exact harsh punishments.

Lieutenant Governor Hamilton and Judge Dejean saw their roles in a different light. Operating within a gap of formal governmental oversight, they tended to settle minor disputes among residents in an ad hoc, heavy-handed, and even authoritarian manner. No regular court proceedings were held in Detroit in the transitional period between French and British rule, but Dejean did assemble a jury of twelve to hear the case of Wyley and Contencineau. Charles Landry, a third suspect in the Abbott & Finchley robbery, had escaped prosecution, having confessed to stealing "some beaver and otter skins . . . in the company of the said Jean Coutancineau." Landry was viewed as a bit player in the crime. But Ann Wyley, according to Contencineau's testimony, was the mastermind of the entire scheme. Contencineau testified that "he knew nothing whatever concerning the cash box that was in the storehouse; that he only saw the negress, Anne, who belonged to Messrs Abbott and Finchelay carry a little box into the kitchen, the day after the fire, but that he did not know what she did with it, and the instant later . . . the negress crushed the cash box with her foot and threw it into the fire." While claiming no personal responsibility for the fire or missing money, Contencineau "confessed, nevertheless, and acknowledged that he stole a beaver skin, conjointly with a man named Landry who was making packs with him for Abbott and Finchelay." Contencineau also stated that when he carried stolen items (the shoes, cloth, and handkerchief) to the house of a soldier's wife, he did so at the direction of Ann Wyley who was "afraid that her master was about to look up his trunk."[12]

Contencineau represented himself as someone who had made a mistake in the petty pilfering of furs and knives, but who lacked the premeditation, insider knowledge, and craftiness of his black female companion. Upon further examination in a second statement to the court, Contencineau even suggested that Wyley had planned the fire, placing "some powder in a horn . . . together in a piece of cloth with a piece of tinder" and "while her master was dining" giving the kindling to Contencineau to "place it upon a piece of English cloth" in the storehouse. He stated further that "after the negress had given him the six dollars [from the cash box], the negress threw the box to him and said 'Empty it and throw it in the fire.'"

In the scant pages of testimony that have survived the centuries, Ann Wyley is only attributed two lines of speech: a directive to her accomplice to hide the evidence, and her own paraphrased testimony in which she "declared that she had given the four silver dollar to Mr Cenette, one of the paper dollars to Mr Chatelain and the other to Mr C Enfant" and that she "had given three pounds in paper to Jean Coutencineau, which said three pounds he carried to Samuel Denny" at her request.[13] Ann Wyley, according to her testimony, was compensating Frenchmen of means with the stolen funds of her masters.[14] Could she have been paying down debts, paying for silence, or purchasing the promise of future assistance in an even larger scheme, such as the theft of her own person from those who claimed her and her release from lifelong captivity?

Jean Contencineau's attempt to shield himself from the worst of the charges did no good. He was viewed as equally culpable with Ann Wyley. In Justice of the Peace Philip Dejean's makeshift court, "the prisoners were found guilty only of the trivial offense of stealing property of a total value of about fifty dollars and there was grave doubt whether the woman was guilty at all." The charge of arson could not be substantiated, as the jury only found circumstantial evidence to support it. The pair was therefore acquitted of the more serious of the two crimes. Nevertheless Philip Dejean determined that the penalty for theft in this case should be death, a decision approved by Lieutenant Governor Henry Hamilton. The punishment was to be carried out on the town commons (at Detroit's present-day Jefferson Avenue) on March 26, 1776.[15]

The handwritten note scribbled by Philip Dejean on the back page of the verdict in French revealed the tenor of his thinking about this harsh decision: "You shall be hanged-hanged-hanged, and strangled until you be dead," he wrote of the pair. And then he entered more intimate words directed toward Contencineau, a fellow French Canadian and likely fellow Catholic whom Dejean addressed as "my dear brother." "You see, my dear brother," the justice penned on his notice of execution, "that it is neither the jury nor myself that has condemned you to death—it is the law that you violated. It is for domestic theft that you are now going to lose your life. According to the English laws, a domestic who steals a shilling, or the value thereof, merits death." Dejean impressed upon Contencineau, in words that may have been read aloud, that even if "bad examples" had come from the servant's own "masters," Contencineau must "understand that God and the laws will not excuse you, and say with me the Lord's Prayer and Ave Maria."[16] Dejean intended to hold the Frenchman accountable not only to the law, but also to a higher power. As a member of the servant class, Contencineau was ordained by God to mind his place in the social hierarchy. Wyley, too, would hang for her crime as part of Dejean's final judgment, but her soul was not of interest to him, and he penned her no parting words.

Dejean's choice to punish Contencineau just as harshly as Wyley points to the quixotic character of slavery in colonial Detroit. This remote fort had nothing like the regimented racial systems of bondage found in larger and older slaveholding communities in places like South Carolina or even New York. A coherent system of laws organizing the practice of slavery did not exist and would never fully take shape in Detroit. The physical isolation and in-limbo jurisdictional quality of the western settlement, which lacked a stable, rationalized civilian government, led to a form of slavery that was fluid and even capricious until its eventual demise in the first decades of the 1800s. In this unusual instance, a white man faced the same punishment as his enslaved, black female codefendant. And the case would take an even more shocking turn when the day of reckoning arrived.

No hangman could be found to put the condemned Frenchman to death, perhaps due to the extremity of the punishment in relation to the scale of the offense. Undeterred, the justice of the peace devised an ingenious solution. He offered Ann Wyley a gruesome choice in order to avoid her own death sentence. The prisoner "was released and pardoned of the said sentenced judgment of death, by the said Philip Dejean . . . on condition that [she], the said negress, would by herself as executioner, execute and put to death, the above named John Coustantininau."[17] Wyley consented, playing the part of hangwoman in exchange for her life, and according to one source, her freedom.[18] If the sinister deal was solely to save her life, it may have been extended in recognition of Wyley's value to Abbott and Finchley. If the offer did indeed include a promise of freedom, it parallels another example of a French colonial practice of bribing enslaved people with the dearest reward in order to compel them to do the government's dirtiest work. In the same period in New Orleans, a black man named Louis Congo won and maintained his freedom as well as his wife's by serving as the city executioner.[19] Ann Wyley's participation in this ghastly affair hints at the desperation of a life lived in slavery, a desperation that exploded into theft, possibly arson, and finally murder.

According to the historical record, Dejean placed the noose in Wyley's hand because no one else was willing to undertake the deed. Perhaps this is so. And just as likely, this sadistic form of retribution in which a slave was made to kill her accomplice, even an accomplice who had betrayed her in his testimony, had a secondary purpose beyond utility. Judge Dejean was no stranger to slaveholding. He had personal stakes in the practice, as evidenced by a transaction in 1777 in which a man named Thomas William had sent Philip Dejean a bill "for vending a Negro."[20] Dejean and other Detroit slaveholders would have been familiar with the toxic effects of holding people in chains. They may well have known about the New York slave revolt of 1708 when a Native man and black woman murdered their owner's family before escaping, or about the larger New York uprising in 1712 when blacks adopted arson as a weapon.[21] They would have worried about such aggressive tactics, the stuff of outright rebellion, being taken up by enslaved people in Detroit. Dejean explicitly fretted, too, about the "domestic" nature of this crime. While James Abbott had been contentedly enjoying his evening meal, his servant and slave had violated the sanctity of his storehouse, testing the security of the entire merchant class. Together, these offenders represented a threat of symbolic proportions—not from outside the fort walls, but from within. Dejean's harshly creative reprisal therefore served as a warning to slaves like Ann Wyley, who might see arson as a tool of self-liberation, as well as to poor whites like Contencineau, who might perceive an interest in common with enslaved people of color.

On the day that a Frenchman was publicly hanged by a black bondswoman, poor whites and indentured servants living in Detroit could glimpse, in terror, what their fate might be if they dared collaborate with slaves. As late as the 1940s, the descendant of an old Detroit family still recalled the sting of this public rebuke, writing in a family history that: "On the day appointed the Detroit Common witnessed the degrading spectacle of the Frenchman being done to death by the slave woman."[22] Racial categories linked to social status mattered and were monitored, even on the Great Lakes frontier, where a civil official skillfully deployed this social hierarchy to control the behavior of a class-stratified, multiracial populace.

Indigenous people fell into a gray area between the racial boxes taking shape in Detroit, categorized as Negro-like if they were enslaved (as designated by the term "Panis") but viewed as having other essential characteristics that differentiated them from blacks. Unlike individuals of African descent, Indians were members of polities in North America: politically organized groups with military might and economic influence that European imperial powers were compelled to recognize. Pontiac's Rebellion had failed to capture Forts Detroit and Pitt, but did force the British out of several western garrisons and frighten colonial authorities. In order to improve relations with restive Native groups, British military officials restored the practice of gift giving, and the British Crown passed the Royal Proclamation of 1763, which forbade colonial settlement west of the Allegheny Mountains.[23] Because of indigenous political organization and the essential role of Native hunters and traders in the commercial fur trade market that spanned eastern North America and crossed the Atlantic, it was impossible for American Indians as a whole to be reduced to the degraded category of "slave" and hence racialized as a fixed, inferior caste.

Some Natives were being enslaved, but others were free individuals of influence. This did not mean, however, that members of the Detroit elite shied away from trying to control American Indians, even those who were free. The purpose of Fort Detroit, dating back to its founding, had been the formation of a military and mercantile post that structured the presence of indigenous people, strategically leveraging these communities as a source of furs as well as a physical barrier to the advance of European competitors.[24] After ousting the French from their prize western post at Detroit, the British recognized, with irritation, that the Great Lakes Indians had not been conquered or displaced. They then followed the previous prescription of Detroit founder Antoine de La Mothe Cadillac, seeking to keep neighboring Indians amiable and pliable in the interest of building a trade monopoly.

So even as town leaders made an example of Wyley and Contencineau to enforce control over colored slaves and poor white servants, they also sought to exercise authority over free Native people who did regular business in town. Most Indians linked to Detroit lived in their own villages but constantly moved through the fort to engage in trade, attend religious services, and socialize with friends and family members. In the 1770s, at least eighteen free Indians attended Ste. Anne's Church, participating in marriages, baptisms, and burials. Most were identified simply as "Indian" in the priest's registry; three were described as Huron, three as métis, and one as Iroquois. These individuals would have been connected to relatives whose names were not necessarily listed when a religious event was recorded, making the estimated figure of eighteen a certain undercount. The number of free Native people involved in the church amounted to less than half of the "Panis" slaves there, whose population in the church registry of 1770–79 reached forty-six.[25] In a fort that imposed geographical intimacy on its residents and visitors due to its diminutive size and tightly intersecting roads, indigenous people would have made up a highly visible, as well as significant, minority group.

The importance of the indigenous presence in Detroit was readily apparent in the plan and architecture of the town. Negotiating with Native people was so crucial to the security of Detroit that an Indian Council House would be constructed in 1779, long before the existence of a courthouse or school. The wooden building provided a place for military officials to woo Indian allies, for town officials to talk with Native political representatives, and for merchants to meet with Native traders; it also became the only sizeable social gathering spot beyond the austere Ste. Anne's. Trader Alexander Macomb, apparently fond of a lively night out, remarked to Lieutenant Governor Hamilton that the Indian Council House, one of few public buildings other than military structures, was "a very excellent house for haranguing as well as for dancing." Macomb's offhand remark reveals the dependence of Euro-Detroiters on the secondary, as well as primary, benefits of the "Indian trade."[26]

Indians were essential to the mix of diverse peoples that made up

Detroit. Nevertheless, church and civil officials felt anxious about having Indians so near. They balked, especially, at what they saw as the "disturbances occasioned by Indians made quarrelsome by the use of liquors."[27] These liquors consisted mainly of brandy and rum customarily provided to Native people in diplomatic exchanges and traded to Indians by European merchants, a practice that, not coincidentally, often had the effect of bettering terms for whites. In April of 1774, the same season that Wyley and Contencineau robbed the store of Abbott & Finchley, British officials compelled Detroit merchants to limit alcohol sales to just one glass per Indian and to stock all rum in a "general" storehouse in order to prevent trouble. Major firms in the town agreed to the prohibition, including Abbott & Finchley. James Abbott then joined James Sterling, Alexander Macomb, and John Porteous to form a committee charged with penalizing Indian liquor transactions. Restrictions on alcohol consumption became just one way in which colonial officials sought to control Native freedoms.

Land Grabs in the Shadow of War

Soon after a Frenchman was hanged by the slave of James Abbott on the orders of the justice of the peace at Detroit, the Continental Congress of the American colonies proclaimed political independence. It was early July of 1776. From Philadelphia, where the Continental Congress met, to the colonial population centers of New York and Boston, news of the momentous decision to sever ties with Great Britain and throw off the mantle of King George III traveled by horseback and word of mouth. In the public houses of New York, officers of the Continental Army proceeded to "testify our joy at the happy news of Independence." When read aloud on July 9 on the order of General George Washington, the potent words of the Declaration of Independence penned by the young Virginia planter and lawyer Thomas Jefferson reverberated across the Philadelphia Commons.[28]

While rebellious residents of the eastern colonies readied themselves to defend these words that formally commenced the American Revolutionary War, Detroit merchant William Macomb was otherwise occupied, sealing a stupendous land deal. Like Thomas Jefferson and George

Washington, William Macomb was a slaveholder. Unlike these "founding fathers" of the republic, Macomb would develop his wealth on the riverbanks and islands of the Great Lakes fur trade region rather than in the agrarian South. When William Macomb and his elder brother Alexander strode across the Detroit River's largest island in the summer of 1776, they were aware of the fate of the black slave Wyley and the French servant Contencineau, and they knew something of the trouble brewing back East. New York traders Phyn and Ellice had complained to the Macomb brothers about the disruption that mounting hostilities were causing as early as June of 1775, informing them that shoes on order might not be delivered. "Such is the distressed situation of this Country that nothing can be positively promised," they wrote. "We are not allowed to send Riffles [sic] out of the Country there are not any servants to be had." The brothers were likely unaware, however, of the drastic escalation of the diplomatic impasse that led to the Americans' declaration of independence. The catastrophic impact of a burgeoning revolution had barely rippled through the western populace. Great Lakes garrisons at Detroit and Michilimackinac had seen soldiers transported to Boston via Quebec in the spring of 1775, and some of these men had been present at the Battle of Lexington. But news traveled slowly to the interior, and word of America's formally declared intention to break from Great Britain had not yet arrived.[29]

For the Macomb brothers, the pressing matter in July of 1776 was securing the purchase of Grosse Ile, the largest among twenty-one islands in the Detroit River archipelago.[30] In the 1770s and in the wake of increased British immigration following Pontiac's quelled rebellion, leaders of the Potawatomi, the Detroit-area indigenous group that claimed this island, had been selling several stretches of land to newly arrived residents. These transactions were technically illegal, as only the British Crown held the authority to carry out land transactions with Native people in the West. But British settlers elbowed into off-limits areas despite the Proclamation of 1763. In Detroit, a far remove from effective British political authority, even members of the military participated in and sanctioned illegitimate land exchanges. So on July 6, 1776, two days after the American Colonies declared independence, William and Alexander Macomb signed a parchment contract made of smoothed animal skin. Along with fifteen Potawatomi leaders, who entered their signatures beside exquisitely hand-drawn animal symbols representing their clans, and in the presence of two French witnesses, the brothers entered into an agreement. The contract read: "We the Chiefs and principal Leaders of Potterwatemy nation of Indians at Detroit . . . bear unto Alexander and William Macomb of Detroit, merchants . . . that messuage or Tract of Land known by the name of Grosse-Isle, and call'd in our Language Kitché Minishen or Grand Island, situate, lying, and being in the mouth of Detroit River where it empties itself into Lake Erie." No price of exchange is recorded in the document. Soon after this momentous, under-the-table purchase, Lieutenant Governor Henry Hamilton gave William Macomb permission to take possession of the island. In 1780, this vague deed would be affirmed as a "voluntary act of the chiefs of the Pottawatome Nation" by the British commander in Detroit at the time, Captain Arent Schuyler De Peyster, who would later marry into the Macomb family. In 1820, Alexander Macomb would defend himself against stories that the Macombs bought the island with "only trinkets," writing: "I had little to do on that score. We made several purchases of the Indians, which were in a manner forced on us by their importunities. Our influence with the pottawatomies was great & they were the proprietors of the lands below Detroit."[31]

If Alexander Macomb and his future son-in-law, Arent De Peyster, protested too much in the aftermath of the Grosse Ile deal, insisting that the massive sale was the result of the Potawatomis' entreaties and therefore voluntary as well as ethical, William Macomb quietly profited from the land grab, becoming one of the wealthiest men in Detroit by the time of his death in 1796. Owning vast swaths of land as well as several slaves meant that William Macomb could lay claim to the game hunted there, harvest natural resources, extend agricultural development, and charge other residents for rent, creating capital and income streams that would allow him to do more of the same: trade goods, acquire acreage, buy slaves, and put those slaves to work on his property as caretakers, farmers, builders, transporters, and domestics.

The Macomb brothers' conduct is an exaggerated example of the mode of settlement and urban development adopted by most elite British residents in the late eighteenth-century Detroit River region. They moved to the area, imported and produced goods for the local market, processed and sold furs collected by Indian hunters, acquired tracts of Native land under specious circumstances, built homes and operated farms with slave labor, and used slaves to transport raw materials and finished goods from west to east and east to west. The most successful of these men attached themselves to a branch of official government business, principally supplying the British military or serving as Indian agents, and they used the pressure of rising white land speculation as well as wartime violability to further encroach on Native territories. In short, British subjects, who did not want for ambition, combined access to Indian land and Indian-procured furs, slave labor, and government connections to build their businesses, and with these, the town of Detroit. Like the metropolis of New York whose backstory of black slavery is now widely recognized, the great industrial and cultural center of twentieth-century Detroit had its roots in greed, graft, and forced racialized labor. Those roots crossed the cultural lines of British and French elites, whose family trees began to merge in the 1760s and '70s. Some British merchants were wise enough to marry into wealthy French families, like James Sterling, the well-positioned trader whose shop was in place before the outbreak of Pontiac's War, and like Alexander Macomb, who married Catherine Navarre, daughter of the French notary and slaveholder Robert Navarre.[32] Within decades, the bicultural daughters of these first British residents would be attractive mates to incoming American businessmen who eyed Detroit as a space of new opportunity at the turn of the nineteenth century.

The networks and commercial ventures built by British Detroiters linked that interior hamlet to towns and cities near the eastern Great Lakes. Although Detroit was remote on the map of northern colonial settlements and surrounded by forests and Indian villages, it possessed close ties to colonial New York, which sat on Lakes Ontario and Erie. Indeed, Detroit resembled New York in situation and characteristics. Like New York City, Detroit was sculpted by waterways that moved around and through the town, forming a series of inlets and islands. Like broader New York, Detroit adopted an urban-style slavery oriented around skilled trades, manufacturing, shipping, and small-scale agriculture. Decades into the future, Detroit would follow the ambivalent and stuttering lead of New York in the development of gradual emancipation for its enslaved population.[33] And consequentially in 1776, like New York City,

Detroit was a British military and loyalist stronghold. Although they lived at "the edge of the West" and deep inside Indian territory, Detroiters were no country bumpkins as some easterners at the time liked to think.[34] Detroit's intrinsic relationship with the people, goods, and ideas of New York was one essential way in which this fortified frontier town was "poised at the intersection of East and West, empire and frontier, core and periphery, and imperialism and localism."[35]

The power brokers in Detroit at the outbreak of the American Revolution were cosmopolitan British traders who trafficked in slavery and misappropriated indigenous lands. They were also members of a tight-knit economic and social circle, aiding one another, intermarrying, trading goods, and exchanging the bodies of slaves. British loyalists nearly to a man, these English, Scottish, and Irish businessmen found opportunity as well as difficulty as the once distant war for independence exploded, drawing ever nearer to their Great Lakes enclave.

War Comes to the Northwest

William and Alexander Macomb were sons of the British Isles, born to Scottish parents who were living in Ireland in the late 1740s and 1750s. Their father, John Gordon Macomb, relocated the family to Albany, New York, in 1755. There the Macomb men entered the brisk business of trade. With the blessing and financial assistance of their father, the adult-aged Macomb sons moved to Detroit in 1769, where they set up shop as traders and merchants, taking advantage of their father's contacts and access to suppliers in the east. The Macomb, Edgar & Macomb mercantile company supplied British military personnel and other residents in Detroit with imported goods, plunged into the pelt trade that was Detroit's chief commercial activity, and acted as local bankers. Besides the profitable land of Grosse Ile "purchased" from Potawatomi leaders, Alexander Macomb attested: "the Ottawas & Chippewas also granted us large tracts back of the Settlement & from the River." The Macomb brothers did well for themselves despite the eventual refusal of the American Congress to affirm these latter land purchases. While Alexander would move back to New York after the Revolutionary War, William established a strip farm immediately west of Detroit's fort pickets and, later, had a large log home built on Grosse Ile.[36]

In the summertime, William Macomb occupied the "Mansion House," his breezy island abode on Grosse Ile, with wife Sarah Jane Dring Macomb and their children. In cooler weather, the Macombs resided at their townhome on seven acres beside the fort, sending their enslaved woman, Charlotte, to manage the island house.[37] And William Macomb found no shortage of bondspeople to task with work on his various properties. He steadily increased his slaveholdings in the 1770s, '80s, and '90s. In November of 1776, "Mr Macome," a Protestant, had a Panis male slave buried at Ste. Anne's Church. In 1788 he was paying off the price of a "negro wench" to Detroit merchant James May.[38] Macomb would come to own scores of slaves by the time of his death in 1796, and many of these had been acquired in the tumult of the Revolutionary War era. That massive conflict disrupted stability and threw lives into disarray, providing a golden opportunity for Macomb and other prominent Detroiters to snatch up slaves, mostly African Americans from the Upper South who were forced to Detroit at the hands of British soldiers and their Native allies. Gradually, over several years between the Declaration of Independence and the Treaty of Paris that cemented the war's end in 1783, Detroit's enslaved population increased by nearly a third.[39]

Although William Macomb was focused on acquiring land rather than fighting a war in the summer of 1776, by 1777 he and other Detroiters felt a mounting anxiety. William and Alexander Macomb's father, John Macomb, was being frightfully harassed back in Albany for his Tory allegiance. By the summer of 1777 John Macomb was fleeing the Rebels, having, as he described it in an appeal for help to the Governor of Quebec, "just time to leave his House when the Rebels enter'd and Plunder'd it of every moveable thing also every living creature & thing out of doors to a very large amount." John Macomb requested placement in Detroit as "commissary for that garrison," for which he would "Relinquish his Salary." He explained that "all his Family are now settled at Detroit [and] he wishes to live there with them."[40] He also hoped this move would bring relief from Rebel assaults. But given the strategic position of Detroit, the brawl between American revolutionaries and British loyalists would soon extend even there.

General George Washington had firmly felt, since 1775, that the northwestern forts were key to a Continental Army victory. He had written to General Philip Schuyler (uncle of Detroiter Arent Schuyler De Peyster, who stood on the opposite side of the conflict and would marry into the Macomb clan), saying: "If you carry your arms to *Montreal*, should not the garrison of *Niagara, Detroit* & c. be called upon to surrender, or threatened with the consequences of a refusal?"[41] Although a Rebel attack on Quebec had failed in 1775, the prolonged conflict and a competition between the Crown and Continental Congress over the allegiance of various Native nations increased Detroiters' fears that they could be targeted. Indigenous people figured prominently in the struggle between the Rebel and British forces, with each side desperately attempting to recruit Indian allies and fretting over the damage that Native warriors could unleash. While British leaders in Detroit managed to secure the support of the Detroit Potawatomies, Ohio Shawnees, and various bands of Ojibwes, Hurons, and Ottawas, they failed to gain the assistance of Potawatomies in Wisconsin and Illinois. By July of 1778, Lieutenant Governor Hamilton in Detroit had succeeded in passing a war belt to Shawnee, Ottawa, Mingoe, Wyandot, Potawatomi, Delaware, Mohawk, and Miami representatives, cementing an alliance that greatly distressed the Continental Congress.[42]

With important Native allies in place, British military officials sought to shore up Detroit's defenses as well as prepare the way for offensive action using the fort as a staging ground. The British concentrated strength and strategy in Detroit, moving personnel to the settlement from New York and making Detroit the center of the western theater of war. Captain Richard Lernoult, reassigned from Fort Niagara in 1776, would oversee the building of a substantial new fort in Detroit located on higher ground behind the dwellings and mercantile shops rather than near the riverbank. Lernoult placed responsibility for the details of construction in the hands of his second-in-command, Captain Henry Bird, who had been transferred from Niagara in 1778. Bird served as the engineer for the new fortification, a star-shaped structure named Fort Lernoult, "which dominated the town of Detroit for almost half a century" (and is marked today by a plaque at Fort and Shelby Streets in downtown Detroit).[43]

Meanwhile, the threat of Rebel attack grew, as Virginia militiaman George Rogers Clark launched an aggressive plan approved by Virginia Governor Patrick Henry to strike at the British in the western interior. Clark's advance into the West was spurred by Thomas Jefferson, who held grave concerns about the fort at Detroit. Jefferson saw Detroit as a pocket of strength that would facilitate Great Britain's ability to maintain Indian allies and attack American settlements in the East and South. "It becomes necessary that we aim the first stroke in the western country and throw the enemy under the embarrassments of a defensive war," Jefferson wrote to Clark on Christmas Day of 1780. "We have therefore determined that an expedition shall be undertaken under your command into the hostile country beyond the Ohio, the principal object of which is to be the reduction of the British post at Detroit." According to Jefferson's instructions, Clark and his men should be ready "at the Falls of Ohio by the 15 of March," when "the breaking up of the ice" on the Wabash River and nearby lakes would allow for water navigation. And Jefferson had more than military strategy in mind when he considered Detroit. He was also thinking forward about financial gains that America would reap. If Captain Clark could successfully capture the post at Detroit, Jefferson wrote, "we shall be at leisure to turn our whole force to the rescue of our eastern Country from subjugation, we shall divert through our own Country a branch of commerce which European States have thought worthy of the most important struggles and sacrifices." But this would depend on the Indians, to whom Jefferson told Clark to "hold out either fear or friendship as their disposition and your actual situation may render most expedient."[44] America, Jefferson imagined, could control the posts of the profitable western fur trade, displacing the British, who had displaced the French only decades prior.

Commander Clark partly succeeded in his invasion of the western front, taking control of former French towns in eastern Illinois including Kaskaskia, which had a large intermarried Native-French population, and Cahokia (where visitors today can tour a reconstructed indigenous Mississippian village). While holding control of the Illinois posts, Clark issued a Christmas Eve statement aimed directly at black and Native slaves. This population, Clark opined in his proclamation of December 24, 1778, had "too great a liberty . . . that prevents them from accomplishing the different pieces of work in which their masters employ them." Clark stated that the mostly French slaveholders of Illinois had "begged" for help, as their slaves' lack of productivity was "causing a total loss of this colony." He intended to crack down on such license by prohibiting alcohol sales to "red and black slaves" and by disallowing "any red and black slaves" from renting private homes or public buildings in which they might gather for "dancing, feasting, or holding nocturnal assemblies." In order to prevent robberies, he planned to forbid "red and black slaves" from leaving their masters' homes after curfew without permission. He would also prohibit them from trading, selling, or buying items such as wood and pigs in exchanges with free residents without a master's permission. Clark's dictate included an enforcement measure, to "enjoin all captains, officers of the militia, and other individuals to enforce the execution of the present proclamation, and all white men to arrest the red or black slaves whom they shall meet in the streets of each village."[45]

George Rogers Clark's proclamation, a wartime slave code, reveals the extent to which enslaved people of Illinois, a Great Lakes area more connected to the South than was Detroit, were biracial in ways similar to Detroit's unfree population. While indicting enslaved people for practicing "disorders, abuses, and brigandage," Clark repeatedly emphasized their color as "red and black." He also called for "white men" in the towns to help police this unruly colored population. Importantly, Clark was highlighting race in a way that had not been so clearly defined in the French and British periods of holding "Panis" slaves. In the eyes of this Virginian, there were categorical differences between "reds and blacks" versus "whites." Indigenous people had been reduced to a color category and thrown in with African Americans, which occluded the tribal specificity of Native backgrounds. Even the French term "Panis" that flattened some Indian people into one subjugated group had been derived from a series of indigenous tribal names (such as Pawnee) and recognized an Indianness—albeit an unfree Indianness, that was not yet reduced to purportedly biological difference. Clark, a southern military man who had penetrated the Great Lakes at a time when "only a handful of American soldiers and settlers" had ever been there, focused on skin color as integral to caste. In his detailed proclamation we can glimpse the beginnings of the American racialization of Native people as "red" in this region, and the yoking together of redness and blackness as inferior states of being.[46] On the cusp of the nineteenth century in the western interior, Americans were already exaggerating these fixed understandings of red, black, and white racial difference.[47]

Captain Clark saw "red and black slaves" as a group gone out of control, but his formal attempt to manage them revealed their own self-actualization, their social ties to one another, and their ability to negotiate with white residents even within a society that held slaves. If Clark had to pass a code prohibiting trade, space rentals, dancing, theft, and evening strolls around town, enslaved people must have been engaging in these activities and finding the wherewithal to gain bargaining power. They were turning to their advantage the needs of white settlers in an isolated environment where slaves were harder to come by and labor was dearly sought. Although Commander Clark stated that enslaved people in Illinois had been fomenting "disorders" "of so long duration," it is probable that they, like enslaved black people in the eastern states, had seized upon the war as an opening for increased disobedience, recalcitrance, and escape. Clark never took the Michigan forts during his campaigns, and so we have no similar record of what he might have witnessed among the unfree population in Detroit. It is possible, though, that enslaved people in that town also used wartime disruption as an opening to push for a greater scope of action.[48]

While George Rogers Clark proved that he could march his men through the dense western territory, British military commanders in Detroit anxiously anticipated a Rebel advance further north. To stave off an attack by the Continental Army and weaken "a wedge of colonial settlement thrust into the heart of Indian America, Captain Henry Bird led expeditions deep into Kentucky."[49] Marching with 150 soldiers and volunteers, hundreds of indigenous allies, and forty-three men charged with carrying supplies and armaments, Bird set out from Detroit in May of 1780, heading for Ohio. The soldiers, most of whom hailed from French families, were being paid by none other than the Macomb brothers, whose company, Macomb, Edgar & Macomb, held the government contract for fiscal agent to the British military. The number of men counted in the supply chain convoy most likely included enslaved blacks. By the time Bird and his contingent reached Kentucky, they comprised a force of one thousand men, large enough to crush the rural settlements of Ruddle's Station and Martin's Fort. And this they did, destroying homes, seizing booty, and taking more than three hundred prisoners.[50]

Bird would write to his superior officer in Detroit, Major De Peyster, that the Indians were the ones responsible for cruelty in excess that had occurred during these raids. While Bird had "entreated every Indian officer that appeared to have Influence among the Savages, to pursuade [sic] them not to engage with the Fort until the guns were up—fearing if any were killed it might exasperate the Indians & make them commit crueliities when the Rebels surrendered," he claimed that he could not control "the Savages" who "tore the poor children from their mothers Breasts, killed a wounded man and every one of the cattle, leaving the whole to stink." Nevertheless, Bird and his men, as well as their besmirched Indian allies, stood to gain from these attacks in the form of prisoners and plunder. Bird wrote of the grueling journey back to Detroit: "I marched the poor women & children 20 miles in one day over very high mountains, frightening them with frequent alarms to push forward, in short, Sir, by water & land we came with our cannon & c 90 miles in 4 days."[51] Although neither Bird nor the other officers mentioned enslaved blacks among the prisoners, several were seized in Kentucky and claimed by these men, as well as by Native combatants.

Bird acquired "the Wench Esther" at Martin's Fort "whereby the Inhabitants and Defenders agreed to deliver up their Blacks and moveables to the Indians as their property, on condition that their persons should be safely conducted to Detroit . . . the said Esther became my Property by consent and permission of the chiefs."[52] Here, as in his earlier report on the raids, Bird disassociates himself from Indian actions that might be viewed as uncivilized. It was not Bird who took this woman in his account of events; rather, it was the Indians, who then bestowed her on Bird, in all likelihood, to strengthen that alliance. Perhaps Bird was aware of the Rebels' penchant to smear British soldiers by describing them as virtual "savages" and used rhetorical distance to protect his reputation. Certainly by 1780, Detroit officials such as Lieutenant Governor Henry Hamilton had come under special attack by American illustrators and writers, charged with barbarity and with accepting the scalps of colonists from bloodthirsty Indians.[53]

The Americans as well as the British positioned Indians as scapegoats, seizing on cultural practices as well as skin color as markers of difference increasingly defined as race-based. While disavowing the Indian allies that were so crucial to his campaign, Captain Henry Bird personally profited from them. He soon turned Esther, the slave he had acquired during a Kentucky assault, into human capital. And by the time Bird sold Esther in 1784, she had borne a son to an unnamed father. Bird decided, as recorded in the deed of sale, to "Make over and give way my right and Property in the said Wench and her male child to William Lee in consideration of his having cleared for me Sixteen Acres of Land." William Lee was a free black man, which raises uncomfortable questions about his purchase of Esther. Was Lee planning to treat Esther as valuable exchange commodity just as Bird had done, or was Lee seeking to help Esther? Perhaps William Lee was a relative or lover of Esther's and sought to secure her freedom by trading his labor. We can only hope that her situation improved, as Esther's documentary trail ends here, with the transfer of herself and child to William Lee. But the cleared land she was traded for, the land that Captain Henry Bird sought, has a traceable future in the record. The parcel would later become part of the ground upon which the defeated British military built a stronghold in their remaining Canadian territory: the town of Amherstberg, home to Fort Malden.[54] In this transaction in which the future of a woman and her child hung in the balance, the value of slaves, as well as land, was paramount to British settlement. Each form of property reinforced and enhanced the other, as slaves were used as capital to acquire land and then to make that land habitable and profitable.

Pathways to Wartime Detroit

When Henry Bird and his compatriots returned to Detroit in 1780, they dragged along "the largest body of people ever gathered in the wilderness of Kentucky . . . about 1,200 of these consisting of the invading force, and about 470 miserable prisoners, loaded down with household plunder from their own cabin homes." Many of these captives, like Esther, were enslaved. Prisoner Agnes LaForce owned thirteen slaves seized by the British and their Native allies during the raids.[55] After having been relocated to Montreal, LaForce, who it turned out was a loyalist from a prominent Virginia family, enlisted the aid of Sir Frederick Haldimand, governor and commander in chief of Quebec, Canada, to recover her slaves. "On the 25th of June last year," she wrote in her appeal, "your petitioner together [with] her five children and thirteen negro slaves belonging to her, were disturbed in their (as they thought) safe retirement by a party of Soldiers and Indians of his Majesty, and were by them taken Prisoners and carried to Detroit where on their arrival said negro slaves were sold and disposed of without your petitioner's consent or receiving any benefit thereby to her great detriment said slaves being her only resource she had and her only property in this country."[56] Despite the governor's effort on her behalf, the petitioner did not recover her slaves, who constituted a valuable infusion into Detroit's labor force. Agnes LaForce's African American property included Scipio, Tim, Ishener, Stephen, Joseph, Keggy (Kijah), Job, Hannah, and Candis—now in possession of French traders, British officers, and Indian interpreters in Detroit—as well as Bess (Betty), Grace, Rachel, and Patrick—now in possession of Indians. Joseph, the son of Bess, and his sister Keggy, were held by Captain Matthew Elliott, who would soon grow rich on such acquisitions. Job, the son of Hannah, fell to Jacques Duperon Baby, one of Detroit's most successful French traders and an Indian interpreter for the military.[57] These black captives joined a Detroit population swelling from an influx of American prisoners (such as Daniel Boone, the famed Kentucky frontiersman, and Jean Baptiste Pointe du Sable, the successful black trader who had married a Potawatomi woman named Kitihawa and became the first non-Native settler of Chicago), as well as many more black southern slaves whose names would never be recorded, and Native refugees from villages devastated by Rebel attacks.[58]

Just as captives, slaves, and exiles were crowding into Fort Detroit, two high-ranking officials were fleeing. Justice of the Peace Philip Dejean and Lieutenant Governor Henry Hamilton saw their past deeds catch up to them. The pair had lost favor by meting out harsh punishments to residents. Their authoritarian bent had irked influential Detroit merchants, like James Sterling and William Macomb, who served as witnesses to a Montreal grand jury that indicted Dejean and Hamilton for "divers unjust and illegal, tyrannical and felonious acts, and things contrary to good government and to the safety of his Majesty's liege subjects."[59] The protest may have begun with an anonymous letter, likely penned by James Sterling, in September of 1777.[60] The letter called Hamilton "cruel and tyrannical" and expressed "how unhappy we are under his government." The complainant then listed among his grievances "the cruel manner in which he [Hamilton] treated Mr. Jonas Schindler, silversmith" as well as the appointment of "a certain Philip DeJean." With Hamilton's approval, Dejean had taken out an "Advertisement" in 1777 announcing that German silversmith James (or Jonas) Schindler had been imprisoned in the garrison and would be driven out "with infamy and sent in the country below" for practicing without an apprenticeship.[61] Dejean had, further, according to the whistle-blower, "passed sentence of death" upon a furrier named Joseph Hecker, accused of killing his brother-in-law in a "quarrel," and "condemned and hanged, also, Jean Contancinau, a Canadian, for having stolen some money &c. from his master, and being concerned with a Negro wench in attempting to set fire to his master's house." While the writer allowed about the servant and slave, that "these criminals deserved death," he angrily queried: "but how dared Lieutenant-governor Hamilton, and an infamous Judge of his own making, take upon them to try them, and execute them without authority?"[62] Even loyalist Detroiters seem to have caught the revolutionary zeal that led them to question undue assumptions of power.

Amidst the turmoil of war, Dejean and Hamilton chose to run rather than face questioning in Quebec. They used the conflict as cover to escape, eluding officials in 1778 by marching out with British troops traveling to Vincennes, Indiana, to retake Fort Sackville from the American army. It was there, in 1779, that Hamilton, caricatured by Rebels with the scathing epithet "the hair-buyer general" for purchasing American scalps, was captured. Captain George Rogers Clark marched him toward Williamsburg, Virginia, where Hamilton, a man who had overseen the jailing of Detroiters, would take his turn as prisoner.[63]

Detroit was tense and full to bursting by 1782, when the enslaved population had increased to 180 souls, when desperate, hungry indigenous people pressed into town seeking assistance and shelter, and when Native military allies came to receive dramatically increased quantities of British gifts, including alcohol.[64] At this moment, slaves of color and free Indians shared a slice of experience, all having been driven to Detroit by the chaos of combat. Native refugees did not always find a warm reception in Detroit. Put off by the expectation that they would support displaced Indians, even though those nations were their allies in battle, military officials sent Native men to attack southern settlements as a means of reducing population pressure in the fort.[65] These attacks led to the capture of slaves from the South, and the vicious cycle of violence, captivity, and disruption continued.

During a period of intense growth born of upheaval, trader John Macomb joined his sons, Alexander and William, in Detroit. He had not been able to secure the commissary post that he had requested as a means of escaping Rebel assaults in New York. Nevertheless, he worked to advance his sons' endeavors throughout the war. Trader John Askin also saw wartime Detroit as a refuge. In 1778, he had suffered the indignity of being fired as deputy commissary at Fort Michilimackinac, for "dispens[ing] the King's stores too loosely." Under Askin's watch, quantities of rum, flour, pork, and butter had come up short, raising the suspicion of his boss, the newly appointed (since 1775) superintendent and lieutenant governor of Michilimackinac, Patrick Sinclair. Sinclair had replaced Askin with local physician David Mitchell, who would later be a supplier of slaves to Detroit, since the role of fort commissary in the Great Lakes came with a secondary, implicit duty: the role of slave trader.[66] Just as historical research on slave traders in the South has found that, unlike the popular stereotype of uncouth and outcast brokers popularized in works like Harriet Beecher Stowe's *Uncle Tom's Cabin,* these men had close ties with the planter class and often became planters themselves, in the Great Lakes, slave-dealing was not a marginal or socially sullied enterprise. Well-positioned fort officials engaged in the practice, and supplying customers with slaves became part and parcel of supplying them with wheat, rum, and other necessities.

As professional tensions about the distribution of military wares in Michilimackinac grew, John Askin cast his eyes south to Detroit. He was deterred, though, by the hostilities between Great Britain and the colonies, writing in 1778: "I have changed my plann of settling at Detroit untill the war is over, indeed in the present Situation of affairs, it's hard to undertake anything."[67] Moving to Detroit, giving up his farm, and transferring his fleet of trading boats seemed a gamble to Askin, but so did remaining in Michilimackinac, where "everything [was] so scarce and so high-priced" and where he had lost his government position. Disgraced and financially weakened, Askin decided he could not wait out the war after all.[68] He relocated his family and slaves to the hometown of his wife, the French Detroiter Marie Archange Barthe Askin. Archange Askin was a Barthe on her father's side and a Campau on her mother's side, and thus descended from one of Detroit's oldest slaveholding families. Due to the influence of his in-laws, Askin acquired a choice piece of land east of the fort pickets in 1780. This ribbon farm, described as Lot 1 "above the fort" in a 1765 survey of Detroit, had been in the possession of the Barthe family prior to the war. Askin also relied on the help of his friends, like Commander Arent De Peyster, who vouched for Askin's character, and James Sterling, who had been Askin's local agent on the ground in Detroit during Askin's Michilimackinac days. Gradually, Askin rebuilt his trade and mercantile business, as well as his thriving farm, with the essential aid of key local contacts and highly skilled slaves.[69]

Back at Fort Michilimackinac in the 1760s and 1770s, Askin had acquired a handful of African and indigenous people whom he held as property. The Native domestic, Charlotte, cooked and served in the house. Askin's possessions also included two adroit black men, Pompey and Jupiter Wendell, whom Askin had purchased from Abraham Douw of Albany in 1775 for "the Sum of One Hundred & Thirty five Pounds Lawfull Money of the Province of New York." Jupiter Wendell fashioned barrels, an essential task in an economy oriented around the storage and shipping of goods, and he also labored as a maritime crewman. Pompey was a skilled sailor who operated Askin's trading vessels. A man named Toon, whose race was not identified in Askin's records, also worked Askin's ships and lost his life doing so, as Toon "was Drowned out of a small canoe coming from the Vessell" while laboring on the lakes. These ships on which Jupiter and Pompey drudged, and on which Toon had died, skimmed the Great Lakes and interconnected rivers, moving goods from Michilimackinac, north to Sault Ste. Marie, northwest to Grand Portage, and southeast to Detroit, where military Commander Arent De Peyster was a regular customer.[70]

John Askin was fastidious about satisfying those he supplied, holding the view that: "We must never disappoint people in the matter of shipping goods." This is why enslaved men with construction and transportation skills were essential to Askin's enterprise. Pompey was especially valuable, and Askin at times could not "do without him," preferring to hold Pompey in reserve for vital tasks while finding others to fill Pompey's shoes for certain outings. When Pompey sailed Askin's ships, he did so with a multiracial crew. One of Askin's employees, referred to as "the Indian," was a free Native sailor, "a good man," according to Askin, "if one could only understand what he says"; another crewman, Mr. McDonald, was a white employee, "somewhat overbearing," but kept on by Askin due to a wartime labor shortage. Askin supplied all of the men with rum during these trading trips "as an incentive to good work besides keeping them from helping themselves from the cargo." However, "Pomp," as Askin called him, only received "half that quantity," a lesser amount than the free white crewmen on the boat. Pompey was crucial to Askin's outfit, but still a slave, entitled to neither his freedom nor equal rations.[71]

During his time as commissary at Fort Michilimackinac, John Askin had done double duty as a slave broker. In 1778, he informed Jean Baptiste Barthe of Sault Ste. Marie: "I sold your panis to Lavoine for 750 livres. He is too stupid to make a sailor or to be any good whatever." A month before he so crudely sold this man using language that may hint at a burgeoning racialization of "Panis" Indians as unintelligent, Askin also sought to procure young Native female slaves. He wrote at the end of a missive to Mr. Beausoleil in which he had already addressed the need to "divide the merchandise equally" among merchants and reported the delay of a shipment of "liquor and provisions" from Detroit: "I shall need two pretty panis girls of from 9 to 16 years of age. Please speak to these gentlemen to get them for me." The attention paid to the girls' youth and appearance in this order suggests their intended purpose for household ornamentation and eventual sexual service in an eroticized gutter of the Great Lakes slave market. John Askin himself had kept an enslaved Indian woman, Mannette, as a sexual object before freeing her in 1766. These "panis girls" may have been sought by Askin for undisclosed personal reasons, or through him for local male associates with illicit designs on the victims of this trade. The direct reference here to physically appealing Native girls stands alone in the extant Detroit records. However, we can read into the silences in this regional history a pattern that has been confirmed in the southern states. In the U.S. South, white men developed an extremely profitable "fancy trade" in which African American women, most often of mixed-race ancestry, were sought for sexual slavery. Marketed at exorbitant prices, these women referred to as "fancy girls" or "fancy maids," were sexually abused by slave dealers in slave pens, markets and prisons along trade routes, as well as by a string of buyers. While we do not have a record as explicit in its ugliness as that which exists in the South, this particular order for young girls in Askin's letter whispers of unseemly ends, especially when viewed in the context of the numerous Native women who were bearing babies to unknown fathers in Detroit. We have now come to recognize the horrendous trials and compromised survival strategies of "fancy girls" in the southern slaveocracy. On the shores of interior lakes and rivers of the West, women sold as "pretty panis" likely suffered similar fates. And in the Great Lakes, as in the South, protected white women benefited from wealth derived from the sale of "pretty panis." In the same month that John Askin was ordering up Indian girls to satisfy himself or his clients, he was also ordering twelve pairs of fancy shoes in the "French fashion" for his French Canadian wife. But the reality was not so simple in its color coordination; women of Native descent could also be members of the slaveholding class. While attending to his white wife's specialty footwear, Askin also ordered in from Montreal a wedding gown of "light blue Sattin" in "the french fashion" for his daughter, whom he affectionately called Kitty. Kitty was a girl of mixed Euro-Native parentage and herself the daughter of an Indian slave. She nevertheless luxuriated in the lifestyle generated by the sale of other indigenous girls, whose impending sexual subjugation allowed her to enjoy a proper continental wedding.[72]

In another transaction that year, Askin attempted to protect one Native slave at the expense of another whom he deemed less valuable. Askin informed Charles Patterson that an Indian boy in whom Patterson should have an interest was in the possession of Ottawas. This boy was Patterson's son conceived with a Panis mother. Askin, who had claimed and cared for his own children from an Indian slave, including the favored Kitty, wrote in rebuke to his friend: "there is a Boy here who was sold

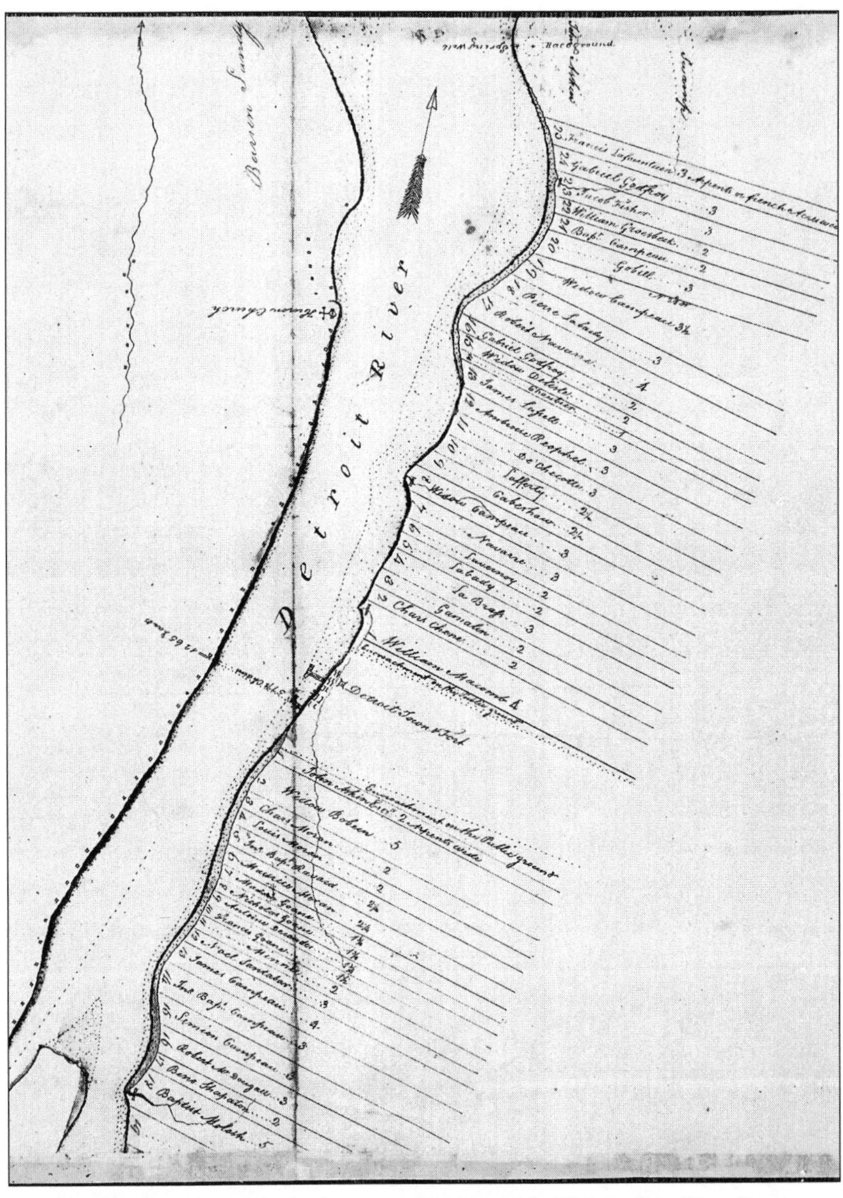

Patrick McNiff, *A Plan of the Settlements at Detroit and Its Vicinity from River Rouge Upwards to Point au Ginglet on Lake St. Clair,* 1796. Courtesy of the Clements Library, University of Michigan. This map depicts French-style ribbon farms as strips along the river and individual farmhouses as squares on the opposite bank. The farms of wealthy slaveholders William Macomb and John Askin, as well as members of the Campau family, are prominently located near the fort.

to the Ottawas, that every body but yourself says is yours, he suffered much [,] poor child [,] with them. I have at length been able to get him from them on promise of giving an Indian Woman Slave in his Stead—he's at your service if you want him, if not I shall take good care of him untill he is able to earn his Bread without Assistance." In concern for this mixed-race child, Askin got the boy back by trading an "Indian Woman Slave" for him, proving again the vulnerability of Native women in the Great Lakes slave market. One wonders if this unfortunate woman was the rescued boy's own mother. John Askin's letters reveal nothing of her identity. This indigenous enslaved woman, a member of a class of people whose bodies were "routinely violated," also became disposable in the historical record.[73]

At Fort Michilimackinac, John Askin built his wealth by diversifying his interests: serving as a commissary on the payroll of the Crown (while allegedly misappropriating military provisions); managing the infusion of Indian furs from the privileged vantage point of his government position; securing land and operating a farm; acquiring boats for the shipment of goods; and using, selling, and placing slaves to strengthen trade and satisfy desires. He would seek to reproduce this winning pattern in his new home at Fort Detroit, which he made with his wife Archange and their multiracial household of young adult Anglo-Ottawa children (the progeny of Askin and his former slave, Mannette), Anglo-French children, and black and Indian bondspeople. John Askin settled near William and Sarah Macomb, whose farm was located on equally prized riverfront property immediately west of the fort.

The Macombs and the Askins, who would become business associates and family friends, were transplanted Detroiters in the opening years of the American Revolution. Also new to Detroit, but not of their own volition, were Protestant missionaries of the Moravian Church who had run afoul of the British authorities. Accused of harboring an allegiance for the Rebels despite a profession of pacifistic neutrality, Moravian ministers David Zeisberger, John Heckewelder, and others stationed at the church's Ohio missions were captured by pro-British Native warriors in 1781. In 1782, the ministers were ordered to appear in Detroit on suspicion of "sympathy and complicity with the American cause." And indeed, the ultra-observant Moravians *had* been operating as pseudo-spies, passing along messages to Rebel leaders about intended attacks on a nearby Ohio fort. This may have been why the Moravian's "taciturn" leader in the region, Reverend David Zeisberger, expressed relief when Native combatants burned mission diaries and letters, confessing he was "glad that they fell into the flames and not into strange hands." While their writings escaped capture, the Moravians themselves did not. A forced relocation to Detroit swiftly followed the assault on their missions.[74]

The Moravian Church, which was founded in Moravia, Central Europe, in the seventeenth century and retained a strong German cultural heritage, had its northern American headquarters in Bethlehem, Pennsylvania. A fervent commitment to evangelism had led Moravians to carry the word of their faith into American Indian communities in the West and Southeast in the late 1700s and early 1800s. It is from Pennsylvania and in service of this cause that the Reverend David Zeisberger had set out as the lead minister on a proselytizing expedition to the Ohio country, once depending on an "old Mulatto" who had lived with Shawnees for twenty years "to translate for them." The Moravians made successful forays into Delaware and Shawnee country and saw their Ohio missions enlarged by Native converts who formed a string of small Christian Indian towns. Pro-British forces ransacked these settlements as the Moravian leaders were seized.[75]

On the arduous march from central Ohio to southern Michigan, Reverend Zeisberger described trudging through "deep swamps and troublesome waters" and passing by a constant stream of people in motion: "a multitude of Indians of various nations, who were all bringing from Detroit horse loads of wares and gifts." These were individuals who had spent time in Detroit, trading goods and receiving presents from British officers as tokens of goodwill meant to secure economic and military alliances. When the Moravians finally reached "the city" and saw "the whole country round about, on both sides [of] the river . . . about a mile wide," they had passed through a territory made wild by the vagaries of a natural water-rich environment as well as by the vicissitudes of an unpredictable war.[76] The Moravians had likewise passed through lands inhabited by indigenous people whose villages and trade routes surrounded Detroit from as near as the Detroit River to the southern reaches of Ohio and into the Cherokee territory of the Southeast. The scene was similar far north of Detroit where Fort Michilimackinac was situated and far west of the city at the southeastern shores of Lake Michigan: Native people and Native lands encompassed Detroit, a center for distributing goods, passing information, and crafting wartime strategy that pulled in people of various colors, cultures, and creeds.

At Fort Detroit, Commander Arent De Peyster summoned Reverend Zeisberger and members of his congregation, including Delaware Christians, for questioning. He released the group soon thereafter, apparently convinced of their innocence, but ordered them back to Detroit within a matter of months to hedge his bet. While this subset of the Ohio Moravians was being held captive at the fort, Native converts to the faith back in Ohio faced a horrible fate. In March of 1782, American militiamen from Pennsylvania had attacked two Delaware villages at Salem and Gnadenhütten, taking the lives of nearly one hundred unarmed Indian Moravians in a senseless massacre. Heartbroken by this crime perpetrated by Americans that they had once secretly assisted, the Moravians could do nothing. They stood at the mercy of the British commander at Detroit, who treated them well, according to Zeisberger, but would not let them leave the area. With their remaining missionaries and a smattering of Indian followers, the Moravians moved to the outskirts of Detroit by order of the British, who wished to keep them under surveillance and had secured a parcel of land from a band of Ojibwes on which the Moravians could reside.[77]

Captives of the power-center at Detroit and refugees from the western theater of war, the Moravians established a mission and farm on the Huron River (now the Clinton River), twenty miles northeast of Detroit near the edge of Lake St. Clair. They resumed their longtime habit of diary-writing, observing the soldiers who had intended to keep a watch on them, and jotting notations about the activities of Detroit traders and farmers that offer clues about the slaves these men and women held. Mourning the loss of their fellow congregants, the Moravians and Delaware converts watched developments of the war from their vantage point on the Huron River. In late spring of 1783, upon returning from a supply trip to Detroit, the Moravian Brother Edwards "brought word that peace would certainly be made." One month later, the Reverend Zeisberger penned in the mission diary: "from the articles of peace it is plain to be seen that Niagara, Detroit, and Michilimackinac will be ceded to the States."[78] But even under the coming sway of an upstart nation that had risked all for liberty, slavery would remain a feature of the Detroit landscape as prominent as the river.

3

The Wild Northwest (1783–1803)

> By an ordinance enacted by congress, dated July 3, 1787 . . . there was a clause in Article VI saying that "there shall be neither slavery nor involuntary servitude in the said territory." This was a safeguard by congress to prevent the extension of slavery northwest of the Ohio River. Notwithstanding this wise provision, our ancestors paid little attention to it, for whenever a spruce young negro was brought by the Indians he was sure to find a purchaser at a reasonable price.
>
> —*General Friend Palmer,* Early Days in Detroit, *1906*

The Great Lakes region could have been different. Acquired by the United States after a bloody revolution that had championed the principles of equality and liberty, and separated from the entrenched slaving stronghold of the South by physical distance, cultural makeup, and economic interdependencies that leaned northeastward, this might have been a place where freedom won in full-throated fashion, matching hot revolutionary rhetoric with reality. In the northern states, the Revolutionary War had generated a sense of disquiet about holding human beings as chattel. Enslaved petitioners and plaintiffs in Massachusetts had exposed the blatant hypocrisy of this upstart would-be country espousing ideals of liberty while maintaining a slave society. Prompted to act by burning desire and the opportunities afforded by wartime disarray, thousands of slaves in the North as well as the South had escaped during the war, evidencing the "contagion of liberty."[1] New England colonists who had employed the rhetoric of slavery as a metaphor to describe their political relationship to Great Britain could not help but see the irony in Americans owning humans as things. This recognition of hypocrisy, and indeed, immorality, at the center of American life fed the gradual abolition of slavery in the New England states, with Vermont at the lead in 1777. In the northern mid-Atlantic states, including New York, emancipation would come even more incrementally as legislatures adopted molasses-like plans for bestowing upon enslaved people the right to personal liberty.

America was no innocent when it came to the beast of slavery. When we look back on decisions made at the founding moments of this nation, we cannot in good conscience claim that political leaders were ignorant of scathing critiques of the practice. Slavery had in fact been a subject of fierce debate in the Constitutional Convention of 1787. Some of the country's leading men were sickened by the vile mistreatment of a whole subset of the populace; others saw slavery as an unfortunate but necessary economic practice that should be phased out over time, and still others felt that slavery was a social and financial good, ordained by a Christian vision of paternalistic social hierarchy based on natural strengths and deficiencies that fell along racial lines. These differences in points of view were mainly, but not fully, regional, with New England and southern states chafing against each other's interpretations of how the new nation should be imagined. But the seeds of deep division that would later explode in a Civil War were buried by the state representatives who met in Philadelphia that May to September in order to establish the nation's governing text. Flushed with their unexpected military victory over a global superpower and chastened by the grave import of their collective task to build the legal scaffolding of a free democratic republic, northern and southern attendees found their way to compromise. They banned the ugly international trade in slaves after the passage of twenty years and developed the callously creative Three-Fifths Clause, which counted enslaved people as equivalent to three-fifths of free people toward congressional representation for the states. This meant that slaveholders, especially those in the South where the majority of unfree laborers lived, could deny enslaved people freedom and citizenship while using these same enslaved people's presence to amass greater congressional power for white male citizens with property. This three-fifths provision, in the words of the historian Edward Countryman, "made slavery the only special social interest that the new national order explicitly recognized."[2]

The freshly acquired region of the Great Lakes, or Northwest, as it came to be called, also triggered tension over the place of slavery in the nation and the boundaries of slavery's expansion into the West. Two months before the delegates of the Constitutional Convention finalized that foundational document in preparation for ratification in the states, the Confederation Congress had laid out a plan for western terrain ceded by Great Britain. Building on a document drafted by Thomas Jefferson and his committee in 1784 that had not been adopted due to perceived insufficiencies, the final legislation written by a new committee in 1787 provided for the division of these lands into three to five states and created a process for the admittance of those states (later, Ohio, Indiana, Illinois, Michigan, Wisconsin, and a portion of Minnesota) into the Union after a temporary territorial stage. The previous text penned by Jefferson's committee had addressed the difficult matter of slavery, recommending that: "after the year 1800 of the Christian aera [sic] there shall be neither slavery nor involuntary servitude in any of the said states, otherwise than punishment of crimes, whereof the party shall have been duly convicted to have been personally guilty." The final legislation adopted in 1787 included this language nearly verbatim, principally to encourage the immigration of white northeasterners into the region.[3]

In July of 1787, during the Constitutional Convention, representatives adopted the Ordinance for the Government of the Territory of the United States North-West of the River Ohio, handily shortened to the Northwest Ordinance, with a prohibition against slavery modified but intact. Always reaching for compromise, architects of the nation's founding documents made the ban on slavery immediate in the Northwest and added a fugitive slave clause. The finalized language of Article 6 included reassurance for southern slaveholders: if their human property should abscond to western lands, that property would be returned. The text also legalized the bondage and forced labor of convicted criminals as a form of punishment. On the issue of slavery, Article 6 of the Northwest Ordinance declared: "There shall be neither slavery nor involuntary servitude in the said territory, otherwise than in punishment of crimes whereof the party shall have been duly convicted: Provided, always That any person escaping into the same, from whom labor or service is lawfully claimed in any one of the original States, such fugitive may be lawfully reclaimed and conveyed to the person claiming his or her labor or service as aforesaid."[4] (The logic of this careful wording that managed to prohibit slavery while simultaneously protecting some forms of it still operates today in the legal use of prison labor to perform some of the country's most dangerous jobs.)[5] But what of the hundreds of Native and African-descended slaves in Detroit who were not runaways from the states and had not been convicted of crimes? They found no safe haven in this new Northwest. As legal historian David Chardavoyne has baldly put it: "The arrival of American rule and enactment of the Northwest Ordinance did not emancipate any slaves in Michigan—on the contrary, for many black and panis slaves, the words of Article VI of the Ordinance were just words, seemingly incapable of freeing them."[6] Riven with loopholes that revealed its ultimately equivocal stance toward slavery, the Ordinance, functionally a constitutional document for the region, left people of color at the mercy of previous customs.[7] Under American jurisdiction, the Northwest would become a wild, wild West for enslaved people, who had very little protection under legislation that upheld a compromised form of abolition and included no enforcement provision. Colonialism and slavery would remain braided together in the new national terrain, as this "foundational document of American expansionism" was careful to protect the property rights of southern slaveholders and to legalize the theft of prisoners' labor on lands still claimed by Native societies.[8]

While the Northwest Ordinance banned blatant slavery in what would later be called the Midwest, it protected access to slave labor. It was not long before the region's slaveholders and would-be slaveholders devised strategies for taking advantage of wiggle room in the federal law. They interpreted the prohibition of Article 6 as applying only to incoming residents in the territory (not to previous settlers) and aided in the seizure and return of fugitives. The Northwest Ordinance, which is often imagined today as outlawing slavery in the interior North, actually allowed for "a *de facto* slavery through a system of long-term indentures, rental contracts, enforcement statutes, and the recognition of the status of slaves who had been brought to the territory before 1787."[9] In a Revolutionary era characterized by radical talk of natural rights, American leaders came close to abolishing slavery in the new western territory that was, by right of prior occupation, indigenous land—but "close" was not good enough to make an immediate, meaningful difference for those enslaved in Detroit.

Betting on Detroit

To elite Detroiters, the settled peace in 1783 represented a startling turn of events. The Treaty of Paris, negotiated by John Adams, John Jay, and Benjamin Franklin at the behest of the Continental Congress in 1783, called for the relinquishment of the interior region east of the Mississippi to the nascent American government. The specter of occupation by a foreign military force and unfamiliar political authority, and the threat of draconian laws and taxes, hung like a scrim over British Detroit. In a place peopled mostly by loyalists and an even larger longtime French population, the loss carried the potential for political unrest and social instability. Worse, in the aftermath of the war, inflation and a scarcity of goods were ravaging the local economy.

One slice of luck for Detroit's white settlers was the physical soundness of the settlement. Detroit had been a military hub during the conflict but had seen no immediate fighting, which could have devastated buildings and cropland. With the town structurally intact, trade could resume as soon as the market recovered. A second boon was the promised protection of colonists' property under the new American government. Even before the end of the war, Thomas Jefferson, hoping for a capture of Fort Detroit, had directed Commander George Rogers Clark to safeguard the inhabitants' material possessions, writing: "Should you succeed in the reduction of the Post, you are to promise protection to the Persons and property of the French and American inhabitants, or of such at least as shall not on tender refuse to take the Oath of fidelity to this Commonwealth."[10] Clark would have seized upon this directive, especially regarding the security of human property, as he had already demonstrated in his Illinois Proclamation of 1778 that he believed "red and black slaves" should be kept in their place as chattel. Beyond Jefferson's dictate to an officer in the field to guard the property rights of previous settlers from New France and newcomer Americans, the formal

Treaty of Paris sought to further ensure Americans' investment in slaves, insisting that: "his Brittanic Majesty shall with all convenient speed, and without causing any destruction, or carrying away any Negroes or other property of the American inhabitants, withdraw all his armies, garrisons and fleets from the said United States."[11] Although the British did in fact remove from American territory former slaves who had been promised freedom for serving on their side of the conflict, Great Britain did not yet condemn slavery unilaterally. Neither did the United States, which would permit certain forms of slavery on Great Lakes lands just as Great Britain had done. Weighing out all of these factors—politics, economics, infrastructure, and slavery—British merchants had to determine whether making a life in Detroit still made sense.

Some British-identified residents, such as John Macomb and his son Alexander Macomb, chose to leave Detroit for New York after the end of hostilities; but others, such as John Askin, stayed on. Askin's neighbor and fellow Scotsman William Macomb wagered on Detroit as well. While the political terrain on which they planted their personal flags was still uncertain, the legal terrain was secure enough in one key respect: the protection of present colonists' right to hold slaves. This proved providential for Detroit's Anglo elite. Men like John Askin and William Macomb would benefit from the weak prohibition on slavery, numbering among the town's eighty-four slaveholding households and steadily accruing more human chattel to work or sell at a profit in the 1780s and '90s.

The slave trade among Detroit merchants boomed during these postwar decades. In 1789 William Macomb was attempting to sell two African Americans belonging to Alexis Masonville for £200. The black woman, he vowed to Charles Morrison, the recipient of his letter, was "very handy & a very good cook." The black man was "a very smart active, fellow and by no means a bad slave." Macomb wanted them "disposed of," preferably by the fall and not on "a longer credit than the first of June." He added in a postscript that he hoped Morrison could purchase him "a very good Carabois [caribou] skin" while he was out making trades, as their "hair" was "most esteemed." Directing the sale of "disposable" black bodies in this letter, Macomb then immediately turned to procuring the skins of valuable beasts whose numbers were then in decline due to overhunting.

Macomb was less than pleased a month later about the intended sale of the slaves to a Mr. Ceré and wished Morrison had instead accepted Mr. Ainse's offer. Morrison corrected his error, soon responding that he had indeed made the better sale to Ainse but "had not seen a Carabois skin."[12] The black man and woman had been passed on to other owners in the Northwest. The woodland caribou had perhaps escaped with their lives farther north where their habitat still remained intact.[13] In 1794, James May sold "a certain negro man, Pompey," to John Askin for £45. The next year, Askin made a profit by selling Pompey to James Donnelson for £50.[14] In 1801 John Askin received a request from James Mackelm, a colleague downriver, to "part with your Negro (who can do every thing)." After asking to be informed of Askin's "price" and "line of payment," Mackelm promises to "look for the feathers and Cyder" already on order. In a follow-up letter, Mackelm again presses for the black man, asking if "he is a slave for life, how old he is, and [if] his price [is] payable six months after Delivery." Those who held on to their slaves rather than selling them in a hot market used them to keep business brewing, especially through the transport of goods, including Elijah Brush, Dr. Thompson, and Robert McDougall, who all sent "their" black men and boys to Joseph Campau's general store to pick up silk, bushels of corn, rum, flour, and gunpowder.[15]

Askin, Macomb, and others in their circle also seized the opportunity to grab more indigenous land. The American Revolutionary War had been waged not only between the British and the Americans but also between both these powers and scores of Native nations that strategically fought with either side or strove to remain neutral, all with the goal of maintaining indigenous strength on a rapidly changing continental map. The Revolutionary conflict had therefore been "a continuation of the struggle about Indian land and who was to get it."[16] Now that the United States had proved itself the victor, indigenous lands were among the spoils. The Crown granted the United States sovereignty over the original thirteen colonies as well as over western territory that was predominantly occupied and claimed by Indians, drawing national boundaries between Great Britain (Canada) and the United States across the Great Lakes and northwest waterways. The negotiation of this treaty in Paris neither included nor consulted indigenous leaders, whose lands—at least on paper—were diced and distributed by European and American colonial powers.[17]

Land lust took hold in Detroit as elsewhere. The region became a microcosm of the larger American bid to obtain huge swaths of Indian ground on the cusp of a new century defined by westward expansion. As the historian Alan Taylor has noted, U.S. leaders relied not only on territorial enlargement at the federal level through treaty provisions and massive acquisitions like the Louisiana Purchase of 1803, but also on the actions of individual Americans who sought private land purchases. There was, Taylor writes, a "power of property lines in weaving a settler society." Along the Detroit River, this effective power of private property to extend the footprint of what would become white America was well underway at the turn of the century. William Macomb already owned Grosse Ile and was raking in proceeds from tenants on the island. Before his death he would purchase Hog Island (now Belle Isle, the beautiful island park known as the "gem" of Detroit), which had served as a commons for settlers who kept pigs there during the French period. John Askin purchased land on both the northern (American) and southern (British-Canadian) sides of the Detroit River and engaged in numerous land speculation schemes, including an attempt to purchase the entire Lower Peninsula (the "mitten") of present-day Michigan.[18]

The war would end with a surfeit in slaves and shifts in land ownership that further secured the powerful position of British merchants. And for them, another blessing sailed on the horizon. Despite Americans' wishful plans for the governance of the Northwest, the British Crown did not keep its promise to relinquish control over Great Lakes forts. Instead, the Red Coats stood their ground, defying the terms of the Treaty of Paris while claiming that Americans still owed unpaid debts.[19] And the Americans, now crippled with war debt, a spent army, a citizen revolt against taxes in Massachusetts (Shays' Rebellion), and a barely formed, untested national government, had little power to force the issue. Throughout the 1780s and most of the 1790s, Detroit and the interior Northwest were American in name only. British authorities, now officially ensconced at Fort Malden in Ontario, brazenly ran Fort Detroit. The British were even so bold as to include Detroit in a new political district in 1791—the District of Hesse, located in the province of Upper Canada, Quebec. And the British would continue the practice of slavery in the posts they so blatantly held. In 1793 the Hesse district government official, Detroit military commander, and mapmaker Major David William Smith wrote to his colleague John Askin to share news of a Canadian legislative meeting in Niagara. "We have made no law to free the Slaves," Smith exclaimed in relief. "All those who have been brought into the Province or purchased under any authority legally exercised, are Slaves to all intents & purposes, & are secured as property by a certain act of Parliament."[20]

Slaves to All Intents and Purposes

Despite a spectacular American victory in the Revolutionary War, little had changed on the ground in Detroit, especially for the enslaved. French, Euro-Native, and Native residents still made up most of the population. British military officials dominated the governing structure of the town. Slaveholding merchants constituted the economic elite. African-descended free people of color (*gens de couleur libre*), who comprised sizeable communities in the culturally French towns of New Orleans and St. Louis, were absent in the Detroit records before 1800 and were likely only present in very small numbers. Few people claiming a declarative American identity were anywhere to be seen. And now, from the perspective of those who wished to get ahead through the mechanism of owning slaves, there were even more unfree inhabitants available to operate the town's shops, storehouses, kitchens, industries, ships, wagons, and farms. Ste. Anne's Church records show "Master Girardin, baker of the town" with a "Panis" named Antoine in 1786, and "Mr. Payet, Parish Priest of Detroit," with a black enslaved woman called Catherine in 1785. British military officers also had slaves, acquired through wartime raids and recent trades within slaveholding circles. "Mr. Grand (Grant), commandant in the navy" buried an unnamed black woman in 1784 and baptized a "Panis" man, Jean Baptiste, in 1793 and another "Panis" man, Paul, in 1794. Grant had married into a prominent French Detroit family in 1774, a reliable way for British residents to increase wealth in slaves.[21]

In addition to individual ownership, corporatized groups of Detroiters could collectively leverage their resources in slaves, as when William St. Clair and a "Co of Detroit Merchants" sold Josiah Cutten (also known as

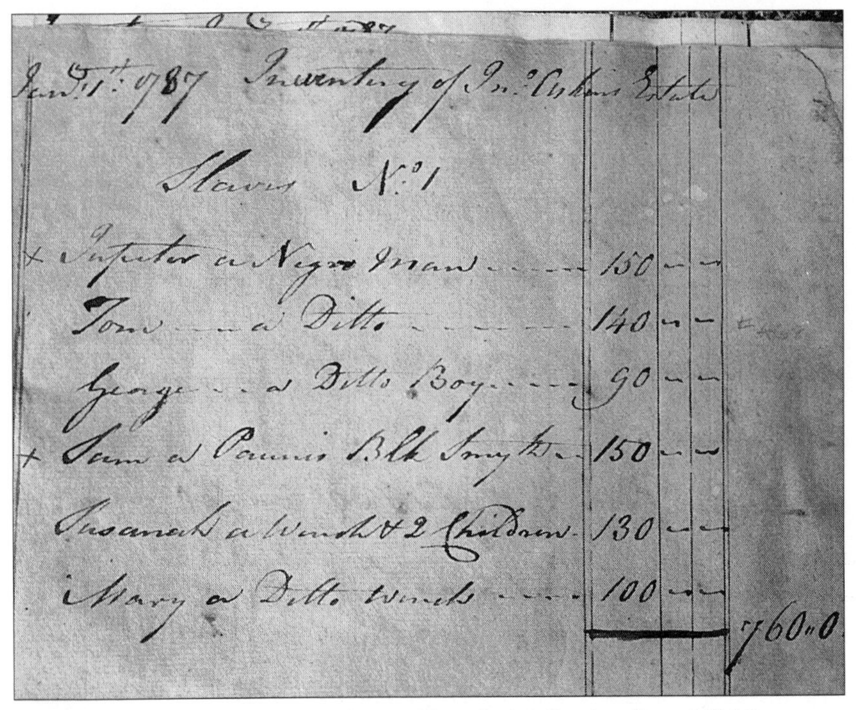

Jan.y 1st 1787 Inventory of Jn. Askin's Estate

Slaves No. 1

× Jupiter a Negro Man	150	– –
Tom a Ditto	140	– –
George a Ditto Boy	90	– –
× Sam a Pawnis Blk Smyth	150	– –
Susanah a Wench & 2 Children	130	– –
Mary a Ditto Wench	100	– –
		760..0

John Askin Estate Inventory. The Burton Historical Collection, Detroit Public Library.

Joseph Cotton), a black man, to Thomas Duggan, an officer in the British Indian Department. The price for Josiah Cutten was "One hundred and twenty Pounds New York Currency payable . . . in Indian Corn & Flour." By the time that he was traded for corn, Cutten had already been sold at least once in Montreal. He would later become the property of John Askin, who pledged £50 for a half share in Cutten in 1792 while Cutten languished in prison for robbing Joseph Campau's store. Askin insured this risky investment such that he did not owe when Cutten, a young man just in his twenties, was later executed for theft in Upper Canada.[22]

While a greater supply of slaves existed in Detroit after the war, there was also a higher demand for their labor. Captain Alexander Harrow, an officer of the British navy who had previously manned the king's ships in Great Lakes trades, owned slaves in Detroit but tried and repeatedly failed to acquire more in the 1790s.[23] In 1794 he sent a 33.6 pound payment to Dr. Mitchell at Michilimackinac, the man who held Askin's former job as commissary, for "a little Pawnese" the doctor had sent. In 1794

Harrow wrote to Mitchell about sending "the boy he mentioned of 12 or 16 years old" and added "if the Boy was a little negro the better." As in earlier decades, a preference for difficult to acquire black boys showed in Harrow's request. The preference was, in some ways, irrational, as Indian slaves from the same locality would be better skilled in working the waters or traveling across the region. But the blackness of an enslaved child conferred a certain status upon an owner in Detroit, showing that the person could obtain rare commodities and marking, through oppositional skin tone difference, a starker social division between the owner and the owned. Black slaves were also far less likely to be confused for free people than Indian slaves in a region peopled mainly by Indians, and were less likely to make successful escapes due to a greater distance from their original homes. In May of 1795 Harrow was seeking a "Slave man or woman, Negro or Pawnee," indicating by word order his racial preference but stressing his willingness to buy any slave. Two months later he pressed Dr. Mitchell at Michilimackinac for "a wench for country work" and "a Slave Boy of 10 or 15 who would suit me." In May of 1796 Harrow was expecting "the Pawnese & 2 children if settled by Mr. Robertson for me." He hoped this Indian would prove "a good Kit[chen] wench." In July he was also trying to get "Black Bet and 3 children to get them by all means," and by August, Harrow's demands rose to a fever pitch of desperation, as he was "still looking for a wench, black or Yellow, young or old."[24]

Most Detroit slaveholders continued to hold just one or two slaves after the Revolution, but members of the merchant elite, their pocketbooks fattened by government-military contracts and Indian land purchases, owned several. In 1787 John Askin inventoried his slaves, listing Jupiter and Tom—both "Negro" men, George, a "Ditto [black] Boy," Sam, a "Pawnis Blk Smythe [blacksmith]," Susannah "a Wench & 2 children," and Mary "a Ditto Wench." The combined value of these individuals totaled £760. The women in the inventory whose races went unmarked were valued at just £100 each, but the skilled male laborers of different races—Jupiter, a black boatman, and Sam, a Native blacksmith, were each worth £150.[25] Across the span of Askin's preserved ledger and personal papers, more than thirty enslaved people of indigenous and African ancestry appear, fleetingly, in the non-emotional mentions of acquisitions, sales, tasks, and deaths. Even John Askin's daughter, Catherine or "Kitty" Askin, had a slave of her own. A young mixed-race Ottawa and Scot woman herself, Kitty Askin possessed a female "Panis" named Cecile.[26] The outlines of Cecile's personal history are unknown, omitted from the record that has preserved minute detail about the color and fabric of Kitty Askin's blue satin wedding gown. And as was the case decades earlier under French rule, Kitty Askin was not alone as an indigenous woman with slaveholdings in Detroit. The most flamboyant Native American woman in town, Sally Ainse, was a savvy trader and slave-owner.

Merchant Slaveholders and Misplaced Missionaries

Sally (or Sarah) Ainse, an Oneida woman from Pennsylvania, had ventured into the business of trade back east alongside her husband, the French-Native trader and interpreter Andrew Montour. A "remarkably tall and elegant" woman who dressed in "English mode with a long gown and hair flowing behind," Sally Ainse moved to Detroit during the Revolutionary War after a separation from her husband. There she found ample opportunity to establish her own networks for trade. Ainse acquired a prime lot within the fort next to Ste. Anne's Church, where she had a wood frame home, kept livestock, and produced flour, corn, and cider for the market. Ainse owned three slaves in 1779 and one female slave in 1782, having likely sold part of her human property to others in the interim. Since Ainse had a previous business relationship with John Askin from a period when they both lived in Michilimackinac, and since she had extensive kinship ties through her former husband in the area, Detroit was a fitting place for the reestablishment of her female-run trading venture.[27] Her clothing in the Anglo style was an indication that Ainse adopted as well as flaunted the accoutrements of cultural intermixture. Ainse, like the French and British traders in town, was caught up in the "skin trade" of dual meaning catapulted by the capitalist enterprise of European exploration, colonization, and slavery. A brief notation in John Askin's account book for 1781 notes that "Sarah Anis" (Ainse) received "1 smoaked skin from Thebeau for a boy at Mackina." This exchange of a Native child for a finished animal pelt that transpired between an Indian woman and white man captures in elliptical snapshot form the intricate nature of slavery in the Great Lakes.[28] American Indians participated in this practice as both perpetrators and victims, while navigating changes, challenges, and chances wrought by the meeting of diverse peoples, the advance of European settlement, and the unseemly ravages of war. Indeed, one of Ainse's indigenous neighbors in Detroit was the Shawnee leader and British military ally Blue Jacket, who, according to a white woman taken captive by a different Shawnee warrior in the war, had married "a half French woman of Detroit" and lived there "in great style, having curtained beds and silver spoons" and "Negro slaves" to serve tea.[29]

Sally Ainse, also privileged with tea and slaves, prospered as a businesswoman in Detroit, living at times with a white man named John Wilson, yet acting as an independent trader. She received boatloads of goods and held accounts with various merchants, including her old associate John Askin and William Macomb. At one point the grand sum of her accounts reached over £2,000.[30] The well-being of the bondspeople owned by Ainse is, in contrast, impossible to determine. They are noted by number, and not by name, in the Detroit city census that lists their "elegant" Oneida mistress's property.

Perhaps Sally Ainse ventured out to visit the Moravian missionaries to diversify her business affairs in Detroit. She had proven herself to be an ambitious and capable entrepreneur, and she was no stranger to the Moravian faith. Ainse had hosted missionaries from that church back in Pennsylvania when she shared a household with her former husband, Andrew Montour. She also had family connections to the Moravians of Upper Canada through her ex-husband and to the Moravians of Ohio as well as Detroit through her brother. The Moravians and their German ways would therefore have been recognizable to her, and the Delaware members of the Moravian congregation even more familiar. In addition to being Oneida, Ainse claimed an identity as Shawnee, an Ohio woodlands nation culturally close to the Delawares.[31] Sally Ainse's ability to identify a growing market for her trade goods may have been what previously led her from Michilimackinac to Detroit in the middle of a war. And the Moravians did need all manner of things. They had been forced to rebuild a settlement and seed a farmstead from scratch after their relocation from Ohio. While they had the benefit of Ojibwe lands and wooden "boards" for building that Detroit officials had negotiated for their use, the Moravians required a constant infusion of supplies and cash from town. Indian men of the congregation crafted bark canoes that they sold at the fort to provide "themselves clothes for the winter." Indian women fashioned baskets and brooms, which they likewise sold to townspeople or traded for apples. In order to sustain families in this new environment, Moravian community members gathered wild cherries and whortleberries, dug wild potatoes, and hunted deer and bears. This nascent Protestant community outside of town represented a promising market for Detroit traders like Ainse, some of whom owned acreage near the mission on either side of the Huron River but, according to Reverend David Zeisberger, had "never seen it," as this rural area near Lake St. Clair was considered "the bush" by Detroit urbanites, who rarely ventured so far out into "Indian land."[32]

Whether or not his business associate, Sally Ainse, beat him to it, John Askin was one of Detroit's first merchants to trek into the marshy wilds north of town. He immediately drew the Moravians into his commercial orbit, offering them credit for provisions sourced in Detroit and becoming one of few white visitors to the mission in 1782. Over the next few years, other Detroiters began to stop by to view the Christian settlement, often traveling by sleigh or "sledge" across sheets of heavy ice that connected the Detroit River to the Huron River by way of Lake St. Clair. Visitors came to take in the sights of the mission, including its 117 resident Christian Indians; they also were keen to assess the valuable lands around the establishment, to set terms of trade, and to have marriages and baptisms performed, as, in the words of Reverend Zeisberger, "there [was] no ordained preacher of the Protestant church in Detroit." The desire for Protestant religious services was one sign that Detroit's population was gradually shifting, becoming more Anglicized as British officers, soldiers, and traders put down roots in the former French territory. Still, there were numerous French residents within the fort proper and living on farms alongside waterways, some of whom sold corn to the Moravian Delawares in exchange for venison.[33]

In the winter of 1784 British Captains Alexander McKee and Matthew

Elliott came "with two sleighs" to see the Moravian mission for themselves.[34] Both men had accompanied Captain Henry Bird on his raids into Kentucky and come away with valuable African American slaves that they promptly moved across the river after the conflict. McKee, now an official of the British Indian Department, was among the individuals sought out by the slave-hungry Captain Alexander Harrow, who begged McKee for "a wench for kitchen and country work [or] a Black boy or man to dispose of."[35] Elliott, a trader and Indian agent for the British, styled himself like a southern planter with his stolen Kentucky bondspeople. He established a sizeable farm on the Canadian side of the Detroit River where, according to the Moravians, "an overseer and several blacks lived." Elliott's "Indian wife" enjoyed the niceties of an upper-class life and lived in a style even higher than that of Oneida trader Sally Ainse. Slaves attended to this Shawnee woman's needs, and when she was out visiting, the Moravians observed, Matthew Elliott "sent his Negro" to pick her up "with a sled."[36] Trader William Macomb became friendly with the Moravians too, forwarding parcels of "letters and papers from Bethlehem, together with Scripture-verses and texts" for the missionaries. The Moravians surmised that packages from their home church town in Bethlehem, Pennsylvania, which brought them such "joy," had arrived on Macomb's ship.[37]

A comfortable farmer named William Tucker was the most frequent British visitor to the Moravian mission. Like Askin, Elliott, and Macomb, he was a slaveholder deeply entangled with Indians. Originally from a Virginia family, Tucker had been taken captive by a group of Ojibwes along with his brother when they were just boys. After killing the boys' father, the Ojibwe captors adopted the eleven-year-old William and his brother Joseph, eventually bringing the children to the Huron River where the Ojibwes had a settlement. While a young man, William Tucker served as an interpreter at Fort Detroit and worked as a trader for George Meldrum, a Scottish merchant from Schenectady, before returning south to Virginia to marry in 1773. He moved back to Detroit with his wife, Catherine Hezel (or Hazel), and, according to county history, with "a family of slaves, consisting of father and mother and several children." William Tucker's Ojibwe friends then bestowed on him a large tract of land along the Huron River, making him one of the first white settlers in the area. As retold in local lore, the acreage William Tucker acquired amounted to "all the land he could walk around in one day." Tucker built a one-story log house tucked among old-growth trees near the "mouth of the river." He planted apple, pear, and cherry orchards, kept boats for transporting his crops for trade in town, and "settled on his farm with his bride and slaves." His route to prosperity followed the usual pattern for European settlers in the Great Lakes region: trade, government work, Indian land, slaves—except that his enslaved labor force was fully black rather than Native.[38]

William Tucker made his living as a farmer on Indian land "eight miles down the river" from the Moravians, who were among his closest neighbors. Tucker befriended members of the Christian sect and acted as their advocate in tense conversations with nearby Ojibwes, who began to feel that the missionaries were overstaying their welcome on the borrowed parcel of fertile land. While Tucker served as a buffer between the missionaries and local Indians, he also found that he needed the help of Moravian Delawares. In 1783, Tucker came to the mission with his wife, Catherine, asking "for an Indian sister to be at the lying-in of their negro woman." This unusual request revealed not only the expertise of Delaware women as midwives but also the everyday proximity of diverse peoples on the waterways: Europeans of different backgrounds, Native people of various ethnicities, and enslaved African Americans from the South. As the Reverend Zeisberger would record in the mission diary, whites as well as blacks began to attend Moravian services in the 1780s.[39] One of these attendees of African descent may well have been the woman on the verge of giving birth on Tucker's farm in 1783.

Events that unfolded at the Tucker family homestead are hazy, yet pivotal to the larger story of slavery in Detroit. The enslaved woman who gave birth in 1783 with the aid of a Delaware woman was most likely Hannah Denison, mother of the first African American family to file a freedom suit in Michigan. The conflicting nature of limited evidence makes the Denison family's origins difficult to reconstruct. According to probate records, William Tucker owned one black family upon his death in 1805: Hannah Denison, her husband Peter Denison, and their four children: Elizabeth (Lisette), James, Scipio (Sip), and Peter Jr. Local oral history conducted by the historian Isabella Swan in the 1960s suggests that the first child in the family, a girl called Judy, was not listed in this official record. Slaveholder Catherine Tucker would later report that William Tucker had purchased Hannah in 1780 from "Joseph Mantour" at Detroit and bought Peter for "three hundred pounds" in 1784 from "Mr. Paulding," also in Detroit.[40] After Peter's arrival, Hannah and Peter coupled. If there was indeed a first baby within the Denison family whose name was left off the record, she may have been the child born with the aid of a Delaware midwife in 1783. The identity of this child's father is not noted in any source. The spare existing record only reveals a description of Hannah's owner, William Tucker, rushing to the Moravians' farm for assistance with the delivery. The secret of the infant's father may have been intimately known to him and, on an isolated farm, to his wife.

Catherine Tucker's record of the purchase of Hannah and Peter Denison tied the members of this couple to two different routes into slavery. Hannah had been sold by the Montours, in-laws of the Oneida trader Sally Ainse, and she may even have briefly belonged to Ainse.[41] Hannah was therefore a woman who had lived among Native and French people and whose own family history may have stretched back multiple generations in the Great Lakes, tracing to Montreal, Quebec or some other northern urban locale.[42] Peter Denison, in contrast, came from a black family not many generations removed from the Upper South. County histories of the Tuckers trace the origins of the family they owned back to a purchase in Virginia before the Revolutionary War. This information is revealing, but not in the way that it at first seems. Based on a wildly expansive 1609 charter from King James I, the colony of Virginia claimed as part of its territory lands stretching past Lake Michigan. Since Virginia "held" this land until the Treaty of Paris concluded the Revolutionary War, enslaved people born in the Michigan region could, technically, be defined as having been born in Virginia. Peter Denison may have been "Virginia-born" right in Detroit with parents who had been seized from the South. William Macomb of Detroit had among his slaveholdings a man named Scipio, valued at £130, and a woman named Lizette, "Wife of Scipio," valued at £80. It cannot be coincidental that this man and woman bear the names of two of the Denison children in such a small community. The elder Scipio and Lizette were likely captured in southern raids during the war and acquired by William Macomb. They then had Peter, who was later sold to Tucker by a man named Paulding, a broker or subsequent owner.[43] The origin of Peter's surname is unclear. Perhaps his parents carried the name from the South (though Macomb's records do not state as much), as "Denison" does trace back to Scots-Irish settlers in southwestern Virginia.[44] While Hannah had compulsory ties to a French-Native slaveholding circle, Peter came from a British household in which his southern parents were held as slaves. The range in the couple's backgrounds, together with the wide network of people their lives had touched, broadened their combined experience as well as their social connections, positioning them to face a future of drastic change.

The Denisons were essential to the smooth operation of William and Catherine Tucker's farm. While Hannah handled all manner of domestic and gardening chores, as well as helping to care for the Tucker children, Peter performed agricultural and manual labor. Peter may also have honed specialized carpentry and boating skills of the kind evidenced by John Askin's enslaved men, Pompey and Jupiter Wendell. Peter probably rowed Tucker's boats to deliver wheat and fruit to Detroit, affording mobility that allowed for the maintenance of ties with relatives on the Macomb farm. The Denisons were likely conversant in local Native languages, including bits of Anishinaabemowin spoken by the Ojibwes who originally owned Tucker's farm as well as Delaware spoken by the Moravian Indians. Hannah probably spoke French. Hannah and Peter's children would have been linguistically adept by necessity, growing up as the only slaves on a large farm among a diverse population in the Indian country outside Detroit.[45] As a young black couple with multiple skills and cross-cultural literacy, the Denisons were well known, highly valued, and frequently sought after. During the time that William Tucker owned the pair, Captain Alexander Harrow angled to buy them, writing in his journal that he had asked if Tucker "would sell his negro man and woman and at what price for the whole."[46] Years later, Tucker's neighbor across the Detroit River, Matthew Elliott, would also try to claim the Denisons as his property. The Denisons clearly possessed ample talents, which would prove consequential when the town of Detroit finally succumbed to American territorial rule.

Postwar Land Dispossession

After the Peace of Paris was signed and the war formally closed, the Ojibwes on whose land the Moravians lived intensified their complaints about the arrangement. They had agreed to host the newcomers while hostilities ensued and had continued to access the Huron River lands for hunting during that time, sometimes leading to tense competition for game with the Moravian Delawares. But now that the war was over, Ojibwe leaders pressured the Moravians to pack up their things and move on. Reverend Zeisberger was anxious about the increasing pressure, imagining that certain Detroit merchants who wished to become "masters of our settlement" were "the real instigators of the Chippewas" and using the Indians "as tools." While Zeisberger's hunch about merchant land lust was accurate, he too easily dismissed the Ojibwes' own motives. In January of 1786, Ojibwe leaders warned the missionaries that this was Ojibwe land, and the settlers must depart. When the governor at Detroit advised the missionaries that prudence suggested they heed this warning, the Moravians relocated, with reluctance, to Chatham, Ontario.[47]

The contest north of Detroit between the Moravians and local Ojibwes was a microcosm of larger tensions still at play in the decades after the Revolution. Native nations that had been yanked into a devastating colonial war refused to accept the outcome. Many lake country bands had sided with the British, who had been less preferable than the French but better than the Americans when it came to the protection of Indian lands. At the close of the war, the British surrendered to the Americans, whose rising power the western tribes witnessed with a stubborn rage. Native Americans recognized that with the defeat of the British, "a new era had begun." And this transformation worked to the detriment of indigenous land claims and political independence. Groups of Indian warriors in the Great Lakes as well as in the South refused to recognize American authority in their own homelands. They led attacks on settler settlements, continuing the revolutionary fight—this time for their own nations' liberty.

Native people's discontent with the shifting balance of power in North America cut into commercial transactions in Detroit. Due to overhunting and some Native men's focus on attacking American settlements rather than hunting, the number of available pelts plummeted. Deteriorating living conditions worsened economic trials resulting from the scarcity of furs. The winter of 1784 proved relentless, described by "Old settlers" as the hardest they had ever seen. Poor crop yields and famine in 1784, 1787, 1788, and 1789, as well as a scourge of smallpox in 1785 and "pestilence and sickness" in 1789, wreaked more havoc, taking the lives of numerous Detroit River residents.[48]

President George Washington and U.S. leaders in the East grew alarmed at the recalcitrance of Native people in the West, who far outnumbered white settlers in the interior and were organized as well as armed. The Moravian missionaries continued to observe developments from their new settlement on the other side of the river, recording the stealthy advance of American soldiers into the country. In 1791 Zeisberger wrote, "From Capt. Elliott, who came from Detroit, we learned that they had news that a strong army from the States was on the march out against the Indians." In 1793 he recorded "news that those at Detroit fear the Americans under Gen. Wayne might attack."[49] Led by General "Mad" Anthony Wayne, a veteran of the Revolutionary War, American soldiers were tasked with crushing Native military resistance, which had coalesced into a confederated, pan-Indian force centered in the Ohio Valley. In August of 1794, Wayne and his men defeated Miami, Potawatomi, Shawnee, Delaware, Ottawa, Ojibwe, and Iroquois fighters, whose ranks had been depleted by long-distance travel and hunger.[50] One year later, in August of 1795, representatives of seventeen western Indian bands and nations signed the Treaty of Greenville with the United States. The treaty called for Native relinquishment of massive swaths of land in Ohio, Indiana, Illinois, and Michigan, including "the post of Detroit, and all the land to the north, the west and the south of it." This left little else in the way of Indian land in Detroit, and those portions remaining would be taken by 1807. As indigenous people had suspected throughout the long years of war, the Americans fully intended to dispossess them, as the "revolutionaries who fought for freedom from the British Empire in the East also fought to create an empire of their own in the West."[51]

Although the indigenous western resistance seemed to have been quelled after the Battle of Fallen Timbers, one final barrier stood in the way of American expansion into the inland West: the British occupation of Great Lakes forts. A new treaty negotiated by John Jay in London won the Crown's forfeiture of these forts and signaled to Native people the final withdrawal of their British ally. The U.S. Senate ratified the Jay Treaty in the summer of 1795, just before the ink dried on the Treaty of Greenville. One year later, Jay's treaty would take effect. The border established between the United States and Great Britain that separated territory with "lines drawn upon the water" would now be recognized by each country.[52] The Detroit River was no longer a thoroughfare that joined settlers on both banks under the shared identity of Detroiters. On one side of the waterway, American stars and stripes would fly; on the other bank, the Union Jack would sway in the rippling wind.

In 1796, thirteen years after the official close of the Revolutionary War, America would finally seize control of the Northwest Territory won back in 1783. "The States," Reverend Zeisberger penned, "have occupied Detroit." After his decisive victory over the western Indian nations with a force of just over a thousand men, General Anthony Wayne swaggered into town to oversee the departure of the British military. Zeisberger noted the transfer-spectacular in his mission diary: "When Gen. Wayne marched in with the garrison by water, and, when Wayne got to the city, the English commandant discharged his cannon from the ship, and was saluted in return, in like manner, from guns great and small, whereupon the new owners moved in."[53] Despite the fanfare, British officers did not remove a great distance away. They simply resituated across the Detroit River at Fort Malden in Amherstburg, Ontario, on land cleared after the war in exchange for an enslaved woman named Esther. Their close proximity and ongoing ties with indigenous groups meant that tensions between the British and the Americans, while lessened, would not disappear until a second major war purported to settle them.

Meanwhile, the "new owners," or American officers, to whom Zeisberger referred now commanded Detroit. Zeisberger would have described the "old owners" as British officers, but there is a second, more accurate meaning of that phrase. The "old owners" were also Detroit's French and British merchant elite who now faced a concrete changing of the political guard but held a core notion in common with the

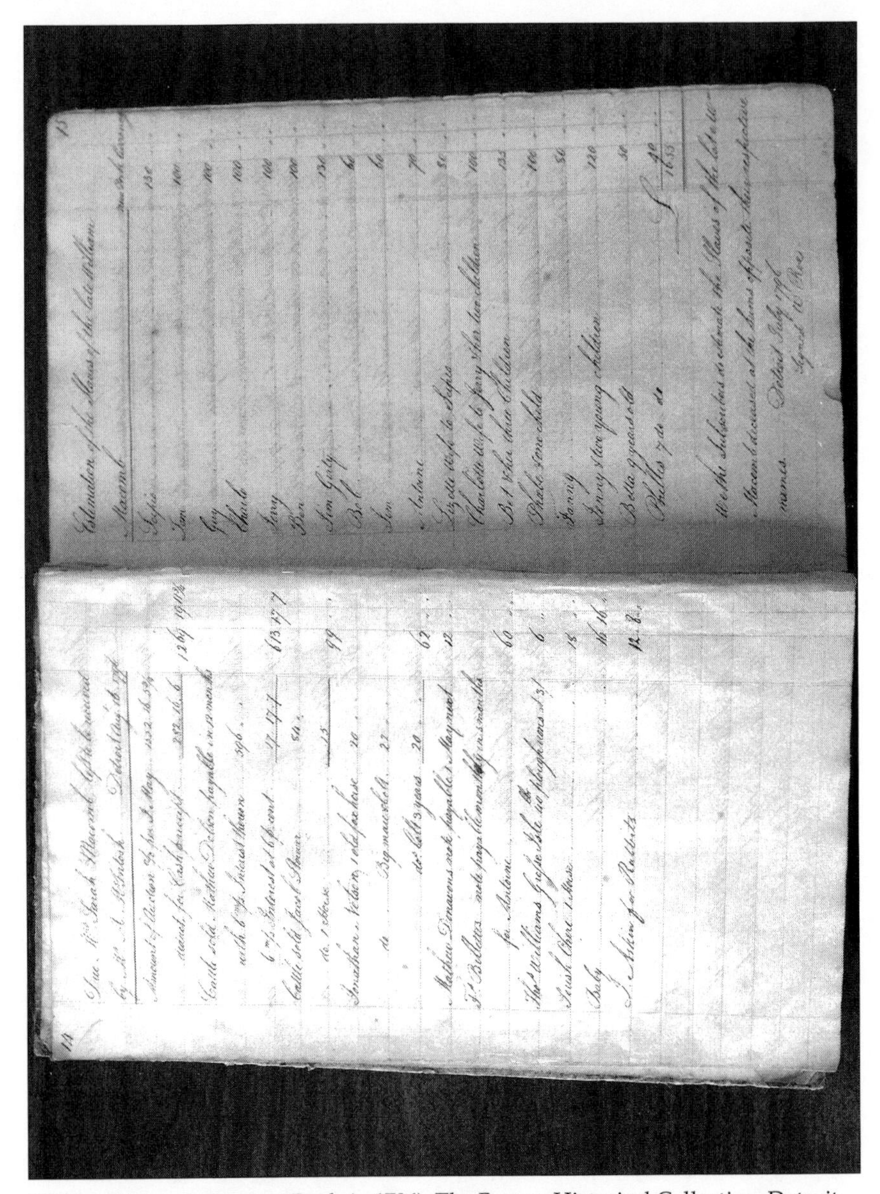

William Macomb Account Book (c. 1796). The Burton Historical Collection, Detroit Public Library. A list of enslaved people with their individual monetary values is included in this bound record of Macomb family accounts.

provisions of the Jay Treaty. Their status as "owners" of people in a slave society would continue to be safeguarded, and now even more emphatically, into the American era. The Jay Treaty, which defined the rights of Detroit's prior residents of European descent, guaranteed: "All Settlers and Traders, within the Precincts of Jurisdiction of the said Posts, shall continue to enjoy, unmolested, all their property of every kind, and shall be protected therein."[54] Now it was not only French slaveholders whose rights to their slaves would be formally honored; British slaveholders could claim the same protections. And any of these Europeans could shift their loyalties to the United States and gain recognition as American territorial "citizens" under the Jay Treaty. They had only to maintain residency for a year or to swear an oath of allegiance if they preferred.[55] The Jay Treaty opened the gate to American belonging for longtime Detroiters and broadly sanctioned their continued possession of Native and African-descended slaves. In a painful irony for enslaved people owned by French Canadian old settlers, France had abolished slavery in its colonies in 1794.[56] Together, the fundamental legal documents of the territory—the Northwest Ordinance of 1787 and Jay Treaty of 1794—functioned in a way that allowed Detroit to become a hub for slaveholders and a prison for captive people decades into the nineteenth century. As Christopher Phillips, a historian of the borderland Midwest and self-identified descendant of slaveholders there, has put it, "slavery and white supremacy were interwoven into the fabric of the entire western region."[57]

Preserved property records of Detroit merchants demonstrate the robust continuation of slavery. In 1787, when John Askin inventoried his human chattel in a ledger book along with his other accounts, he enumerated eight persons: three men, two boys, two women, and two children of unspecified gender. Half of these individuals were identified as "Negro"; both of the women and a "Pawnis" blacksmith were most certainly Native. In 1796, when the executors of William Macomb's estate estimated his property holdings in the wake of his death, they listed twenty-six slaves: ten men, six women, and ten children. Charlotte was the wife of Jerry and mother of two. Bet (or "Black Bet," as Captain Harrow called her in his bid for purchase) had three children. Betta, listed alone without a family, was nine years old; Phillis, also listed alone, was seven. Most, if not all, of these individuals were African American. The racial breakdown of the souls counted among the assets of two of the most prominent British traders, Askin and Macomb, revealed a shift in Detroit's enslaved population. Before the war, indigenous slaves had vastly outnumbered those of African descent, who made up a tiny portion of the captive population. During the war, raiders into southern settlements seized African Americans who then became the property of traders, merchants, officers, and farmers. In the postwar years, the number of captive people reached an apex in Detroit. City census records from 1773 listed eighty-five enslaved people; in 1782 that number had jumped to 180. By 1796, 298 enslaved people lived in Detroit. The registry of Ste. Anne's Church adds precious detail to these raw census numbers. In the decade of the 1780s, ninety-seven enslaved people appeared as principal entrants in the priests' record book; sixty-eight of these were Native American, and twenty-six were African American. In the 1790s, Ste. Anne's priests noted eighty-five enslaved members; fifty-six were Native, while twenty-four were black. In short, over the three decades since James Sterling had been the first British slaveholder to appear in the Ste. Anne's registry with black slaves, the church's African American population had increased nearly eight-fold.[58] British settlers' desire for black slaves and their access to New York markets, together with wartime raiding to the South, gradually shifted the color of Detroit's unfree class. The enslaved population was now approximately two-thirds Native and one-third African American. As the settlement moved into its "first American century," slavery persisted as a more evenly divided biracial phenomenon, shaded black as well as red.[59]

Theft, Fight, and Flight

After the Revolutionary War, enslaved people in Detroit carried on much as they had in prior decades—fighting for dignity, liberty, and a decent quality of life, trying to beat the odds in a frontier community that presented openings as well as barriers. In 1792 a "Panis slave" named Francois stood accused of stealing "two bed covers, two shirts, and some other things" from a house, the mode of rebellion taken by black bondspeople Ann Wyley and Josiah Cutten in previous years. Francois, who lived in "a hut in the rear of the house of Baptiste Meloche," armed himself "with a knife" after the incident. When the homeowner, Michael Houde, pushed into Francois's "hut" looking for evidence of the crime, he promptly withdrew upon seeing the weapon. Afraid to confront Francois directly,

Houde took the matter to court. Hearing the case against Francois was none other than John Askin, who was enjoying a new appointment as "one of His Majesty's justices of the peace for the District of Hesse" along with new buildings that he had conveniently acquired on the Huron River after the Moravians' departure.[60]

Besides stealing from wealthy merchants, unfree people attempted escapes from and to Detroit in the 1790s. On a snowy autumn morning in 1794, an enslaved man fled Detroit and made his way to the Moravian mission in Ontario. The Moravians did not aid the runaway, who was captured by "Mr. Parke" (of the prominent Meldrum and Park trading firm in Detroit) and then returned by Park to the town center.[61] In 1798 John Askin lost a slave to escape. His daughter Madelaine Askin attempted to aid in the recovery of the man and wrote to her "dear Papa" in French: "I gave notice to several people that if they see your negro, to arrest him and take him to you, and I told them what reward you would give." Madelaine reported that she had secured the aid of other settlers, who would help to capture the runaway "with pleasure." Sampson, a black man owned by the slave-hungry Captain Alexander Harrow, fled in February of 1797. Sampson's escape plagued Harrow for over a year, and Harrow was not quite sure if he wanted the difficult Sampson back. He determined in March of 1797: "I wish Sampson could be sold for £50 rather than have any more trouble with him." By the summer of 1798, Sampson was working "in the service of Mr. Wells Attorney-at-Law" in Cincinnati. Harrow drew up a bill of sale for Sampson to Wells for "100 Dollars" and tried to hedge by getting Joel Williams of Cincinnati to purchase Sampson if Wells would not. In March of 1799, Harrow had still received nothing for Sampson, and he had not managed to have Sampson sent back to Detroit. Sampson's trail in Harrow's record ends here. Perhaps Harrow eventually collected funds for Sampson; likely, he did not. To engineer his escape, Sampson ran south to Ohio through the swamps rather than toward the legendary North Star. During Sampson's lifetime and that of other slaves in Detroit prior to the turn of the nineteenth century, Upper Canada was as much slave territory as the United States, which meant fleeing either north or south held equal promise and risk.[62]

Before Sampson seized his freedom, plaguing his frustrated owner who dared not enter Indian country to track him, a fugitive from Kentucky took the reverse of Sampson's course. This man fled north into Detroit, where he formed a partnership with a Wyandot hunter and entered the fur trade between Detroit and Ohio. Unnamed in the record, this black trader represented an infinitesimal free black population in eighteenth-century Detroit. Another free man may have been the "coal maker" in town described as "Will the Negro" in John Askin's ledger that recorded a debt Will owed.[63] Perhaps this was William Lee, the man who had cleared acreage to purchase Esther and her son from Captain Henry Bird during the war. If so, and if William acquired Esther to free her, they may have become one of Detroit's scarce free black families.

But many more enslaved people, both black and Native, remained in the town and its satellite communities, failing to find their longed-for freedom in the aftermath of the war. A significant number of Detroit's still-captive bondspeople worked on the farms and river islands of William Macomb, which included: a "farm near the fort . . . on the Detroit River" a "farm at the Grand Marrais," "Hog Island," a "farm on the south east side of [the] Detroit river," three houses "in the fort," "lands in the Ohio," and "Indian grants" at "Grosse Isle, Stony Island & other small islands," and lands "on the north of the river." Before his death in April of 1796, Macomb ensured that his "moveable estate . . . Slaves, Cattle, Household furniture, Books, Plate, Linens, Carriages, and all [his] utensils of Husbandry" would be duly accounted for. He appointed as executors of his estate merchants from New York and Detroit and named his wife, Sarah, followed by their eight children, as heirs. The items listed in Macomb's itemized account of "moveable goods" would be passed down or auctioned off for the proceeds. In September of 1796, the executors began to liquidate by shedding human chattel. They sold Antoine to F. Billettes, transported Ben and Guy to New York, sold Bet and her "three boys," Sam, Isaac, and Charles, for £135, and sold the "Negro girl Betta" for "fifty."[64]

Settling the Country in the Lakes

William Macomb may have been Detroit's wealthiest resident upon his death in 1796, but he would not be among those to lead the town into its first American century. That task fell to men like James May, a slaveholder; Solomon Sibley, a non-slaveholder; and Elijah Brush, a man with two "indentured" slaves. Born in Birmingham, England, in 1756, the nineteen-year-old James May had journeyed to Detroit in 1778, where he married a French woman, Rose St. Cosme, and began to engage in the chief business of the frontier: trade.[65] A man of massive stature, fine tastes, and "a strong virile intellect," May had achieved solid middle-class merchant status by the time that William Macomb died. May further improved that status when he turned up among the crowd at the Macomb family estate auction. On that hot August day, John Askin bought rabbits; Jonathan Nelson bought a fox house, a mare, and a colt; Matthew Dolson and Jacob Flower bought cattle and a horse; and Francis Billettes bought the black man, Antoine, "payable monthly on 5 months." It was James May, however, who made the largest haul. At a time when coins and bills were scarce and most economic transactions were made through a barter and debt system kept track of by local merchants, May paid 252 in "cash" on the spot and still owed 1,269 for the things he bought from Sarah Macomb. Because of the size of May's purchase, his sundry items were not detailed in the Macomb family ledger book like Askin's rabbits or Nelson's fox house, but the purchase probably included unfree people whose lives were devastated by the death of the trader who had formerly owned them. For men, women, and children in bondage, the passing of a master meant certain change: often sale and separation from loved ones. And James May, like many of Detroit's leading residents, dealt in slaves as both an owner and purveyor. In the 1790s, May owned a black woman named Jenny, acquired from a man named Grauchin "in payment of a debt," as well as Jenny's sister Chloe, and an unnamed "Negro boy."[66] May sold John Anderson "a negro woman" in exchange for "200 good raccoon skins + 50 more if he is satisfied with her work." And since Detroit merchants served as bankers for their customers, keeping logs of complex accounts, debts, and exchanges, among May's business records are several transactions that he tracked for other Detroit slaveholders, including John Askin, who owed May for "a Negro Man named Pompey sold you," William Hands, who owed May for "making a pr of shoe packs" (moccasin-like boots) for a "Pawney Girl," and James Abbott, who owed May for "1 oak plank taken by your negro last fall."[67] While some Detroit merchants were struggling in the postwar period when

Lieutenant Edmund Henn, *A View of Detroit. July 25th, 1794. E.H.* Courtesy of the Burton Historical Collection, Detroit Public Library. This image, rare in its lively depiction of the high level of activity on the Detroit River and its shores prior to 1800, appears to show people of color in the canoe in the foreground.

furs decreased in availability and value, May was enterprising enough to continue his upward climb by acquiring more property, leasing what he already owned, and becoming indispensable to the new American government.

Chief among James May's calculated moves was the strategic use of his schooner the *Swan*. In 1796, the year the American military assumed control in Detroit, May leased his ship to the U.S. government to transport soldiers to the fort, making the *Swan* "the first vessel in the lake region to fly the stars and stripes." The next year, May followed the proven European settler pattern of getting hold of cheap Indian land. With two partners, he purchased "several thousands of acres" in Macomb County from six Ojibwe "chiefs" for $50, clothing, and corn.[68] While May was doing well under the occupying government, he lived in an unpredictable place still characterized as western and wild by most Americans in this era, a place where the population was small and culturally heterogeneous, the nearest city (Cincinnati, Ohio) was three hundred miles away, and the raw forces of weather and water could disrupt lives as readily as fluctuating commercial markets.

In the fall of 1801, James May learned what it meant to lose in a contest with the great inland seas. May's schooner *Harlequin* had set out in late July with its captain, Joseph May, at the helm. Two months later, the ship had not reached any port and James May feared "that her and the Crew" had wrecked. Among the crew lost at sea were three sailors, including May's brother Joseph, and three passengers. "The stroke," May wrote to his colleague John Askin, "is a very severe one for me, the effects of which I shall feel for a long time; perhaps the rest of my days."[69] Askin could commiserate with May. Askin had lost two ships of his own to storms and rough waters back in 1798 and had expressed the agony that ensued when "*madame bad luck* took a passage" on one's vessels.[70] For May and Askin, the financial losses went beyond damaged ships and included human property never to be recovered. One of May's sailors was an enslaved man, whose death, May feared, would have a disastrous domino effect. "The loss of the Negro man," May confided to Askin, "will probably be the cause of my losing the negro woman, who ever since the misfortune happened, has been delirious and is now very ill, in bed." May reached out to his friend for help in the form of a slave order, writing: "Being now deprived of two of the best servants, in this country, my sittuation [sic] is very distressing, unless you will condescend to let your Boy George, remain with me until I can have time to look about for a servant, his Mother is very anxious to have him stay with her, & says it will be the only comfort she has in this world now she has lost her Husband, to have her son with her."[71]

The tragedy of the shipwrecked *Harlequin* unveils an extraordinary, if blurry, picture of an enslaved family's circumstances in early American Detroit. James May owned the black father and mother of this family, while John Askin owned the couple's son, George. Although they lived in the same town, this family was physically separated. George's parents did not have the luxury of raising and caring for him. George's mother, a domestic servant in Askin's home, was crushed by the loss of a loved one at sea. This was a feeling she would have shared with other women attached to unfree men who plied the dangerous lakes not by choice and sometimes lost limb or life in the process. A man owned by William Macomb had injured a foot jumping between two vessels, a sloop and a canoe. John Askin's bondsman, Toon, had died at sea while working Askin's trading fleet. Other enslaved men had died in shipwrecks, clung to trees rooted in bare rock along the storm-swept lakeshores, and frozen to death while delivering letters in the harsh northern winter weather.[72]

The wife of James May's drowned sailor, named either Jenny or Chloe (May does not take the time to specify which of his enslaved women he means), was valuable enough to her owner in a town where slave labor was a sought-after commodity that she had a built-in bargaining chip. James May was willing to buy the mother's son to assuage her pain, cut short her mourning, and get her promptly back to work. It is notable that this black family's crisis dominates May's letter to Askin rather than May's own familial loss, the death of his brother Joseph. May revealed to Askin that he could not promise "Money down" on the black boy, but would "endeavor to give you the worth of him some way or other." But despite his feelings of camaraderie with May, business was business. Askin did not make the sale, preferring instead to keep little George among his own property holdings.[73]

John Askin had been living well since the war but was nevertheless anxious about his financial status. He watched the roller-coastering price of animal furs as beaver became scarce, values fell, prices rose slightly (for deer skins but not the more plentiful raccoon skins), and fell again.[74] He chafed at the American government's imposition of duties on trade goods. By 1800, Askin was carrying uncomfortable debts and bemoaning the commercial opportunities in Detroit, woefully penning in his letters: "this Country is Over-done" and "Ruin, Detroit is not far from you."[75] Discouraged, he shifted into semi-retirement and contemplated a move that would mean leaving behind his Detroit landholdings.

James May was not so pessimistic, even after the wreck of his ship *Harlequin*. He doubled down in Detroit, identifying with the fledgling American nationality that John Askin was loath to embrace. May became a justice of the common pleas court of the Northwest Territory and in 1801 accepted an appointment as Wayne County's militia captain. A forward thinker, he obtained a ferry license to transport passengers across the Detroit River—the newly established border between the United States and Canada. He also kept the accounts of Detroit's only printer and continued to trade in furs and goods.[76] May did well in those turbulent years when soldiers, territorial appointees, and incoming settlers from New England transformed Detroit into an American-run place, at least, by all outward appearances. His granddaughter recalled that the family sipped from "solid silver wine cups." May himself remembered Detroit's early American years as a grand string of parties. "The citizens all lived like one family," he fondly reminisced. "They had assemblies for dancing and social intercourse, and the ladies never went without their silks. As a rule assemblies were once a week, and sometimes once a fortnight. Dining parties were frequent, and they drank their wine freely."[77] It would have been black women like Jenny or Chloe who dressed white ladies in rustling silks, tended to guests at these balls, and laundered linens after scrubbing dance hall floors. And while enslaved women lived in close quarters with their owners in what was a densely packed urban environment, they may have differed with May's portrayal of Detroit residents as one big, festive family.

James May became a pillar of Detroit civic society after the American assumption. He championed the rule of law and building of roads and became impassioned about bringing education to the territory. May accepted U.S. authority with little sign of reluctance, but his long tenure in Detroit and close affiliation with British loyalists made him a Tory in the eyes of eager American newcomers moving in from the East, such as Solomon Sibley and Elijah Brush. Sibley, a native of Massachusetts who had been trained at Rhode Island College (now Brown University) viewed May as a pompous Brit and referred to him sarcastically as "Sir James." Sibley had first moved from New England to Marietta, Ohio, where he pursued the practice of law. He then relocated to Detroit in search of opportunity, and, by all indications, a wife. The move to Detroit would have made for dramatic change. Although Sibley had spent time within the Northwest Territory, he had resided in one of the areas most developed by Americans, where flagship Ohio River towns like Marietta and Cincinnati attracted settlers from New England as well as the mid-Atlantic and southern states. As a place where thousands of acres had been wrested from Native people in the Battle of Fallen Timbers and Treaty of Greenville, Ohio would soon become the first state to emerge from the Northwest Ordinance. The southern parts of Ohio, Indiana, and Illinois were nothing like most of Michigan, where indigenous societies still held oceans of land and the infamous Black Swamp that stretched from Michigan to Ohio made land travel treacherous. To a polished man like Sibley, the isolated fort town of Detroit was like another country. Indians, whose motives Sibley would have been unsure of, lived in large numbers in villages across the watershed; French, a tongue unknown to Sibley, was the common language of local residents. But on the bright side for Solomon Sibley, when he arrived in 1798, professional competition in the field of lawyering was slight in Detroit. His arrival made for a sum total of two lawyers working in town. He had hardly been practicing a month when the attorney general of the Northwest Territory, Arthur St. Clair II (son of the territory's governor), took advantage of fresh talent and named him deputy attorney general for Wayne County.[78] Promoted nearly upon arrival to a plum government post, Solomon Sibley, recognizing his good fortune, tried to settle in. He found Detroit rustic at first, complaining that the town was "without taste or elegance," but he also called the bucolic scene of the fortified village at the river's edge "exceedingly pleasing as you approach it." Soon Sibley was writing: "I should feel myself quite contented to spend the residue of my days in this Country—But for one thing, we have no ladies here that I care a fig

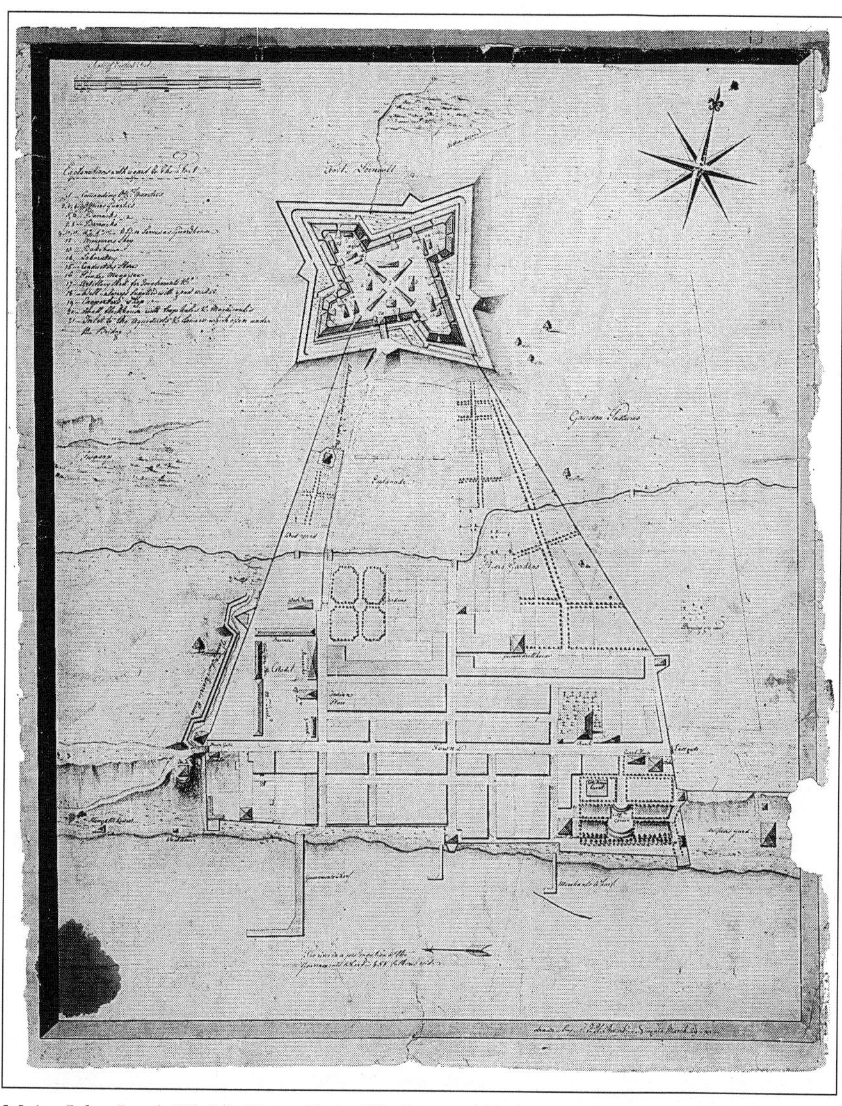

Major John Jacob Ulrich Rivardi, Artillerists and Engineers, March 29, 1799. *Plan of Detroit, 1796–1797.* Courtesy of the Clements Library, University of Michigan.

for—have been in company with some of the young French . . . but take no pleasure in listening to their French nonsense—They speak no English & I speak no French."[79]

As one of few American civilians in town—they numbered less than twenty at the turn of the nineteenth century—Sibley found himself in a foreign cultural environment. Detroit was not yet culturally American, and the Northwest region as a whole was far from being racially white. The Second Continental Congress had set in place legislation for "a territory that had practically no white population and which, in a sense, did not belong to the United States at all."[80] Most of the 327 inhabitants within Detroit's walls as well as those along the riverine suburbs were still predominantly French when Sibley arrived; even the British settlers who had chosen to stay and, through residency, become de facto Americans outnumbered American patriots.[81] Along the banks beyond the fort's wooden pickets, hundreds of French farmers extended Detroit's social circles, as did indigenous families in settlements stretching beyond Lake St. Clair to the north and Lake Erie to the south.

An alliance of kinship existed between the early French and British settlers since many families were intermarried. Of the leading traders in Detroit during the British era, few wedded women who were not local. John Askin, who coupled with a French Detroiter, wrote many of his letters in the French language. But Solomon Sibley, a high-collared Massachusetts man with broad shoulders and a long patrician nose, was among an American professional class that did not care to mix intimately with the French *habitants*. French ladies, in turn, had their own reservations about "Yankee" men. Miss Navarre, a member of a French first family in town, had the misfortune of sitting in tobacco juice spat in her pew at Ste. Anne's Church by young Americans Frederick Bates and George Wallace. She later opined that these men "had more ill-manners & less decency than even the Yankees generally had."[82] The cultural mosaic of Detroit confounded some Americans and delighted others. Frederick Bates, a quartermaster in the U.S. military, became smitten with the daughters of Commodore Grant, the British naval commander and slaveholder who had married a French wife. Bates, a handsome officer with wavy dark hair, thought Grant's bicultural daughters were "the finest girls in this country." He recognized his disadvantage, however, complaining that "the French girls" thought of Americans as "a rough, unpolished, brutal set of people."[83]

Solomon Sibley had difficulty finding a spouse in the remote French and Indian town with a British influence now ruled by the Americans. If French women thought themselves too sophisticated for the Americans, Sibley thought himself too ambitious for the French. Shaped by a Protestant work ethic honed by a New England upbringing, Sibley characterized the French as "exceedingly ignorant and lazy."[84] Certainly he would not have agreed with James May that luxurious parties once a fortnight were fitting or even proper for a tiny town built of wood on muddy, narrow roads. Detroit left much to be desired when compared to the Americanized cultivation of New England, or even Ohio, in Sibley's eyes.

Although he had been thus far unlucky in love, Solomon Sibley may have taken heart in his immediate rise in politics. The Northwest Territorial Legislature required a representative from Wayne County, where Detroit (and most of present-day Michigan) was seated. Although Judge James May seemed an obvious choice for the spot and ran with the backing of British loyalists, the Americans and, surprisingly, the French as well supported Solomon Sibley. Sibley won the seat in Detroit's first American election, perhaps, May charged, because Sibley's supporters provided free alcohol to voters and turned away others for being unfit for the ballot box. Victor nonetheless, the thirty-year-old Sibley began journeying back and forth to Cincinnati, Ohio, the seat of the Northwest Territory, and Chillicothe, Ohio, a second meeting place of the legislature. He once lost his way while traveling to attend a meeting, passing through forests and swamplands on buried paths.[85]

As Sibley's travels southward show, Detroit reoriented politically toward Ohio (even while continuing to favor suppliers in New York). The majestic Queen City on the Ohio River that bordered the slave state of Kentucky, Cincinnati was the source of the mail in Detroit (which was extremely slow to arrive) and also the source of the news (even more sluggish). Because there was only one newspaper circulating in Detroit and the whole of the territory, the *Freeman's Journal* published in Cincinnati, Detroiters posted public notices in French and English and dispatched a drummer to the streets when announcements were urgent. None of this sat well with Solomon Sibley. He saw the necessity for drastic change in Detroit, starting with the layout and position of the settlement. He felt that the picketed town was "exceedingly crowded with buildings leaving no room for further improvement." He was aware that his constituents fretted over the proximity of Native communities on the fragments of land that they still held. They urged Sibley to ask the "U. States" to "settle the lines between them & the Indians." These free residents also wished to see more white Americans moving to the area, being "desirous the United States would give full encouragement to the settlement of the Country on the lakes." A fair portion of Indian lands ceded in the Treaty of Greenville had not yet been occupied by whites, and Detroiters of that stripe were anxious to see the acreage settled, thereby "enableing" their region "to defend itself against their Indian neighbors, should a war take place." Not twenty years had passed since the close of the Revolution, and Detroiters were anxious about the start of another major conflict that would set indigenous people lately dispossessed of the bulk of their land base against the village.[86]

Sibley took this desire for local development seriously. His first order of business as Wayne County's representative was to see Detroit recognized as a full-fledged town. On January 18, 1802, the territorial legislature approved Sibley's bill for Detroit's incorporation.[87] Upon returning home from Ohio after this victory, Sibley was greeted by candles lit in every window and a "general jubilee" in Detroit.[88] Loyalist John Askin watched these events unfold with vigilance, wariness, and a bit of pride, writing to an associate: "This place is incorporated. Mrs. Macombs farm and mine are in the Town. The legislature honored me so far as to make me one of five trustees . . . to whom they gave great authority."[89] The French fur trading post and military fort established by Cadillac in 1701 was, one hundred years after its birth, an American town of the new Northwest.

By 1803, Solomon Sibley was scribbling sunny missives too, as he had found a fitting spouse and brought her back to his adopted hometown. "I am now settled at Detroit having removed the whole of my family, To wit, Mrs Sibley, to this place," he wrote in August of that year. "The journey was fatiguing due to the heat of the weather & the lowness of the waters." Despite the tiring travel, Sarah Sproat Sibley, formerly of Chillicothe, Ohio, was "pleased with the Country & its habitants," according to her husband.[90] But while Solomon Sibley no longer felt lonely in Detroit, he was vexed by crucial changes taking place in Washington. In March of 1803, Ohio became the first state to emerge from the Northwest Territory. As a result, Congress placed Wayne County within Indiana Territory, the first territory to be carved from the larger Northwest in 1800. Detroit was now even farther away from the seat of regional government. The territorial circuit court judges who traveled to various locations hearing cases rarely made it to the Great Lakes interior. Sibley himself now had to travel an even greater distance—southwest to Vincennes, Indiana, in order to attend legislative sessions.

At these regional gatherings of territorial representatives, Sibley witnessed the tension that swirled around the subject of slavery. While existing records on Detroit do not reveal internal debates over slavery among town leaders who had mainly emigrated from the Northeast, other white settlers in the Northwest Territory, especially in Indiana and Illinois, vociferously resented the legal prohibition against slaveholding. Some of these individuals already owned slaves, and many of them hoped to acquire some to work in their salt and lead mines, convoys, and corn fields. Local officials on the ground in these parts of the Territory that had closer ties to southern states therefore interpreted Article 6 of the Northwest Ordinance as going into effect at some indeterminate future time. Settlers there submitted petitions to the territorial legislature and U.S. Congress pushing for a repeal or modification of the antislavery clause at the federal level. At a special convention of representatives in Vincennes in 1802, pro-slavery officials asked for the right to bring slaves into the Northwest Territory for the next decade, arguing that they should be "permitted to enjoy their property." In 1805, Illinois residents requested their own separate territorial government and the allowance of slavery. Although acquisitive settlers did not achieve these formal means of legalizing slavery, they concocted and regularized long-term arrangements of indenture that amounted to "de facto" slave ownership in sections of the Northwest Territory.[91] Territorial leaders passed laws to make a virtual system of slavery possible by leaning on the fine line between involuntary and voluntary servitude.[92] Supported by the wink and nudge of local officials, residents found ingenious ways to circumvent the general slavery prohibition of Article 6, principally by filing paperwork in the courts to transform slaves into indentured servants who were said to have freely consented to their status. It was possible, these Illinois and Indiana settlers realized, to find hundreds of "voluntary" servants among the enslaved population who had very little power of self-protection. Solomon Sibley may well have attended the meeting in Vincennes where the slavery issue was most hotly debated, but his own views on slavery are not disclosed in his papers. Sibley's New England background and later assistance to the eldest child of the Denison family suggests that he may have looked askance at underhanded attempts to extend slavery northwestward. Even if this was the case, the son he raised in Detroit, Henry Hastings Sibley, would later become a slaveholder (and the first governor of the state of Minnesota).[93]

Regardless of his personal views, in Sibley's adopted home of Detroit, slavery was a system with deep roots, protected by French and British custom as well as by American law and international treaty. According to U.S. dictates, then, the eighty-four French and British families who owned slaves in Detroit before the close of the Revolutionary War had every right to continue possessing them after the passage of the Northwest Ordinance.[94] Their children could also inherit this human property. The one population legally barred from owning slaves in Detroit was the very small number of newly transplanted Americans. They could not bring slaves into the territory or buy slaves once they were in Detroit without violating the Ordinance. But they *could* marry into slaveholding French or British families, contract slaves through indenture, and hire the slaves of other residents at will. Although they were never so extreme in the pursuit of slavery as their Northwest territorial neighbors to the south, free Detroiters with an interest in maintaining or accruing wealth also found ways to evade the constraints of Article 6. At the same time, enslaved people in Detroit were pondering what this changed legal context meant for their prospects of freedom. As rules came down from the federal and territorial levels, and in the absence of any local laws structuring slavery in Detroit, unfree blacks and Indians in the town and surrounding suburbs prepared to capitalize on the fresh set of terms.

Between the unpredictable years of the Revolution and the heady first sessions of the Northwest Territorial Legislature, borders had been established and territories occupied in the Great Lakes region. New flags had been planted. Imperial rivalries had cooled. But in the wake of a movement loudly proclaiming that "all men are created equal, that they are endowed by their Creator with certain unalienable Rights, that among these are Life, Liberty, and the pursuit of Happiness," couples like Charlotte and Jerry, children like Betta, and families like the Denisons were still enslaved in Detroit.[95] Today, reminders of the prominent people who stole the lives, livelihood, and labors of others dot the greening landscape of southeastern Michigan. The home of William Tucker, owner of the Denison family, still exists on the Clinton River, its original plainspoken farmhouse architecture occluded by a modern addition. Macomb County, where the Tucker home stands, carries the family name of Detroit's largest slaveholder. Just off of Belle Isle, the Detroit River island wrongfully procured by the Macombs and later purchased by the Campeaus, a street named after Joseph Campau bisects the city. And Detroit itself is situated within Wayne County, named for the famously "mad" General Anthony Wayne, who proudly dispossessed southern Great Lakes indigenous peoples, laying the groundwork for American ascendance in the Old Northwest and the world.[96]

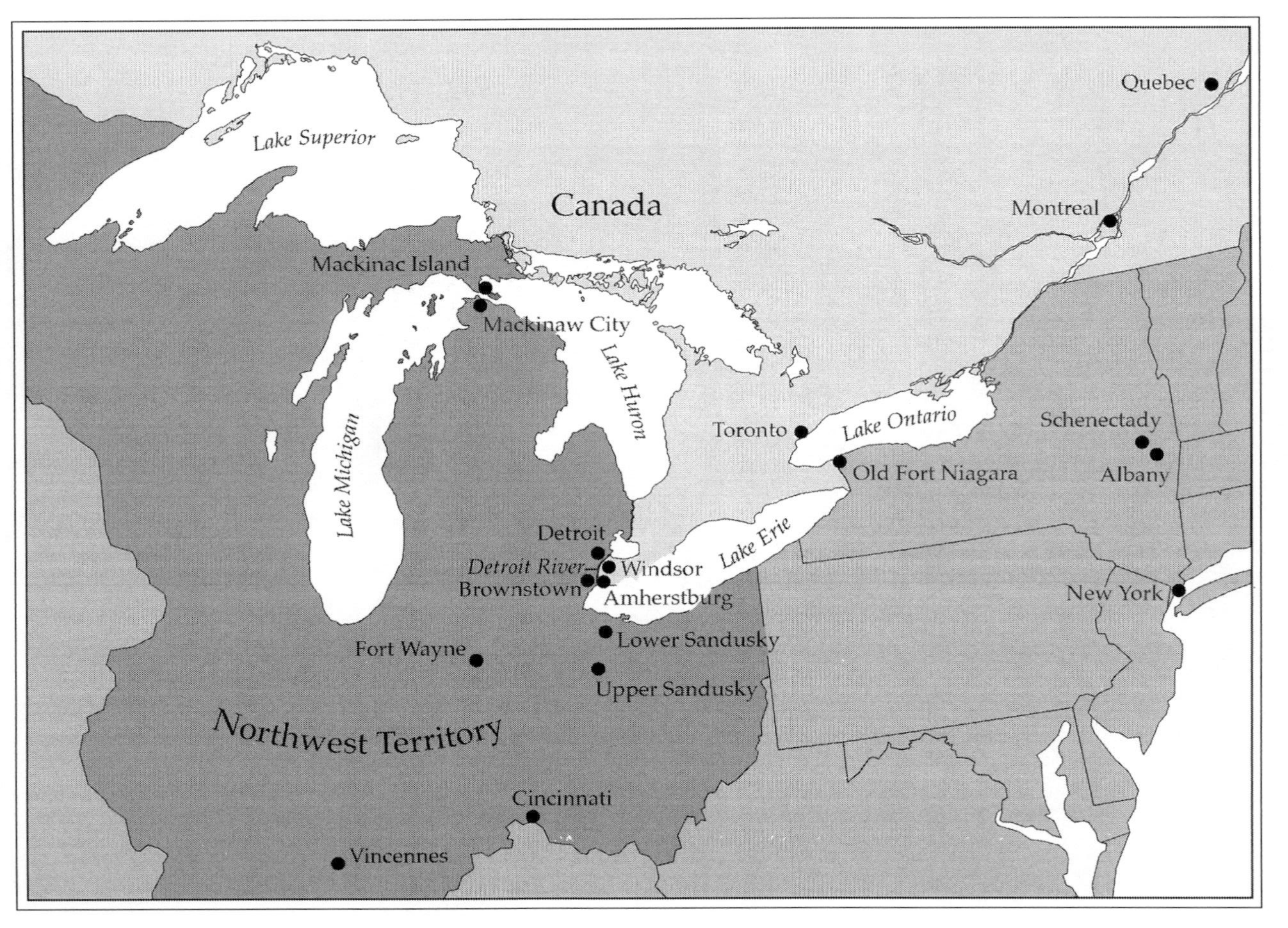

Detroit and surrounding area, 1799.

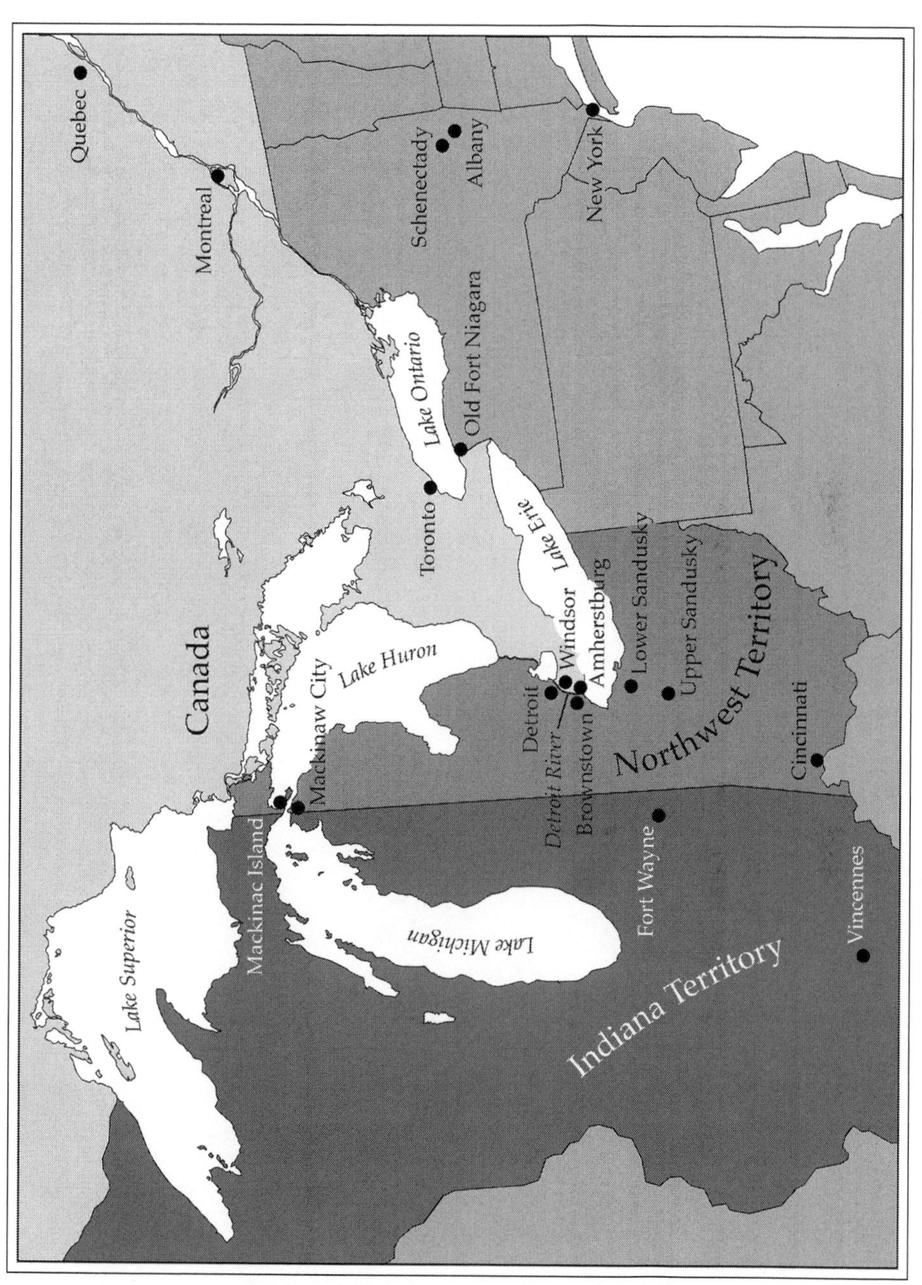

Detroit and surrounding area, 1800.

4

The Winds of Change (1802–1807)

Ruin, Detroit is not far from you.

—*John Askin, April of 1800*

When the Northwest Ordinance finally went into effect after the American occupation in 1796, Detroit had no applicable laws of its own. French civil law, overlaid by British common law, had previously operated in the settlement. And unlike many towns that would soon crop up in the sparsely populated Northwest region, Detroit stood on an international border and housed a large European settler population with rights protected by the Jay Treaty between the United States and Great Britain. The town was also surrounded by indigenous peoples, whose lands, though greatly reduced by warfare, treaties, and hasty sales pressured by the threat of a coming wave of non-Native migrants, still extended for hundreds of miles between Euro-American settlements. According to the Northwest Ordinance, these remaining Indian lands could not be taken without "consent," except in the case of "lawful wars authorized by Congress," language that anticipated and justified further territorial expansion by the U.S. government. Turn-of-the-nineteenth-century Detroit was a mind-boggling morass of murky rules and unspoken expectations. It was therefore a thrilling place to be a bright-eyed lawyer looking for the challenge of a lifetime, which is exactly what Elijah Brush was when he arrived, eager and unmarried, in the year 1798.[1]

Elijah Brush had been born in Bennington, Vermont, in the early 1770s and educated at Dartmouth College in Hanover, New Hampshire. He came to Detroit to practice law and soon found fortune by making the

Part of St. Anne's Street in 1800. Engraving by Silas Farmer from a watercolor by Lieutenant Colonel Jacob Kingsbury or George Washington Whistler. Silas Farmer, *The History of Detroit* (Detroit: Silas Farmer & Co., 1884), 368. Courtesy of the Clements Library, University of Michigan. This drawing of Detroit's main thoroughfare depicts the French village aspect of dwellings prior to the 1805 fire.

marriage match of the season. The twenty-something Brush swiftly wooed Adelaide (also called Alice) Askin, the youngest daughter of John Askin and Archange Barthe Askin. Pampered through her girlhood, Adelaide Askin simply adored cosmopolitan fashion and finely crafted things. Despite her physical isolation from urban centers like New York City, London, and Paris, she was always in the know when it came to cutting-edge style. This was in part due to a steady flow of information from her older sister, Archange Askin, who lived in London and was married to a British military officer of the Royal Artillery Regiment. Archange penned letters to Adelaide spilling over with fashion advice and shipped them across the ocean to Detroit. Informed of the latest transatlantic trends by her sister, like the rage for gloves and turbans made of silk, Adelaide eagerly sought out premium fabrics and elegant designs. Ready-made clothing was unavailable in the shops of remote Detroit, so much of Adelaide's wardrobe would have been imported from elsewhere or meticulously hand-sewn by enslaved black women. Beyond being fashionable, Adelaide was well educated, having studied at L'Assomption de Sandwich in Canada. She was fluent in both French and English and had grown up enjoying the domestic services of indigenous and black women who had been stripped of their freedoms.[2]

By catching the eye of Adelaide Askin, the enterprising Elijah Brush inserted himself into a well-heeled, landholding, bicultural, multilingual old Detroit family. No wonder Brush was filled with "exceeding great joy" at the "prospects of speedily being married to Miss Askin," according to his friend, the fellow New English attorney Solomon Sibley. And Brush was equally enthused, Sibley added, about "a fair way to realize a fortune," which Brush believed was on the near horizon at Detroit, as he had heard that a "New County" was being designated with "the County Town . . . established on the Pra[i]rie."[3] Brush's impending nuptials and Detroit's bright future were intertwined in the eyes of the observant Solomon Sibley.

Elijah and Adelaide chose the festive annual celebration of Mardi Gras, observed enthusiastically in French-Catholic Detroit, as the season for their nuptials. Father Levadoux performed the service at Ste. Anne's Church on a February evening in 1802. The newlyweds, whose wedding had been the social event of the winter, next endeavored to establish their household together. Adelaide Askin likely brought a slave with her into her home with her new American husband, while Elijah Brush busied himself with procuring imported dishware and delicacies for his bride. "I have lately [entered] into a matrimonial life with Miss Askin," he wrote to the merchants he frequented in Albany, New York, "and find myselfe [sic] under the further necessity of troubleing [sic] you again with a further commission, which I expect to be obleiged [sic] to repeat annually." Brush ordered, among other things, from the shop of Robinson & Martin: "one Set of fashionable guilt chinea [sic] complete with coffee cups & c One barrel of loaf Sugar and Coffee, one fourth chest of best hyson tea; 1/2 barrel of best 4th proof 1 dozen handsome knives & forks." While most Detroiters made use of goods provided by merchants in town and could not afford personal imports, Mr. and Mrs. Elijah Brush preferred items of distinction, no matter the expense and waiting time. Elijah Brush ordered one dozen silver teaspoons engraved with his initials from New York, quipping about the low quality of local craftsmanship: "if you give a Silver Smith in this Country Silver to work you'll never get either work or Silver." When his wife was displeased with the color of Rusha sheeting fabric sent by Martin & Robinson's shop, Brush "disposed of it and ordered another piece." He sent to New York, as well, for Adelaide's accessories and clothing, ordering a "fashionable Summer cloak," a "fashionable Bonnet for Summer," and enough kidskin ladies shoes for Adelaide to change her footwear twelve days in a row. When the couple's first son, Edmund, was born nine months after the winter wedding, Elijah ordered shoes for the boy as well. For himself, Elijah requested "1 Superfine fashionable coat Dutch cloth," "1 pair of black Striped Velvet pantaloons and Vest of the finest quality," and "1 fashionable beaver hat" from New York, closing the loop of the fur trade that was his new town's chief enterprise.[4] Detroit produced furs and shipped them East so that cosmopolitan professionals like Elijah Brush could wear the beaver hat as a status symbol all across the coasts of the Atlantic.

For the Brushes, the buzzword was "fashionable," and as a leading lawyer in the town, Elijah Brush could afford to wrap his young family in luxury. In 1803, he ordered an elegant two-wheeled carriage with a folding roof, called a *caléche,* from Robinson & Martin's firm in New York. The next summer two copycat carriages appeared on the narrow roads

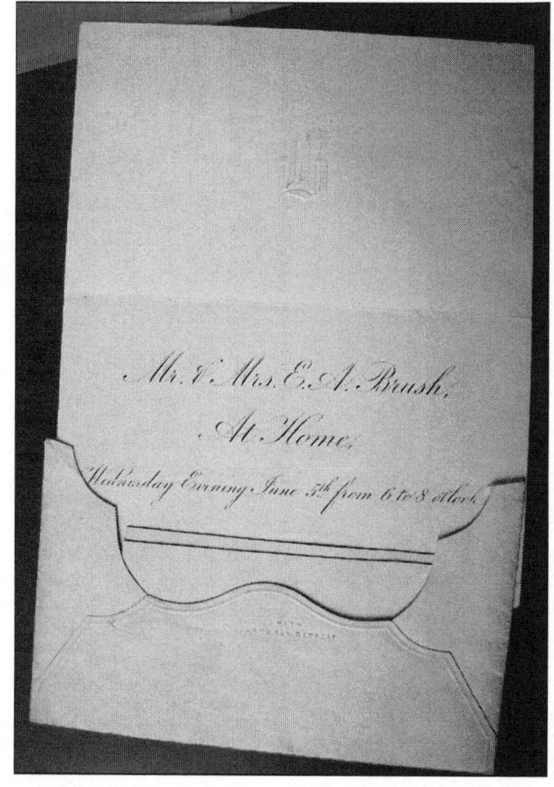

Elijah and Adelaide Brush House. *Detroit, 1852* by R. Bürger. Library of Congress, Prints and Photographs Division, LC-DIG-pga-00350. The Brushes purchased this farm from Adelaide's father, John Askin, before he moved across the river. Enslaved people lived here with both families.

Mr. and Mrs. Elijah Brush calling card. Benjamin F.H. Witherell Papers, 1791–1924. The Burton Historical Collection, Detroit Public Library. Adelaide and Elijah Brush were members of Detroit high society who enjoyed convivial entertainments and cosmopolitan fashion. Adelaide was the child of a British merchant and French socialite. Elijah was an American attorney from New England.

of Detroit, ordered by officers at the garrison.[5] The Brushes had become the town's "Joneses," trendsetters who influenced norms and sparked the competitive desire to "keep up." And in a place where slavery was still widely practiced despite the territorial law that curtailed it, the couple's eye for the next best thing soon turned to bondspeople. Peter and Hannah Denison, an African American couple toiling away on the Tucker farm in the countryside of the Huron River, had developed a reputation in the area. Before long the Brushes would seek the same kind of distinction in their choice of servants as they did in consumer goods. They would import Peter and Hannah all the way from the sticks to work in their fashionable urban household.

The self-confident Elijah Brush met with approval from British-identified John Askin, who wrote to a friend about his American son-in-law: "he promises fair, has a good character and [is] reckoned a good lawyer which is not a bad profession in this quarter."[6] To a business partner, the practical Askin also expressed his approval of young Elijah, writing that Brush was "an able Lawyer, has considerable practice is sober and industrious therefore I believe Alice has made a good choice."[7] Askin's respect for Brush would have made the dilemma that Askin was weighing a little easier to settle. Despite his positive observations that "the Gentlemen on this side" of the river treated him with "nothing but politeness and civility" and "debts are recovered here without delay which is a great Object for a Merchant," Askin had misgivings about continuing to reside in American Detroit.[8] He preferred to live in British territory and, consequently, to avoid American taxes on his business transactions across the border. He therefore elected to relocate with his wife, sell a portion of his real estate, pay off debts, and leave his youngest daughter and son-in-law behind in Detroit. "In the course of two weeks we remove over the River," Askin soon told an associate, "but I will be a great part of my time here to attend to the lands and [etc.] on this side."[9] Near his departure date, Askin wrote to a trading partner, perhaps referring to livestock, perhaps referring to human chattel: "Part of my stock are sent over the River and in about two weeks we will move after them." According to a traditional history of the early American period in Detroit, the town had "lost a grand old man" upon John Askin's leave-taking.[10]

Askin's enslaved laborers, who would now become residents of Canada as well, may have thought otherwise.

By the spring of 1802, John Askin was off to Canada, but the relocation to British turf was bittersweet. Settling in at his new abode, charmingly named Strabane after his birthplace in Ireland, meant abandoning the beloved Barthe-Askin farm along the north side of the river. Askin was therefore buoyed by the news that "Lawyer Brush" was "desirous of purchasing" the family estate in Detroit. The newlyweds lacked cash on hand to pay John Askin's £2,000 asking price, but they moved into the home with Askin's blessings and paid taxes on the property. In part because Adelaide Brush wished to remain in Detroit rather than relocating to the Ohio Country as Elijah had at first intended, by 1805 Elijah was planning to "sell some lands he has in the States" and pay Askin for the Detroit property. Adelaide longed to keep the French farm in the family, and Elijah sought to please his nostalgic bride. "She has the same desire of being perpetuated in it that Mrs Askin [her mother] has on account of the family tradition it has already passed through," Brush explained to Askin, his approving father-in-law.[11]

Brush finally purchased the farm at the price of $6,000 U.S. after living there rent-free for nearly four years. He would obtain the "premises with all the appurtenances, privalages and Commodities to the same." The Askin farmland, "being on the Detroit or Streights of Lake Erie" lie "mostly in what is now called the Town of Detroit," and boasted a royal pedigree. It had been "ceded and granted by Charles Marquis-De-Beauharnois knight of the Royal and Military order of St. Louis . . . and Gilles Hocquart Knight and member of the King's privy counsil . . . to Eustache Gamelin . . . and Granted by Piquotee Belestre Military and Civil Commandant for the king at Detroit unto Jaques Pelet" before coming into the Barthe family. Layered into this legal record of land exchange dating back to 1747 are decades of colonial presence and the selling of land as a commodity. Nowhere in the document is an original purchase from Native people indicated. Neither does the sale of the Brush farm reveal the consent of any woman. For this coveted parcel had fallen first into the possession of a British male in-law, and then an American male in-law, the lucky Brush. Handed down in the families of French women, the land would be legally retained by English and American men. Brush could thus buy his own wife's family farm and make this transfer of landed power seem like a gift to her. During his time on the farm, Elijah Brush built his legal practice. Brush and his father-in-law grew all the closer, and Brush began to represent John Askin in land deals that remained essential to free white men's success in the region.[12]

While Askin family members then in Upper Canada sent pleasing treats like an "Indian sack full of Cramberry [cranberry]" over to their cherished Adelaide, Elijah traversed the frozen river many a time to visit with his father-in-law in cold weather months.[13] They were a tight-knit clan. And while Brush may have preferred deep down to strike out for Ohio, where he already owned land, it was plain to see that he had found a plum situation in Detroit. Just as John Askin had benefited from marrying a French wife and settling on her family's farm beside the fort a generation earlier, Elijah Brush married into prime property when he wed Adelaide Askin, daughter of one of Detroit's most prominent traders and largest slaveholders.

Recalcitrance and Rebellion

In order to improve his circumstances, John Askin only needed to sell his properties, tidy up his finances, and move to one of his other plots across the Detroit River. And while this was not a simple proposition given the losses he had taken in the fur trade as well as his failing health due to elder age, it was a readily achievable goal that did not entail the risk of life or sacrifice of loved ones. The lives of enslaved people were entirely different and considerably more constrained. Black and indigenous men and women held in bondage also carefully assessed their situations in the first American years of the late 1790s and early 1800s, scrutinizing shifting structures of governance, flows of capital, and social relationships. The transition from French to British rule at the end of the French and Indian War had meant few changes for unfree Detroiters. Raiding during the American Revolutionary War had brought larger numbers of African Americans from the South into the region, making the 1780s the high mark of slavery in the town in numerical terms. The Americans' passage of the Northwest Ordinance had meant little in the decade when

British officials had refused to relinquish western posts. But the wheels of political power, as well as the century, had now turned. What changes would the British withdrawal and the official American presence usher in for those who lived in slavery?

British loyalists who moved to Canada, such as John Askin and Matthew Elliott, brought their bondspeople along with them, increasing the enslaved population along the border with the United States. An ordinance passed in 1793 by the lieutenant governor of Upper Canada, John Graves Simcoe, outlawed the importation of new slaves to Canada and introduced gradual emancipation but permitted British subjects crossing the river to retain their human property. Slavery would be legal in Canada until the British parliament ended it throughout the territories of Great Britain forty years later in 1833.[14] By the time John Askin arrived, former Detroiter Matthew Elliott and his fellow British military officers, Alexander McKee and Henry Bird, had already moved to present-day Ontario and established homes on land bestowed on them in 1783 by Native allies from the Revolutionary War. Elliott "was given the allocation nearest to Lake Erie, and his home and farm were soon to become a landmark for those approaching Detroit via the Lake Erie-Detroit River route." He steadily expanded his land holdings, resulting in a "home and farm that became a show-place in Upper Canada." An unforgettable aspect of that "showplace" to some observers was its striking resemblance to a southern plantation. Matthew Elliott, a British Indian agent with a Shawnee wife (one of several Native women he partnered with in customary marriages or informal liaisons over the years), possessed more than eight hundred acres by the early 1790s and presided over a magisterial farm where "he did not directly engage in farming himself, but ran it as a plantation with a steward or overseer to supervise his Negro and Indian slaves."[15] To a commander at the nearby fort in Amherstburg, Captain Hector McLean, this slaveholding Indian agent was infamous for his wealth. McLean wrote that Elliott "lives as I am informed in the greatest affluence at an expense of above a thousand a year. He possesses an extensive farm not far from the garrison stock'd with about six or seven hundred head of cattle & I am told employs fifty or sixty persons constantly about his house & farm chiefly slaves." Another, more favorable observer traveling through the area enthused: "The farm belonging to our friend, Captain E . . . contains no less than two thousand acres. . . . His house, which is the best in the whole district, is agreeable situated, at a distance of about two hundred yards from the river; there is a full view of the river, and of the island of Bois Blanc, from the parlour window." Elliott's bucolic riverside farm was the setting for whippings of enslaved people who were secured to a locust tree with an iron ring and shackles.[16]

On the American side of the Detroit River, slavery also continued apace. The federally appointed governor of the Northwest Territory and slaveholder, Arthur St. Clair, had widely publicized his view that the provision of the Northwest Ordinance limiting slavery was ideational and meant to curtail future, rather than present, activity. He had written in 1793, and announced to Illinois residents prior, that "the declaration that there shall be neither slavery nor involuntary servitude in the said Territory . . . was no more than a declaration of principle . . . but could have no retroactive operation whatever." In the Northwest Territory, French and British residents still owned slaves, and Americans had access to bondspeople owned by prior settlers. Some free residents across the Northwest Territory took advantage of this flexible situation, attempting to acquire slaves. But ambiguity had its costs. Would-be slaveholders in Detroit felt discomfort about whether their intentions would be legal. They carried the angst of residing in a gray area between the letter of congressional law and common practice on the ground. Governor St. Clair's statements about the "principle" of the Ordinance had been intended to allay such anxieties, but in Detroit, a northerly border town with a stream of New Englanders trickling in, such worries could not be fully assuaged.[17] Slavery in American Detroit was persistent but unstable, reflecting the "fragile legal constructions" that characterized northern slavery in the post-Revolutionary "gradual emancipation era."[18]

Enslaved people in the town and closest farmsteads, counted at thirty-one in the 1796 Wayne County census (after many had been removed by their masters to Canada), saw little immediate improvement to their situations following the passage of the Jay Treaty. But a few years later, by 1800, unfree people were doubling down on their acts of defiance. Just as they had before the Americans took charge, enslaved men and women fought the injustice of exploitation with the limited mental and physical weapons available to them: withholding compliance, pilfering property, battling members of the master class, and stealing themselves away. Attempts at escape increased in both number and boldness. The papers of Detroit merchants who were dissatisfied with their slaves, as well as of Solomon Sibley, who managed local legal complaints, offer glimpses of the range of rebellious actions unfree people took at the turn of the nineteenth century. In 1801, a "Pawney man" belonging to the Frenchman "Mr Barth" was accused of assault against a J.B. Nadau. In March of 1802, Jaco, "a Pauni" owned by Frenchman Simon Campau, acted "contrary to the obedience due to [Campau] as his master." Jaco had "absented himself and doth still absent himself from his said Masters Service." Campau entered a formal complaint in the matter, seeking the territorial circuit court's intervention. Toby, a "Panisman," was arrested and jailed in 1807 for absconding and was returned to George Cotteral, who "claim[ed] the Said Toby as his Slave, and acknowledge[d] that he hath humbled himself to his Satisfaction." Mary Abbott, an Englishwoman, complained in the summer of 1802 that "her slave Susan a Panie has resisted and refused to obey her lawful Command contrary to the obedience due her mistress." Mary Abbott turned to the courts as did other slaveholders, with the result that constables equipped with a warrant were ordered to "apprehend the said Susan a Panie . . . to be further dealt with according to Law."[19] It was a difficult stretch of years for Abbott women in terms of trouble with recalcitrant bondspeople. Elizabeth Audrain Abbott, wife of Robert Abbott, found herself threatened with a whipping by her slave. A black woman named Mary, described as a "negro wench" in the court record, was jailed after "beat[ing] and abus[ing] her mistress, the same Mrs. Abbott." Robert Abbott then endeavored to sell the black woman to Thomas Jones, who declined another offer of a "Pawny Boy" from Mr. Pattinson in order to buy this woman who had been promised as having "no fault except beating his [Abbott's] wife." However, when Jones discovered that the jailed Mary "was rotten with the pox," he took Abbott to court in order to break the contract.[20]

In American Detroit governed by the Northwest Ordinance, longstanding resident slave-owners like the Campaus and the Abbotts had in their favor a more functional judicial system to which they appealed for intervention in controlling their human property. Now masters could use territorial courts to enlist police power in the correction and apprehension of unruly or runaway slaves. But at the same time, the Ordinance limited how enslaved people could be held and transferred in Detroit. Solomon Sibley's handwritten notes on the *Jones v. Abbott* case, which he argued in court, open with the lines: "1 point—By the common law a negro is no[t] a slave or the subject of property. . . . The Statutes and laws of this Country, do not recognize slavery—But on the contrary expressly negative such a state in society—Vide the ordinance of Congress passed 1787. Article 6." Based on this reasoning, Sibley contended that Abbott was unable to "establish his right in this property," meaning Mary, and therefore the contract was null and void.[21] While Sibley's sense of clarity in interpreting the Ordinance was not shared by everyone, his trial notes hint at the raincloud the Ordinance represented over the heads of slaveholders, whose only umbrella was the Jay Treaty.[22]

Enslaved people in Detroit also proved aware of the import and potential of Article 6, and they were learning to effectively use the courts just as slave-owners had. The case of the Smith family, though sketchily preserved, provides a glimpse into the first documented use of legal strategy by African Americans seeking freedom in Detroit. Antoine and Anna Smith, an African American couple with children, leveraged the law to put an end to their harrowing experience of varied forms of captivity dating back decades. The Smiths were attendees at Ste. Anne's Catholic Church, where a priest recorded fragments of their story. Father Gabriel Richard described the pair as "free negroes ransomed in the past few years from the said Indians who had made them prisoners in their youth." Antoine and Anna had been captured by Native people, probably during the Revolutionary War. They were freed from captivity at Fort Wayne in Indiana and "taken to be husband and wife." For reasons left out by the priest, the couple came to Detroit where they seemed to have a brighter future ahead. In 1803, Anna gave birth to a baby girl, Therése, who was baptized at Ste. Anne's. But by 1805, the Smiths were in dire straits yet again. Anna and the children had been snatched by a local slaveholder, or perhaps sold to him in violation of the Northwest Ordinance. In response, "Anthony Smith, a black man," hired a lawyer to contact the offender who "h[e]ld them as slaves." A.J. Hull, attorney for the plaintiff, wrote to the Frenchman Jacques Laselle that Smith demanded the "release" of "his wife and children, from slavery." Hull's letter continued with the lightly veiled threat: "As you must be sensible as well as myself, that slavery is prohibited, by the ordinance which forms this territory, you cannot hold them as such. By giving his wife and children to him now, you will save yourself much trouble and expense. If you refuse I shall immediately commence my suits, which will be expensive to you, and will surely recover them in August."[23]

Lasalle's reaction to this letter demanding the release of the Smith family does not survive. He probably relented, given the absence of further court documents in the case and the blatant machinations of other local slaveholders to appear as though they were complying with the Ordinance. The Smith family's legal strategy won the day, but their anguish lasted months. Anna and the children were in the hands of Lasalle at least as early as June 5, 1805, when Hull wrote his letter. Hull did not expect to recover them until August. Antoine, a husband and father, must have agonized each passing hour about the suffering of his loved ones during that extended wait.[24] Following their ordeal, the family returned to the multiracial community of Ste. Anne's Church, where a handful of other blacks also worshipped. In 1816 church records show that Anne Smith, "a free negress," gave birth to another daughter named Angelique.[25]

British captain Alexander Harrow, who had already lost a man named Sampson to an escape in the 1790s, encountered difficulties for the second time when Robert Taylor, a black man, absconded from him in June of 1802. Harrow had a warrant issued for Taylor's arrest. But by the next month, an exasperated Harrow was offering Robert Taylor a contract of indenture, in which he attested: "I Alexander Harrow of River St Clair of Wayne & Territory North-West of the Ohio, being willing and desirous that Robert Taylor, a negro man of about Thirty years of age, and a slave servant of mine for life . . . should at a future day & within a reasonable time, obtain, possess & enjoy, full and entire freedom." The term of indenture was set at four years, during which time Taylor was to "well and faithfully, work, labour and serve" Harrow and "at all times during said Term, behave himself, honestly, uprightly and faithfully." If Taylor failed to meet these conditions, his status would revert back to slave for life. If he complied, he would receive at the end of four years "A suit of cloaths adapted to his Station in Life," courtesy of his former master.[26] Harrow, who was losing valuable property to escape, thought it wise to offer a promise of future freedom in exchange for the loyal service of his African American bondsman. Against his preference to simply hold humans as chattel outright, Harrow had been compelled to negotiate with Robert Taylor in a new legal environment that limited slavery.

Captain Alexander Harrow slowly grasped the reality that it had become harder to keep slaves in Detroit, a town where New Englanders were gaining more influence. As enslaved people grew aware of the opening that the Northwest Ordinance created and the changing demographics on the ground, they ran more frequently and refused to return unless they could negotiate better circumstances. Harrow therefore resorted to the practice of indentured servitude, which other slaveholders in Detroit adopted as a method of holding de facto slaves at the same moment. Correspondence regarding John Reed, a black runaway from Kentucky, points to indenture as a tactic used by Detroiters, like others in the Northwest, to take advantage of the language in Article 6 of the Ordinance, which did not prohibit *voluntary* servitude. After being advertised as a runaway by his master, Reed was "taken up and confined" by Detroit slaveholder James May, now a U.S. marshal, "in the Common Prison of said County of Wayne." Daniel Ransom, an agent of Reed's owner, owed May $200, a price that included the reward money for Reed's capture and the cost of his incarceration. The agent, Ransom, worried about whether the enslaved man could be kept captive in Detroit and therefore included a contingency in the contract for Reed's return. Ransom would not pay May, the contract stated, "should the negro escape."[27]

Reed's plot thickened. Deputy Attorney General Solomon Sibley wrote to John Reed's former owner, Colonel Grant of Licking, Kentucky, detailing the situation and commenting that the bounty hunter, Ransom, wanted to purchase John Reed for himself. This, however, would be difficult in Detroit, as new slaves were not supposed to be bought and sold in the territory. It would likewise be tricky in Canada, where the importation of slaves had been prohibited since 1793. Sibley explained to the Kentucky colonel: "The Negro if he purchase cannot by him be held as a slave on either side. Mr Ransom's only method will be to get the fellow to endent [sic] himself for a term of years. It will rest with you to determine whether it is not better for you to sell him for a much reduced price to what he would command in Kentucky rather than risk taking him thither thro' the Indian Country." Sibley's frank assessment confirmed a further complication in this case: there was a great chance of losing Reed altogether if Colonel Grant sought to transport the bondsman southward. In order to reach Kentucky, Reed would have to be brought through Indian territory, and Reed was "an arch lad" who had "acquired a knowledge of the Indian language."[28] Since Reed could not be sold in Detroit and was a flight risk due to his linguistic skills and Detroit's location in Indian country, Sibley suggested that Reed be pressured into indenture while he languished in jail awaiting an uncertain fate.

Under the Northwest Ordinance and American authority in Detroit, enslaved people had attained a status ambiguous enough that slaveowners now had to think twice about how to transport, retain, and claim them. In addition, the formation of a newly defined international border along the Detroit River highlighted pathways for escape that made calculated risk-taking more possible for bondspeople. Enslaved men and women could run south to Ohio, they could go east and cross the river into Canada, and they could hide out in adjacent indigenous territories that lay between the town of Detroit and both of these routes. Tensions between the U.S. and British governments, as well as between various Native groups and the Americans, meant that enslaved people had now gained an advantage that indigenous tribes had long employed in the region: playing imperial powers off of one another.[29] Slaveholders, wary of both Indian hostilities and the unknown wilds of lake-country nature, were hesitant to track enslaved people into the swamps and Native villages surrounding Detroit. And back inside the wooden pickets of the town, a novel legal environment was leading would-be slaveholders to pursue indentured servitude instead of clear-cut slave ownership.

A record from 1799 further indicates Detroit slaveholder strategies in this altered political context. In order to avoid legal complications for selling a slave, Charles St. Bernard, a merchant of Hamtramck Township, contracted an "indenture" with Henry Berthelet, a merchant of Detroit. In actuality, the document entails the sale of a small child, the "young negro girl, Named Veronique, about five years of age," rather than a time-limited labor agreement. According to the contract, Berthelet is: "TO HAVE & TO HOLD the said young negro girl above bargained & sold, for and during her natural life" for the "Sum of SIXTY POUNDS

New York Currency." Bernard and Berthelet take pains to explain that Veronique was "born within this County, when under the Dominion of his Brittanick Majesty, and has never been out of it since the United States have taken possession of same." Carefully spelling out the child's place of birth and permanent residence in British Detroit allows the men to demonstrate that she can be held under the rules of the Northwest Ordinance. Further, to hedge their bets, the merchants introduce their bill of sale by describing it as "this INDENTURE made at Detroit." Their contract was signed, sealed, delivered, and recorded by the Wayne County court.[30]

Too young to fend for herself or broach an escape, Veronique became the property of Berthelet. But John Reed, a grown man who had already shown that he would run, may have been offered a more forthright contract of indenture, as this was the best means for the would-be buyer/bounty hunter to hold on to him, as well as for his Kentucky owner to redeem some value from the loss of him. While being an indentured servant in Detroit could not have been Reed's desired outcome when he first fled, it was a status that offered greater potential for the future than lifelong slavery in the American South.

Elsewhere in the Northwest Territory, indenture was also being employed as a secondary form of confinement. The practice was common in Illinois and Indiana, where a "terrain of unfreedom" developed on the shadow side of the Ordinance. Often, enslaved people were pressed into servitude contracts with only a veneer of consent. In Marietta, Ohio, in 1802, "a negro boy under the age of twenty-one" named Bob signed a contract of indenture with Dudley Woodbridge, using an X as his mark. Stephen Wilson, a man from Virginia, had previously owned Bob but attested: "I have this day received of said Woodbridge the sum of two hundred dollars for a relinquishment of my claim to the said negro boy." Woodbridge paid Stephen for Bob, who then agreed to serve Woodbridge as his master until he reached the age of twenty-one. In Wilson's words, a "bill of sale" was made granting Bob "his freedom, to enable him to bind himself by indenture to Dudley Woodbridge." Bob was sold to "free" him up to sign an unpaid labor contract. Bob did manage, however, to extract something of value for himself in these negotiations. According to the agreement, Woodbridge would: "At the age of twenty-one years . . . provide and furnish the said Bob with good, comfortable and sufficient apparel, meat, drink, washing, & lodging; and will learn him the said Bob to read." If Woodbridge kept this promise, Bob would be literate by the time he attained his actual freedom. The documents describing Bob's sale and indenture found their way into the archives of Detroit when the Woodbridge family moved to town in 1814.[31]

While enslaved blacks like John Reed were able to slightly improve their status through indenture, several individuals held as slaves in Detroit found other ways to inch toward autonomy. They began to collect wages for their work as a trickle of American migrants moved into town in need of labor. Eager American lawyers, merchants, and doctors kept farms in addition to practicing their professions and sought skilled agricultural and domestic workers. This included compensating enslaved people who were hired out by their owners and allowed to retain some of the income, or who were permitted to hire themselves out. David Maney paid Elizabeth Burnett "for her washing" in September of 1802; she attested to the receipt of this sum by signing with her mark. Evidently a practiced washerwoman, Elizabeth was also a seamstress. The man who owned her, William Burnett, had been owed "Cash to your woman to pay for mending" two years earlier. Merchant James May recorded that William Robertson owed "half pay of Pomps wages for attending cattle [in company] with John Askin" and that Charles La Leavre was owed "By 1 days work of his Man helping to kill pigs By work for self." A woman called Black Betty owed in May's ledger for five pounds of beef, which she may have planned to pay off through the exchange of her labor. This was probably the same Bet sold with her two sons by Sarah Macomb after William Macomb's death in 1796. In the Macomb family account book several individuals received pay for services: Charity for washing, Suana for washing, Sisco for masonry, and Will for chopping wood. A woman called Black Patty, who may have attained her freedom, was earning enough to accrue livestock and pay her debts in cash. In 1801 Patty conducted business with or through James May, had an "account" on file with him, and had paid "10 dollars + Cash 3 dollars" toward "a cow + calf 17 Dollars + 50 Cents."[32]

Beyond creating a market for finite indenture contracts as well as paid work, American jurisdiction in Detroit had a third unexpected benefit for the enslaved: an enlarged geographical community. Raiding during the Revolutionary War had increased the black population in town, which meant more available free labor for slaveholders. But higher numbers also meant the black community as a whole was bigger, potentially more robust and resilient. Having a greater number of African Americans in the area—most of them enslaved, a few of them free—increased the chances for social alliance, communal collaboration, and organized rebellion among blacks as well as among unfree people of indigenous ancestry. One truncated but telling example points to a growing black community in the southern Great Lakes that may have channeled its collective energies toward a radical challenge of slavery in the area. In 1803, a fatigued British captain outlined the "cares" of his French wife in a letter to John Askin, his relative by marriage. The unruly behavior of her slaves had driven his wife to distraction, groused Captain Alexander Grant. Mrs. Grant's bondspeople were "very ungrateful and turbulent," and her "Cursed negroe wench" along with a black man lately purchased from Matthew Elliott, were both in jail for theft. Grant complained that the jailed pair were suspected of carrying "information of a great number of vagarents hovering about here to bring off as many negros as they can And as I am told forming a Town on the other side of Sandusky. at present there is forty Black men there."[33]

Grant's grumbling letter reveals that African Americans clustered south of Lake Erie were rumored to be easing into Detroit River settlements, stealing items, sharing strategic intelligence, and encouraging enslaved people to escape. The specific community described by Captain Grant in 1803 may have been the same one encountered by Moravian missionaries who followed the Miami River to Lake Erie in 1808 and were the first to document the settlement by name. "After we had passed through a place where twenty years ago an old Wyandotte town had stood, we came to Negro town where about six or seven Negro families live. They have been among the Indians for a long time, and have taken over their way of life," penned one of the fascinated Moravian brothers. After entering the Wyandot-African village just outside of Upper Sandusky near the mouth of the Sandusky River, the traveling missionaries were served by a black woman host, who "spoke English very well," and gave them "cornbread and coffee," the latter being a preferred drink among the villagers. The Moravians took care, while in the home of their host, to follow "Indian custom" and accept the victuals she offered. A Methodist minister called Benjamin Larkin passed through two years later, and remarked upon the same settlement where "some Negroes and Indians dwelled."[34]

These survivors of war, slavery, and migration encountered by the missionaries had come north by various routes in the late eighteenth century and resided with Wyandots, members of the Wendat (Hurons, Petuns, and Neutrals) diaspora set in motion by wars with the Iroquois in the middle 1600s. Some blacks in the village had been brought in as captives but later lived as free people; others may have entered as free. Some of these individuals were mixed-race of African and Native ancestry, but seen as "Negro" by the Moravians due to their darker skin tone. Some may also have preserved African and African American spiritual and folk practices, as not very far away, in Fairfield, Upper Canada, Moravians had observed a black woman with a broom that was "somewhat like the fetishes the Negro in Guinea fashions out of roots" and was believed to bring protection to its bearer from "illnesses and misfortune."[35] This village south of Lake Erie was the same community that produced the free black trader who worked between Detroit and Ohio with a Wyandot partner in the 1790s.[36] When the Wyandots were compelled to sign away territory to General Anthony Wayne after the Battle of Fallen Timbers in 1795, most tribal members moved westward. Several black families who had acclimated to Wyandot ways stayed behind. Tension grew between the groups, as the Wyandots, pressed to remove and take stock of their now meager resources, began to distance themselves from people of African ancestry in the village.[37] The black, mixed-race, bicultural residents who remained rebounded from this rejection and received other African descendants into their midst, especially runaway slaves trickling in from the U.S. South. Negro Town (a name that would stick well into the early twentieth century and later be disparaged as "Nigger Town" by local white Ohioans) became a radicalized community of color out of necessity.[38] Mrs. Grant's black woman and the man with her in jail likely had connections there, suggestive of a free black network based near Lake Erie and the interconnected Detroit River region as early as 1803. In the summer of 1807, James May on the American side complained to John Askin on the Canadian side that his own enslaved man, Nobbin, had escaped and that "a bad set of people about" were also trying to persuade Askin's enslaved boy, George, to run across the river.[39] These "bad people" may well have hailed from Negro Town. Enslaved blacks and Indians in Detroit now had another destination should they take a gamble on seizing freedom: a black village in the remote, semi-protective zone of former Indian lands not yet settled by whites.

Despite the continuation of slavery, circumstances in Detroit had shifted in discernible ways for unfree people as well as their owners several years into the new American era. The disruption of the Revolution had reshaped the racial makeup of Detroit's population, dispersing more African Americans throughout the region. The Northwest Ordinance narrowed pathways to slaveholding for Americans, while the Jay Treaty drew a boundary that highlighted routes for escape to foreign territory for enslaved people. In this environment, captives found greater opportunity for boldness. Escapes were more frequent, and freedom-seekers identified multiple destinations.[40] In addition to fleeing south toward Sandusky or Cincinnati across wild terrain that no white gentleman relished entering, bondspeople made for Native towns, viewed as equally formidable by slaveholders even in the aftermath of the Treaty of Greenville that had stripped indigenous groups of most tribal territory in Ohio. From one community home-base with both a black and Indian imprint, Negro Town of Ohio, clandestine attacks may have been waged against Detroit slaveholders to rile bondspeople, seize goods, and spread the message of freedom. Just as John Askin had sensed when he packed up his things and moved to Canada, winds of change were in the air along the strait.

Legislating Detroit Town

While enslaved people in Detroit pushed for liberty in radical ways, Elijah Brush's professional star continued to rise. His father-in-law, John Askin, wrote that Brush was "an industrious man and except for improvements is by no means extravagant for a man who earns so much for his profession" and noted with paternal pride, "His practice is worth a great deal."[41] In 1803 Brush was appointed as a trustee of the board governing the township of Detroit (as had been his father-in-law before the move to Canada). Brush was responsible, along with a handful of leading men, for devising local rules, ensuring the compliance of the public, and handling complaints. The board's first municipal ordinances addressed fire protection and the sale of foodstuffs. Bread now had to be stamped with bakers' initials and sold for the fixed price of six pence for a three pound loaf. Instead of allowing farmers (primarily French residents) to come to town with carts of eggs, butter, beans, vegetables, and meats on Sunday and commence selling these products following mass at Ste. Anne's, as was the local custom, the board established market days on Tuesday and Friday and designated a set location by the river that would serve as a farmers' market.[42] Tavern keepers were prohibited from allowing "any minors, apprentices, Servants, or Negroes to Set drinking in their houses, at any time, or to have any Strong drink, without Special order & allowances of their parents or masters." This directive indicated the finely graded class stratification in Detroit as well as town leaders' continued efforts to control the behavior of societal underlings. "Negroes," a term nearly synonymous with "slaves," were classed right along with poor laboring whites, minors, and "servants," the latter of which could include members of any racial group as well as lifelong unfree people characterized as indentured servants in contracts.[43]

The absence of the word "slaves" in this edict is representative of all early laws in Detroit, which avoided directly pointing to a class of people held in slavery, likely due to the influence of the Northwest Ordinance and the seriousness with which leading Detroiters, such as Solomon Sibley, took this federal mandate. Detroit would never develop a slave code like other municipalities with slaves; nor did it clearly lay out rules for indenture. Slavery and servitude were old practices instantiated by custom rather than regulated by local law. Enslaved people would therefore fall under the general rules of the community, with their masters held responsible for their infractions. It would take decades before Detroit had a law specifically aimed at enslaved people, which took the form of a Michigan territorial black code, rather than a slave code, in 1827. The territorial legislature seated in Detroit passed "An Act to Regulate Blacks and Mulattoes." This punitive legislation required blacks in the city to provide proof of freedom, register with a clerk of court, and pay a registration fee; it also required newcomers of African descent to pay a $500 bond to a free resident within twenty days to guarantee good behavior, or else be forcibly removed; the law charged fines for anyone aiding runaway slaves. Despite the clause that protected African Americans with proof of freedom from unlawful seizure, this law intended to limit and control the black population, making it harder for free blacks and runaway slaves to call Detroit home. This law would predate a series of similarly harsh local actions following a dramatic act of organized resistance in 1833, in which Detroiters aided the escape to Canada of Thornton and Ruthie Blackburn, runaways from Kentucky. But decades earlier, in 1802, before the existence of Michigan Territory as a discrete place, no such law directed at the black population existed. Blacks and Native Americans held as slaves were legislated alongside people deemed dependents with no reference to enslaved status.[44]

While studiously avoiding the subject of slavery, Detroit's board of trustees spent the bulk of its administrative energies passing and enforcing rules about fire prevention. In a town built almost entirely of wood, fire was a hovering threat and constant cause for anxiety. The board therefore required residents to keep their roofs free of soot, to own ladders tall enough to reach the tops of chimneys, and to maintain personal fire-fighting paraphernalia, including a barrel full of water and buckets. In the evenings, domestic fires had to be covered and candles snuffed. A night watchman patrolled the streets looking for wayward flickers of light and pounded on door planks to question residents about candles left visibly burning. Fire inspectors regularly checked every household for the requisite ladders, buckets, and barrels. Those who broke the fire codes and other regulations were charged by the board and required to pay fines. By 1805 town trustees had put in place scrupulous precautions against a possible conflagration, a regulatory code for the grocery market, fines for noncompliance with municipal rules, and a system of tax collection.[45]

As soon as Detroit's trustees began to make local laws, residents—including those same trustees, began to break them. John Askin was a fire code offender before his move across the river, as was John Dodemead, a relative of James Dodemead, the man in charge of the fire engine. In 1803 merchant-slaveholders George Meldrum, Henry Berthelet, Robert and

James Abbott, and James May were all fined for fire code violations; they failed to keep at their houses the required kind and number of ladders and buckets. Elijah Brush "esq[uire]" was also charged for having a "roof-ladder too Short" but was conveniently "excused" from fine payment.[46]

Town officials policed moral dangers, too. In 1803 inspectors filed a report against Henry Berthelet, the purchaser of little Veronique who would soon attain U.S. citizenship, as well as other "Delinquents" for using "profanity on the Sabbath day."[47] In 1802, Deputy Attorney General Solomon Sibley brought suit against Margaret White, "Spinster," for keeping "a common, ill governed, and disorderly house." At White's residence, "for lucre and gain, certain persons, as well men as women, of evil name and fame, and of dishonest conversation" engaged in "drinking, tipling, whoring, and misbehaving themselves." The growing Town of Detroit now had a social counterpoint to Ste. Anne's Church in the form of a rowdy saloon and brothel. We can surmise that indigenous and black women were present here, as the prostitution of enslaved women by their owners had long occurred in Detroit's sister city of New Orleans.[48]

James May, an elected town board member, was a two-time offender for breaking town codes. He violated regulations by sending beef "not Sound" to market, for which he had to pay fifteen dollars.[49] He also broke the law by proxy, since he carried responsibility for the actions of his slaves. In 1802 May was charged twenty-five cents because his "young Negro boy" was caught "carrying filth out of the S. W. gate of the town," which amounted to littering on the public commons.[50] May was also busy accusing others of breaking the rules; in 1803 he complained that the "Negro-man" of John Michel Yack (of French and German descent) was guilty of "Galloping a horse in the streets of the town of Detroit." Yack was fined a dollar for the transgression of his slave.[51]

Although James May could not have been happy about his own fees, he certainly had the means to pay them. In a tax list for Wayne County compiled in 1802, one hundred and four homes and only seven slaves were counted within the pickets of the fort and just beyond the walls to the west. Several enslaved people who lived in farms outside of town were not accounted for, including the Denison family, the bondspeople owned by William Tucker on a tributary of the Detroit River. According to the records of Ste. Anne's Church, between 1800 and 1809, at least twenty-nine individuals were still being held as slaves within the church community. This included ten blacks, fifteen "Panis," one "mulatto," and three individuals with no racial designation listed.[52] James May, who possessed one slave according to the 1802 census, also owned one of the three most valuable homes, assessed at $1,000. In a tax levied in 1805 for ownership of "mules, calashes, carioles, dogs and studhorses," May was the highest taxpayer, followed by Joseph Campau, James Abbott, and Elijah Brush, all slaveholders or beneficiaries of indentured slave labor.[53] Although William Macomb's widow, Sarah Macomb, was not listed among these men and may not have had a fancy calash or studhorse, she was still prospering in the decade following her husband's death. In the spring of 1806, under a list of "Sundry Expenses for the Family," Sarah Macomb recorded the purchase of "Molly the Wench," for whom she paid "70" in "cash." The acquisition of Molly dwarfed all of Sarah Macomb's other expenditures recorded in the same list, including: honey, eggs, fish, work by the blacksmith, a pig, six hens, linen, and cash paid while "shopping at New York."[54]

The serious-minded attorney Solomon Sibley watched national matters as closely as local issues from his home in Detroit. When Ohio achieved statehood and Congress formed Indiana Territory in 1803, the seat of Northwest Territorial governance shifted from Ohio to Indiana. Sibley, who served as a territorial representative, worried about the fate of Detroit in the aftermath of this consolidation, fearing Detroit would fall prey to neglect now that the regional government was at a farther remove. Therefore Sibley, along with other local leaders, pushed for a separate territory that would prioritize Detroit. Two years later, Sibley saw his dream of independence realized. In January of 1805, President Thomas Jefferson approved a division of the lands then encompassed by Indiana Territory. The newly christened Michigan Territory would occupy the boundaries of what had formerly been defined as Wayne County, a land nestled among flowing rivers and glistening lakes. Even better, Detroit would become the territorial capital, and President Jefferson would appoint commissioners to govern from the town beginning July 1, 1805.[55]

Elijah Brush stood in the thick of local town governance as the infant Michigan Territory took shape. Constantly busy with his law office, he also juggled new roles as fire inspector (an elected position) and lieutenant colonel in the Michigan militia (an appointed position) starting in 1805.[56] True to form, Elijah Brush dressed smartly for his militia post, having ordered in from New York "twelve yards of superfine Buff casimure and four doz[en] of the best trible gilt Coat buttons" as well as a stack of instructive military books: "Hayts Cavalry dicipline—Steven's Artillery, Stubons Exercise for the Militia, [&] Fishers Military tactics."[57] During Elijah's long stints at work, Adelaide Askin Brush, little Edmund, and the newest baby Charles sometimes stayed with family across the river in Canada. Adelaide may have been visiting at the home of her father when the greatest calamity since Detroit's founding unfolded. One morning, from the safety of Strabane, his stately home across the river, the venerable trader John Askin witnessed flames leaping across the rooftops of Detroit.[58]

The Great Fire of 1805

It had begun at ten o'clock in the morning of June 11 in the year 1805: the fire that would destroy the original French fort town made charming by shingles and diminutive glass window panes.[59] John Harvey, a baker by trade, kept a stable behind his business where sparks of a mysterious origin ignited, possibly from the pipe tobacco of an employee at the bakery falling into hay. Robert Munro, a witness to the events that would transpire, was employed as the storekeeper at the Indian Factory, where government goods were sold to Native traders. The factory site was located opposite the bakery in Detroit's compressed town center and so made for front-row viewing of the impending disaster. When Robert Munro caught sight of "flames bursting through the doors and windows" of the bakery's outbuilding, he wildly shouted the alarm.[60] His calls, along with the panicked screams of others, were answered by the town's single fire engine, a souped-up horse-drawn wagon manned by twelve volunteers. The bucket brigade, a line of men passing buckets overflowing with water, fell hurriedly into position. Despite the frenzied efforts of community firefighters, a robust wind carried the flames from building to building. Townspeople began to flee, lugging all they could from their homes and making their way to the commons beyond the pickets near the river. Robert Munro at the Indian Factory grabbed what he could and ran. At Ste. Anne's Church, where mass was in session that morning, Father Richard fled as Father Dilhet, with the help of a few devoted worshippers, salvaged "vestments and sacred utensils." Their actions to save cherished church items may be the reason why the Ste. Anne register, in which so many fragments of enslaved people's lives were notated, has been preserved to this day. The church, along with every other structure inside the town walls with the exception of the fort (British Fort Lernoult, soon to become Fort Shelby) at the rear of the settlement, burned to the ground within a few hours.[61] Three days later, Robert Munro opened a letter to William Henry Harrison, governor of Indiana Territory, with the solemn words: "Sir,—I have the painful task to inform you of the entire conflagration of the town of Detroit." He ended lamenting: "I can hardly hold the pen to write these few lines, and my mind is equally affected with the distressing scenes I have witnessed."[62]

Robert Munro was among the first victims of the disaster. Close enough to the fire when it broke out to be injured, he later bore the psychological scars. Canadians like John Askin, at a safe distance along the opposite bank but with friends and relatives remaining on the Detroit side, watched the ominous dark smoke mushroom into the sky with near equal panic that morning. The first Detroiters to escape the smoldering town jumped into rowboats and pushed out onto the waterway. From the sanctuary of the river, they watched, in the words of an early Detroit historian, Clever Bald, "the flames sweeping from house to house across the narrow streets, fire-fighters stubbornly working at their hopeless task, women and children streaming out on the Common, and above, like an angry storm cloud, the thick black smoke hiding the sun."[63] Munro, who had barely escaped the Indian Store with his papers and two thirds of the goods, reported to Governor Harrison that "In less than two hours the whole town was in flames, and before three o'clock not a vestige of a house (except the chimneys) visible within the limits of Detroit. The citadel and military stores were entirely consumed. . . . The situation of the inhabitants is deplorable beyond description; dependence, want, and misery is the situation of the former inhabitants of the town of Detroit."[64] Another eyewitness, awestruck by the incident, described it as "at once sublime and painful, exceeding in awful grandeur perhaps almost any spectacle of the kind which has happened since the world began."[65] But two important people did not see the conflagration and were late in even learning of it. William Hull and Augustus Woodward, Michigan Territory administrators appointed by President Thomas Jefferson, were en route to Detroit from the East while the great fire burned.

William Hull had agreed to serve as the governor of Michigan Territory and Augustus Brevoort Woodward as one of its two active supreme court justices. By the time the men arrived at the seat of their new territorial government, scheduled to become official the next month in July, they found nothing there but the shards of a colonial settlement. The buildings were gone with most of the contents destroyed, and the people were severely distressed. On the cusp of its grand moment as capital of Michigan, Detroit lay in a pile of debris. John Askin may have thought that his prognostication of Detroit falling into "ruin" seemed to have come to pass, though not in the financial realm where he most expected it. Disaster sparked by human hands, rather than an unfavorable business environment, proved to be the first undoing of Detroit. The original French Canadian dwellings were lost to wisps of memory, leaving the town orphaned from its eighteenth-century architectural heritage and its residents orphaned from their sheltering homes.

Out of the Ashes

Judge Augustus Woodward was the first of the incoming U.S. administrators to arrive on the scene after the fire. Judge Frederick Bates was already present, as he lived in the town, had served in the military, and, as his letters have revealed, courted French ladies.[66] Woodward appeared on June 30, having departed from Washington days before with the formal appointment from President Jefferson that he had long sought in hand. Woodward was born in New York City in 1774. He studied at Columbia College and soon made his way to Washington where he began the practice of law and served as a member of the city's first municipal governing council. A voracious reader and fiercely analytical thinker, Woodward found interest in all manner of subjects, from the study of languages (he wrote in Latin, French, Greek, and Spanish as well as speaking fluent French) to literature and poetry, science, leadership, politics, and governance.

A staunch Jeffersonian Republican, Woodward admired Thomas Jefferson and wrote forthrightly that Jefferson was, in his view, "undoubtedly the second character in America in every thing which forms a component part of a great man. Washington alone is his superior." Woodward's handwritten notebooks, full of pictorial foreign language word-trees, a self-made map of Washington City, English word sounds and stenographic shorthand notes, classical quotations, and principles of chemistry, show Woodward to have had much in common with the supple-minded Jefferson, known for his interest and competence in a dizzying array of subjects. In 1790, soon after Jefferson was elected to the presidency, Woodward sought a clerkship with him. But Jefferson informed the avid young student by mail that "I am not able to serve your wishes. . . . There neither is, nor has been a single vacancy in the clerkships in my office since I came to it."[67]

It was not until six years had passed that Woodward had the chance to meet Thomas Jefferson in person. A critical observer who treated Jefferson to the closest scrutiny, Woodward wrote down "Notes on My Visit to Mr. Jefferson," in which he found fault with the president's comportment. Jefferson was too "lively" and attentive, which "detracted from that calm & sublime dignity, which the imagination always attributes to a great & elevated character." Woodward continued in his critique: "Calm & composed he should have waited my approach without an advance on his part; my salutation & accessions . . . should have been readily reciprocated with a mild & engaging condescension." Jefferson was, in other words, too willing to engage Woodward and failed to display a social distance that underscored Jefferson's higher status.[68]

Woodward's desire for Jefferson to politely remind him of his place reveals the young lawyer's own belief in social hierarchy and graces. But at the same time that Woodward disliked Jefferson's outgoing manner, he accused the president of being overly self-promoting. "I rather tho[ugh]t he spoke of his own notes a little too often: he ought not to have presumed that I had read them or had ever seen them," Woodward harped.[69] But Woodward *had* read Thomas Jefferson's bestselling *Notes on the State of Virginia*, published in 1785. Jefferson's *Notes* contained the now well-known passage in which Jefferson lambasts African Americans for being unintelligent, unattractive, and unfit for assimilation into white society. Woodward, writing his own thoughts on blacks in an essay titled "On Habits," had expressed views remarkably similar to Jefferson's. In the essay, Woodward wrote: "in our own country—One sees all the negros in slavery—from his cradle he has known nothing else; the impression made by this custom has habituated him to imagine some kind of natural connection between the Africans and slavery. They are such black ugly creatures with such big lips & flat noses that surely God who is a wise Being & does every thing right w[ould] never put rational Souls into them—They must be hewers of wood and drawers of water forever—At any rate, they must not be put on a par with that dignified being a white man."[70]

Augustus Woodward was certainly influenced by Jefferson's writings in this opinion of African Americans as a subspecies created by God with an inbred irrationality. Nevertheless, he thought it arrogant for Jefferson to assume familiarity with Jefferson's popular book. Woodward's skittish interaction with Thomas Jefferson upon their first meeting was an indicator of his social awkwardness more generally. A tall, reedy man with a prominent, irregular nose and small, piercing eyes, Woodward believed deeply in his own self-evident intelligence and was quick to defend against slights. That he could sharply judge a man whom he admired and whose ideas he incorporated suggested that Woodward readily turned an exacting eye toward those who did not measure up to his standards. Still, Woodward's intellectual gifts and passion for knowledge caught and held Thomas Jefferson's interest. Jefferson became an associate to the younger attorney, lending him an encyclopedia and seeking Woodward's aid in identifying sources on topics of interest to them both. On one occasion, Woodward promised to send Jefferson a work that he would "shortly procure from alexandria" [sic] containing "a great deal of information on the domestic jurisprudence of France."[71] This relationship led to Woodward's appointment as one of Michigan's first two supreme court justices, for which he would take an oath of fidelity to "support the constitution of the United States."[72]

As the first appointee to the court, Woodward became chief justice of the Supreme Court in Michigan Territory. He brought his prejudiced views on race with him to the work as surely as he carried along his educational training and legal experience. The driving intellectual force in a territory that was only required by local law to have one judge present for cases, Woodward would become the only justice to write opinions for the court during his eighteen years on the bench. Several of these cases involved disputes over slavery, a practice limited by the Northwest Ordinance but not explicitly addressed in Michigan Territory laws (that Woodward himself would first pen in 1805) or in Detroit Town edicts established by the board of trustees. Woodward's decisions on slavery cases would soon show his investment in establishing a legal culture in Detroit that reflected the principle of the rule of law, protected U.S. sovereignty over its territory, and maintained peace at the border.[73]

Augustus Woodward arrived in Detroit one day before Governor William Hull, with a personality guaranteed to irk his superior. Woodward was self-posturing, self-important, and spoke in multisyllabic words so as to display his fine education.[74] He was also prominent and fortunate enough to immediately find shelter with James May, whose expensive home was located beyond the borders of the fallen town. From there, Woodward, whose "office and his friendship with President Jefferson gave him prestige in the Territory, and his own imperious nature demanded respect," began to steer the distressed inhabitants.[75] Together with Judge Bates, Judge Woodward convinced Detroit residents to await the arrival of the governor before rebuilding their homes. With no permanent shelter, the townspeople created a refugee camp on the common land beside the river, squatted in the homes of nearby farmers, and depended on the charity of local merchants, like Jacques Girardin, a slaveholder, who provided the people with loaves of fresh bread.[76]

One day after Woodward's appearance and two weeks after the massive fire, Governor William Hull finally reached Detroit. He arrived with his wife Sarah Hull, a son, two daughters, a personal secretary, and the secretary of Michigan Territory, Stanley Griswold. "Shocked and appalled to find his intended capital in ruins, and the inhabitants encamped round about," Hull went about the difficult business of managing a proto-state.[77] Unlike Augustus Woodward, Hull was not able to secure the best of temporary accommodations. Hull wrote to James Madison, secretary of state: "On my arrival (July 1st) every house was crowded, and it was more than a week before I could obtain the least accommodation. I am now in a small farmer's house about a mile above the ruins, and must satisfy myself to remain in this situation during the next winter, at least."[78]

Although an unfortunate man in the summer of 1805 and on key occasions thereafter, William Hull had been born into privileged circumstances in 1753. He hailed from Connecticut, trained at Yale College, and served honorably in the Revolutionary War under General George Washington as well as General Anthony Wayne. Hull had been appointed by Jefferson as governor of Michigan, which also made him military commander of the territory. But any grand hope that he may have harbored for his new western post was dashed from the beginning. Hull was described by his descendants as "a man of considerable ability . . . handicapped in his new job by his total lack of acquaintance with frontier life and problems."[79] As he struggled to recover Detroit from overwhelming disaster, a task that stretched on for years, William Hull would learn too late about the pressure that the Indian presence would foment and the cohesion of the large French population, whose language he did not even speak.

But in the days immediately following the fire, Hull forged ahead with drawing the beleaguered populace together. He called a meeting beneath the pear trees of slaveholder Sarah Macomb's fruit orchard and gave a rousing speech.[80] Hull vowed that a committee would be formed to request aid from the U.S. government, assured the people that they would be made financially whole, and expressed his desire to rebuild the town according to a "Judicious and enlarged plan."[81] Governor Hull saw opportunity in the ruins of Detroit. Some local leaders agreed with his vision of an expanded settlement, such as Solomon Sibley, who had always judged Detroit to be too tight and too French. Stumbling out from the ashes of catastrophe, certain Detroiters began to see strategies for growth that today might be termed "disaster capitalism."[82]

Elijah Brush also approved of the governor's notion of building a bigger and better Detroit. One year after the fire in 1806, Elijah Brush, James May, and John Anderson wrote a letter to President Jefferson representing a view that they described as having been sanctioned "by all the inhabitants here who are in the least Degree interested, or affected thereby."

Governor Hull was, in the letter writers' estimation, running "a System of Territorial Government as much to our perfect satisfaction." But the men nevertheless had pressing concerns and urgent requests. They appealed to the U.S. government to recognize all land claims obtained and held during the French and British periods; they wished to see "the Indian Title in this Territory . . . extinguished." They wanted "to open the door to Emigration" and thus see more white settlers enter the country, and they sought "some support and Releif [sic] for the unfortunate sufferers by the late conflagration at Detroit." Finally, they hoped to see "the Plan of the New Town of Detroit" enacted—a town that would marginalize indigenous people and reward settlers of European descent, who by hook or by crook had gained title to those lands in the colonial period. If these measures were not taken, especially regarding land, "our Ruin is completely sealed," the authors proclaimed in defeatist language about Detroit that was already beginning to sound like an echo in the early nineteenth century.[83] Early settlers may have found the wood-shingled village charming and may have tolerated indigenous neighbors to further the fur trade, but the new Americans had another vision in mind. The catastrophe of fire on the heels of the establishment of Michigan Territory created an opportunity for drastic change. The rustic French fort town that hugged the banks of the narrow river could now be remade into an "authentic" American city.

Judge Augustus Woodward was tasked by Hull with designing a spatial layout for the New Town Plan. He seized upon the assignment with gusto, imagining the future Detroit as a grid of long, diagonal streets punctuated by graceful spokes at regular intervals. Much of the design was inspired by the work of a Frenchman, Pierre Charles L'Enfant, who had planned the majestic Washington City for President George Washington.[84] Woodward had kept a hand-drawn map of Washington in his pocket notebook while working as a lawyer there. Perhaps he pulled out that map, worn at the creases of the folds, to examine its specifics before sketching a design for Detroit. He also may have dusted off his reading notes from Columbia College, which included the titles *On the Best Plan for Building a City*, *Improvements on the Plan of the City of New York*, *Description of the City of Philadelphia*, and *Description of the City of New York*.[85] Surely this moment was one the intense man who compulsively sketched in his notebooks had been waiting for all his professional life. In addition to calling upon his broad base of multidisciplinary knowledge as well as his love of the liberal and applied arts, Woodward relished playing a dominant role in the refashioning of Detroit. His ardent belief in nationalism and patriotism, and the need to build up both in America, suggest he would have welcomed the challenge to remake Detroit into the pride of an American West.[86] Although he spoke fluent French and admired French politics of the Revolutionary era, Woodward cared little for English ways.[87] He had created a table in his plentiful notes in which he compared American and British characteristics, the latter group faring poorly in the tally. While American "Patriots" could be counted on for "Modesty, Intelligence, Morality, Eloquence, Decency, Family Ties, and Plainness," the British displayed "Hauteur, Science, Gluttony, Ratiocination, Prostitution, Pride of Birth, and Splendor," in Woodward's humble opinion.[88] Detroit's New Town design rested in the hands of a man who wished to imprint an American stamp with an invisible touch of French influence.

Enslaved Detroiters in Disaster's Wake

Governor William Hull's New Town notion depended upon the wreckage of old Detroit. But he was not the first to realize that disaster presented economic openings. As Detroit's priceless eighteenth- and early nineteenth-century buildings lay in smoldering heaps of ash, merchant James May picked his way from lot to lot, where he "gathered the stones of which the chimneys in the houses were built . . . and built a stone house with them." May's palatial stone home, located on May's Creek, a waterway that once spilled into the Detroit River, was complemented by a gristmill, tannery, and barn. This became the new hub from which May managed "a big business" with his partner, Valentine. May and Valentine rustled cattle from Ohio and Indiana back to Detroit, supplied the military post at Detroit as well as others, and provided "salt and fresh pork and beans" to households along the strait. Later, the large stone building that May called home became a courthouse and a hotel.[89] But the early account of May's stone salvage project raises pointed questions. Who, exactly, waded through the ash and rubble looking for choice chimney stones? Who carried those stones to the undisturbed creek bank miles outside of town? Who built the stone manor house? Who ground the corn in the mill? Who raised the cattle? Who tanned the hides? May's slaves and hired laborers surely performed these tasks, though they garner no mention in the historical record.

Not one existing narrative of the "great fire" of Detroit notes the presence of unfree people during or immediately following the incident. Despite this void, it stands to reason that enslaved people—both black and Native—would have been severely affected by the calamity. Many would have been homeless alongside their owners yet directed to the worst of temporary lodgings. Bondspeople faced hunger and bodily need just like other Detroiters but likely received lesser portions of donated food and none of the funds delivered by the relief ships dispatched from Michilimackinac and Montreal and distributed by wealthy residents.[90] Lots and roads had to be cleared, pickets reconstructed, and new homes and gardens established. Certainly slaves would have been tasked with this work as well as their customary labors. But at the same time that unfree people would have been especially disadvantaged in this moment of crisis—more vulnerable to the vagaries of chance and the burden of excess work in a town struggling to rebuild in the aftermath of destruction—they, like James May and William Hull, could find and exploit hidden opportunities. For enslaved people, disaster could be double edged—painful, but also productive. The Revolutionary War had shown that chaos and disruption could be a boon in slave communities, creating new routes to freedom. In enslaved circles where lifelong servitude was the condition of existence, events defined as crises could spur constructive change.

The Denison Case

Peter and Hannah Denison, a black couple enslaved on the Huron River twenty miles north of Detroit, would have heard about the fire as soon as news could travel. They surely worried about what the loss of the area's central settlement would mean. But even more pressing in the lives of the Denison family than total town destruction downriver was an event that transpired just a few months before the fire. The Denisons' owner,

William Tucker, had died in the spring of 1805, and his passing put the Denisons in extreme danger. The death of an owner, as the bondspeople of William Macomb had experienced, often meant the disbursement of slaves. William Tucker left his wife, Catherine Tucker, the bulk of his property, which consisted of "six hundred acres whereof 60 acres are supposed to be leased and under fence . . . With a dwelling house, barn, stable, out houses, and orchard thereon." William also wished Catherine to have: "my Black man and Black woman—Peter and Hannah his wife" who would receive "there [sic] freedom after the decease of Catherine Tucker my wife provided they shall behave themselves as becometh to her . . . during her life." Tucker revealed in his will that he "always meant to give their freedom" to Hannah and Peter. Perhaps William Tucker had even told the couple as much and led them to believe he would free them upon his own death. If so, the pair would have been sorely disappointed upon hearing the specifics of Tucker's will. Peter and Hannah would not obtain liberty yet. For that, they would have to await Catherine Tucker's demise. But their main, heartrending concern as Tucker's estate was settled would have been for their children: Elizabeth, Scipio, James, and Peter Jr., also left to Tucker's wife in the will. Unlike Peter and Hannah, the children would not be freed upon Catherine Tucker's death. Rather, "one sixth share of the negro children" would be inherited by six of the seven Tucker children—all of them boys. (Tucker's only daughter, Sarah, was to receive two cows after her mother's death.) How could four African American children be subdivided into six equal parts? Unless the Tucker sons (William, Edward, John, Jacob, Charles, and Henry) planned to work these slaves on a time-sharing plan, there was just one method: sale and division of the proceeds.[91]

William Tucker's last testament was chillingly clear. He had bequeathed: "unto Catherine Tucker my Trusty and well beloved wife the farm I now live on together with all building stock (I mean, oxen cows sheep young cattle hogs farming utensils household furniture my Negro man and woman Peter & Hannah & their daughter and three sons). The sole use and benefit therof [sic] for & during the whole term of her natural life."[92] As soon as Catherine Tucker died or had the inclination, the Denison children could be sold. Their fate rested entirely in the hands of Catherine Tucker and her male heirs. Peter and Hannah Denison would have felt deep unease and even rage at this revelation. Their family was still together following the death of a man who had claimed mastery over them. But for how long?

It is impossible to know exactly how events began to turn next, who said what to whom and when. The records of Detroit are silent on which person in the transaction initiated the contract of indenture. Perhaps Catherine Tucker sought fast cash to balance the finances of her estate, or perhaps she feared that a resentful Peter and Hannah would run. Maybe Elijah Brush saw the need for skilled labor following the fire and approached Catherine Tucker about acquiring her black man and woman. Whatever the impetus, in 1806, Catherine Tucker transferred Peter and Hannah for an undisclosed signing fee. She "indented" the couple "to Elijah Brush for one year, at the expiration of which they were to have and enjoy their freedom."[93] Elijah Brush had probably paid Catherine Tucker hundreds of dollars to make this deal for the Denisons' removal. The couple's children would remain with Catherine Tucker, however. This loss of their family must have dominated the thoughts of Hannah and Peter as they rowed the river to the remains of the old French port town where they had been purchased in 1780 and 1784 and separated, then, or prior, from their own parents.[94]

The home occupied by Elijah and Adelaide Brush, as pictured in a drawing from the middle 1800s, took up the better portion of a city block. Sprawled across lush park-like grounds surrounded by pickets, the large two-story farmhouse had multiple front-facing windows framed by wood shutters and a long, covered front porch secured at the corners by columns. Crisscrossed by walking paths, the land supported shade trees, fruit trees, and thriving gardens.[95] The house would have had stone chimneys. The doors may have been painted an emerald green, a color at that time viewed as "evidence of the taste and wealth of the householder."[96] The Brush farm, as it came to be known after John Askin's move to Canada, encompassed more than a mile of land with 386 feet of frontage along the Detroit River just outside the fort.[97] When the Denisons walked onto that land and into the home where they would work, they could not have helped but compare it to the more modest farmhouse of William Tucker. The Denisons also would have been quick to perceive the high social status of their new masters: Adelaide, the elegant daughter of a prominent trader, and Elijah, a big man in local affairs. At the time of the Denisons' arrival, Elijah Brush's stature, and hence his influence, were steadily expanding. He had been appointed co-mayor of the town in 1806 along with Solomon Sibley, and he was serving as treasurer of Michigan Territory as well as lieutenant colonel of the Legionary Corps.[98]

Within the wooden walls of the home constructed on land purchased by Adelaide's maternal ancestors in the period of the French and Indian War, the Brushes and the Denisons must have sized one another up.[99] Hannah would have been told to keep the kitchen, clean the house, sew and wash linens and clothing, and serve Mrs. Brush as other enslaved women had done before her, while Peter would have been ordered to take on many of the regular duties of male slaves in Detroit. This included heavy agricultural work, construction and repairs about the place, delivery of parcels and letters, and the application of any specialized craftsman skills. Because Elijah Brush did not engage directly in the fur trade but instead represented clients in the industry, Peter was not dispatched to sea, made to clean and pack furs, or directed to transport malodorous skins across great distances. Instead, he was likely assigned to help clear the rubble in Detroit. All through the year that the Denisons lived with the Brushes, town residents were still homeless due to the fire. During the winter of 1806 and into that spring and summer, Detroit resembled a tent city, with temporary lodgings half open to the elements teetering among refuse piles.

As days turned into weeks and weeks into months, the Brushes may have come to appreciate the particular attributes of the Denisons. We can wonder what the exacting Adelaide first noticed about the capable Hannah. Perhaps Hannah spoke often of her children in the French language, pulling on Adelaide's heartstrings. Or perhaps Hannah, a woman handy with the needle, even claimed the superior skills of a dressmaker and could craft the fashionable clothing that Adelaide so adored. And Elijah may have recognized in Peter a self-possessed nature that indicated an unusual force of inner strength. Elijah may even have regretted the other man's forced condition of servitude, feeling a flash of sympathy for the difference that class and color made. His father-in-law, John Askin, had after all once described Elijah Brush as a "warm hearted fellow."[100] So during the long winter months, when Detroiters relied on fires for heat, stories for comfort, and sleds for transport across icy waters, the Brushes and the Denisons may have gotten to know one another, slowly laying a fragile foundation for common cause. Even given the unequal power relations in place, something transpired between these pairs—perhaps a sense of mutual dependence, recognition, or even respect. By the time the calendar turned to the fall of 1807, the Denisons were suing for their children's freedom, and they had secured as their attorney Elijah Brush, Esquire.

Or maybe this story is inside out as I have told it, with emphases on the wrong elements. Maybe actions less romantic, but more heroic, actually occurred in Detroit that year. Perhaps Peter Denison had an unusual asset that he was able to leverage to change his family's circumstances. He had relatives on the Macomb farm, which was parallel to Brush's place on the other side of town. He was not unknown to Elijah Brush. The two men had probably met and even conversed in the past. Elijah sensed what Peter was made of. So upon the death of William Tucker in 1805, Brush and Denison negotiated an agreement. In exchange for something special from Peter, Elijah Brush would ask Catherine Tucker to release the Denisons under the auspices of a one-year indenture contract that would soon see the whole family freed. But then, a hitch. Catherine Tucker refused to let the children go. So while Peter and Hannah Denison lived in Detroit and worked for the Brushes, they strategized with the Brushes to challenge their former mistress's right to continue holding the children as slaves. Like other enslaved people who engaged the services of attorneys, Peter Denison likely paid Brush's fees by trading even more of his own labor. The case brought forward by Elijah Brush on behalf of the Denisons would test the court system of Michigan Territory as the first freedom suit to be heard there. Brush, in his own words, "had always considered the Subject of Slavery as very doubtful in the Country, and as highly necessary to be Setled by Some judicial decision." He wanted to be the one to argue the matter, "but had no clear idea what the ultimate decision was likely to be" in the suit described many years later by a scholar of African American history as "Michigan's Own Dred Scott Case." *Denison v. Tucker*, decided in the fall of 1807 by a single judge, constituted the rationale that regulated slavery until Michigan statehood in 1837.[101]

Established in July of 1805 upon the birth of Michigan Territory, the Michigan Supreme Court was a "loosely organized, often whimsical bench." As no physical courthouse existed, sessions were held in any available structure, including the Indian council house, offices, taverns, "and sometimes on a Woodpile."[102] The rough-hewn quality of this arrangement suited Chief Justice Augustus Woodward, whose focus on the life of the mind led him to bathe seldom and dress with scant attention to polish or presentation.[103] Perhaps in part because he was known as "quarrelsome" and "slovenly," Woodward never married, concentrating his energies instead on the tasks and problems set before him as a manic, conceited, and some have said "brilliant" visionary of the territory.[104] One of the mottos scrawled into the pages of his notebooks read: "Tis better to excel in knowledge than in power."[105] While Woodward's pursuit of government posts over the course of his career shows that he was not immune to the allure of status, for him, research, reading, and knowledge in the quest for "patriotism" and "virtue" were paramount endeavors and essential ends.[106] So when Elijah Brush entered a motion on behalf of Peter and Hannah Denison, Woodward—a man who had written just over a decade earlier that blacks "must be hewers of wood and drawers of water forever," consented to hear the case. The Michigan territorial judiciary had borrowed from Ohio law to establish the supreme court with "exclusive jurisdiction" over cases involving land title, matters exceeding $200, crimes allowing capital punishment, divorce, and appeals from the district courts. The Denison children would have been valued at far more than $200 and closer to $2,000. This case therefore fell squarely into the supreme court's purview. Dutifully, Woodward issued a writ of habeas corpus, a right to inhabitants guaranteed by the Northwest Ordinance along with trial by jury. With the use of the writ, Woodward summoned Catherine Tucker into court to present the Denison children and testify as to her claim on them.[107]

Habeas corpus had been applied over the centuries of Anglophone legal culture to prevent wrongful imprisonment and allow captive people to appear before a judge who would determine the reasons for their detention. No person, the practice presumed, should be held without just cause. In the 1700s, the writ became a tool for slaveholders to demand the return of fugitive slaves. The application of the writ in protection of enslaved people was more unusual, and in requesting it, Elijah Brush pursued an edgy legal strategy fit for his location on the borderland-frontier. Catherine Tucker was thus compelled by Judge Woodward to bring him the "bodies" of the Denison children.[108] Unlike most freedom suits, which became more common in the nineteenth century, the Denison case would not turn on whether the Denisons could prove a "free maternal ancestor."[109] Instead, the future of these children would rest on the fine-grained interpretation of territorial and international law.

In the case of *Denison v. Tucker,* Catherine Tucker's statement on September 24, 1807, began as follows: "In obedience to the commands of the annexed writ of *Habeas Corpus ad subjiciendum* I have brought before the Supreme court of the territory of Michigan, the bodies, of Elizabeth Denison, James Denison, Sip Denison and Peter Denison Junr . . . together with the cause of their detention by me." Tucker, represented by attorney Harris Hickman, claimed that she held the children "in Servitude, under the Authority of the Ordinances and Laws of Upper Canada, which existed prior to, and at the time of, the surrender of the Post and Settlement of Detroit." Tucker was a British subject who had remained on the American side of the river. She argued that she was therefore due the protection of property guaranteed by the Jay Treaty, as the children were born to Peter and Hannah, slaves of her husband purchased for "a valuable consideration." Because the children "were all born, within the precincts & Jurisdiction of the Post of Detroit, while it was a part of (and subject to the Laws of) the province of Upper Canada," Tucker believed "she was entitled to hold them." She signed this statement with her mark rather than her name, an indication that Catherine Tucker's level of formal education was no higher than that of her bondspeople.[110]

A beneficiary of slave labor who regularly represented his father-in-law and other members of the slaveholding class, Elijah Brush fought hard for the Denisons, arguing their case "at full length" a day after Catherine Tucker's attorney presented hers.[111] The text of Brush's argument does not survive in the Michigan Supreme Court records, but we can intuit the outlines of his position. Peter and Hannah were now free following the year-long term of their indenture contract with the Brushes. Their children should be free as well according to the dictates of the Northwest Ordinance. Brush's allegiance in this case was not to a principle of emancipation but, rather, to individuals with whom he had ties. Brush was loyal to those he claimed as part of his circle, and the Denisons could be counted as such for reasons both altruistic and self-serving. But neither Brush's commitment nor his connections could win the day in court on such a consequential matter as property ownership. This case, as Judge Woodward saw it, went straight to "the question of Slavery" in the territory. And as he wrote in his final decision issued on September 26, 1807: "The question is novel, it is important, it is difficult."[112]

Augustus Woodward devoted thirteen pages, covered in a tight cursive scrawl with numerous lines of crossed out text and length-wise additions in the margins, to thinking through the complexities of the *Denison v. Tucker* case.[113] Maybe he once again dusted off his books from Columbia, referencing his copy of *On the Abolition of Slavery, Plan of a System of Jurisprudence for the United States*, or *Commentaries on the Constitution of the United States*, as he struggled through his deliberation.[114] He solicited information from James Wood, a colleague in Canada, and perhaps from legal associates back East or elsewhere in the western territories. Wood explained in a letter to Justice Woodward that: "Prior to the Conquest of Upper Canada by Great Britain, an Ordinance was passed by Mr. Raudot, Intendant of Canada, dated the 15th of April 1709, by which it was ordained that, under the good pleasure of his Majesty (the King of France) all *Panis* & Negroes which had been or which should thereafter be purchased, should belong in full property to those who had or who should purchase them in quality of Slaves." Wood also disclosed that Elijah Brush was well informed of this precedent, suggesting, "if you will call on *Mr. Brush* he will give you a Volume containing the Laws of Upper Canada which I left with him this Spring & in which the Statute you allude to is contained." Wood's letter, dated August 18, 1807, six weeks before the Denison case came to court, is indicative of forethought. Elijah Brush was preparing his case months in advance, and Judge Woodward was expecting the charge against Catherine Tucker. Both men may have been influenced in their actions by a statute passed in Missouri, Louisiana Territory, just months prior in June of 1807, which permitted individuals being held as slaves to sue for freedom on the basis of wrongful captivity.[115]

Augustus Woodward sought information from a Canadian regarding a nearly hundred-year-old French edict and may have looked westward for instructive territorial law. Deciding this slavery case in Detroit required as much. Because Detroit was positioned on a border and at the intersection of territorial, national, and international laws, Woodward had to contend with the legal history of two empires and one aspiring imperial nation, including layers of law dating back to the French colonial period. He had to grapple, as well, with the moral mire of slavery, the citizenship status of Catherine Tucker, and the birthdates and places of the Denisons. Woodward's lengthy written decision began with a history of slavery in Europe (England, Spain, and France) as well as the United States, reviewed the Northwest Ordinance and Jay Treaty, defined the meaning of property, discussed "principles of the law of nations on the Subject of Slavery," quoted the French ordinance on slavery of 1709 and the Canadian act of 1793 preventing the importation of slaves. While weighing all of these matters, Woodward professed that he held absolute the Constitution and authority of the United States. "The American government has promptly, Steadily and uniformly manifested its disposition to introduce its own forms of government, and to apply its own laws," Woodward proclaimed. His chief aim was to affirm and strengthen America's position as an independent nation. He therefore determined that his territorial court must resolutely uphold the international treaties of the federal government. Woodward acknowledged that the Northwest Ordinance mandated: "In this territory Slavery is absolutely and peremptorily forbidden." Nevertheless, he also asserted: "the federal constitution required that provisions in a duly ratified treaty prevailed over any contrary local laws."[116] For him, the U.S. Constitution and treaties ratified by Congress trumped the quasi-constitutional nature of the Northwest Ordinance, which he saw as comparatively "local." Woodward determined that enslaved people born before the effective American era that commenced in 1796, even "after the application of American laws," could be held in a "State of *qualified* slavery." He accepted that Catherine Tucker was a British citizen, entitled to protections of personal property as spelled out in the Jay Treaty cemented between Great Britain and the United States. He therefore decided that Catherine Tucker was entitled to hold the Denison children as her property.

Woodward rendered a complicated ruling that drew on the Jay Treaty, the Northwest Ordinance, gradual emancipation schemes in the Northeast, and British Canadian slave law. He issued a partial, graduated emancipation decision in which some slaves and slave descendants would never be free, others would be free after twenty-five years, and some—those born after the American assumption of control in the Northwest Territory—would be born free. The ruling stipulated:

> The Laws of France and Upper Canada ceased to have any effect in this Territory almost immediately after July 11, 1796, but under Jay's Treaty settlers continue to enjoy their property of every kind. The term property as used in Jay's Treaty includes slaves, as slaves were recognized as property by the countries concerned. Slaves living on May 31, 1793, and in the possession of settlers in this Territory on July 11, 1796, continue such for life; children of such slaves born between these dates continue in servitude for twenty-five years; children of such children, and all born after July 11, 1796, are free from birth.[117]

Because the eldest Denison children had been born between 1793 and 1796, they were consigned to slavery for life; their younger brother, Peter, would be relegated to slavery for another twenty-five years.[118] The devastation in the aftermath of that court session must have been profound. Elijah Brush had lost the case, and Peter and Hannah Denison had lost their sons and daughter to a lesser demon politely deemed "qualified slavery."

Word traveled swiftly along the banks of the river. Catherine Tucker's success in court spurred other slaveholders on. It was only three weeks after this decision that the Detroit slaveholder George Cotteral used the writ of habeas corpus to have the runaway Native man Toby arrested and returned to him. One week after Toby was apprehended, on October 19 of 1807, Judge Woodward had before him another slavery case. Canadian merchant Richard Pattinson petitioned the court to forcibly return his runaway slaves who were living in Detroit. Jenny, a mixed-race woman of African descent, and Joseph Quinn, a Native man, had run away from Pattinson's home in Sandwich, Upper Canada, a year earlier, in the fall of 1806. The two had made it to safety across the river and managed to evade recapture for months. Pattinson described Jenny as a "certain Mulatto girl . . . about the age of twenty years about five feet Six inches high straight and well made." One wonders what the relationship was between Pattinson and Jenny, a young woman whose figure he admired and who, in his words, "refuse[d] to return to his services." Joseph Quinn, the young man Jenny absconded with, was close to her age, at eighteen. He may have been a friend, lover, or relative of Jenny's, such that the two vowed to make their break together. Pattinson asked the Michigan court to arrest both young people and return them to his possession.[119]

Pattinson likely expected a positive outcome given the precedent of the Denison case. But that situation was entirely different in Judge Augustus Woodward's view, which was filtered through a lens of upholding American sovereignty. In the Pattinson case, Woodward emphasized that while the Jay Treaty compelled the recognition of British property rights in Michigan, no such treaty existed between the United States and Canada regarding Canadian slaves. He decided the court had no obligation to return persons held as property who were fugitives from a "foreign jurisdiction."[120] Woodward's decision in this case set important precedent for slavery law in the territory and the strength of U.S. jurisdiction at the border. He later received notice from the postmaster of New York City that copies of his decision on the Pattinson case were circulating in New York, where it was printed in *The American Citizen* and *Republican Watchtower* newspapers and sent to the Speaker of the House.[121]

On the same day that the Pattinson case reached the court, a slaveholder in similar circumstances filed a petition. Matthew Elliott, who "had remained at Detroit until about the time of surrendering said Post to the American Government, when he removed to Amherstburg," had lost several of his slaves. He claimed that "Hannah, Peter, Abraham, Scipio, Candus, and James who were born the slaves of said Matthew Elliott of female slaves belonging" to him, had run away to Detroit "last winter and spring." In addition, Elliott stated that Pompey and Jane, whom he bought from John Stockwell, who bought them from George Meldrum, had also "deserted" at the same time.[122] Elliot brought suit for the arrest and return of eight people. Given the replication of several names from the Denison family and the vague time window in which these slaves were said to have escaped, Elliott may have been chasing financial gain by claiming people he did not actually own and taking advantage of what he saw as an opening signaled by the Denison decision. Judge Woodward denied Elliott's request, citing the Pattinson ruling that he had issued that same day.[123] Woodward saw no legal obligation to find, arrest, and return the slaves of British Canadian subjects. Elijah Brush, who argued and lost all of these cases, first on behalf of the Denisons' freedom and then on behalf of Pattinson's and Elliott's right to recover their slaves, confessed he had never been "Sanguine" in his "expectation of Success" in any of the suits.[124] The relationship between slavery and the law in Detroit had been too hazy for Brush to predict an outcome. And Woodward's supreme court decisions may have added still more confusion, as he protected the right to hold slaves for the class recognized as old British settlers, but rejected the right of British-Canadians to recover their slaves with the aid of the court.

Despite his previously expressed views of black inferiority, Augustus Woodward criticized slavery severely in these decisions. In Pattinson's case, he empathized with the runaways as "human beings escaping from chains and tyranny" who "Could find no place in the whole earth to rest."[125] In the Denison case, he approved of the Northwest Ordinance's ban on slavery, writing: "Nothing can reflect higher honor on the american government than this interdiction. The Slave trade is unquestionably the greatest of the enormities which have been perpetuated by the human race. The existence at this day of an absolute & unqualified slavery of the human Species in the United States of America is universally and justly considered their greatest and deepest reproach." These ardent feelings, which seem to represent a change for Woodward over time, had no practical bearing on his decisions for the Michigan court. In the end, he addressed these cases legally rather than morally, or rather, with a view of maintaining American sovereignty as the highest form of his moral duty.

The Denisons surely had little regard for the subtleties of Judge Woodward's musings on the ugliness of the slave trade and assuredness of America's failing. For them, the judge's final decision that stole the liberty of four of their members was what mattered most. The next generation of their family would remain enslaved, most for their entire lifetimes. The Denisons would not abide this. By late October, the Denisons knew Tucker would have trouble recovering the children from Canada, just as Pattinson and Elliott had failed to recapture fugitives who had crossed the international border into Michigan Territory. This was all the incentive the Denison family needed. In the fall of 1807, they fled across the river to Sandwich, Upper Canada, keeping their family unit intact against all odds.[126]

As the Denisons ran *from* Detroit in search of liberty and security in their personhood, other black and Native captives ran *to* Detroit from Canada. The river that had once connected two sides of a single settler community but now divided two adversarial nations was being used as a bridge yet again—this time for fugitives escaping the grip of slavery. Detroit saw a surge of freedom suits and runaway slave cases between 1807 and 1809, as enslaved people, and those who claimed them, watched to see how the legal winds would blow. *Denison v. Tucker* was the first slavery case decided in Michigan Territory, but it would not be the last fight for freedom at the riverside. Before long, Peter Denison would return to his birthplace of Detroit, armed and politically dangerous.

5

The Rise of the Renegades (1807–1815)

The whole territory is a double frontier.
The British are on one side. The savages on the other.

—*Memorial of the Citizens of Detroit, 1811*

Maybe the story was inside out. Perhaps Peter Denison, the black man formerly enslaved by William and Catherine Tucker, was never really a servant indentured to Attorney General Elijah Brush. The legal record of the Michigan Supreme Court tells us otherwise, explicitly stating that Catherine Tucker indentured both Peter and his wife, Hannah Denison, to Elijah Brush following the death of William Tucker in 1806. But the odd events that soon ensued on the heels of that contract indicate a more intricate and unusual course of events that unfolded in the borderland vortex of turn-of-the-century Detroit.

The onset of the 1800s was difficult for Detroiters. A raging fire had destroyed the old town within the walls and scattered residents across the countryside in search of shelter. Political leaders for the newly designated Michigan Territory, mostly hailing from more refined eastern cities and townships, struggled to find their footing in a frontier environment peopled by inhabitants who spanned a cultural range, including, most especially, indigenous North Americans and French Canadians. The first session of the Michigan Territorial government, led by Governor William Hull, was held two months in the wake of the fire in the corner tavern of Richard Smyth, who, in addition to selling spirits, crafted hats.[1] Enslaved people, often in groups, were making bold bids for freedom by crossing the international borderline that was the Detroit River, a movement that led to a series of controversial cases in Chief Justice Augustus Woodward's outland court. French-speaking *habitants* harbored suspicions of the radical plan for rebuilding the town put forward by American leaders. Because of the need of constant translation between French residents and the governor, "the intercourse of the heart," Judge Woodward wrote, "seldom pass[ed] through." Neither the British nor the French actually liked easterners, Woodward confessed. The British referred snidely to Americans as "Yankees," while the French maligned them as "Bastonnois," "Sacre Bastonnois," or "sacre cochon de Bastonnois" (Bostonians, blasted Bostonians, or filthy swine of Boston).[2] Eastern newcomers, for their part, often viewed the old western settlers as uncouth and "half savage."[3] The landed elite, many of them from longtime merchant and slaveholding families, pushed for a federal government that they distrusted to recognize existing land claims and mark a fixed boundary between white and Indian territory that would swell the former and shrink the latter. And even as Detroit dragged itself out of the ashes of manmade disaster and negotiated internal social as well as political strife, new threats gathered on the horizon that presaged the possibility of yet another imperial war.

Incoming governor William Hull may have once thought that he was equipped to untangle such a tight knot of conflicts and pressures. Hull was a man possessive of an imposing physique, as well as an impressive military and judicial background. His full girth, patrician nose, and slightly downward turned eyes might even have intimidated those who worked with and beneath him. His history of outstanding service in the Revolutionary War helped him win the appointment as governor of Michigan Territory. Hull had risen to the rank of lieutenant colonel in that conflict and was roundly recognized for his brave and brutal handling of the bayonet, even receiving a personal commendation from General George Washington. After retirement from the military in 1786, Hull served as a common pleas court judge in Newton, Massachusetts, and as a member of the Massachusetts state senate. Being a Democrat and staunch supporter of Thomas Jefferson also buoyed Hull's rise, as it was President Jefferson who tapped Hull for the gubernatorial post that included responsibility for Indian Affairs in the region. For a salary of $2,000 per year, William Hull made plans to move "to a rough frontier society made up of French-speaking settlers intermixed with a sprinkling of Americans who were primarily westerners of an independent spirit." After taking the oath of office in Albany, New York, in the spring of 1805, Hull set off for Detroit with his family by way of a water route. Travel across Lake Erie was unpredictable, with the speed of the crossing entirely dependent on the winds. Nearly two long months after their departure, the Hulls had arrived to find Detroit "vanished."[4]

Sarah Hull, William Hull's wife of twenty-four years, entered a waking nightmare when she arrived with a son, Abraham, and two daughters, Nancy and Maria, by way of the Detroit River. Four years later, she would describe the arduous trek from the Northeast as "a long and perilous journey through the wilderness of six hundred miles." Responsible for the management of her upper middle-class household in a period that elevated white women's roles as Victorian wives and mothers of the Republic, she was expected to create a proper and uplifting home while her husband attended to politics. But there was no home to make in Detroit. The settlement was an ash bin. Sarah Hull and her children were virtually homeless, living with a farm family a mile out of town in crowded conditions worse than those suffered by her husband's headstrong chief justice.

Sarah had not been groomed to live in a refugee zone on the western edge of American expansion. The daughter of a judge in Newton, Massachusetts, she would have been expected by fellow ladies of the genteel class to instill virtue in her children, host teas and charm guests, and lubricate the social wheels of her husband's bright political future. Frontier Detroit promised nothing resembling this picture. The people there were isolated, insular, ethnically oriented toward French and Indian ways, and accustomed to making do in the most extreme of circumstances. In 1805, the population amounted to just 274 souls within the walled village, and most of those residents had been displaced to makeshift lodgings. Outside the central footprint of the riverine fort, farmers, "almost exclusively French," dug in along the various waterways. Sarah Hull could not have missed the precarious nature of Detroit Town: "a long, narrow column of settlers . . . flanked by the British on one side and by the woods and the Indians on the other." But she had shown fortitude in accompanying her husband to military encampments during the Revolutionary War. She had been present at the Battle of Saratoga and helped to tend the wounded. This was exactly the kind of grit that she would need to muster, and more, in adjusting to her new environs of Detroit.[5]

While Sarah Hull struggled to keep her family fed, clean, and morally upright in their temporary, substandard quarters, she observed her husband weighing out the innumerable threats to the territory he now governed. Indians, their large and persistent populations and outstanding claims to Detroit area lands, plagued William Hull. His most active supporters, merchants of an American cast, wanted Native people pushed back and contained. Even more foreboding than the Indian encampments outside Detroit were the hundreds of clans, tribes, societies, and confederations of indigenous people spanning the Great Lakes region from New York to Minnesota and into British Canada. These original inhabitants of the inland seas, chain-linked rivers, fertile coasts, and forested hunting grounds had shown themselves to be fierce protectors of their lands and life ways. Indians had attacked this very settlement and held it hostage in the 1760s. Then they had fought with their former foes—the British military—against the Americans not twenty years later. During the Revolutionary War, Indian warriors had gathered at Detroit in order to collude with British officials and plan attacks on patriot settlements. They were everywhere, the indigenous people of the Great Lakes. These Indians had their own minds. They had a generation of young men itching to retake what had been lost in the Treaty of Paris in which they had had no representation. They also had the friendship of the British who lay in wait, ready to use them as a first line of offense against their former American colonies that had dared to break away. While William Hull pondered the Indian threat that never quite receded, he anxiously watched as tensions between the United States and Great Britain simmered to boiling.

The main issue was impressment. Great Britain boasted the greatest navy in the world and depended upon its ferocious fleet for global financial primacy as well as homeland security. The British navy enabled the small island nation to dominate much of the globe in international trade. But as Britain fought a protracted war with France during the French Revolution and Napoleonic Wars that followed, the country's navy was severely overstretched. The British navy desperately needed more sailors even as British subjects and Irish resisters were defecting to American ships in the hope of better wages, greater independence, and shorter terms at sea. Determined to preserve its military might on the oceans and to put the upstart United States in its place, Great Britain got its back up. The navy ramped up a program of impressment led by burly "press gangs" that searched port town pubs and social spaces, and even private homes, for British defectors. These men were taken aboard British ships and compelled to work for the navy in conditions that approached indentured servitude, with low pay, long terms lasting until the ends of wars, and little if any shore leave. After 1803, the British navy became even more aggressive in its impressment practice, challenging American merchant ships, searching the decks for defectors, and forcing into military service men who claimed American identities by way of affiliation, naturalization, and birthright.[6]

This was the cast of William Hull's mind when an incident foreshadowing the War of 1812 unfolded in the summer of 1807. On June 22 of that season, an American warship floated near the Virginia shoreline with no military mission and only light weaponry. The frigate U.S.S. *Chesapeake* captained by Commodore James Barron was simply scheduled for a routine commercial trip to the Mediterranean. The deck was loaded with cargo, the ship's cannon stowed away. So neither the captain nor the crew saw the blow coming when the British warship *Leopard* attacked by cannon at close range. The *Leopard* struck the *Chesapeake* thrice as the American captain tried but failed to launch an effective defense. Commander Barron had no choice but to surrender while a party of British naval officers forcibly boarded the ship, physically inspected the bloody crew, and kidnapped four men accused of desertion from British service. Only one of these prisoners, Jenkin Ratford, had actually been born in Britain. Three Americans were killed in the *Leopard* assault; eighteen were wounded. The *Chesapeake* was a bundle of shattered boards when finally released to limp back to port. The British defector, Ratford, was punished for his crime with a hanging on board the ship that he had fled months prior. The captured Americans from the *Chesapeake* crew soon joined the six thousand American men who had already been impressed by the British.[7]

News of the *Chesapeake* affair leapt across eastern seaboard states as well as western territories. The offended American populace fumed with outrage. President Jefferson declared a risky trade embargo, crippling commercial exchange and the country's overall economy. The American Republic and British Crown were squaring off against one another as events slowly spiraled toward war. The British lords of the sea were on the offensive, and Governor William Hull was steward of an untamed land bordered by massive waters. Michigan Territory was a virtual peninsula with three quarters of freshwater coastline accessible to an aggressive British Provincial Marine. Moreover, the land over which Hull had formal American authority, but not by Native American consent, shared a border with British Canada that was uncomfortably close. A few stone throws across the Detroit River sat in wait Fort Malden, the encampment built by the British military after these same men had begrudgingly vacated Detroit just over a decade prior. And only one month before the *Chesapeake* incident, Hull had received an alarming letter from an officer stationed at Fort Mackinac, on the island above the Straits of Mackinac. The captain warned that neighboring tribes were communicating by wampum belt and likely planning to attack. So Governor Hull felt the breath of danger when he cast his thoughts to the corners and borders of Michigan Territory in the summer of 1807. The Indians could assault Detroit. The British could besiege Detroit. And the two could join their nefarious forces to fall upon America together, just as they had in the Revolutionary War. Biographers of William Hull have tried to convey and contextualize his fear of an Indian attack fired up by British instigation. For it was this fear (in hindsight, strategically misdirected) that led Hull to act in unpredictable ways that shocked his white contemporaries.[8]

The Renegade Militia

William Hull determined that he needed a strong defense, the best defense that could be obtained in a hinterland settlement with a dangerously low population of free white men. His attempt to organize the local French farmers into a formidable militia, as required by law for every new territory organized through the Northwest Ordinance, had dissolved into conflict when locals complained that the uniforms Hull required were far too expensive. Through a newly devised Michigan law modeled after a New York code, Hull and the judges had bestowed upon Hull the right to dictate militiamen's dress. A proper New Englishman with a penchant for formalities, Hull decided that each member of his militia should don: "a long blue coat . . . white plain buttons, white underclothes in summer, white vests and blue pantaloons in winter, half boots or gaiters, round black hats, black feathers tipped with red, black cartridge and bayonet belts."[9] Hull was more than slightly out of touch with his new frontier environment, judging by his dress code. Elijah Brush, the flashy attorney turned militia leader, was perhaps the only soldier more than happy to comply. Brush had ordered a uniform ready to wear from New York the moment he received his commission. But the majority of Detroit residents who were compelled to defend the settlement could not afford to purchase the fabric that Hull required for uniforms (which he had ordered wholesale and personally sold), let alone spare the time from farmhouse labors that would be required for their wives and daughters to stitch the peacockish outfits. The down-to-earth French residents of Detroit were disaffected. The eager beaver Americans were small in number. Who could Hull turn to, then, as threats outside the town walls mounted? Who, in Detroit, had nothing but their lives to lose?

Governor Hull had no choice that did not involve invention. He was in dire need of new and untried ideas. He might have sought out, in this circumstance, someone like Elijah Brush, an influential American with local ties, a formal role as lieutenant colonel of the territorial militia, and experience in the settlement dating back several years. *I know a man*, Elijah Brush might have whispered to William Hull, following a meeting of militia leaders in Richard Smyth's candlelit tavern. For surely Elijah Brush did know Peter Denison, the enslaved black laborer of William Tucker famous enough that various Detroiters had tried to buy him. Peter Denison was broadly skilled in physical work and river navigation; he had an unusual strength of mind that inspired respect in others. A man of talents masked in the historical record that paid little attention to slaves, but apparent to all who encountered him in his time, Peter Denison was soon envisioned by Governor William Hull as a chief defender of Detroit. The challenge was getting access to the man when he belonged to Catherine Tucker, a piece of human property bequeathed by her husband.

Elijah Brush must have approached Denison first. Then came the contract of indenture with Catherine Tucker, and the move of Peter and Hannah Denison into the elegant riverside home of Elijah and Adelaide Brush. Peter, in consultation with Hannah, must have extracted a promise for his dangerous work on behalf of the town: freedom for himself and his wife, and probably for their children as well. For in August of 1807, months before the *Denison v. Tucker* freedom suit was brought before Judge Woodward, Peter Denison was leading a company of men of color whose task it was to defend Detroit.[10] Members of the prominent Askin family were among the first to nervously notate the strange sight of black men drilling with arms right across the waterway. James Askin wrote to his brother Charles from Strabane, the family abode on the Canadian coast of the Detroit River: "at Detroit they are making great preparations. The Town of Detroit is Picketed in from the Water Side until it joins Fort Lernoult. A Company of Negroes mounting Guard, The Cavalry Patroling every night, Batries Erecting along the Settlement, and the Militia called out frequently." James's father, John Askin, was displeased at this unwelcome turn of events, writing to a business colleague in Montreal: "our run Away Negroes have had Arms given them & Mount Guard."[11]

The Askins may not have been taken by utter surprise at this unusual turn of events. They could have been warned of developments by their in-law, Elijah Brush. But British military officials at Fort Malden in Amherstburg necessarily learned of the news through formal channels of command. On August 17, 1807, Lieutenant Colonel Jaspar Grant informed Secretary James Green of Quebec that he had heard from Colonel Isaac Brock of trouble brewing in Detroit. Grant's description was even more detailed than the following excerpt reveals, as his intention was to expose Detroit's advantages and weaknesses should a military conflict unfold. Grant wrote to Green in a lengthy letter:

> As the affair of the Leopard and Chesapeake has occasioned much ferment at Detroit, and has also induced the Governor the Territory of Michigan, who resides there, to take steps by no means indicative of friendly intentions, I conceive it my duty to acquaint you . . . [of] what is going forward there. . . . The Militia of Detroit have been constantly assembled for the pur-

> pose of Drill, they amount to about 400, are much better disciplined than could well be supposed, are very well appointed, and two Companies are kept in constant pay. There is, besides, a company formed of Renegade Negroes, who deserted from Captain Elliott and several Gentlemen at this side. This company consists of . . . 36 in number, and are kept for such desperate services as may be required at this side.

These armed black men defending Detroit were joined, as Grant described the scene, by a force of "inhabitants . . . called in from the distance of 30 miles."[12] Governor Hull had been inventive indeed, forming a special militia of nearly forty former slaves; and so, it seems, had Peter Denison, their designated leader.

Appointed as the head of a defensive force made up of enslaved men of color, Peter Denison had fished for his men across the river among the farms of Upper Canada's largest slaveholders. Denison's recruitment strategy of enticing enslaved men to Michigan was the unspoken cause behind Matthew Elliott's lawsuit in October of 1807, in which Elliott attempted to recover several fugitives who were living in Detroit. Elliott had listed the Denisons as part of his absent human property although the family had not formally belonged to him. His action may have been as emotional as it was economic, a vindictive attempt to punish Denison for leading away Elliott's bondsmen. Inside and outside the courtroom, Elliott met resistance. His overseer, James Heward, had been tasked with finding the runaways, but met sharp recriminations from white working-class Detroiters when he arrived in town to give testimony. The overseer stopped in at Smyth's tavern "to get a drink of grog," and found himself being verbally accosted by a carpenter named William Daily and a navigator named Peter Curry. As half-pints of brandy made the rounds, Daily called Heward a "British rascal" and "threatened to pull off his wig." The tavern filled with more working men from Detroit. Heward's situation grew dicey. In a defensive move that begged greater forethought, Heward called the men "a damned rascally set of beggars," which they rejoined by calling him "a damned British rascal." By the time the dust settled, Heward had been tarred and feathered on the face and head, his wig tacked up by a nail on a post at a public street corner. In an irony that again revealed the intense social dynamics of Detroit, a thirteen-year-old enslaved boy belonging to the father of Heward's host sounded the alarm that "they were killing Mr. Heward."[13] Heward was not in lethal danger, as it turned out, but his dignity took a blow, and "he had tar on his face" and "his hat full of feathers" by evening time. James Dodemead, a witness to the whole affair who testified before Judge Woodward, said he could think of no motive for the tavern patrons' aggression except for the "offense given by Mr. Heward . . . [in] coming over to give testimony respecting Mr. Elliott's slaves." The only item the attackers took from Heward was his wig, the witness reported—the chief symbol of the victim's social class and national identity.[14]

In addition to throttling Heward outright, the men at the tavern threatened the absent Matthew Elliott with a tarring and feathering and boasted that "if the Court decided the Slaves of Mr. Elliott Should be restored, the Court should be tarred and feathered" too. Attorney General Elijah Brush, who was deposed in this case, said he was told by an irascible Mr. Smyth that Elliott was also targeted for "formerly taking an active part with the Indians against the United States" and that the threat of tarring and feathering extended to "the judge." Harris Hickman, counsel for Matthew Elliott, swore that "Richard Smyth, tavern keeper in Detroit . . . made use of a great deal of violent and abusive language . . . relating to the Case of Mr. Elliott's Slaves" and "Swore very bitterly that they Should not be restored to their master, and that he would Kill any person who Should come to his house to take them, or Should attempt to arrest them, and to carry them across the river." Smyth made this promise on "several other Occasions since," Hickman testified, "with violent language and threats of the Same Kind."[15]

The men in the tavern disdained the forcible seizure of slaves. Richard Smyth, a justice of the peace as well as a hatter and barkeep, was sequestering some of the runaways in his own house. As shown by the ire of these workers, an antislavery spark was flaring in the city along the strait. But objecting to the return of fugitive slaves to the Brits was not just rooted in a rejection of the notion or practice of bondage; it was how these men could sense as well as demonstrate their burgeoning identity as American Detroiters. It offended these residents to see rich slaveholders cross the river and try to enlist the Michigan courts to arrest black bondspeople. The British elite, once occupiers of this soil, were now intruding on these tavern-goers' turf. Defending fugitive slaves in their midst was an act of nationalism, which is why Judge Woodward admonished them in patriotic terms. In court, Woodward chided: "he did not believe any American citizen would So much disgrace their Country" as these men had in insulting Heward and Elliott, "at a time when the United States had so many good Causes of Complaint against the British government." Matthew Elliott, Woodward said, "had a right to be a Suitor in the Courts."[16]

The conflict between the tavern-goers and the slaveholders, between the tradesmen and the justice, was spurred by border tensions. These tensions led Smyth and his mates to see black people held captive by the British as fellows and potential allies. The presence of black runaways stoked political and class consciousness among the white workers, giving them clear ideological adversaries: British slaveholders who sided with Indians, and a pompous eastern judge who might be tempted to side with slaveholders. Slavery became a screen against which these men could project a proud national identity. Daily, the carpenter, Curry, the navigator, Smyth, the hatter, and the several men who joined them, including William Watson, Austin Langdon, Abraham Geel, and others, tested their ideal Americanness against the foreignness of British slave-owners, and even against the definition upheld by Augustus Woodward in which "Americans" should be cautious of causing "offence." Upon witnessing the tarring and feathering of Heward, one among them had cheered his fellows on by shouting: "hurraw my boys." They likely roared at the news that Governor Hull was arming fugitives, including some of Elliott's own bondsmen. But Augustus Woodward saw escaped slaves as "disorderly characters who had Come from the British dominions" and decried Hull as having "resorted" to "low intrigues." To the chief justice, black slaves, unruly workers, and jumpy territorial governors were the real threat to America.[17]

While Smyth and the men at his tavern jolted the establishment, enslaved men of color were crossing the strait to fight in defense of Detroit. Peter Denison resided on the Michigan side of the border, but his men lived on the Canadian side and had pledged their "desperate services" in order to seize freedom in the United States. When they traversed the river and armed themselves beneath a rival national flag, these men were joining a tradition set by enterprising men of color in colonial wars past. During the French and Indian War as well as the American Revolution, black men had fought, mostly for the British, in exchange for promises of freedom. Even that very summer of 1807, as hackles rose in the aftermath of the *Chesapeake* incident, enslaved black American men had escaped their owners to board British naval ships.[18] But the Detroit militia of formerly enslaved men deviated from this more typical arrangement. Led by officers of African descent, these men had crossed an international border to fight for the other side.

In the Revolutionary War, the War of 1812, and the Civil War fifty years into the future that would divide America from itself, black men were rarely shown the respect of being named officers of their military units. But William Hull, according to a scornful Judge Augustus Woodward, had audaciously formalized black men's martial leadership. Woodward wrote in a complaint to the secretary of war, William Eustis, "Mister Hull had issued three commissions to captain Denison, lieutenant Burgess, and ensign Bosset, black men, not under any law of the United States or this territory." In Woodward's view, Hull had been "insolent in the extreme" when challenged about this course of action and had taken as his authority "some ex parte correspondence with mister dearborne, then secretary of war."[19] Hull made a show of defending his deeds in a letter to Colonel Grant at Fort Malden meant to calm escalating fears that these armed former slaves might attack. "The permission which I have given to a small number of Negroes, occasionally to exercise in Arms," Hull wrote, "I am informed has excited some sensibility among the Inhabitants on the British Shore. Be assured Sir, it is without any foundation, for they only have the use of their Arms, while exercising, and at all other times they are deposited in a situation out of their control."[20] Hull's reassurance that the formerly enslaved Canadian men did not always have access to their rifles and bayonets would have been cold comfort to the British military leader, as well as to the slaveholders in his province, whose human property was not just absent but also armed.

Governor Hull cut a new groove into the pattern of using black fighting men in colonial and early America. Under his auspices, the "first black militia" was formed in the United States.[21] The military titles that Hull bestowed upon leaders in this unit—captain, lieutenant, and ensign—indicate that he viewed the group as akin to a company in the Michigan militia.[22] And very likely, Elijah Brush, or Peter Denison himself, had driven Hull to formulate this arrangement. The fear of an Indian attack was so great at Detroit that Hull hired desperate men for desperate measures. How these rebels must have relished scoffing at their former masters, drilling with weapons in plain sight right across the waterway. Primary accounts describe this unusual militia company variously as a group of men made up of "Negroes" and "slaves." Although the record does not state as much, some of these men may have been Native or mixed-race Afro-Native people enslaved by the British. Their object would have been freedom, rather than allegiance to any single slaving nation, be that nation European, American, or indigenous.

Governor Hull had authorized an unprecedented military organization. Judge Woodward stridently objected, viewing Hull as having gone a bridge too far when he armed the slaves of the neighboring nation. Woodward directed his concerns to Secretary of State James Madison in July of 1807, writing: "There is however one point on which the inhabitants of the different sides of the river are at variance. This is the desertion of the slaves. I expect complaints will be made to you on this head by the British minister. I do not approve the temper, principles and conduct of the inhabitants of this side, on the subject. I thought something ought to be done to check it."[23] In a set of resolutions addressed to a Michigan territorial special committee in 1808, Judge Woodward continued to criticize Governor Hull on this issue, stating that Hull had been responsible for the "embodying of slaves belonging to the subjects of his Britannic Majesty residing in the province of Upper Canada into a militia company, and the issuing of commissions, or other authority, to such persons, or other slaves, or black persons, to be officers in such militia company." Woodward viewed Hull's actions as stoking the flames of discord between the United States and Great Britain and, most importantly to him, of violating American civil law. In order to have gone forward with a plan to arm escaped slaves, Hull should have sought higher legal approval. "In our government," Woodward asserted, in a separate letter of complaint to the secretary of war, "we had no masters but the law."[24] Although Woodward's comment was not consciously ironic, it highlights a difference in status that fueled the dispute; the enslaved men in Hull's militia could not have made so bold a claim to having just one master in the abstract form of law. Their masters were men and an immoral slave system wielded by men that sometimes bested the law. The special committee responded to Woodward's complaint that Hull had acted out of bounds by quoting the territorial dictate regarding the governor's military powers. "'The governor, for the time being, shall be commander-in-chief of the militia, appoint and commission all officers in the same below the rank of general officers,'" the committee reminded Woodward, then stated further that they had paid "particular attention" to Woodward's charge that Hull had "formed negroes, who were slaves, into a military company." The committee found it to be "true that the governor has given permission to the black male inhabitants to exercise as a military company; that he has appointed a black man by the name of Peter Denison to command them; and has given him a written license for the purpose; though not in the form of a military commission. . . . This company has frequently appeared under arms, and has made considerable progress in military discipline. That they have ever conducted in an orderly manner, manifested on all occasions an attachment to our government and a determination to aid in the defense of the country whenever their services should be required."[25]

Not surprisingly, the territorial special committee (made up of the judges and Hull himself) sided with Hull, but, remarkably, the committee heaped praise on the discipline and patriotism of black men. The committee's response went on to assert that Woodward's emphasis on these men's status as slaves was an irrelevant point: "With respect to any of them being slaves, the committee only observes that they were black persons, who resided in the Territory, and were not claimed as slaves by any person or persons in the original States." The committee members had decided against Judge Woodward, but by using the same logic as Woodward's own legal decisions in the Pattinson and Elliott cases: if these black militiamen were runaway slaves of British owners, it was not Michigan Territory's affair. Michigan was only beholden to slaveholders from their own nation: the United States. "Under this view of the subject," the committee report concluded on this matter, "the committee is of the opinion that the conduct of the executive in availing the country of the services of their black people, was not only proper but highly commendable; especially as it was at a period when the safety and protection of the Territory appeared to require all the force which could be possibly collected." Black men formerly from Canada would now be considered "their," meaning Michigan Territory's, "black people," members of "the country." Woodward was not convinced. He rebutted this finding in a letter to the federal government, noting again his doubts about the "propriety of organizing a military company composed of slaves who had run away from gentleman residing opposite" and of "negroes commanding the company as officers being alike unauthorized by the town and the gen. [general] gov. [government]."[26]

Augustus Woodward's pointed criticism of the formation of a black militia in Detroit exposed the issues of racial bias, slave status, international relations, and military readiness in a way that forced a clear and revealing response from territorial representatives. These men, like Governor Hull, viewed the defense of the border as utmost in importance and would not protect human property rights of British slaveholders on Michigan soil. Black men in Michigan Territory were presumed free unless an American owner from the slave states made a claim. Despite this deference to U.S. slaveholders regarding fugitive slaves that meant the continued, legalized threat to black people in the Northwest, the committee's response was an avowed rejection of slavery as an assumptive state for all black men. These legislators affirmed Michigan's fledgling political identity as a free American territory and lauded black men as responsible and even patriotic. No other city, state, or territory within the nation had yet made such a bold defense of black men's collective honor. It happened first in Detroit.

But also central to this story is *why* it happened in Detroit, an environment characterized by frontier conflict and borderland contingencies. The violent threat of Indians was assumed to be so great that black men not legally freed should be armed to fight against them. While their recognition of the talents of African American men might be viewed as progressive, if self-serving, William Hull and the territorial committee at the same time reinforced an oppositional ideology of "Americans" versus "Indians." Indigenous people were perceived as bogeymen in the wilderness, a terrifying, outsized threat requiring radical containment. At least these militiamen of color were not prone to taking scalps, territorial leaders may have thought, in a slanted view of reality that failed to recognize Euro-American brutalities against Native people. Here, in this circumscribed imaginative space of the colonial psyche, black men had an advantage. They could be viewed as co-combatants rather than age-old enemies. A conceptual line was now being drawn between Native Americans and African Americans that favored blacks in the pre–War of 1812 years. Black men had one thing the Michigan Territory needed more than almost anything else: the willingness and strength to defend Detroit and America's borders. But the effective difference between being "black" versus being "red" was far from clear cut in every interaction or circumstance. Members of each group were still enslaved in Detroit, sometimes within the same households. And the racialized categories ("negro," "black," "mulatto," and "panis") used to serve as shorthand for their naturalized subjugation were sometimes viewed as overlapping or interchangeable by officials. In 1808 John Askin recorded his contract of indenture with Charlotte Moses, "a mulatto or pawnee Girl of Detroit," who signed her X mark to "truly observe and obey" him as "her Said Master."[27] Another example of multiple or confused racial identifiers appears in a criminal case that wound through the Michigan courts in the summer of 1814. Monique, a woman charged with stealing a valuable bedspread from the shop of Andrew Elliott, was found guilty by a grand jury in the territorial supreme court. The district court record in Detroit, where Monique resided, describes her as "a certain Black woman," while the supreme court record describes her as "a Pawny Woman." Notably, both the district and supreme court sessions were held in Detroit where Monique was personally known. Perhaps Monique was mixed-race; perhaps her sliding racial identification signaled her enslaved status more than any concrete racial designation. Precisely recording her racial identification was clearly not essential to the case or a matter of importance to the court. Similarly, individuals of Native ancestry or of mixed-race Afro-Indian descent were very likely to have been present in the so-called Negro Militia.[28]

Judge Woodward thought the risk of Indian attack was being exaggerated and said as much in his critique of Governor Hull. Colonel Grant on the British side of the river also expressed disbelief at William Hull's fired-up rhetoric: "They have picketed in the whole town of Detroit," Grant wrote. "Every military preparation is going forward there, and every violent declaration against this side . . . the Governor of Detroit declares, if an Indian fires a hostile shot in Detroit or in the Territory, he will treat the Canadians with the utmost severity. The apprehensions circulated at Detroit appear to me to proceed more from Policy to freighten the Inhabitants into labour without food or reward, than from any real sense of danger from Indians." Grant went on to disclose to his superior that any alliance between the British at Fort Malden and western tribes was unpredictable. "The Aid I should expect there from Indians and Militia is of a very precarious kind," he wrote. "Indians can never be brought to act within pickets."[29]

Grant's canny analysis painted a picture in which Hull was using the fear of Indians to compel undercompensated military labors, and in which Native people hardly stood at the ready to passively take orders from the British regarding designs on Detroit. As progressive as William Hull's actions seem with regard to black militiamen, they were also strategic in a way that furthered the consolidation of American authority within the town and beyond. Hull could use the deep desire for freedom among men of color to entice them to work for little or no pay, even as he used the specter of a Native assault to pull French farmers into town from thirty miles distant. William Hull's stated terror of Indians may have included an element of cold calculation, but he was right on one score—Native people had not yet been contained and could not be controlled. Just as American and British relations were a seething cauldron of suspicions, American and indigenous relations were far from settled in the Northwest.

The black militia authorized by Governor Hull remained active in Detroit for years, prepared, according to the territorial committee, to defend "the country." But which country would those men favor as they considered their political allegiances? Did they subscribe to any national identity at all when both countries that warily met at the Detroit River border held blacks and Native people as slaves? Peter Denison, the sole member of the black militia whose story we can access through the documentary record, demonstrated loyalty to his family rather than to Michigan or the United States. He had agreed to lead William Hull's unconventional military unit in exchange for freedom. But in the summer of 1807 while his men drilled in plain sight at the fort in Detroit, Peter Denison's children were still being held as slaves by Catherine Tucker. Peter and his wife Hannah took the case to court that autumn with the aid of Peter's fellow militia leader, Elijah Brush. Judge Woodward, who had never approved of the black militia, issued the writ of *habeas corpus* as Brush requested but refused to free the children of the militia's well-known leader. Peter Denison must have felt that his trust had been betrayed—by the town of Detroit, the territory of Michigan, and perhaps Governor Hull himself. But he did not settle for this theft of his family's natural rights, any more than the Native peoples who continued to live around Detroit settled for the theft of their land base. Peter knew the rough terrain of the border; he had already crisscrossed the river in order to gather his men. In the fall of 1807, he abandoned Detroit's black militia, and likely his formal protection of freedom issued by the governor, to flee with his family to Canada.

The Denisons had held, and lost, a legitimate route to freedom. Now they were on the run as fugitive slaves. But Peter Denison had won a partner in Elijah Brush, not resulting from Brush's sympathy or guilt, or even an antislavery stance adopted by the attorney. These men had spent months as comrades in arms, serving in segregated units of the Michigan militia. Peter Denison and his wife had lived with Elijah and Adelaide Brush, in the intimate quarters of the couple's urban farm. Although Elijah could not have felt the anger, fear, and humiliation experienced by Peter Denison, whose children were counted as chattel, he could have shared Peter's sense of moral outrage. Hadn't Peter been willing to risk his life for Detroit, the capital of Michigan Territory? And yet the court of that territory refused to protect his children as full-fledged persons. When Peter Denison rowed the river with Hannah, his daughter Lisette, and his sons James, Sip, and Peter Junior, he was not without friends. A note in the Michigan Supreme Court record indicates, in just one line, that Denison family members "took refuge with Mr. Askin." Elijah Brush came through for the daring Denison family, convincing his father-in-law, once among British Detroit's largest slaveholders, to extend a hand.[30]

Red-Lining Detroit Lands

Immediately following the series of territorial supreme court suits that tested the limits of slavery in Michigan, Governor Hull set his mind to the problem of Indians and land. Local white property holders had been complaining about Native Americans living too close to town and had expressed worry about a lack of formal federal recognition of their preexisting land claims. The loss of more than three hundred buildings to fire and the unsettled issue of how to reapportion lots within the town pickets raised the stakes of land competition all the more.[31] And the shadow of possible war with the British placed a continuous pressure on the military readiness of Detroit, which, in the view of U.S. officials, entailed managing where Indians were on the landscape and what actions they engaged in.

In his dual capacity as governor and superintendent of Indian affairs for Michigan Territory (a conflict of interest when considered from the indigenous standpoint), William Hull started on the difficult task of reorganizing Detroit area lands by wresting more ground from Native people on the direct order of President Thomas Jefferson. Jefferson had been desirous of extending America's hold at Detroit beyond the immediate fort town. He informed the senate that "the posts of Detroit and Mackinac" had been designed as "mere depots for commerce with the Indians" by "the government which established and held them." Jefferson, in contrast, wanted to extend the land base around these forts for military purposes. Hence, he "thought it would be important to obtain from the Indians, such a cession in the neighborhood of these posts as might maintain a militia proportioned to this object." Already a veteran of the Louisiana Purchase with a keen understanding of the power of holding contiguous terrain for settlement and economic advancement, Jefferson had in mind acquiring lands in Michigan "so as to consolidate the new with the present settled country."[32]

In December of 1807, Jefferson's secretary of war, Henry Dearborn, conveyed the order to William Hull to "hold a treaty with the chiefs of such Indian tribes or nations as are actually interested in the lands hereafter described." While Dearborn pointed out that it would be "difficult" for Hull "to ascertain, with any tolerable degree of certainty, the quantity of acres," Hull should expect to net in the ballpark of six hundred thousand acres, for which he was "not, on any condition, to exceed two cents per acre" and should endeavor to find it unnecessary to "exceed one cent per acre."[33] Hull was convinced of the soundness of this aim and began to plan the treaty council. "I probably shall not hold the treaty until about the first of June," he wrote to Dearborn, "They are now on their hunting grounds, will soon be employed in making their Sugar, and in the month of May, will be engaged in their planting—In the meantime, I shall be making the preparatory arrangements." Hull's reply conveyed his own implicit awareness of Native people's wide-ranging use of their lands—for maple sugaring, hunting, and farming—necessities of cultural meaning and subsistence. Still, he expressed in his letter to Dearborn, in the interest of progress and economics, this land should be finagled for the United States at less than the cost Dearborn had set. "If the treaty can be effected," Hull penned, "and the lands can soon be opened for sale, it will be of vast advantage to this Country, and likewise to the United States—The more I see of the Country, the more valuable I consider it." Hull added in a postscript to his missive that he thought it advisable to extend the boundary "so as to include the islands" in the land cession.[34]

Governor Hull called a meeting of Ottawa, Ojibwe, Wyandot, and Potawatomi leaders in the Wyandot village of Brownstown, south of Detroit, later that year. On November 7, representatives of the various tribes gathered and agreed to cede what is now all of southeastern Michigan and a sliver of northwestern Ohio. The payment for these lands was set at $10,000 in "money, goods, and implements of husbandry." Native people were to retain fishing and hunting rights and to receive "two blacksmiths," provided to the tribes as evidence of the U.S. government's "liberality." Several small portions of land, ranging from one to six miles square, were to be "reserved to the said Indian nations" for their villages and agricultural pursuits. William Hull reported to Thomas Jefferson in December of 1807 that all had gone smoothly, and that he had "heard of no complaint from a single individual of the Indians" regarding the treaty. He attested, too, with his jacketed chest puffed slightly out, that he "believe[d] a treaty was never made on fairer principles."[35]

Governor Hull accomplished his objectives in this carefully orchestrated treaty council, and his description of the outcome may have faithfully reflected how he felt about the negotiations. But these treaty proceedings were not as pleasant as Hull's description implies. While the treaty itself details only land, monies, objects, and expertise to be exchanged, Hull's speech to the gathered Native leaders in advance of the treaty signing focused on an entirely different subject: warfare. When addressing representatives of the Ottawa, Ojibwe, Wyandot, and Potawatomi nations who held land and interests in Detroit, Hull highlighted themes of weapons, conflict, death, and danger. He addressed the gathered leaders as "My Children," and directed them to listen "with attention" for "the good of [their] women and children." Hull then offered his talk as a representation of the views of "Your father, the President of the United States" who "desires to recall to your minds the paternal policy pursued towards you by the United States." Referencing the mounting tensions between the United States and Great Britain, Hull explained that "a misunderstanding having arisen between the United States and the English, war may possibly ensue." In the event that war did break out, it was the president's wish that "the Indians should be quiet spectators." Hull's purpose in this speech, in addition to attaining land, was to keep Native people from fighting with the British against the Americans. He assured his listeners that if they did not express "intentions hostile to the United States," they would be left unmolested by the United States, and indeed, protected by the nation. But if they did harbor ill intentions, the United States would "lift the hatchet" and "never lay it down till that tribe is exterminated, or driven beyond the Mississippi." He warned them that if the Indians dared to challenge the U.S. militarily, they "will kill some of us; we shall destroy all of them." He then summarized these pertinent points by emphasizing "the interest your Great Father takes in your welfare; how anxious he is to promote your happiness; how desirous he is to prevent you from taking any measures, which will involve you in ruin." Hull concluded with the disclosure that this degree of candor was actually an act of kindness, "warning you of the fate of any tribe, who shall have the hardihood to raise the hatchet against us." He then advised the leaders to render "a plain and decided answer" on their political allegiances.

The content of Hull's speech, as submitted by him to Thomas Jefferson, did not dwell on the Detroit area land cession. It did not have to, when the threat of extermination and removal was implicitly leveraged as context for the treaty negotiations. How broadly would the U.S. president interpret "hostile intentions" on the part of the gathered nations? Would agreement to the requested land sale insulate the tribes from deadly accusations of hostility? Certainly the gathered Native leaders must have thought so; they proved themselves unwilling to take the chance for the sake of their families. One Ojibwe leader who signed the treaty, and whose name is recorded as Pooquiboad in the proceedings, stated: "Our solemn determination is, never to raise the hatchet against the United States. We too well know the fatal consequences of it."[36] From the middle 1600s onward, indigenous people of the Great Lakes had fought valiantly and strategically for their homelands, autonomy, and relative positioning in a seemingly never-ending series of imperial wars. They knew the cost of losing in such battles, and many in the Ohio Valley had recently lost nearly all in the American revolutionary conflict and postwar campaigns of General Anthony Wayne. So William Hull was successful in achieving the Indian land cession desired by the president as well as propertied residents in Detroit. The negotiation that he viewed as utterly fair had been peppered with language steeped in threat.

The 1807 Treaty of Detroit is rarely mentioned in histories of Detroit, of Michigan, or of the Midwest, but it was critical to American officials' plan for defending against British and Native aggression on the northern U.S. border and to Michigan territorial leaders' hopes for fostering white settlement in the march toward statehood. This drawing of a broad boundary around the capital of Detroit and its environs set in place the pattern for the eventual relinquishment of most of what we now know as the state of Michigan by the early 1840s.[37] The reduction of Native territorial sovereignty immediately around Detroit also had dire consequences for enslaved people who used indigenous spaces as routes of escape with the knowledge that slaveholders were unlikely to follow them there. The shrinkage of Native landholdings strengthened U.S. military positioning, flung the door wider for American settlement, and smoothed processes of surveillance and recapture for American slaveholders. A win for Governor Hull and U.S. settlers was a loss for Native people as well as for the enslaved.[38]

William Hull found that in Detroit success and setbacks followed one

George Winter, *Pottawattamie Indians Crooked Creek Indiana*, 1837. Winter sketched this scene of a Potawatomi community near Logansport, Indiana, in August 1837, prior to the group's removal. Courtesy of Tippecanoe County Historical Association, Lafayette, Indiana.

another like the tumbling waves of the lakes. While Native leaders had consented to sell hundreds of thousands of acres in the deciduous lands of southeastern Michigan, French Detroiters were resistant to the reassignment of land lots via government auction. The great fire and mass exodus from the immediate town site had left the settlement in disarray and thrown the ownership of private land, much of it purchased from Native people or allocated in the French colonial period, into confusion. The nearly sixty homeowners who used to live within the town walls had been displaced; farmers outside of the walls along the river worried about whether the United States would view their eighteenth-century claims as legitimate. Augustus Woodward had crafted a plan for the redesign of the town that was approved by Congress in 1806 but disliked by local residents, who objected, in part, to Woodward's naming a main thoroughfare Woodward Avenue, after himself. (Woodward later denied this accusation, saying that he had named the street after the forests around Detroit. Only a portion of Woodward's design, between Grand Circus and the river, was ever realized.)[39] Governor Hull and Judge Woodward established a Land Board to hear residents' claims and assign lots, then successively hired and lost three surveyors (then rehired the first) to plot out town lands. In addition to acreage within the town pickets that would be allotted to former residents who had lived there (at a small fee if lot sizes were larger than the originals), territorial leaders had gained permission from Congress to distribute by auction 10,000 acres north of the village to adult residents over the age of seventeen.[40] Much of this new acreage had in the past been used as a commons by the townspeople, who shared the swath of cleared land surrounding the pickets for daily access and pasture land, and who likewise used the land of Hog Island (now Belle Isle Park) to let their livestock roam. U.S. officials in Washington saw this "quantity of vacant ground" around the walls as "valuable" federal land that could be sold. Detroiters complained in a formal memorial to Congress in 1808 and in a petition to the governor in 1811 about the loss of the public lands that had once been equitably shared by the community. Their petition specified that they wished to see the area "held by the inhabitants of the town forever as a commons." In valuing communal use of the land, the descendants of Detroit's oldest white settlers of the farming and working classes shared a view with Native people in the region diametrically opposed to the federal position that land should be sold for profit. The old settlers' vociferous protests, rendered in French and in English, yielded no change in policy, however; the land would be divided and "liberally" sold, making lots available to newcomers, to British residents who had not even sworn allegiance to the United States, and, remarkably, to the "wives and slaves" of some former in-town homeowners. Some residents were dismayed and even offended, feeling that struggling farm families and working-class laborers lost the use of the commons unless they could meet the "humiliating conditions" of paying for it.[41]

The designation of land lots took decades to settle due to unceasing conflict. While American and British residents benefited from the new system, so too did individuals designated as their subordinates: current and former bondspeople. Among the recipients of deeds were several individuals described as "negro" or colored, including, Pomp ("a negro man"), Thomas Parker ("a negro . . . employed in the Hull family"), Pompey Abbott, Cato ("Dodemead's Negro"), Harry and Hannah ("Dodemead's negroes"), London and Mary (living at the Watsons'), Margrett (at the Voyers' home), Susan and Nell (at Mrs. Abbott's home), and Hannah ("Coate's Negro"). Joseph Cooper, "a negro," was noted as not having drawn a lot. This record of black land ownership demonstrates two interconnected, critically important facets of life for African American Detroiters in the early 1800s. They were eligible for in-town land and were hence treated as municipal residents on par with Anglo settlers. They were at the same time usually noted by first name only, designated by race, and attached by the use of possessive punctuation to white Detroiters. The Land Board record does not indicate whether these individuals were enslaved or free at the time. Some were certainly free by this period but particular individuals (like Pomp) appear as slaves in previous town records. Still others held an even more ambiguous status poised between slavery and freedom. Hannah, described as "Dodemead's Negro" in the land records, had evaded John Dodemead's claim to her in court in 1809. While John Dodemead had requested a writ of *habeas corpus* to hold Hannah, a "black woman," and Thomas, a "Mulatto" boy (probably her son), several witnesses, including Elijah Brush and Solomon Sibley, testified that Dodemead had previously declared that the two "were not slaves of him or any other person." Perhaps Dodemead had been involved with Hannah, had a child with her, and intended to free them before changing his mind. Since prominent witnesses were aware of his past declaration of the woman and child's freedom, Dodemead was unable to retract it. Augustus Woodward decided in this case that Hannah and Thomas were "free persons" who must be "discharged out of the Custody of the Marshall of this territory and of Said John Dodemead." The appearance of Dodemead's name next to Hannah's in the land grant entry suggests that black land recipients depended upon a connection with or patronage from past or present white owners and employers, regardless of how tangled or contentious such relationships might be. Another black woman, also named Hannah, may have had a more constructive relationship with a patron, as she had the explicit help of Austin E. Wing, a Land Board official, in making her application. Significantly, Native people do not appear as designated by tribe or race in the Land Board lists.[42] Mixed-race Native-French and Native-English town residents would be noted under their European surnames, and many other indigenous people had moved to different locations by the time these lots were assigned. The prominent Oneida woman trader, Sally (Sarah) Ainse, who had once owned a house and second lot in Detroit, had relocated to the Thames River in Upper Canada prior to the American assumption in 1787.[43] And through the Treaty of 1807, most other free Native Detroiters had been red-lined, so to speak, outside the district through land cessions. While Governor Hull had made it a priority to build a stone Council House for trade and political meetings with the Indians in 1807, he did not wish to see those same Indians dwelling too near as neighbors.[44]

Even as the Native population within the town proper was dwindling, by 1810, rates of enslavement had also dropped dramatically in Detroit due to a bundle of factors. A number of black and Native bondspeople had been transported across the river by retreating British owners. The liquid international border, crossable by boat, was encouraging escape attempts. The ban on slavery legalized by the Northwest Ordinance made it more difficult to buy and sell human beings. In accordance with Judge Augustus Woodward's decision in the Denison case, babies born to enslaved residents would now be free, and his decisions in the Pattinson and Elliott cases meant fugitives from Canada would also be treated as free people in Detroit. American Detroiters, such as the patrons in Richard Smyth's tavern, began to connect slavery with a previous British colonial administration and supported black runaways as a means of distinguishing themselves from the British. But whether enslaved or free (a phrase containing a vast magnitude of difference), most of the black people in town were working for, living with, and viewed as possessions of white residents. As a result of this mix of multiple causes, the 1810 census enumerated forty-three "free colored" residents in Detroit Town proper and only four "slaves." The tally for riverside suburbs totaled as follows: Cote du Nord-Est: six free colored; Cote de Poux: ten free colored and two slaves living within two slaveholding households; River Rouge: ten free colored and eight slaves living in two slaveholding households; Grand Marais: seven free colored and one slave; Grosse Pointe: three free colored and two slaves living in one slaveholding household. Several suburbs did not have residents listed in either of these categories. A tally of the census numbers indicates seventy-nine free people of color and seventeen enslaved people within a total population for the District of Detroit of 2,355.[45] The 1810 census did not note the race of these enslaved individuals. The use of the term "Negro" so frequently in Land Board records suggests that most people within the categories of "free colored" and "slaves" were black or of mixed African descent. The population of enslaved Native Americans had dropped significantly since the 1790s, but several people categorized as "Panis" were still present into the first decades of the new century. The registry of Ste. Anne's Church (which had lost its original site due to the fire and Woodward's town plan that ran Jefferson Avenue straight through the burial ground) notes twenty-nine enslaved congregants between 1800 and 1810. Ten were black; fifteen were Native; one was "mulatto," and three had no racial identifier noted.[46] The term "mulatto" could indicate a person of mixed African descent of either white or indigenous parentage, and any of the non-identified individuals could have been indigenous.[47] Even as the practice of slaveholding faded in the second decade of the American era, unfree indigenous people still outnumbered unfree blacks in Detroit.

Enslaved and free black residents in the town saw their position improved through a land allotment process that included them. But longtime French inhabitants were vocal critics of the American attempt to rebuild the old town through a regularized layout, the grid that now characterizes much of the Midwest. It seemed to them that newer arrivals, namely influential Americans, were being awarded the choicest lots along the river and closest to town. Elijah Brush was a case in point; he had procured the first available farmland east of town in 1807. In February of 1808, Elijah and his wife Adelaide sold a prize parcel to William Hull, who made a series of personal purchases from previous settlers, many of them French, between 1808 and 1811.[48] But even as Governor Hull increased his wealth through land ownership and commissioned the first brick house in Detroit for his family, he operated in a state of constant conflict. Hull withdrew his previous support of Woodward's newfangled town plan, and the two became political adversaries. Their argument over the black militia, which raged on from 1807 to 1811 and sparked Woodward's testy missives to Hull's superiors in Washington, contributed to the souring of their relationship. While Hull faced complaints from French residents and epistolary attacks from Woodward, he also contended with his wife's anxiety about political tensions in Detroit. During one of William Hull's trips to Washington in April of 1809, Sarah

Hull wrote him a pointed letter that opened with the worrisome line: "My mind has been so agitated in thinking of the perplext situation you are placed in, that I find no relief but in writing. I shudder at the idea of you returning to Detroit, that never can be done with honour to yourself it is gone as much as if your commission was taken from you." Sarah knew her husband was trapped. Detroiters did not like him, and federal officials were using him for their own political ends. "You have experienced enough of the treatment of this people already," Sarah wrote of Detroit residents. And about government leaders in Washington, she warned: "the truth is they are the friends to Mr. Madison, not friend, to your character or interest." Sarah wanted to see her husband "nominated to the senate" and perhaps dreamed of a life in relatively genteel Washington City. She resented influential politicians for not putting her husband forward, despite his sacrifice in traveling "through the wilderness" of the West and "render[ing] services to his country." In large, dark lettering at the top of her final page, Sarah urged William to "Renounce all Politics Be Neuter." In cautioning her husband to avoid political entanglement through a tactic of neutrality, Sarah went so far as to advise emigration: "if you cannot do this in America flee to some other part of the world, at least till a government arises that can estimate your talents and reward your virtue." She concluded her sharp letter with the warm sentiment: "however disagreeable your situation is remember you have one friend that will devote her life to make you happy."[49] Sarah Hull's missive was a Molotov cocktail of smart analysis and tough advice that recognized her husband's tenuous position. Within a few short years, William Hull would wish that he had followed Sarah's sage, if fiery, direction and left the leadership of Detroit to some luckier soul.

The Denisons on the Border

While Sarah and William Hull brooded over their unstable situation in Detroit, Hannah and Peter Denison had accomplished, by propulsion of unjust circumstances, just what Sarah Hull had recommended to her husband. The Denison family had moved to another country by crossing the river into Canada. In Sandwich, a town more modest than Detroit with "fifty log or frame houses built near the Old Huron Church, a small shipyard, two small wharves, and a small government warehouse," the Denisons made a new home. Several former Detroiters loyal to the British Crown had reconvened there, sometimes referring to Sandwich as "South Detroit."[50] In Sandwich, the Denisons joined St. John's Anglican Church, where they participated in the social and religious rites of baptisms, weddings, and funerals. Choosing a Protestant denomination after having lived in a Catholic town, the Denison parents soon formalized their commitment to the faith. In October of 1808, nearly a year to the day after their failed freedom suit in the Michigan Supreme Court, "Peter and Hannah Donnison Adults, free Negroes" were baptized at St. John's. Elizabeth Denison, the couple's eldest child who went by the nickname "Lisette," served as sponsor for several Denison baptisms in the church. The merchant John Askin may have witnessed these baptisms, as he and other slaveholders who had recently moved from Detroit were also members of the congregation.[51]

While the Denisons had full lives in the province of Upper Canada, they also became denizens of the border, expertly navigating the river that separated the United States from British Canada. They crossed and recrossed the strait by choice between 1807 and 1812, never once being caught and arrested as fugitive slaves. Catherine Tucker did not fight to retrieve the children, seeing, perhaps, a lost cause since the Denisons could readily run. Neither did William Hull dispatch men to find the black militia leader who had abruptly deserted his company. Hull may have felt, morally, that Peter's flight was just, or recognized, pragmatically, that the Denisons had influential friends on both sides of the border. Peter Denison found work as a "Negro servant" in the household of former Detroit slaveholder and lawyer Angus Mackintosh.[52] Although life would never be for the Denison family what it was for a free white family there, and although the differences of race and class still structured their lives (as indicated by the limited work options available to Peter), the Denisons were integrated into a tight-knit network of Detroit River People: white and black, slave-owners and slaves, old settlers and new Americans.

In the years before the next conflict with Great Britain that Detroiters were anxiously anticipating, various members of the Denison family depended upon and renewed personal ties around Detroit steeped in a vexed history of slavery. In 1810, Elijah and Adelaide Brush were raising four boys in Detroit. Several people of color also resided with them, according to the Detroit town census. Six free "colored" people and one "slave" were listed by tally (with no names given) beside Elijah Brush's entry. There is no indication of that single enslaved person's identity, but precedent suggests this was an indigenous woman, a personal servant of Adelaide's dating back to the Askin family slaveholdings. The free people of color in the Brush household were the Denisons, who also appear in Detroit account ledgers in these same years. An anonymous merchant's sales ledger locates Peter Denison in town, describing him as "Peter Tucker's negroe man" in 1808. Over the next two years, Peter purchased "Sundries" and flour from this shopkeeper, regularly settling his account "in full." He also purchased 1¼ yards of "Humhum," a cotton textile used for lining coats. Peter's procurement of this fabric is a telltale sign that the Denison women were sewing for the family and perhaps for market. In 1809, the anonymous shopkeeper refers to Peter Denison as "Peter, Brush's black man," a shift indicative of the local acceptance of the Denisons' separation from the Tuckers two years after the pivotal freedom suit. The Denisons acted like and were treated as free people despite Judge Woodward's decision, benefiting from what legal historian Rebecca Scott has described as "the alchemy of creating status out of circumstances."[53] But what had not changed in the time since the family fled to Canada and circled back to Detroit again was an insistence on the dependent attachment of black residents to white merchant elites. The use of possessive grammar and racial terminology to describe Peter in both ledger entries underscores the social hierarchy rooted in race and class that was still firmly in place in early 1800s Detroit.[54] Looking for work, for respect, and for the best hope for their future, the Denison family spanned the border, living at times in Sandwich under the auspices of the Askins and living at times in Detroit with Elijah Brush. For this African American and Afro-Canadian family, Detroit was experienced on the ground as a place that bridged the river, regardless of differing national claims to lands on each side. In both locations, white patronage was a necessary element of the Denisons' personal security and livelihood. Their act of rebellion in taking Catherine Tucker to court and refusing to let the border box them in to slavery could only get the family so far in a larger society shaped by notions of racial difference and territorial conquest.

The Denisons returned to a place of compromised familiarity within the old town of Detroit, finding steady work with the Askin family, once among the largest slaveholders around. From 1808 to 1811, the Askin family ledger of credits and debits includes several mentions of the Denisons. Lisette (Elizabeth) is the most visible Denison family member in this record, followed by her next younger brother, James. Born in the mid-1780s, Lisette was in her twenties by this time. Her baby brother Scipio appears in the ledger too, as does her father, Peter. The absence of her mother's name suggests that Hannah worked from home at the Brush farm rather than crossing to the Askins' nearby property to provide domestic services. In the course of his accounting, John Askin carefully recorded the racial and caste status of the Denisons. In 1808, "James Dennison Negro Boy" is listed. In 1809, "Lisette negroes man & woman" appear, followed in that same year by an entry for "James and Lisette servants." In 1810, an entry for "Lissette & Jm. Denniston formerly slaves" simultaneously reveals John Askin's heightened awareness of the family's past state of bondage and his acceptance of their current status as free people. Despite Judge Augustus Woodward's legal affirmation of Catherine Tucker's right to the children in the 1807 court battle, his decision was not being applied on the ground where human relations played out in the nuanced exchanges of the everyday. The Denisons were treated like free people in Detroit, albeit free people of color with a lower standing than whites that upper-class community members took pains to inscribe in the cramped pages of their ledger books.

The Denison family, especially the children, did all manner of paid work for the Askins. Lisette Denison was compensated most often for spinning and sewing work; various entries noted items she produced with "thread," "purple cloth," and "gray coating," a fabric used for making coats. For a mixed variety of products, Lisette was paid in wages, sums for set purchases, as well as in bartered material goods. In June of 1809 she was due two months' worth of pay, a frustrating situation that may have influenced the care she took later in life with her finances. In August of that year the Askins gave Lisette "cash" to "buy shoes." In 1809 John Askin registered frustration with Lisette in a rare ledger entry composed in complete sentences rather than dry lists of services, credits, and debits. Lisette had managed to make herself unavailable to Askin, who complained that Lisette was: "Employed in the whole of the winter nights for herself & Brother without [permission] having refused to twist worsted saying she must mend her Brother's clothes which time must be [nearly] 3 Hours Every night in winter." Although John and Archange Askin wanted Lisette to spend time making the tightly twisted "worsted" yarn that the family could use or sell, they found that Lisette "has only spun or twisted yarn three times this winter though frequently desired to do so." During the cold winter months when days were short in the Great Lakes, Lisette was spending her evenings as she chose, helping her brother—or at least, that is what she told the Askins. Lisette possessed three quite valuable skills that she must have learned in apprenticeship to her mother, Hannah. She could spin; she could sew, and she could also bake. Recognizing that her specialized labor was prized enough that she would not be let go by the Askins even if they grew frustrated with her, Lisette controlled her own productivity. When it came to meeting her employer's intense demands, Lisette demonstrated a self-protective and even stubborn streak that would continue to characterize her personality into late adulthood and set her on a path to owning fine apparel of her own.[55]

The Denisons provided essential services for the Askins. Under an 1810 ledger subheading titled "Lissette & Jm. Denniston formerly slaves," John Askin entered a note with a tally of the payments owed the Denison family: "James his credit for services with 4 [1/2] Bushells of corn . . . his father . . . & Lisette." James was performing agricultural labor on the Askin farm, and his father likely did the same. John Askin sometimes paid Peter in "bushelles of wheat," "whiskey," and "brandy." At times he paid Peter, as well as Lisette, by way of Elijah Brush. Twice he paid Lisette in "alms," church contributions that went to the pastor. Sometimes he paid in cash. John Askin regretted, though, that he was paying James more for fewer days of work than the slaveholder Captain McKee was paying "Geo" (George).[56] The Denisons, as a family, were skilled and versatile laborers who knew how to drive hard bargains after years of experience with the Tuckers, not to mention the Brushes, the Askins, and even Governor Hull.

In addition to their exchanges with the Denisons, the Askins maintained a series of economic relationships with people and families they had once owned or who had been previously enslaved in Detroit. John Askin recorded trades for labor with "Mary," "Tom," and "George formerly my slave." Mary was paid an "allowance" and found herself in a similar situation as Lisette Denison when John Askin fell behind in paying her. In response, Mary, who was provided with leather supplies to make "shoe packs," "said she would work for nothing" during this period, suggesting that she occupied an ambiguous status between slavery, indentured servitude, and freedom, much like the Denisons. The Askins also continued to own enslaved people, though fewer than before, in these years. In 1810 John Askin recorded paying "4.8" in "expenses for Jim my negero."[57] The Denisons and other liminal laborers in Detroit of black or Native ancestry and ambiguous or former slave status were intertwined within a web of community economic relationships that allowed them to make a living but continued to privilege the European and American elite. "Negro" workers and former "slaves" constructed, baked, fixed, and made all manner of things on Detroit farms, at Detroit shops, and inside Detroit households. They cut wood and planks, worked with ice and powered through snow, sewed textiles, and made durable shoes for the harsh weather conditions. Peter Denison likely resumed leading the black militia once he was back in the home of Elijah Brush. By 1809, Peter had purchased a muff, three blue handkerchiefs, more than thirty yards of blue flannel, and one pair of "worked mockasons" for which he paid in full. The bulk flannel order may have been for uniforms. Peter also bought "8 plain flat plates," butter, snuff and tobacco that year. Peter often paid cash for his items, and he accepted cash intended to go "to Hannah," and "to wife," for seamstress work. Peter's expenditures were recorded in the anonymous merchant's ledger among a mix of purchases made by diverse Detroiters. French old settlers like Pierre Chêne and Madame Macabe appeared in this record book, buying tobacco and calico, as did American professionals like Solomon Sibley, who purchased a lady's parasol for his wife and two pairs of "fine kid gloves." An indigenous man listed as "Na'auguaijigue Chief" paid for ten plugs of tobacco with "muskrats in full." And two African Americans besides the Denisons were listed in the ledger: a woman described as "Mary Ann Negroe

Wench," who was paid for one month of "services" and a boy called "Jack the little Negro," who was paid for his "services" of delivering green tea and sugar. While procuring household goods as "Brush's black man," Peter Denison seems to have been ever mindful of his unstable status. In the winter of 1810, Elijah Brush wrote to John Askin, explaining that "Peter goes across to see if he can get any allowance from Lisette to assist in the purchase of his liberty if you should happen to owe him anything and wish it I will endeavor to furnish the money." That season, Elizabeth Denison borrowed £14 from Askin, which Askin passed along to Brush "on acct [account] of Lisette my letter." Peter and Hannah, aided by their industrious and effective daughter, moved out on their own, leaving Adelaide Brush to bemoan to her brother: "Peter and his wife [left] us this fall therefore, I have nobody to depend upon." [58]

Formerly enslaved people—many of them now viewed as free people of color—were an integral part of the social and economic fabric that knit Detroit together in the years before the next war. The legal conditions of Detroit's location in Michigan Territory of the Northwest, together with the town's continued geographical isolation, meant that relationships had to be carefully negotiated. Such mediations provided a legally vulnerable family like the Denisons with the cover to live as free residents. At the same time, formerly enslaved people's need for cover created opportunity for merchants and landowners, who could contract work for delayed pay or no pay at all, lend money or withhold it, to continue exerting significant influence over disadvantaged people's lives. The Denisons met this overlay of obligation and control with a remarkable creativity and adroitness that simultaneously bespeaks their own aspirations as well as those of Detroit's liminal working class of color for whom detailed accounts do not survive.

The Black Militia and the War of 1812

Governor Hull first said no when asked to accept the position of brigadier general of the Northwestern Army. He repeated his refusal upon the second request from Secretary of War William Eustis. Hull was not eager to take the highest western military commission on the eve of America's second war with Great Britain. Perhaps age was an issue uppermost in his mind. A local hero of the Revolutionary War for his brave bayonet work, Hull was now fifty-nine years old and far less nimble. His wife Sarah's warning must also have rung in his head as he weighed this momentous decision. She had told him three years before to beware the manipulations of Washington insiders. Or maybe Hull was feeling miffed, as he had offered to serve in the military during the preceding winter and was told his service was not necessary. A final barrier to Hull's acquiescence was his reluctance to relinquish his gubernatorial post. But upon the third request of Secretary Eustis in the winter of 1812, and with the promise that he could hold both the civilian and military titles, Hull relented, agreeing to lead the forces of all federal troops in Michigan against a concerted British and Indian assault that was sure to come before long.[59] War had not yet been declared, but tensions were rising feverishly in hot spots around the country. First the attack of the *Leopard* upon the U.S.S. *Chesapeake* off the coast of Virginia had dramatically symbolized the campaign of British impressments and the Crown's practice of bullying American ships and blockading American trade. Then the striking, Ohio-born Shawnee leader Tecumseh had gathered influence among several western and southern indigenous nations.

Tecumseh was organizing a coalition around the spiritual vision of his brother, Tenskwatawa, also known as the Prophet, in which indigenous people renewed their cultures, reclaimed their faiths, and took back their homelands. Tecumseh's aim, fed by Tenskwatawa's vision, was for Native independence won through a confederation of tribes, but he would ally with the British in order to achieve this goal. The Prophet had received permission from Potawatomi and Kickapoo residents to found a multitribal village of proponents on the Tippecanoe River in their territory of Indiana. A spiritual, intellectual, and organizational hub of the Native revolution, Prophet's Town was a bright red flag waving in the face of a bullish American government. As Prophet's Town drew adherents, Tecumseh, whose mother was Creek, traveled south into Cherokee and Creek territory sharing his two-pronged message of "prophetic nativism" and "intertribal unity."[60] Watching the spread of Tecumseh's message and the political and spiritual gathering of nations in the western interior pushed the Americans to the offensive. In 1811 troops led by Indiana governor and future U.S. president William Henry Harrison had closed in on Prophet's Town, the source, Harrison believed, of a series of raids on Indiana settlers.[61] Aware of Harrison's approach, the warriors struck first and were counterattacked by Harrison's men, who then burned the empty settlement to the ground, making Harrison into a frontier folk hero for segments of the American populace and inspiring the future pro-Harrison campaign rallying cry: "Tippecanoe and Tyler Too!" Tenskwatawa would not be deterred by American reprisals; he rebuilt Prophet's Town and grew its size to eight hundred warriors. Tecumseh, who had been traveling during the battle as an ambassador of the Native resistance, had survived to fight another dawn against the Americans.[62]

Governor Hull had been keeping track of these dire developments from the capital in Detroit, as had been local residents. As Tecumseh and the Prophet's notoriety mushroomed with news of the Battle of Tippecanoe traveling across the forests and prairies, Detroiters were growing ever more fearful of an Indian attack on their town. In 1811, leading citizens drafted a memorial to the "president, senate, and house of representatives" in Washington, voicing their fears and urging "an increase in military force." The memorial writers described "dissatisfactions with the aboriginal inhabitants of these countries," which had "been kindled into an open flame." They begged the government not to allow "conflagration" to spread "along the whole line of the frontier," as "the Savage mind, once fully incensed, once diverted from the pursuit of their ordinary subsistence, once turned upon plunder, once inflamed by the loss of their kindred and friends, once satisfied with the taste of blood, is difficult to appease, and as terrible as subtle in vengeance. The horrors of savage belligerence description cannot paint. No picture can resemble the reality." But paint it these authors did, and with a self-focused, stereotyping brush that refused to see the legitimacy in Native people's defense of their original homelands and ways of life. This memorial, signed by Solomon Sibley, Augustus Woodward, George McDougall, Harris Hickman, and Richard Smyth, was the work of Anglo American professional and working-class men, who stressed the need for government "protection" in "their exposed and defenceless situation."[63]

Governor Hull, who may not have exactly appreciated the pattern Detroiters had set of going over his head with their letters and memorials, agreed with the townspeople's diagnosis and prescription. The

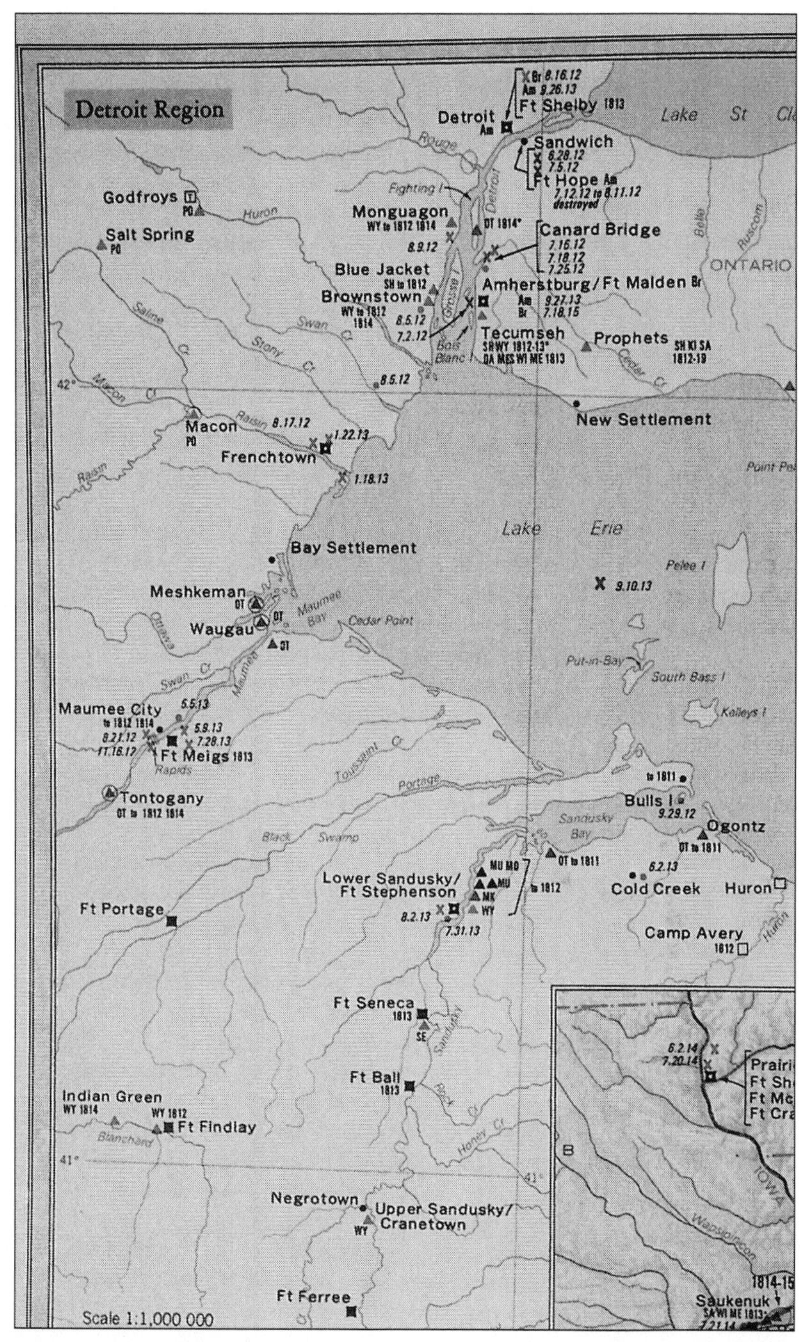

The War of 1812: Indian Involvement 1811–1816. Map originally published in *Atlas of Great Lakes Indian History*, edited by Helen Hornbeck Tanner. Copyright © 1987 by the University of Oklahoma Press, Norman. Reprinted by permission of the publisher. All rights reserved.

borderland northwest, Hull predicted, would be a front line of the international altercation to come. The British had already shown a willingness to abuse the power of the Royal Navy while carrying out their impressment policies. As a peninsula surrounded by coastline, Michigan was especially exposed to maritime attack, far more vulnerable than southern territories like Ohio, Indiana, and Illinois. A terrestrial threat also existed, deep inside the western woodlands. Although indigenous people had been pushed beyond a boundary in treaties at Greenville, Fort Wayne, and Detroit, they were inspired by spiritual renewal and outraged at the continual loss of land, and they were increasingly organizing across tribal lines. Hull, as historian Michael Witgen has put it, was "painfully aware that the United States, in stark contrast with the Canadians, had a troubled and violent history with the Native peoples living within the borders of the territory he claimed to govern . . . and assumed that the peoples of Anishinaabewaki [Ojibwe, Ottawa, and Potawatomi country] would turn against the United States."[64] Back in 1807, a wary Governor Hull had ordered the Michigan militia to rebuild the pickets surrounding the town to a height of eighteen feet. Lately, he had been fixated on the notion that the government should immediately build a naval fleet to patrol the Great Lakes. In March of 1812, he wrote to Secretary of War Eustis recommending that "A force adequate to the defense of that vulnerable point [Detroit], would prevent war with the savages, and probably induce the enemy to abandon Upper Canada without opposition. The naval force of the Lakes would in that event fall into our possession." In April of 1812, Hull accepted his commission as brigadier general, but he never received the enhanced naval force he longed for.[65]

While Hull was lacking in full support from the federal government on the waterways, he did have at the ready Ohio militiamen, Michigan militiamen, and, one rare source suggests, the black militia of Detroit.[66] Hull first had to gather his scattered troops from Ohio before preparing a defense of the northwestern border. According to a dispatch from New York written on July 18, Hull "arrived at Detroit, with 2,300 men, after a tedious march through the wilderness."[67] In order to get there, Hull and his troops had been compelled to cut a trail through a portion of the thick and formidable marshland of northern Ohio's Black Swamp, watered by the Maumee River and greater than one hundred miles in length.[68]

Facing the acute challenge of traversing a difficult landscape weakened Hull's army before the war had officially begun. At the Miami River, Hull chartered a private boat, the schooner *Cuyahoga,* to transport the wives and children of officers as well as trunks of records and medical supplies to Detroit. Because the War Department sent notice that the United States had formally declared war on Great Britain via the sluggish regular post, Hull found out the news days after British military leaders knew of it in Canada. Thus prepared to engage, officers at Fort Malden on the British side of the Detroit River dispatched a longboat, which captured the ship Hull had commissioned and commandeered Hull's supplies. Even as a Washington writer cheered Hull's arrival in Detroit, exclaiming Governor Hull "had arrived at Detroit on [July] the 5th, with his army amounting to nearly 2,500, all in good health and high spirits," Hull had been disadvantaged by geography and his own government and bested by the British command.[69]

The fate of the *Cuyahoga* foreshadowed the nature of this off-kilter conflict that tested, but in the end left in place, territorial boundaries established by the Revolutionary War. The War of 1812 was a series of odd engagements, missed opportunities, unfortunate accidents, and unanticipated atrocities, especially in Michigan Territory. Governor Hull, as well as the town of Detroit, would suffer from both mistakes and misfortune in a war that many Americans, especially Federalists in New England, were not even in favor of. But in the Great Lakes, from New York to Michigan Territory, fear of a Native alliance with the all too proximal British troops in Canada, fed a hawkish orientation. In New York, rumors circulated about the rise of an Indian force in league with the enemy. "Great exertions were making by the British at Fort Malden, to array the Indians against us," a letter writer exclaimed, "Previous to the declaration of war, a tomahawk, stained with blood, had been sent from Malden to all the neighboring tribes."[70] The United States planned to forestall attack by launching an assertive invasion of Canada from Detroit. Directed by Secretary of War Eustis to prepare to wage an offensive war, Hull and his officers began to plot a frontal assault on British targets. Eustis commanded: "By my letter of the 18th inst. You were informed that war was declared against Great Britain. Herewith enclosed, you will receive a copy of that act, and of the President's proclamation, and you are authorized to commence offensive operations accordingly. Should the force under your command be equal to the enterprise, consistent with the safety of your own posts, you will take possession of Malden, and extend your conquests as circumstances may justify."[71]

Hull and his men made an auspicious beginning for the American strategy by crossing the Detroit River and occupying the tiny town of Sandwich in July. Black militiamen may very well have been among this force. On July 20, 1812, an unsigned journalist's dispatch written in Ohio described the scene at Sandwich based on an eyewitness account: "We are further enabled to inform our readers, that we have since our last learned from a gentleman direct from Sandwich . . . that the army crossed the river without opposition; that the inhabitants generally fled, but on receiving the proclamation they returned to their houses, and resumed their businesses." After giving the account of the Sandwich campaign in which Hull had posted a proclamation inviting residents to join the American cause and assuring their protection, the writer of this piece made the following observation: "Previous to the army's leaving Detroit, a company of the black infantry associated and requested to accompany the army in support of America and freedom. Governor Hull accept[ed] the offer and gave commissions. The captain is said to be a very intelligent man, and the company perform well."[72]

In a dispatch full of precise detail about troop movements, artillery pieces, and the eighty barrels of flour secured from the king's commissary at Sandwich, the black militia was entered into the written record of the War of 1812. The "intelligent captain" must have been Peter Denison, who had spent ample time in Sandwich but had resettled in Detroit with Elijah Brush, colonel of the First Regiment of the Michigan Volunteer Militia, before the war began. The reporter from Ohio noted in his commentary that these black men offered to fight for "America" and "freedom." However, the history of the Denison family, and of all enslaved people in the Detroit border zone, whether of black, indigenous, or Afro-Native ancestry, indicates a strategic lack of national allegiance. These were "revolutionary renegades," who fought for freedom, for independence, and for dignity of life, in ways that could sync with or diverge from the aims of any particular colonial or state power.[73] As the first black military company on American soil authorized by a government official and commanded by black officers, the men of the black militia fought for the right of their families to be free from tyranny in any form.

Hull's taste of victory in the occupied Detroit River town did not last long. On July 17, the British along with Ojibwe and Ottawa allies captured the American fort on Mackinac Island. Hull heard this portentous news from two Ojibwe travelers whose route took them through Detroit. Judge Augustus Woodward wrote about the loss of the fort in the concluding lines of his July 28 letter to Secretary Eustis: "You will, no doubt, have received, through other channels, the information which has arrived here of the capture of Michilimackina by the enemy." It was in this same letter that Woodward complained about Hull issuing "three commissions to captain Denison, lieutenant Burgess, and ensign Bosset, black men."[74] Would not these black soldiers have continued on through the next engagement of the war that unfolded in the town where they were stationed? In all likelihood, former slaves and men of color based in Detroit fought in the War of 1812.

On August 12, a British force led by Colonel Isaac Brock together with a Native force led by British Indian agent and slaveholder Matthew Elliott set sights on Detroit. At 1:00 p.m. on Saturday, August 15, Brock sent a message to Hull by way of a small vessel demanding Hull's relinquishment of the fort. "The force at my disposal authorizes me to require of you the immediate surrender of Detroit," Brock insisted, catching Hull by surprise. And then Brock's letter included a line meant to stoke the latent fears of Hull and his constituents. "It is far from my intention to join in a war of extermination," Brock wrote, "but you must be aware, that the numerous body of Indians who have attached themselves to my troops, will be beyond controul the moment the context commences." Hull stalled, hoping for reinforcements that never came from troops that he did not realize were located just miles outside of town. At 3:00 p.m., Hull rejected Brock's demand. By 4:00 p.m. the British were firing canons across the river. The Northwestern Army counterfired from artillery positioned in the heart of downtown Detroit. Hull directed Elijah Brush to guard the northern edge of the town, backing into the woodlands. If the black militia was activated, they were likely assigned a similar duty, positioning Peter Denison to coordinate with his colleague, Elijah Brush.[75]

The British assault continued unabated into the night. Fitful residents who dared not sleep may have recalled stories of the siege of the village by the Ottawa warrior Pontiac two generations prior. The terrified occupants of Detroit Town desperately buried money and silver, or directed their slaves to do so. Women and children fled to the enclosed stockade at the fort as cannonball shots splintered the wooden walls, killing two soldiers.[76] Lisette and Hannah Denison would have been among these women, clustered, perhaps, with Adelaide Askin and her children. Resourceful and independent, Lisette may have joined local women in nursing the wounded. Her brothers, James and Scipio, may have been defending the fort with her father, Peter, and other men of the black militia.

With ammunition running low, no reinforcements, and the threat of Indian reprisals against the civilian population that he was duty bound to protect as governor, Hull decided, in a fateful choice that military historians continue to analyze and debate, to surrender the town. Elijah Brush was among the four officers who drafted the statement of Detroit's capitulation, an American defeat that resounded across the country and brought harsh recriminations for Hull. Within forty-eight hours of the commencement of Colonel Brock's attack, old Fort Detroit was British once again. Imagine the fear of fugitive slaves who had escaped from Canada, the rage of Richard Smyth and the men who frequented his tavern. As the outlying farmhouses along the river were plundered by Native warriors, the disgraced Governor Hull moved into his former brick home, now occupied by his daughter and her family, where he was placed under armed British guard.[77]

On the following Monday, August 17, Hull, his officers and staff, and members of the regular army were taken as prisoners of war to Quebec. Elijah Brush was among them. The military historian Gene Allen Smith has written that "Peter Denison was taken off with other white and black prisoners to Canada before being paroled." Although no apparent document directly points to this outcome, it is certainly plausible, as the British paroled nearly four hundred prisoners seized at Detroit.[78] If Peter was taken to Quebec but released early, he died just days later. On August 27 of 1812, Reverend Richard Pollard of St. John's Church entered into the registry: "Peter Dennison . . . departed this life and was buried."[79] The archival trail of Detroit's black militia ends here, with him.

But the war went on after the death of Peter Denison in 1812 and after the death of Elijah Brush in 1813. The families of these men lived through the British occupation of Detroit that lasted for more than a year, during which time Augustus Woodward intervened on behalf of the populace and won protections from the British commanding officer. In the winter of 1813, British troops and Tecumseh's warriors attacked French Town on the River Raisin in Michigan, a settlement that had formed when several French families migrated from Detroit in the 1780s. American troops were defeated, captured, and tortured there, a low point for American morale and a rallying point for demoralized U.S. soldiers who would take up the cry: "Remember the Raisin!" But by the next summer, U.S. forces were landing significant blows against the British. In 1813, after hanging his battle flag commemorating a quote by felled captain James Lawrence—"Don't give up the ship!"—naval commander Oliver Hazard Perry won a dramatic sea contest against vessels of the British navy on Lake Erie, a body of water where William Hull had first said an American force was needed. In 1814, General William Henry Harrison, who directed the Northwestern Army in Hull's wake, led troops to recapture Detroit for the United States. A series of clashes ensued in which British troops, Native forces, and American soldiers confronted one another but did not score victories decisive enough to tip the scales of war. In the Battle of New Orleans, which took place in January of 1815 just after American and British diplomats meeting in Belgium had signed the Treaty of Ghent in December, Commander Andrew Jackson amassed a multiracial force, including black and Choctaw soldiers, that prevented British troops from entering the city.

It was not until February of 1815 that Congress ratified the treaty and most Americans heard the good news that the war had formally ended. But neither the United States nor Great Britain had been victorious in the conflict. No territory had been gained or lost by either nation, though Canadians could take pride in having successfully fended off multiple American incursions. Native Americans in the region saw their influence severely reduced with the death of Tecumseh at the Battle of the Thames in 1813 and the reinstatement of American power at western forts at the war's end. The War of 1812 would be the last moment when indigenous forces allied across multiple tribal lines to challenge the United

States militarily. In the northern reaches of Michigan, western reaches of Wisconsin and Minnesota, and great west of the high plains and Rocky Mountains, hundreds of Native populations still organized autonomous societies outside the reach of American colonialism.[80] But in the Ohio Valley, the lower peninsula of Michigan, Illinois, Indiana, and the Southeast, the outcome of this war was "most ominous to the Indians."[81]

While devastating for indigenous people, the conflict was a virtual "draw" for Great Britain and the United States, which has caused it to fade in memory for citizens of both these nations. But the War of 1812, often called the "forgotten" war of American history, marks a watershed moment for the story of slavery in Detroit.[82] By the time war began, the number of enslaved people in the town and riverine suburbs had shrunk to a handful of individuals listed in the Ste. Anne's Church register. In 1812, a black woman named Nansey was described as the slave of Jacques Laselle, as was her son, Jean Baptiste Rémond, conceived with an "unknown father." Abraham Ford, a black man, was married to Marie Louise, a free Native woman of French and Native parentage, whose mother was "of the Sauteur nation" (Ojibwe); they had a child, Julie Ford, born in 1813. Abraham Ford is described in the register as "negro of Colonel Matthew Elliott." By the end of the war, slavery in Detroit had nearly met its demise. In 1820, no enslaved people were listed in the Ste. Anne's Church register or the Detroit census. The 1830 census noted one enslaved person within the borders of Michigan. Two years prior to Michigan statehood, in 1835, two enslaved people lived in Monroe and Cass Counties, Michigan.

Warfare, political struggle, and territorial laws had weakened the practice of slavery in Detroit during the late eighteenth and early nineteenth centuries, but enslaved people themselves dealt the final blows. Adopting a renegade politics, traversing the border in pursuit of freedom, and fighting against those who claimed to own them with legal as well as lethal weapons, enslaved people undermined the corrupt, fraying, suspect system until it snapped. They no doubt shared the view of fugitive slave J. Levy, who wrote a letter back to his master from Canada in 1852, boldly proclaiming that "liberty is ever watchful" and "security" to "self" "demanded the sacrifice."[83]

During the War of 1812, hundreds of black men fought for the British as well as for the Americans, seeking freedom and respect for the priceless risk they took with their lives and futures. In the United States, African Americans sailed with Perry's troops on Lake Erie, spying Canada just across the waters.[84] What these men learned about the secrets of the border, what enslaved Detroiters and black militia members had long known, became prized information for disparate black communities, especially after 1833 when Britain abolished slavery in its colonies and Canada became free soil. The stories shared by these revolutionary renegades traveled with military men of color and fugitives from slavery, adding a shimmering thread of hope to the collective consciousness held by African Americans and other oppressed peoples.[85]

Conclusion: The American City (1817 and Beyond)

> The drama continues, but it does so with wrenching twists and turns, fervent disjuncture, and dizzying prospects.
>
> —*June Manning Thomas and Henco Bekkering,* Mapping Detroit, *2015*

After the dust in Detroit had settled following the War of 1812, Elizabeth Denison, known to her family by the nickname Lisette, continued on in the household of Adelaide Brush, widow of militiaman Elijah Brush. Lisette and her siblings lived as free residents of the city. But limitations that the Denison family and all free people of color had faced continued into mid-century; theirs was a hard-won and consistently compromised freedom. Lisette would spend the rest of her working life in the most common employment for free black women in the 1800s: as a domestic laborer in the homes of white Americans. In August of 1816, Lisette shared the joyful occasion of her brother Scipio's marriage to the seventeen-year-old Charlotte Paul in Detroit. In December of that year, Scipio and Charlotte had a daughter, Phoebe, who was baptized in 1817 across the river at St. John's Church in Sandwich. Lisette served as a sponsor for her baby niece's baptism, as she and the rest of the Denison family's younger generations continued their frequent crossings of the U.S.-Canadian border in what was, essentially, a transnational way of life. In 1819, a son named James was born to Scipio and Charlotte and baptized at St. John's, sponsored by his aunt Lisette, his uncle James, and his father Scipio. The absence of Hannah Denison's name in these church records of the 1810s suggests that she followed her husband, Peter

Denison, into her final rest before these new grandbabies entered the world. If so, Hannah Denison missed Detroit's surge of growth in what one privileged Detroiter called an "auspicious era."[1] Like Hannah and Peter Denison, and Elijah Brush, many of the most prominent figures in Detroit's slaveholding history had passed away or relocated by the 1820s. William Macomb, the town's largest slaveholder in the eighteenth century, had died before 1800. In 1817, his widow, Sarah Macomb, and son, David Macomb, were advertising nearly five thousand acres of land for sale, including plots in Upper Canada, "most excellent Land, on Grosse Isle," and an "elegant and pleasantly situated farm on the border of the Detroit River." The two other Macomb sons, William and John, had begun the process of selling their Detroit River and island lands in 1810, with John and his nephew William preferring to run a coffee plantation on the Caribbean island of Cuba where slavery was still patently legal. John Askin would pass away in 1818 at his home on the river, and James May would leave this life in 1829.[2]

An Auspicious Era

As Lisette Denison searched the deep brown eyes of her baby nieces and nephews who just one generation ago would have been born into slavery, she may have cast her mind to the shadowed reality of that past, and then to the possibilities of a brighter future in Michigan. Certainly other talented Detroiters, especially those who enjoyed racial privilege, social position, and a reassuring measure of wealth, scanned the eastern horizon for signs of opportunity. In the newly launched *Detroit Gazette* newspaper, established in July of 1817, tavern owner Richard Smyth was announcing a "meeting of the citizens of Detroit" to discuss "important matters relating to trade and the general prosperity." The Abbott family's merchant business, established in the 1770s and burgled back then by the company's slave woman and servant man, was still going strong in the fall of 1817, when James Abbott advertised blankets, sundry cloths, and "fine" flour for sale on credit in the *Gazette*. In the spring of 1817, John R. Williams, also a merchant in Detroit and descendant of the slaveholding Campaus on his mother's side, wrote to Samuel Abbott, a lawyer at Mackinac, to conduct business and share big news. Williams's letter bridged the old and new character of the city—the Detroit of colonial and Revolutionary War times that relied on systems of unfree labor and the post–War of 1812 Detroit that was increasingly modernizing and expanding its economy. In his missive, Williams solicited "Panis" labor and at the same time sounded a ring of ebullient optimism about industrial development and growth. Williams opened by disclosing his "difficulty of procuring servants" in Detroit and telling Abbott: "I am informed they can be procured at Mackinac, of the Panis Nation of both sexes." Specifically, Williams "would be glad to have a boy and girl from 12 to 18 years of age, Bound under indentures to serve for a limited number of years, say to the age of 30." If Abbott would do Williams the service of sending him a "boy and girl . . . of good moral habits and tractable disposition," Williams would clear the account on Abbott's "draft at sight." John Williams's request bespoke his close association of Native people with servitude, such that he believed the French term for an Indian slave, "Panis," designated a particular tribe of people. In the 1810s, Williams's entreaty smacked of old patterns. Many an indigenous person defined as property had been ordered from the straits of Mackinac by Detroit merchants in the century past. While Williams did not propose to buy these children outright, and could not have done so under Michigan law, he could pay Abbott a sizable fee in the form of debts eliminated for procuring their indentures such that they would be bound to him until mid-adulthood. Williams made no mention of indigenous parents or tribal leaders in his letter. A complacent consumer of Native labor, he fully expected these children to be easily plucked from their families and offered up for his use.[3]

After dispensing with the prosaic business of getting hold of "Panis" servants, Williams turned readily to the "news." He informed Abbott that "The President of the U.S. has signified his determination to visit us this summer. I look upon the event as an auspicious aera in the prospective improvement of this country, and anticipate more alteration within the next five years than the country has undergone since its first settlement. The projected canal to connect the waters of Lake Erie with those of the Huron, will no doubt greatly acclimate the population & prosperity of this country." John Williams, who would become the first formally elected mayor of Detroit seven years after writing this letter, had the keen eye of a futurist. The Erie Canal, completed in 1825, would indeed open the floodgates of Euro-American settlement in Michigan and set Detroit on the path to becoming "a truly American city." For Williams, this modern version of Detroit would, and should, coincide with an older colonial order in which "tractable," or readily managed, indigenous children could be ordered like items in a catalogue. When President James Monroe visited the city for five days that August, "a period of great glorification for the small city," he might have witnessed the enduring imprint of this colonial history inscribed in the menial class status of Detroit's residents of color.[4]

Beyond the growth of the white population and support of trade through federal infrastructure, residents of John Williams's ilk looked toward higher education as a means of uplifting Michigan Territory to the level of existing states. Citizens began rallying for the formation of a local university and launched into avid fundraising. Leading men stepped immediately forward in a "rapid and liberal manner," according to the *Gazette*.[5] On the first day that subscriptions were collected, more than £1,000 of funding had been pledged for the cause that all upheld as worthy. Judge Augustus Woodward, who had always been fond of serious interdisciplinary study, and who, according to two nineteenth-century chroniclers, still kept one "pawnee" servant as "one of the last slaves in Detroit," introduced a bill to establish the school and delved into the development of a "System of Universal Science" to organize areas of study for the university.[6] James May, the merchant whose wrecked ship in 1801 had killed a man he owned, made a payment of $5, the initial installment toward an overall pledge "to be paid in money." According to the record of the university treasurer, May agreed to pay this amount each year over five years in "the aid of the University of Michigan." James Abbott, also a slaveholder, pledged $315.32. Attorney Solomon Sibley, whose son would later own slaves and rise to political prominence in Minnesota, promised $625.67. The Detroit freemasons, in which slaveholder Joseph Campau served as treasurer, contributed an undisclosed major gift to the school. The university also drew support from a public relief fund dating back to the fire of 1805 that had not been fully exhausted. Hybrid from the outset, the school's financial foundation was sourced from both private and public wealth. Tuition was set at "a small sum," but "certified" students unable to pay would be supported by the territorial treasury.[7] Members of Detroit's old slaveholding network were among those who contributed the earliest designated contributions, making public education in Michigan possible. The original list of trustees for the school included surnames of some of Detroit's earliest and largest slaveholding families: the Campaus, the Abbotts, and the Macombs. Organized as a "Primary School" linked to a "Classical Academy" with training through the high school level, the University of Michigania (also known as The Catholepistemiad) was formally established by territorial Governor Lewis Cass with the Reverend John Monteith serving as president and Father Gabriel Richard serving as vice president. Augustus Woodward, the main mover behind the ambitious initiative, laid the first cornerstone for the inaugural campus building in September of 1817. Two decades later, in 1837, the institution would spread its wings, gliding southwest to the forested hamlet of Ann Arbor.[8]

This relocation to Ann Arbor, and the university's institutional and intellectual maturation there in the second half of the nineteenth century, depended on a large swath of land acquired through an unexpected chain of transactions. An agreement known as the Treaty of 1817 had cemented a transfer of approximately 4.2 million acres of land from indigenous to Euro-American hands in the aftermath of the War of 1812. The story was by then a familiar one in the Detroit River region and Ohio Valley: land speculation and government pressure pushed indigenous peoples to treat or sell, lest they be smothered by incoming settlers or driven out following violent battles with militiamen and military officers. But in the negotiations of this particular treaty, leaders of the Ojibwe, Ottawa, and Potawatomi nations specified that they wanted a portion of their land to be directed toward a certain purpose. They granted territory along the River Raisin in southeastern Michigan to the state, to be used or sold in order to support educational opportunities for their children. These Native leaders wished to see an extension of Ste. Anne's Church in Detroit and the "corporation of the college of Detroit" (Michigania) in order to better prepare their own children in a moment when territorial administrators had their minds set on statehood and a citizenry defined mainly as white. Michigan officials would later trade a portion of this original 1817 land grant on the River Raisin for acreage in Ann Arbor near the Huron River. Here, the college was relocated from its original site in downtown Detroit and expanded to offer advanced courses of classical study.[9]

An iconic Midwestern and American educational institution, the University of Michigan was born of a compromise made by Native people in the context of a century of colonial warfare and land dispossession in the Great Lakes. Built on ill-gotten lands and funded, in part, by family wealth derived from slave labor, the University of Michigan system now shines as a cultural star of the state. In 1976, the Michigan State Legislature adopted Public Act 174, a law authorizing tuition waivers for tribally enrolled Native Americans who reside in Michigan and have been admitted to any of the state's public universities. This redistribution of public resources to citizens of indigenous nations is an ethical response to troubled historical relationships. Tuition for Native people has been, in the words of an undergraduate student at the University of Michigan from the Grand Traverse Band of Ottawa Indians in northern Michigan, "prepaid in land and blood."[10]

The Mammon of Unrighteousness

Lisette Denison may have wondered, as talk of a university bolstered town pride, whether her nieces and nephews would ever study there. Records indicate they would not. The first African American student, Samuel Codes Watson, was admitted to the University of Michigan medical school in 1853; the first African American woman, Mary Henrietta Graham, was admitted to the college of literature in 1876.[11] In the 1810s and 1820s, the livelihoods of Lisette and her family members still depended upon domestic labor and close connections with prominent white Detroiters. But Lisette had shown in her dealings with John Askin, when refusing to twist worsted yarn for hours on end, that she was capable of shaping the terms of such domestic employment. In the early 1820s, Lisette left the household of Adelaide Askin and began working for the family of prominent attorney Solomon Sibley. Lisette cooked for the Sibleys and provided care for their children. When Solomon Sibley's daughter, Catherine, left Detroit to attend Emma Willard's finishing school for girls in New York, she wrote back to her mother: "Tell Lisette I often wish

I could visit her cookie jar." The Sibleys appreciated Elizabeth Denison's finely honed skills in the kitchen. And Lisette, by all appearances of what transpired over the next decade, appreciated Solomon Sibley's facility with the law.[12]

Elizabeth Denison had grown up enslaved on a farm in the Detroit River hinterlands. She had no formal education and never learned to read or write. She had come of age during the era of Detroit's transformation into an American town and watched as Detroit area lands were extracted from indigenous people, divided up into lots, and sold for government profit. With the growing influx of eastern and southern settlers, Lisette saw Detroit transform into a small city with three thousand residents by 1817.[13] She recognized the value of land and, like many white citizens around her, sought to acquire it for herself, even though moral title, she might have realized in her heart, belonged to the Native peoples who increasingly lived on small parcels of reservation lands north of Detroit near the Saginaw River, at the straits of Mackinac, and toward the western banks of Lake Michigan. As she matured, Lisette managed to redefine herself as a financially savvy urbanite at the dawn of Detroit's industrial metamorphosis. Beginning in 1825, Solomon Sibley's papers show a series of land purchases made by Lisette Denison and facilitated by Sibley. She bought 48.5 acres (four lots) in the town of Pontiac, due north of Detroit, from Sibley's business associate Stephen Mack, becoming the first black landowner in the city. She then leased these lands to her brother Scipio. Scipio and Charlotte Denison soon had another daughter, who was baptized in Pontiac. When their family needed a loan of $5, Scipio turned to his sister Lisette, who had herself married by then, in 1827, to a man who shared her brother's first name: Scipio Forth.[14]

Lisette's marriage was short-lived. Her husband vanished from the historical record and, presumably, from her life soon thereafter. The mystery of her husband's disappearance was likely a source of sadness for Lisette, but she rebounded, taking a job in 1831 in the home of the president of Farmers and Mechanics Bank, former Detroit mayor, and War of 1812 veteran John Biddle. Lisette grew and diversified her investments throughout the 1830s. After her brother vacated the Pontiac land, Lisette rented it out. She then bought stock in the steamboat *Michigan* and shares in Farmers and Mechanics Bank. In the spring of 1837, Lisette acquired land in downtown Detroit from Solomon Sibley's son, Ebenezer Sibley. She paid her mortgage off in full in 1842. Like her father before her, Elizabeth Denison had a knack for bartering desired skills that brought her support from prominent whites and then pushing that support to access new and sometimes radical opportunities. A notable cook and seamstress, Lisette had channeled the goodwill and connections of her influential patrons to become a woman of invested wealth. Whether to continue the benefit of these key relationships, to procure liquid assets in the form of cash payments, or to maintain caregiving responsibilities for children she had helped to raise, Lisette continued to work for John and Eliza Biddle as a cook, nanny, and housekeeper into the 1850s. But Lisette did not make her long-term domestic employment with the Biddles easy for the prominent couple. Recognizing her importance to the family, she continued to negotiate her own labor terms. In 1839, a visitor to the Biddle's elegant new home in Wyandotte, Michigan (fifteen miles south of Detroit), commented that she "[did] not know how [Mrs. Biddle] would get on but for Lisette who, notwithstanding her frequent threats of leaving, seems as firmly established as ever."[15]

Fifteen years after this observation was made by a guest in her home, Eliza Biddle was still dependent on Lisette in what was an interdependent, often strained relationship. In 1855, Lisette accompanied Eliza on a trip to Paris in order to "keep house" for her employer. According to Eliza, who mentioned Lisette's cooking and penchant for fine gloves frequently in her letters to relatives and friends, Lisette created buckwheat concoctions that astonished and delighted Parisian high society. Almost forty years before Quaker Oats marketed Aunt Jemima pancake mix, making the stereotyped image of black women's domestic servitude a nostalgic American sensation, Biddle wrote the following about Lisette's cakes: "Lisette is making us quite celebrated in Paris by her buckwheat cakes and I expect some of these days to be invited to come to the Tuileries [Palace] and bring my black cook & her griddle that the Empress may enjoy the American luxury." Eliza Biddle proudly reported that the "Ambassador" himself requested Lisette's cakes. Rather than sending a parcel containing the treats, Eliza Biddle sent Lisette, who startled the "indignant" French chef "when she produced a fire in the furnace and produced her griddle." Eliza Biddle did not forget Elizabeth Denison's race, or shed her sense that a formerly enslaved African American woman could be viewed as a personal possession to be sent around town like a package. Lisette was too sharp to have been unaware of these racially biased attitudes on the part of her employer, or of Parisians' view of her as a folksy relic of America's quixotic slaveholding past. She even allowed her resentment to slip to the surface so that Biddle could glimpse her feelings. Eliza Biddle wrote about Lisette: "She thinks when she is sent for by the Emperor she will not return to our modest ménage but remain at court & perhaps have a carriage of her own." Eliza Biddle recognized Elizabeth Denison's ambition to do something greater than cooking for the Biddles, but she quickly squelched any critical introspection that such recognition might have raised for her. The next line of her letter celebrated the fame of Lisette's cakes while erasing Lisette's name as the creator of the delicacies: "Wherever we go we hear of these famous buckwheat cakes and of course when we invite company it is to sit round the table & enjoy them."[16]

Elizabeth Denison made her griddle cakes, accepted her pay, and saved her Paris earnings. She kept close watch on her house in Detroit with the help of the Biddles and their associate, Mr. Campau, checking on whether the house was rented and if the rent was equal to the value. Eliza Biddle found Lisette's careful habit of saving money to be excessive; she wanted Lisette to hand over control of her earnings to the Biddles and accept a yearly allowance of $25 instead. Eliza Biddle's stated reason for this change was that Lisette was living too frugally and, worse, embarrassing the Biddles by "asking charity when she has really more than she can spend if she were to live till she is a hundred & no one she cares for to leave it to when she dies." Revealing the fissures in her relationship with her "black cook," Eliza complained that Lisette was telling people that she had been "badly used by everybody." The resentment Lisette felt after years of laboring as a domestic and being treated like a mere functionary showed even more in her elder age. Eliza Biddle tried to have her son William, Lisette's favorite among the Biddle children, "cheat" Lisette (Biddle's own choice of words) in order to gain control of her finances. Instead of receiving the Biddle's money in the paid allowance as she would be led to believe, Lisette would be receiving and spending down her own funds. But Eliza Biddle's financial scheme did not work. Lisette

Elizabeth Denison Forth. Photo courtesy of Saint James Episcopal Church, Grosse Ile, Michigan.

Mrs. John Biddle (Eliza Falconer Bradish). By Thomas Sully, Metropolitan Museum of Art, New York, New York. Available at www.metmuseum .org.

Denison maintained her savings and, contrary to Biddle's condescending expectation, made a plan for her bequest that included those she cared for.[17]

One year after the close of the Civil War in 1866, Elizabeth Denison's life ended in Detroit. Her file in the historic Elmwood Cemetery record indicates that she died on August 7, 1866, and was buried in the "Stranger's Ground."[18] She had composed a will (and revision) with Solomon Sibley's assistance and selected William Biddle, who had completed his law degree at Harvard and was then working as an attorney in Detroit, to serve as executor of her estate. In her will dated January 1860, Lisette Denison acknowledged that she was "unable to read and write." She left various sums of money (between $50 and $100) to all of her living relatives: at that point only nieces and nephews, as she had lost her siblings and in-laws and never had children of her own. Finally, she authorized her trustee, William Biddle, to devote the remainder of her estate toward "the erection of a fine chapel for the use of the Protestant Episcopal Church." This chapel was to be a remedy for "the poor in our house of worship . . . humble followers of the lowly Jesus . . . excluded from those courts . . . shut out from those holy services by the mammon of unrighteousness." When Lisette dictated her intentions to Solomon Sibley, she spoke from experience. Lisette had been force-fed "the mammon," or riches, of "unrighteousness." She knew the bitter taste of poverty and the withering touch of slavery. A free woman who had stolen her own life with the loving aid of her family, she now wished to help others who suffered in want. Lisette signed this will, the only surviving document generated by an enslaved resident of Detroit, with her X mark.[19]

In the modern city fashioned by American consolidation and expansion, Elizabeth Denison became a landowner and a shareholder before the onset of the Civil War. Her family's story is the most documentable case of slavery in the city of Detroit. Her will is a rare record of the consciousness and intentions of a member of that long-forgotten group. But even as Elizabeth Denison charted new paths for formerly enslaved residents of Detroit as well as for African American women, she negotiated the circumstances of her life in an environment shaped and colored by a history of slavery and indigenous land dispossession. Despite her noteworthy earnings, Lisette had been unable to prevent the indenture of her own nephew, Eastman Denison, aged eleven, to the son of Elijah Brush, Charles R. Brush, in 1834. She had not been able to avoid patronizing treatment on the part of her employers, or to break through the barriers of race, gender, class, and station that steered her into service as a "black cook" instead of earning her living as the brilliant businesswoman that she might have been a century later. And it is essential to this story that Lisette derived much of her wealth later in life from investments in land that Michigan governors William Hull and Lewis Cass had wrested from the families of the Wyandot, Ottawa, Potawatomi, and Ojibwe nations.

For all the limitations of her choices, of her times, and of her community, Elizabeth Denison's will reflects one clear value, one ethical commitment to be upheld even in death. She believed that it was paramount to tackle poverty, to welcome and tend to the poor who were excluded even in houses of worship. And so she dedicated the bulk of her wealth to the founding of a church that would respect and care for all people.[20] William Biddle, Lisette's trustee, selected Grosse Ile for the site of the church. This was the island vacation spot preferred by his family, where Lisette had once worked as their housekeeper. Saint James Chapel on the island was established as a result of Elizabeth Denison's generosity, which was then enlarged by other contributors. The only existing original portrait of Lisette still hangs today in that house of worship, though Lisette herself had attended Mariners' Church on Jefferson Avenue in downtown Detroit in the last years of her life.[21]

Is it ironic that a church made possible by a woman once enslaved in Detroit was built on Indian land illegally purchased by Detroit's largest slaveholder? Is it unexpected that two of the cities where Lisette Denison labored as a servant and invested as a landlord—Pontiac and Wyandotte—bear the names of an historic Ottawa figure and a tribe removed by the state of Michigan? At the conclusion of this patchwork quilt of an historical chronicle, perhaps not. These apparent contradictions reflect the difficult compromises as well as the unsettling outcomes that abound in the history of slavery in Detroit. While slavery was never the driving force behind Detroit's economy (based on animal pelts and land speculation), enslaved people's labor proved critical to domestic, business, and social functions, even as challenges to slavery were formative for some Detroiters' identity as Americans. A particular kind of society with slaves in early America, Detroit was a remarkable place where a northwestern frontier environment led to flexibility and creativity, even as the town's location along a liquid international border made it more porous than many other slaveholding spaces. As a region where indigenous enslavement was a long and continuous practice, Detroit produced an unusual cross-section of African American and Native American experiences of slavery, revealing slavery's adaptability to various natural and cultural environments and the interwoven processes of black and red racialization.[22] At the same time, the trajectory of the narrative in these pages—from French colonial enslavement of mostly indigenous people to the life of a free black woman on the eve of the Civil War—suggests that even while Native slavery was always more prevalent in Detroit, black slavery emerged as more prominent in the documentary record. As black freedpeople like Lisette Denison made their way in the nineteenth-century city, and as free Native Americans such as members of the Saginaw Chippewa Tribe at Mt. Pleasant (in mid-Michigan) and members of the Ottawa Grand Traverse Bay and Little Traverse Bay Bands (in northern Michigan) fought to maintain their tribal identities and reservations, those indigenous people who were held as slaves faded from historical records but continued to live and "make generations," hidden in "plain view," in and around the City of the Straits.[23]

The Bouquet of Roses

Along the central riverfront, the footprint of colonial Detroit is snug as a vintage pin cushion. Here, where silver spires pierce the powder blue of sky, shiny high-rise office buildings reflecting the cool shades of water, it is difficult to imagine a prior world of French shingled homes and fruit orchards, of canoes and bateaux plying the waters, of Red Coats marching down the roads, of human slavery and beaver frenzy. But these are the same streets, now paved and more densely populated, where an enslaved indigenous woman was forced to give birth in a prison cell, where an enslaved black woman joined with an indentured white man to rob her master's storehouse, where the black family owned by a local merchant mourned the death of a father at sea, where Peter and Hannah Denison were purchased and later fought in the courts for their children's freedom. These striking individuals and their stories have long been erased from the collective consciousness of the city. The physical markers of colonial Detroit, which might have aided in memory, have all but faded from the surface of the landscape. The Macomb farm has disappeared. The home of the Brushes is gone now, too, with only a sign for Brush Street and the square of Brush Park keeping silent vigil. The earliest surviving home in the city, built for Charles Trowbridge and his bride, Catherine Sibley, only dates back to 1826.[24] Lisette Denison would have visited there, as Catherine was the same Sibley daughter who missed Lisette's cookies while off at school in New York, and Charles Trowbridge helped to steward Lisette's papers late in her life. But Lisette's own house in Detroit has now vanished. In its place stands an empty lot, forlorn and riddled with glass shards.

There is currently no historical marker acknowledging slavery in Detroit—revealing that people were bought, sold, and held as property there. And yet, for more than a century spanning French, British, and American rule, Detroit was a place that saw unconscionable bondage, elicited inventive bids for freedom, and shaped lives not devoid of heroism. Where the human-made buildings and memorial plaques have long gone or never existed, the river that first called to Native hunters and French adventurers remains. The waters still flow between the lakes, narrowing at the earthen bend where Detroit City rises into the clear and open atmosphere. The strait stood as witness to all that transpired in this place. We can rely on that river now as a road to history, even as residents in the past rowed across it to survive.

These were the thoughts ice-skating across my mind as I toured Detroit with my friend and colleague, the legal historian Martha Jones, and other scholars invited by Martha to take her informal but much lauded tour of the city in the winter of 2013. It was a frigid day, snow packed and dazzling white, with sun rays gleaming off the blanketed sidewalks and skyscrapers. As I thought these wandering thoughts about rivers and histories, I walked across Hart Plaza to the windy riverbank, where a riveting sculpture now stands in bronze and granite. Built in 2011 for the occasion of Detroit's three hundredth birthday, the International Underground Railroad Memorial, sculpted by Ed Dwight, has a sister sculpture across the river in Windsor, Ontario. Each work of art represents a cluster

Gateway to Freedom, International Underground Railroad Memorial, author photos.

of figures. On the Detroit side, African American freedom-seekers and underground activist George DeBaptiste gaze across the waterway to freedom; on the Windsor side, a family who has accomplished the crossing stares into each other's eyes and toward the heavens.[25] As I walked a slow circle around the Detroit monument, breaking from the tour group, I came across the statue of a woman at the side of the ensemble. She wore a scarf on a head tilted downward as if weary from the journey that had brought her this far; she grasped a small boy lovingly about the shoulders, and from her hand dangled a sculpted basket woven of bronze. The artist had shaped the basket as an empty vessel, perhaps symbolic of want and need, but on this day the bronze container overflowed. A stranger, another admirer of this moving, metal piece, had left behind a dried bouquet of red and white roses. Already touched by the artwork itself, the faces and forms of those silent figures, I was affected upon seeing the petals, gleaming blush and glowing pearl in a coating of snow and winter sunlight. Some visitor to the city or, more likely, a resident, had left a bouquet for a monument. Those roses transformed the sculpture into beautiful still life: Freedom-Seekers with Flowers. I imagined this bouquet was a gift not only for those we remember—the thousands who crossed this river in the celebrated Underground Railroad—but also for those we forget, the hundreds who were enslaved right here, on the streets of old Detroit, and the countless unseen victims of human trafficking at the border today. The disjuncture and even discomfort of the fact of slavery in this place made the gesture of the roses all the more magical. Human connection blooms in the toughest of circumstances. Communities persevere. Resilience triumphs over ruin. In this way, as in many others, Detroit is signpost, symbol, and story—for its denizens, a region, a nation, a world.

A Note on Historical Conversations and Concepts

Every project has more than a single origin story. This one has several, all shaped by a number of influences stemming from my experience as a resident of Michigan and professor at the University of Michigan in Ann Arbor for nearly fifteen years. Teaching a capstone senior seminar for the Department of Afroamerican and African Studies on representations of slavery that included an Underground Railroad tour presented by the African American Cultural and Historical Museum of Washtenaw County led me to discover, along with my students, the rich local history of southeastern Michigan abolitionism. It was delving further into this local history in an investigation of Adrian, Michigan, abolitionist Laura Smith Haviland that led me to review Michigan's 1855 personal liberty law. This protection for Michigan residents who were runaways from the slave states undermined the national Fugitive Slave Act of 1850. Reading it set me on a quest to find earlier laws, opening my eyes to loopholes in the Northwest Ordinance that left legal room for slavery and indentured servitude to exist in Michigan. Intrigued and also disappointed by this latter fact that was at odds with my own ideas about the state, I wanted to pursue the subject focusing on Detroit, where Michigan's practice of slavery was the most concentrated. Serendipitously, an interdisciplinary group of faculty members and graduate students at the University of Michigan began meeting to jointly explore the notion of introducing a new field of scholarly enquiry called the Detroit School of Urban Studies, in line with the Chicago and LA schools coined in previous decades. Our Department of Afroamerican and African Studies was centrally involved in this activity along with faculty in Social Work, Sociology, Urban Planning, and the Residential College, so I sat in on these discussions with urban planners, sociologists of the city, and twentieth-century urban historians, which heightened and sharpened my interest in Detroit. Although my peers were discussing postindustrial society, food deserts, green spaces, mass incarceration, and the pitfalls of gentrification, I could see links between this modern (and postmodern) Detroit and the Detroit of the colonial and early American eras when slavery was practiced. I began to visit Detroit museums and historic sites in southeastern Michigan to try to feel the outlines of a story I might tell even as my imagination was captured by a quotation by a colleague involved in the Detroit School discussions, the historian Charles Bright, who had written the following about Detroit history in an article in the *Journal of American History*:

> The dominant historical discourse [on Detroit] is one of rise and fall, spiked by an immense nostalgia for the city that once (briefly) was. The recent past is often deployed as a cautionary tale about what goes wrong with urban spaces when racism, white flight, and industrial evacuation undercut a city's viability. Such a historical construction places Detroit in a past that is now lost and irretrievable and leaves current residents . . . dangling at the end of history with little hope and no agency.[1]

Bright's passage prompted a number of questions for me. Was Detroit's history really lost and irretrievable? What did it mean to be "dangling at the end of history"? And what kind of historical evidence or narrative would provide the impetus for those dangling on the end to pull themselves back up, into a fuller knowledge of history, community, place, and power relations? It so happened that my considering of these questions coincided temporally with the War of 1812 bicentennial and the Civil War sesquicentennial. There were a number of related events taking place in the Detroit area, and what I observed at the ones I attended indicated to me that the historical thread about slavery and Detroit that the public wanted to hold on to was a story of Detroit's role in the Underground Railroad. I sat in on sessions in which speakers extolled the bravery of their UGRR conductor ancestors and freedom-seeker ancestors, and sessions in which performers dramatically reenacted the feats of locally famous Michigan abolitionists. I also visited a new exhibit unveiled at the Detroit Historical Museum that celebrated the valiant organizers of the Detroit Underground and proclaimed the Northwest Territory to be a free space dating back to its founding in 1787. All of this interest in local history was exciting and even contagious, but there was something missing. Detroit was not only a place that fostered freedom bids as part of the Underground Railroad; it was also a place that fostered slavery throughout the second half of its colonial history and well into the American period. I wanted, then, to explore and share the stories of those who were enslaved in Detroit and to trace the form of slavery that took shape in a northern interior locale with a significant Native American presence. I wanted to understand how slavery and race intersected in early Detroit, how conditions of bondage and the extraction of unpaid labor intersected with gender roles and women's experiences, how enslaved people undermined their condition of unfreedom, and whether remnants of Detroit's history of slavery still existed in the city's landscape.

After beginning research on this project in the spring of 2011, I was stunned to learn just how few scholarly works had been written on the subject of slavery in Detroit. The sum total of dedicated secondary source materials that I uncovered with the help of my talented student research assistants consisted of a 1938 master's thesis completed by Therese Kneip at the University of Detroit, a 1970 article titled "Black Slavery in Michigan" published by David Katzman in the journal *American Studies*, a chapter on "Black Slavery in Detroit" by Jorge Castellanos in the 1981 edited book *Detroit Perspectives*, and an article titled "The Fluid Frontier" published by Afua Cooper in the *Canadian Review of American Studies* in 2000. Cooper's work in particular emphasized the importance of both natural and political borders along the Detroit River and put forward the notion of "the border as a significant unit of analysis" for Canadian-American transnational black history. "One discovers," Cooper asserted about the border, "that Blacks who lived at its edges consciously manipulated it in their 'search for place.'" Cooper's insights about the material and metaphorical role of the border have influenced multiple studies, including my own. But in the year 2000, Afua Cooper's approach was rare; few other works were picking up on the important themes and questions she presented, especially on the U.S. side of the border.[2]

More than a decade later, in 2012, Detroit journalist Bill McGraw released a well-researched newspaper story provocatively titled "Slavery Is Detroit's Big, Bad Secret." I had begun my research just a year earlier and wondered if McGraw had been drawn toward this topic, as I had been, by the groundswell of local talk about the Underground Railroad in Detroit's history during public events marking anniversaries of the Civil War and the War of 1812. Two of these gatherings took place at the Detroit Historical Museum and were the result of a long-term collaboration between scholars based at the museum and at Wayne State University. The historians Denver Brunsman and Joel Stone were central to these endeavors and published edited books in 2009 and 2012 featuring the work of graduate students and linked to museum-based symposia. These detailed edited collections on Detroit during the Revolutionary Era and War of 1812 years touched on the dynamics of slavery and contributed to the small body of existing literature. In addition, David Lee Poremba's scrupulously annotated chronology of Detroit completed for the city's tercentennial in 2001 includes a wealth of detail about key events that contributes to the reconstruction of the context in which slavery unfolded.[3] In fact, the three hundredth anniversary of the city's founding was an important moment that inspired the production of a wider range of Detroit histories and chronicles than had been published since the early and mid-1900s; most of these anniversary works were geared toward popular audiences and fostered an energetic local public awareness of Detroit's long and fascinating history.

During the early stages of my research, I found, as well, that scholarship on African American history in Detroit during the colonial and early national periods was nearly as slim as the literature on slavery in the city. A University of Michigan doctoral dissertation and later articles by Norman McRae on "Blacks in Detroit" (1982), as well as books by David Katzman (1975) and Reginald Larrie (1981), included chapters on the pre-nineteenth-century era of black history in the city. Isabella Swan and Mark McPherson, both local Michigan historians, had written brief (in the case of Swan) and exploratory (in the case of McPherson) biographies of Elizabeth Denison Forth that were essential to this subject matter; both included crucial primary source transcriptions at the end of their books. But overall, as the colonial historian Christian Crouch has concurred in her nuanced papers on Detroit as "the Black City," it was as though blacks were imagined as having just appeared on the Detroit scene during the Great Migration of African Americans from the South and were associated only with Motor City manufacturing, the Motown musical sound, and mid-twentieth-century peaks of social unrest, otherwise known as the riots of 1943 and 1967.[4] While I was in the midst of developing this project, a pivotal edited collection, years in the making, was released by Wayne State University Press. That book, *A Fluid Frontier*, edited by Canadian historian Karolyn Smardz Frost and American literary scholar Veta Smith Tucker, focused on the valiant history of the Underground Railroad in Detroit but also wrestled with the unpleasant fact of slaveholding in the Detroit River region, particularly in the introduction and a chapter focused on the Denison family. In 2011, the Canadian historian Gregory Wigmore published his article "Before the Railroad: From Slavery to Freedom in the Canadian-American Borderland" in a *Journal of American History* special issue on borderlands. A significant piece heralding and indeed modeling a broader discussion that recognizes the northern border as equal in historical importance and social texture as the southern border (with Mexico), Wigmore's work, like earlier publications by McRae and Cooper, emphasized the role of the Detroit River as a permeable border that enslaved people crossed in dual directions. Wigmore skillfully used the theme of river traffic to indicate a pre-history of slave escapes "before the [underground] railroad" as well as a broader context of international political machinations. There is, perhaps, a subtle sticking point between historians such as Wigmore and interdisciplinary scholars such as Veta Tucker over how to carbon-date the activities of the Underground Railroad. Tucker suggests in her opening chapter to *A Fluid Frontier* that every escape in the region can be counted within Underground Railroad history, while Wigmore sets up a strict before-after structure in the language of his piece.[5] It should be noted that the National Park Service's essential and admirable Network to Freedom program also takes a liberal view when determining what to count within the Underground Railroad framework and when to start counting. The historian Manisha Sinha, in her recent sweeping interracial study of the transnational abolition movement, asserts that the history of abolition begins when the first person resisted slavery. This argument is resoundingly convincing; however, the history of abolition (the multifaceted struggle to end enslavement across the Atlantic world) and the history of the Underground Railroad or Railway (organized networks of activists committed to aiding enslaved people's passage to freedom in the United States and Canada) do not fully overlap. On this question, I lean toward the view implicitly advanced by scholars Eric Foner and Stephen Kantrowitz, who describe the concerted organization of antislavery networks as a marker of the formation of the movement in the late 1820s and 1830s. It is relevant, though, as well as revealing for Underground Railroad scholarship, that research on Detroit indicates the existence of such networks in the very early 1800s in references to connected individuals who encouraged escapes as well as to the presence of Negro Town as a base camp for resisters.[6]

Alongside the small but now steadily growing number of publications on slavery and early black history in Detroit, there have been several dissertations, manuscripts in progress, and new books produced by a generation of historical thinkers who are exposing the economic importance, political ambiguity, and cultural complexity of Detroit as a place situated betwixt and between colonial France and Great Britain, Great Britain and the United States, and multiple indigenous nations. In 2001, map historian and curator Brian Leigh Dunnigan released an extensive cartographical study, *Frontier Metropolis,* which reproduced and contextualized maps and images to reconstruct the city's past and serves as a major reference guide for current studies. Dunnigan's interpretation emphasized the international and urban character of this remote frontier settlement across one and a half centuries. Catherine Cangany's *Frontier Seaport* (2014), in implicit conversation with Dunnigan's interpretive graphic collection, emphasizes Detroit's port town character. Cangany's is the first in a series of full-length New Detroit History monographs that seek to move historical literature on the city beyond the scholarship of early twentieth-century antiquarian historians and political historians such as Silas Farmer and Clarence Burton, whose chief interests were in collecting data about the city in order to champion its progress in a rising industrial age.[7] Cangany brings an enlightening Atlantic studies perspective to her analysis of early American Detroit, which she describes as a maritime trading town with economic and cultural ties to urban centers on the East Coast as well as in Europe. Cangany's focus on economic exchange and local politics leads her to notice the presence of enslaved people. Forthcoming histories by Karen Marrero, Andrew Sturtevant, and Kyle Mays will frame Detroit as an explicitly indigenous location where Native American and mixed-race Indian people lived in a nuanced set of relations with European and American settlers and, to a certain extent, African Americans. What I hope this book, *The Dawn of Detroit*, adds to the mix is an explicit and concentrated focus on enslaved people's lives that necessitates seeing African American and Native American history in Detroit as interrelated rather than separate streams of experience.

My work joins with all of these aforementioned texts, and surely others, in the collaborative intellectual project of picturing early Detroit in a way that draws on the conceptual revelations of ethnic studies, women's and gender studies, and studies of the Atlantic world, the movement of trade and capital, and the intermingling of cultures. Somehow, as the reading public has internalized narratives about American national and regional pasts, we have forgotten that Detroit is ancient, that Detroit is indigenous, and that Detroit has a long-standing black presence. We have misplaced the knowledge that most of the Midwest was French, and we attribute anything fascinating in Francophone-American history to New Orleans, or maybe to St. Louis. We have never deeply considered the impact of the reality that slavery existed even in the Midwest and, as Afua Cooper so boldly stated it nearly two decades ago, in Canada where a "mythology" of a black "haven" holds sway.[8] Scholars, while aware of these nuances, have only begun to probe them and to actively present them for public consideration. In our current transnational world where all entrenched human dilemmas are simultaneously local and global, a renewal of studies of Detroit and the U.S.-Canadian borderlands helps return us to a sense of the critical importance of the Great Lakes region to North American histories of extractive and settler colonialism, slavery, racial formation, cultural complexity, and the refusal of subjugated peoples to readily submit to domination.[9]

Remembering the Black Militia

In the small number of studies that assess slavery in Detroit, or early black history in the city, the story of the black militia often rises to the fore. This book has been no exception, for that saga holds within it an explanatory power that captures the unstable racial dynamics produced by Detroit's borderland character. Today Detroit's black militia is commemorated on a plaque in the Detroit Historical Museum that details the biography of its leader, Peter Denison, as well as in literature produced by Ranger Shawna Mazur of the River Raisin National Battlefield in Monroe (the present-day location of French Town) and through historical reenactment at the Battlefield.[10] These are necessary and enlightening interventions into local histories and memories that all too often overlook African American contributions to the state's early past. But even as we remember the historic occurrence of black men forming and leading an American military unit at the dawn of the nineteenth century, we must take care to recall and question the reasons why this special unit was authorized by Michigan authorities in the first place. William Hull imagined the black militia as a defensive force, positioned to fight primarily against Native Americans on whose lands Michigan Territory was located. Black men's seeming willingness to protect the United States raised their esteem in the view of some territorial officials and potentially set them at odds with indigenous people.

In addition to coming away with a lopsided interpretation that valorizes black agency and leaves in place a notion of Native Americans as enemies of the state, it is easy to part historical tracks at this juncture of the story of the black militia, to see Native American history moving in one direction that positions Indian people outside the United States, while seeing African American history moving in an opposing direction that positions black people as (co-opted) insiders. But the picture of what life looked like in early Detroit—what survival for subjugated groups looked like—was never so clearly divided along these kinds of racial lines. People of indigenous and African descent were enslaved both in that town and along each bank of the river. They ran away together, as in the case of Jenney (a mixed-race black woman) and Joseph Quinn (a young Native man) in 1807. They formed families together, as in the case of Abraham and Marie Louise Ford, an enslaved black man and his free Ojibwe-French wife, whose daughter was born in the midst of war in 1813. African Americans and Native Americans may even have been members of the black militia together, given the nature of slavery in the region, the tendency for Afro-Native people to be defined as "negro" in historical records, and the unit's makeup of runaway slaves from Canada. Of course, in addition to forming close connections, Native Americans and African Americans also faced off, across domestic spaces in which one was the owner, the other owned, and across lines of battle in the Revolutionary War and War of 1812. One thing these populations always shared with one another, as well as with settlers of the young American nation that sought but failed to define as well as confine them, was a fierce love of the dignity and autonomy embedded in the principle of freedom.

Borderlands and Frontiers

I have never quite imagined myself as a borderlands scholar, but as a place that birthed surprising events shaped by its location on multiple lines of differentiation and difference, Detroit compels its students to think in these expansive interpretive terms. In framing the parameters of this book in the introduction, I describe Detroit as a "frontier-borderland" environment. With the use of this language, I am calling on at least two streams of historical study: Native American histories of the Great Lakes and Middle West and African American histories of slavery. Histories of the Great Lakes, particularly those that focus on Native people in the region, engage with the notion of borderlands as spaces of cultural encounter.[11] The classic example of this scholarship is Richard White's *The Middle Ground: Indians, Empires, and Republics in the Great Lakes Region,* which captured the multilayered complexities of cross-cultural accommodation. White's concept of a "middle ground," defined as a "place in between: in between cultures, peoples, and in between empires and the nonstate world of villages," was an arena where indigenous peoples and Europeans encountered and negotiated with one another by necessity.[12] He argued that a social and political middle ground, a "mutually intelligible world," formed through a series of misunderstandings between Indians and Europeans who were struggling to compromise through the end of the War of 1812. White's interpretation of inter-group dynamics in the Great Lakes influenced numerous studies to follow, some of which critiqued his argument, all of which built on his work.[13] While I appreciate White's concept, I am inspired by the notion of "the Coast of the

Strait" (described in the introduction of this book) to perceive these social relations differently.

Rather than seeing a *ground* that various historical actors traversed to eventually meet in the middle in a place like Detroit, a metaphor that suggests terra firma beneath all of the historical actors' feet, I imagine Detroiters moving across more than one type of surface as they warily encountered one another: water as well as land. If free Europeans can be said to occupy one kind of cultural ground, and free Native Americans can be said to occupy an alternative kind of cultural ground, where do we place people who fit into neither of these categories? Where do we locate the enslaved? I will suggest that the unfree occupy a precarious position more akin to a shoreline, with one foot on water, the other on land. Located on an unpredictable metaphorical coast where the water and land converged, enslaved people encountered free people of various ethnic backgrounds from a differential position of insecurity. Instead of the "middle ground," a Midwestern landscape peopled by those who were free, we can imagine a coastline dominating early Detroit. This coast was a waterscape in the Great Lakes interior where enslaved people—Native Americans as well as Afro-Americans—strove to negotiate from a groundless position of material and legal instability.[14]

I suppose I differ from many other historians of Native America in the social groups that I hold in view as I scan the Midwestern terrain. I want to insist on the visibility of an overlooked world—a black and indigenous world of bondspeople—shaped by their daily strategies of survival as well as the cultural heritages of their various homelands. This world of the unfree that surely formed in servant's quarters of merchant homes, in farm fields and fur trade shops, on riverbanks and riverboats, was not devised strictly along the lines of race, clan, or tribe; it was a shared social space of the struggling subjugated.[15] With great care, colonial and early Americanists who study the Midwest are beginning to map this world. Jennifer Stinson offers a moving and analytically penetrating study of lead mining districts in Wisconsin and Illinois in the 1820s and 1830s that connects black slavery with Native land dispossession and an expanding culture of white masculinity and gentility that was supported by both. Christian Crouch is tracing the history of black Detroit through successive imperial regimes and analyzing black men's adaptations of indigenous terrain and strategies in the Midwest and Northeast. And in his forthcoming second study of indigenous peoples in the Great Lakes, Michael Witgen is endeavoring to formulate a capacious and exacting theoretical frame that historicizes the racialization of Indians in the age of U.S. expansion and interprets what he calls the "political economy of plunder" that links black and Native trajectories.[16]

In addition to charting complex cultural and political relations between European colonies and indigenous communities, historians of Native America have wrestled with connotations of the term "frontier," rightly contesting the customary meaning of the word derived from historian Frederick Jackson Turner's 1894 thesis of westward expansion.[17] In Turner's work and in American culture more generally, the word "frontier" has long suggested a line of difference between advancing white "civilization" and Native American "savagery," where cross-cultural confrontation ultimately gives way to the perfection of the American character and expansion of the colonial enterprise captured by the idea of "manifest destiny." However, in studies of the history of slavery, particularly work by Ira Berlin, frontier locations have been described as places on the edge of slavery's westward movement.[18] These are locations where populations were relatively sparse, where lands were not fully settled by whites, and where practices of plantation slavery had not yet been systematized and fixed into social and legal practice. As legal historian Lea VanderVelde has so clearly described it: "Frontier slaves were sought for the needs of westward expansion," as "lands were available for settlement in great supply, but labor could not be hired." Because of the need for slave-owners to rely on their bondspeople differently in these rugged locations, frontier environments often left greater room for slaves to negotiate their relationships with masters. The frontier farm in 1820s Missouri, for instance, is a spot where one might expect to see an enslaved man clearing a field alongside his owner. Detroit was just such a place, and hence I have retained the language of "frontier" throughout this book, though with a degree of restraint.[19]

Some historians of Native America and the West also see a utility in the use of the contested term "frontier." William Cronon employs this word sparingly in his environmental history of Chicago because of its ability to convey a macro-level historical relationship between cities and rural areas understood as frontiers in the nineteenth century.[20] In his article on ethnic mixing in the Missouri River region titled "More Motley Than Mackinaw," John Mack Faragher employs the notions of "frontiers of inclusion" and "frontiers of exclusion."[21] He argues that prior to the surge in Anglo-American population numbers and prior to Missouri statehood in 1821, French and Native American residents lived and worked together there, cooperating across lines of difference. With an increased American presence came greater racial differentiation and less political support for Indian land claims. Faragher sees the texture of frontier relations as shifting over time and degrading with an increased Anglo-American influence. While Faragher's emphasis is on change over time, I see an application for his analysis across time as well as across social spaces in the locale of Detroit. Similarly to what transpired in Missouri, free Native people saw their standing in Detroit decline with the diminishment of French power and the imposition of British and then American authority. For free indigenous people, Detroit moved from being something like a "frontier of inclusion" in the French period to becoming a "frontier of exclusion" in the British and American periods. But at the same time, there were always frontiers of inclusion and exclusion operating simultaneously in Detroit. While free Indians were included in French community and social life in noteworthy ways, unfree Indians—Native bondspeople—were excluded. The notion of frontiers of inclusion and exclusion, when viewed in place as well as across time, helps to illuminate social relations in Detroit in a way that keeps the presence of enslaved people of color visible.

Seeing early Detroit through a lens that includes Native Americans and African Americans within the same frame, together with their Euro-American captors and, at times, collaborators, highlights a related set of open and difficult questions that scholars are beginning to fruitfully engage. How can we further explore and understand the attitudes and activities of Native American slaveholders in the North? Did they have practices in common with familiar groups (Cherokees, Choctaws, Chickasaws, Creeks, Seminoles) that are categorized as the slaveholding tribes of the Southeast and Indian Territory? How did varieties of indigenous political organization in the eighteenth and nineteenth centuries shape slave trading and slaveholding practices in the North as compared to the

South, in the woodlands as compared to the plains, and so on? How did earlier patterns of indigenous captive taking and slave labor usage (for instance, in the Fort Ancient and Mississippian archaeological periods and into the sixteenth and seventeenth centuries) affect later practices of slavery in Native communities? What do we do with the knowledge that so many Native women were first held captive by indigenous peoples in the Great Lakes? How do issues of gender, enslavement, and the racialization of Indians as "Panis" complicate notions of indigenous alliance, negotiation, and as it has lately been termed, "mastery" in interior Great Lakes areas where indigenous groups retained staying power well into the late nineteenth century? Does the language of "mastery" (meant to indicate prowess in imperial dynamics in a way that restores Native groups to a place of rightful recognition in international affairs) take on different connotations when we recognize that some of these "masters" actually possessed human beings as slaves?[22]

And in what might be deemed a flip side of the tarnished coin of colonial influences, we must continue to ask the critical question of how we should understand the role of people of African descent within analyses of colonialism in Native American studies and African diaspora studies. Should black people be considered "settlers," a rhetorical move that groups them together with the Europeans who sometimes enslaved them but that also recognizes how black communities do indeed benefit from the dispossession of indigenous lands? The U.S. slavery historian Max Grivno offers a sharp take on this question, noting that in the "Northwest Frontier," blacks found a "liberating potential" due to a number of factors, including a diverse population, slavery's "unimportant role" in local economies, legal challenges to slavery like the Northwest Ordinance, and a high need for labor that increased laborers' bargaining potential. In this context, Grivno argues, "the frontiers' free black[s] and slaves were often most comfortable with white settlers, with whom they shared a language and a similar cultural heritage." While my study of enslaved people in Detroit has led me to see this site in a contrasting way that leans toward commonalities between blacks and Native Americans, I would not deny the fitness of Grivno's argument, especially in places farther west, such as Minnesota, where Euro-American labor and social systems developed later than in Detroit. Canadian indigenous studies scholars

Zainab Amadahy and Bonita Lawrence have wrestled with the question of black settlement in material as well as ethical terms, landing uncomfortably on a notion of "ambiguous settlers" to account for black people's "desperate need to survive after slavery" while acknowledging that black writers on both sides of the border often fail to acknowledge Native land loss. "Black struggles for freedom," the co-authors assert, "have required (and continue to require) ongoing colonization of Indigenous land." In the United States, Native American studies scholars are also starting to think through the ways in which African American relationships to settler colonialism were similar to or distinct from those of Euro-Americans. Jodi Byrd, a Chickasaw literary scholar and colonial studies theorist who has acknowledged her own tribal nation's role in holding black bondspeople, determined that a separate word, "arrivants," is needed to capture the difference between black dwellers and white "settlers" on Native lands.[23] In the domain of western history, public historian Crystal Alegria and Métis/Cree/Ojibwe doctoral student Jill Mackin are working with the term "refugee" in their development of a narrative that describes the experience of Lizzie Williams, a black woman who moved from Kentucky to Montana out of "desperation" following the Civil War. They seized on this language in rejection of the more common term "pioneer" and in the understanding that "refugee" conveys: "one that flees; *especially*: a person who flees to a foreign country or power to escape danger or persecution."[24]

The aspirational language of "ambiguous settlers," "arrivants," and "refugees" strives for a fair and sensitive means of articulating the compromises and complicities of various populations in a painful past. But, as Amadahy and Lawrence suggest, there is perhaps one space in the American-Canadian borderlands in which a radical alterity to colonial and racialized complicity existed: Native communities that accepted blacks via the Underground Railway (or "Railroad" in U.S. parlance). Putting forward Tuscarora "guides" as their primary example (but alas, offering no citation), Amadahy and Lawrence point to those who "risked their lives at a time when Indigenous people could have been enslaved, killed, or dispossessed of their land for helping runaways."[25]

And so it seems we have come full circle. I took up this book project in part because I saw the public commemorations of Underground Railroad history in Detroit as too simplistic and celebratory, as too evacuative of an earlier and more ornery past complicit with racial slavery, but I also concede at this parting moment that the Underground Railroad motif does have the potential to do productive cultural work. The cognitive leap required to see that any operations of the famed Underground Railroad had to take place on current or former indigenous lands compels a respect for first peoples, their land holdings, and their political systems, even within a framework of feel-good popular mythology that obscures the wrongs of the United States, Canada, and the citizens of these nations. If scholars and writers can commit to the serious archival and intellectual project that must accompany such a leap, we can perhaps make progress in urging the publics of which we are part to challenge the intersecting systems and ongoing imprints of slavery and colonialism. The Great Lakes, as the historian Heidi Bohaker has so beautifully put it, was a place of "spiritually charged waterscapes," for humans as well as other-than-human beings. Perhaps here, in this ancient land of glassy waters, anything was, and still is, possible.[26]

Acknowledgments

I could not have taken up this book project, or completed it within the span of six years, without the wonderful collaboration and assistance of many giving people. Tayana Hardin, once a graduate student in American culture and now a professor in her own right, began work on this project as my first research assistant in the spring of 2012. I then applied to a campus program that funds undergraduate work-study students to conduct research with faculty members, invited graduate students in history and American culture to participate, and formed a small research team on slavery in Detroit. Our group of seven worked over a two-year period to find, transcribe, interpret, and present primary sources. The members of this team, Michelle Cassidy, Emily Macgillivray, Paul Rodriguez, Sarah Khan, Kaisha Brezina, and Alexandra Passarelli, were indispensable to the project and a joy to work with. We created a website to share our findings (mappingdetroitslavery.com). I am grateful to our web designer, Ariela Steif, and to the generous scholars who read our website draft and made suggestions for improvement: Veta Tucker, Greg Wigmore, Brian Dunnigan, and Lucy Murphy. An additional bounty of thanks goes to Michelle Cassidy, who designed the website map and worked closely with the French records to translate church register entries and create tallies and graphs, to Michelle's husband, Alex Sin, for assisting her with the charts, and to Michelle and Emily Macgillivray, both, who aided me with this project with patience and prime research as well as translation skills for more than three years.

My brilliant colleagues at UM helped (and saved!) me at every turn, particularly Michael Witgen, who read three chapters of the manuscript; Brian Dunnigan, who shared his wealth of knowledge about Detroit history and images at various stages of the work and helped me fine tune military references; Greg Dowd, who offered clarifying, corrective, and encouraging feedback; and Martha Jones, my dear friend and toughest reader, who pushed me on the legal aspects of this history. Other generous readers whose feedback greatly improved the manuscript include

Michael McDonnell, Jennifer Stinson, and my dear friend Paulina Alberto. Terry McDonald, director of the Bentley Library at UM, shared valuable sources and responded to the links between university history and slavery with absolute openness and a desire to document the facts. As former dean of the College of Liberal Arts & Sciences, Terry was one of the first to encourage me to forge ahead with my book on Michigan history, a subject beyond my past regional focus on the South. I benefited from hearing reactions to and feedback on this work in talks at Indiana University, the University of Minnesota, Pomona College, Harvard University, Northwestern University, the University of Chicago, the University of Cincinnati, Yale University, Johns Hopkins University, Stanford University, and the University of British Columbia. Scholars in the organization Historians Against Slavery helped me to connect past and present in my thinking. Many other people supported me through their input, interest, administrative expertise, inspiration, or quiet encouragement. They include: Stephen Ward, Beth James, Angela Dillard, Karen Marrero, Rebecca Scott, Jay Gitlin, David Blight, Walter Johnson, Christina Snyder, Jodi Byrd, Sherene Razack, Scott Morgensen, Kel Keller, Bill Hart, John Steckley, Andrew Sturtevant, Rachel Whitehead, Phil Deloria, Kristin Hass, Shawna Mazur, Roy Finkenbine, Carol Mull, Del Moyer, Robert Olender, Darryl Li, François Furstenberg, Angus Burgin, Philip Morgan, Liz Thornberry, Father Daniel Trapp, Mark Bodwen and the Burton Historical Collection staff, Lisa Brooks, Christine DeLucia, David Glassberg, Ned Blackhawk, Heather Thompson, Tim LeCain, Brett Walker, Mary Murphy, Susan Kollin, Lucy Murphy, Margaret Jacobs, Christopher Phillips, Nathan Marvin, Emily Albarillo, Wayne High, Judy Gray, Keaten North, Tammy Zill, Mark Simpson-Vos, Eric Crahan, Jesse Hoffnung-Garskof, David Roediger, Patricia Montemurri, Pat Majher, Krista Ewbank and Kate Sullivan of Saint James Chapel, Melba Boyd, Katie Barkel and Brian Short of LSA Communications, Rowena McClinton, Carl Ekberg, Sharon Person, Margery Fee, my co-instructor, Joel Howell, and all of the talented graduate students in the Literature of U.S. History seminar (winter 2016), Deborah Meadows and Shirley Vaughn of the African American Cultural & Historical Museum of Washtenaw County, Kevin Walsh, Pete Kalinski and Thomas Reed of Digging Detroit, Stephanie Wichmann for French lessons (however poor my performance was!), and surely others whose names I may have regrettably omitted. Thank you to my dedicated agent, Deirdre Mullane, who supports my crazy array of projects and found a fitting home for this one. Thank you, as well, to my editor at The New Press, Marc Favreau, who saw the possibilities for a historical project like this to speak to our present pressing social and environmental issues. I am deeply grateful to the Mellon Foundation, which sponsored part of the writing of this book through a New Directions in the Humanities Fellowship, and to the Eisenberg Institute for Historical Studies at UM, which secured for me a teaching release to research the Michigan abolitionist Laura Smith Haviland, an investigation that eventually led to this book.

As always, my family draws me away from the page to live in this beautiful physical world and makes everything I accomplish possible. I am forever grateful to: Joseph, Nali Azure, Noa Alice, and Sylvan David Gone; Patricia Miles King; Erin, Erik, Benny, and Montroue Miles; James and Sean King; Sharon Juelfs; Rakale Collins-Quarells; Steve McCullom, Tyrone McCullom, and Deborah Banks Johnson; Vanessa, Melvin, Amanda, and Alexis Walker; Maryanna Gone DuBois; Stephanie and Baylee Rain Iron Shooter; and Joseph Azure. Thank you also to Luna for being the one by my desk-side at all odd hours.

Bibliographic Abbreviations and Quotations

Because there are three archives and collections that I used repeatedly in researching this book, I have abbreviated references to them in the chapter citations.

BHC: Burton Historical Collections, Detroit Public Library, Detroit, MI.

BHL: Bentley Historical Library, University of Michigan, Ann Arbor, MI.

MPHC: This abbreviation, standing for Michigan Pioneer and Historical Collections, is commonly used in Michigan histories to indicate a massive set of compiled primary materials originally published under the separate titles of: *Pioneer Collections* (1876–1886), *Historical Collections* (1886–1912), and *Michigan Historical Collections* (1915–1929).

Quotations in this book duplicate the original text of eighteenth- and nineteenth-century sources to the extent possible. This includes varied spellings for the same names or places and grammatical errors. I have tried to reduce usage of the indicator "[sic]" to denote an error in the original.

Notes

Introduction: The Coast of the Strait

1. For a history of the use of the racial term "red" by Native Americans as well as Europeans, see Nancy Shoemaker, "How Indians Got to Be Red," *American Historical Review* 102 (June 1997): 624–44.

2. Michael Witgen, *An Infinity of Nations: How the Native New World Shaped Modern North America* (Philadelphia: University of Pennsylvania Press, 2013), 11.

3. Bkejwanong as an Anishinaabe settlement: Michael A. McDonnell, *Masters of Empire: Great Lakes Indians and the Making of America* (New York: Hill and Wang, 2015), 47–48. The persistence of French culture: Jay Gitlin, *The Bourgeois Frontier: French Towns, French Traders, and American Expansion* (New Haven: Yale University Press, 2010), 1, 11, 155. Detroit as a Canadian dependency: William Renwick Riddell, *Michigan Under British Rule: Law and Law Courts, 1760–1796* (Lansing: Michigan Historical Society, 1926), 15. Wild-garlic place: William Cronon, *Nature's Metropolis: Chicago and the Great West* (New York: W. W. Norton, 1991), 23.

4. National Audubon Society, "Detroit River—Facts and Figures," http://web4.audubon.org/bird/iba/michigan/Press/DetroitRiverFactSheet.pdf. Accessed August 9, 2012. "Junction" quote: Jean-Claude Robert, "The St. Lawrence and Montreal's Spatial Development in the Seventeenth Through the Twentieth Century," in Stéphane Castonguay and Matthew Evenden, eds., *Urban Rivers: Remaking Rivers, Cities and Space in Europe and North America* (Pittsburgh: University of Pittsburgh Press, 2012), 147.

5. Jodi A. Byrd, *The Transit of Empire: Indigenous Critiques of Colonialism* (Minneapolis: University of Minnesota Press, 2011). For illuminating analyses of indigenous Americans in the Atlantic world and parallels as well as differences between a "black" and "red" Atlantic, see Jace Weaver, *The Red Atlantic: American Indigenes and the Making of the Modern World, 1000–1927* (Chapel Hill: University of North Carolina Press, 2014). For an astute articulation of the intimate and damaging ties between Europe, Africa, the Americas, and Asia, see Lisa Lowe, *The Intimacies of Four Continents* (Durham, NC: Duke University Press, 2015). Lowe defines intimacies in this book as the "braided" nature of slavery, colonialism, empire, and the rise of liberal ideology across these geographical spaces as well as the close contacts between people originating from the various continents, 38, 34.

6. Quoted in Brian Leigh Dunnigan, *Frontier Metropolis: Picturing Early Detroit, 1701–1838* (Detroit: Wayne State University Press, 2001), 13. René-Robert Cavalier La Salle was the first European explorer to sail the Great Lakes. Father

Hennepin accompanied La Salle on the 1679 voyage and recorded the earliest detailed description of Detroit. The ship was later lost and has yet to be uncovered. Dunnigan, *Frontier Metropolis,* 13. greatlakesexploration.org/expedition.htm. Accessed December 15, 2014.

7. Michelle Cassidy, Emily Macgillivray, and Tiya Miles, "Placing Indigenous Peoples in Early Detroit," in Linda Campbell, Andrew Newman, Sara Safranksy, and Timothy Stallmann, eds., *Detroit: A People's Atlas* (Detroit: Wayne State University Press, forthcoming). Ottawa presence: Gregory Evans Dowd, *War Under Heaven: Pontiac, the Indian Nations, and the British Empire* (Baltimore: Johns Hopkins University Press, 2002), 28. Location of Huron villages: Andrew Keith Sturtevant, "Jealous Neighbors: Rivalry and Alliance Among the Native Communities of Detroit, 1701–1766" (Ph.D. diss., William and Mary, 2011), 24. Detroit as native hunting ground: Karen L. Marrero, "Founding Families: Power and Authority of Mixed French and Native Lineages in Eighteenth Century Detroit" (Ph.D. diss., Yale, 2011), 134–37. Hurons and Wyandots: The development of the Wyandots as a western configuration of Huron people was an involved social and political process resulting from migration. Some Hurons (Hurons being one of the three branches of the Iroquoian Wendat people of the upper Great Lakes, including Hurons, Petuns, and Neutrals) migrated southwest in the mid-1600s in the aftermath of war with the Iroquois Confederacy. The Hurons who settled in northern Michigan near the straits of Mackinac in the 1670s and along the Detroit River in the early 1700s came to be called Wyandots in early U.S. treaties. These Wyandots also included some members of the Petun nation. John L. Steckley, *The Eighteenth-Century Wyandot: A Clan-Based Study* (Waterloo, Ontario: Wilfrid Laurier University Press, 2014), 22–25. "Coast of the Strait" as a translated Huron name for Detroit appears in Silas Farmer, *History of Detroit and Wayne County and Early Michigan: A Chronological Cyclopedia of the Past and Present* (1890; Detroit: Gale Research Company, 1969), 3. According to the Huron and Wyandot linguist John Steckley, the Huron word *Taochiarontkion* does translate into French as "La côte du détroit," and in English as "the coast of the strait." Another Huron word for Detroit, *Karontaen,* translates into English as "where a log lies." John Steckley, email exchange with Tiya Miles, November 17, 2016. Steckley cited the following reference for these early terms as recorded by the French: Pierre Potier, *Fifteenth Report of the Bureau of Archives for the Province of Ontario* (Toronto: C. W. James, 1920).

8. Richard Quinney, *Borderland: A Midwest Journal* (Madison: University of Wisconsin Press, 2000), xiii–xiv.

9. Gloria Anzaldúa, *Borderlands/La Frontera: The New Mestiza* (San Francisco: Aunt Lute Books, 1987), 3.

10. Edmund Morgan, "Slavery and Freedom: The American Paradox," *Journal of American History* 59 (June 1972): 5–29; Edmund Morgan, *American Slavery, American Freedom: The Ordeal of Colonial Virginia* (New York: W. W. Norton, 1975).

11. I have borrowed this phrasing from the African American history scholar

Robin Kelley. See Robin D. G. Kelley, *Freedom Dreams: The Black Radical Imagination* (Boston: Beacon Press, 2002).

12. Brian Leigh Dunnigan, "Charting the Shape of Early Detroit, 1701–1838," in June Manning Thomas and Henco Bekkering, eds., *Mapping Detroit: Land, Community, and Shaping a City* (Detroit: Wayne State University Press, 2015), 18.

13. Cadillac's dream quote: McDonnell, *Masters of Empire*, 70.

14. P. Nick Kardulias, "Negotiation and Incorporation on the Margins of World-Systems: Examples from Cyprus and North America," *Journal of World-Systems Research* 13:1 (2007): 55–82, 68, 70.

15. Anne F. Hyde, *Empires, Nations, and Families: A New History of the North American West, 1800–1860* (Lincoln: University of Nebraska Press, 2011), 19.

16. Richard White, *The Middle Ground: Indians, Empires, and Republics in the Great Lakes Region, 1650–1815* (New York: Cambridge University Press, 1991), 116; Claudio Saunt, *West of the Revolution: An Uncommon History of 1776* (New York: W. W. Norton, 2014), 145.

17. Meaghan O'Neill, "50 Surprising Fashion and Beauty Products Made From Oil That You Probably Use Everyday (Even If You're Green)," www.treehugger.com/style/50-surprising-fashion-and-beauty-products-made-from-oil-that-you-probably-use-everyday-even-if-youre-green.html. Accessed July 26, 2016. Petroleum Services Association of Canada, "Clothing," www.oilandgasinfo.ca/oil-gas-you/products/clothing. Accessed July 26, 2016.

18. Witgen, *Infinity of Nations*, 215–16, 267, 270.

19. Hyde, *Empires, Nations, and Families*, 19.

20. Christof Mauch and Thomas Zeller, "Rivers in History and Historiography: An Introduction," in Christof Mauch and Thomas Zeller, eds., *Rivers in History: Perspectives on Waterways in Europe and North America* (Pittsburgh: University of Pittsburgh Press, 2008), 5. "Inland navigation": J. Disturnell, ed., *Sailing on the Great Lakes and Rivers of America* (Philadelphia: J. Disturnell, 1874), iii.

21. Dunnigan, "Charting the Shape of Early Detroit," 21. The stream behind the settlement, called Savoy Creek, lies beneath the city streets now.

22. White, *Middle Ground*, 117.

23. To my knowledge, it has not been demonstrated through documentary evidence that slaves came to Detroit with Cadillac. Historian of Afro-Canada Afua Cooper asserts that they did without offering a primary source in Afua Cooper, *The Hanging of Angélique: The Untold Story of Canadian Slavery and the Burning of Old Montréal* (Athens: University of Georgia Press, 2007), 74. The presence of slaves in Detroit in 1701 is certainly possible and even likely, since they were already in New France at the time and had been since 1628; Cooper 70, 72, 75. In addition, as Cadillac sought to bring representatives of various subsets of a varied labor force along with him, it would have made sense for him to include slaves. Cadillac's contingent: Brian Leigh Dunnigan, *Frontier Metropolis: Picturing Early Detroit, 1701–1838* (Detroit: Wayne State University Press, 2001), 18–19.

24. Guillaume Teasdale, "The French of Orchard Country: Territory, Landscape, and Ethnicity in the Detroit River Region, 1680s–1810s" (Ph.D. diss., York University, 2010), 214–15.

25. French "northern style" architecture: Teasdale, "Orchard Country," 16–17.

26. F. Clever Bald, *Detroit's First American Decade: 1796 to 1805* (Ann Arbor: University of Michigan Press, 1948), 17, 25; Farmer, *History of Detroit*, 489.

27. Dunnigan, "Charting the Shape of Early Detroit," 22.

28. White, *Middle Ground*, 154–58.

29. The stories of enslaved people surface sporadically in merchant, church, and legal records. A primary figure is Peter Denison, a black man who, together with his wife, Hannah Denison, sued in a court of law for their children's freedom. While the Denison family is described in a number of sources, many other slaves in Detroit can only be traced through the scattered fragments of truncated lists and notations. This is especially and poignantly true for the scores of unfree Native American women labeled *"Panis"* in the records, a term derived in part from the name Pawnee, the horticultural and non-equestrian Missouri River Indians frequently taken in slave raids by Great Lakes indigenous peoples.

30. Benjamin Drew, *A North-Side View of Slavery: The Refugee: Or, The Narratives of Fugitive Slaves in Canada, Related by Themselves* (Boston: John P. Jewett and Company, 1856).

31. Christopher P. Lehman, *Slavery in the Upper Mississippi Valley, 1787–1865* (Jefferson, NC: McFarland & Company, 2011), 1–4, 26, 43, 45. Perhaps because slavery in Detroit and Michigan differed from slavery in other Northwest Territory states in focus, Michigan is often neglected in studies that address slavery in the Midwest. These studies tend to look most closely at the southern-leaning states of Indiana and Illinois as well as at Minnesota, perhaps because of the famous Supreme Court *Dred Scott* decision rendered about a man held in slavery at Ft. Snelling, Minnesota. For more on slavery in the Midwest, see Leslie Schwalm, *Emancipation's Diaspora: Race and Reconstruction in the Upper Midwest* (Chapel Hill, NC: University of North Carolina Press, 2009).

32. For cultural analyses of ideas, rhetoric, and imagery of ruin in Detroit, see Colin Dickey, *Ghostland: An American History in Haunted Places* (New York: Viking, 2016), 256–59; Dora Apel, *Beautiful Terrible Ruins: Detroit and the Anxiety of Decline* (New Brunswick, NJ: Rutgers University Press, 2015); Kavita Ilona Nayar, "Reclaiming a Fallen Empire: Myth and Memory in the Battle Over Detroit's Ruins," (M.A. thesis, Temple University, 2012).

33. Lea VanderVelde's specific description of slave labor on the fringes of westward expansion in St. Louis contributed to my development of a summary of slave labor in the different western location of Detroit; Lea VanderVelde, *Redemption Songs: Suing for Freedom before Dred Scott* (New York: Oxford University Press, 2014), 16. Likewise, Jennifer Stinson's emphasis on the dirty work done by slaves near the Mississippi River contributed to my sense of what a wet and muddy

location meant for the workloads of black women. Jennifer Kirsten Stinson, "Black Bondspeople, White Masters and Mistresses, and the Americanization of the Upper Mississippi River Valley Lead District," *Journal of Global Slavery* 1:2 (October 2016) (unpublished version, cited by permission).

34. VanderVelde, *Redemption Songs*, 12. For a discussion of the use of the term "frontier" in this book that situates the word within Native American historical studies and African American slavery studies, please see the historiographical essay following the conclusion.

35. In thinking about the unexpected nature of slavery in Detroit then and now, I have been influenced by my colleague Phil Deloria, whose book popularized the notion of "Indians in unexpected places" in Native American studies as well as American studies circles. See Philip J. Deloria, *Indians in Unexpected Places* (Lawrence: University Press of Kansas, 2006). The Michigan Human Trafficking Unit was formed in 2011. AG Human Trafficking Cases, State of Michigan Attorney General Bill Schuette, www.michigan.gov. Accessed December 10, 2014. For more on the approximately 1,200-plus cases of murdered and missing indigenous women in Canada that have taken place over a period of more than thirty years, see Jessica Murphy, "Canada Launches Inquiry into Murdered and Missing Indigenous Women," *The Guardian*, December 9, 2015. Audra Simpson, "The State Is a Man: Theresa Spence, Loretta Saunders and the Gendered Costs of Settler Sovereignty," *Theory & Event* (forthcoming: Spring 2017). Sherene H. Razack, "Gendered Racial Violence and Spacialized Justice: The Murder of Pamela George," *Canadian Journal of Law and Society* 15:2 (2000): 91–130. Lisa J. Ellwood, "MMIW: A Comprehensive Report," IndianCountryTodayMediaNetwork.com, February 2016. Accessed April 30, 2016. Toni L. Griffin and June Manning Thomas, "Epilogue: Detroit Future City," in June Manning Thomas and Henco Bekkering, eds., *Mapping Detroit: Land, Community, and Shaping a City* (Detroit: Wayne State University Press, 2015), 211, 213.

1: The Straits of Slavery (1760–1770)

1. Silas Farmer, *History of Detroit and Wayne County and Early Michigan: A Chronological Cyclopedia of the Past and Present* (1890; reprint, Detroit: Gale Research Company, 1969), 221; Brian Leigh Dunnigan, *Frontier Metropolis: Picturing Early Detroit, 1701–1838* (Detroit: Wayne State University Press, 2001), 24. David A. Armour and Keith R. Widder, *At the Crossroads: Michilimackinac During the American Revolution* (Mackinac Island, MI: Mackinac Island State Park Commission, 1978), 3. While Farmer measures the stockade at ten feet high, and Dunnigan says it was made of oak, Armour and Widder describe it as fifteen feet high and cedar. The fort and pickets were reconfigured after Pontiac's siege, which likely accounts for this difference; Armour and Widder, *Crossroads*, 48; Donald Lee, "Clark and Lernoult: Reduction by Expansion," in Denver Brunsman and Joel Stone, eds., *Revolutionary Detroit: Portraits in Political and Cultural Change, 1760–1805* (Detroit: Detroit Historical Society, 2009), 73–77, 74.

2. Farmer, *History*, 367; David Lee Poremba, ed., *Detroit in Its World Setting: A*

Three Hundred Year Chronology, 1701–2001 (Detroit: Wayne State University Press, 2001), 39.

3. Poremba, *Detroit,* 37. Jean Dilhet, *Beginnings of the Catholic Church in the United States,* translated and annotated by Patrick W. Browne (Washington, D.C.: The Salve Regina Press, 1922), 114. Dunnigan, *Frontier,* 38, 19. Brian Leigh Dunnigan, "Charting the Shape of Early Detroit, 1701–1838," in June Manning Thomas and Henco Bekkering, eds., *Mapping Detroit: Land, Community, and Shaping a City* (Detroit: Wayne State University Press, 2015), 22.

4. Quoted in Farmer, *History,* 11. For a full description of Detroit by Cadillac, see "Report of Detroit," Letter of Cadillac to M. de Pontchartrain, September 25, 1802, MS/Cadillac A.deLam, Burton Historical Collection, Detroit Public Library, Detroit, MI.

5. Farmer, *History,* 4.

6. Poremba, *Detroit,* 40; Dunnigan, *Frontier,* 46, 52, 53.

7. Dilhet, *Beginnings,* 114.

8. Quoted in Marcel Trudel, *Canada's Forgotten Slaves: Two Hundred Years of Bondage,* George Tombs, trans. (1960; reprint, Montréal: Véhicule Press, 2013), 30–31. Beavers have two layers of fur: a coarse, insulating outer layer of long strands and a soft inner layer of shorter strands. The strands of this inner layer readily twine together into a matted or felted texture when processed. Because furs worn by Native people as robes were partially pre-processed by human skin as well as the smoke-filled atmospheres of Native homes, worn furs commanded higher prices in the trade; Kardulias, "Negotiation and Incorporation on the Margins of World-Systems," 69, 70, 71. "Fat beaver" could be used to refer to a grade of fur more commonly called "coat beaver" (castor gras), meaning: "that which has contracted a certain gross and oily humour, from the sweat exhaled by the bodies of the Savages by whom it has been worn . . . used only in the making of hats"; *Encyclopedia Britannica or Dictionary of Arts, Sciences and General Literature,* Seventh Edition (Adam and Charles Black, 1842), 478; "The Beaver and Other Pelts," Digital Collections, McGill Library; http://digital.library.mcgill.ca/nwc/history/01.htm. "Beaver Pelts," *Historical Encyclopedia of Canada* (2013), http://www.thecanadianencyclopedia.ca/en/article/beaver-pelts. The term "fat beaver" was also used to refer to beaver harvested in winter when the pelts were thickest. For an engrossing analysis of the use of dress to signal identity in the context of colonization and racialization, see Sophie White, *Wild Frenchmen and Frenchified Indians: Material Culture and Race in Colonial Louisiana* (Philadelphia: University of Pennsylvania Press, 2012).

9. Jay Gitlin describes the swath of French territory in colonial North America as a corridor running from north to south; Gitlin, *Bourgeois Frontier,* 2. Clarence M. Burton, ed., *The City of Detroit Michigan: 1701–1922* (Detroit-Chicago: The S.J. Clarke Publishing Company, 1922), 719.

10. Quoted in Trudel, *Canada's Forgotten,* 57; Therese Agnes Kneip, "Slavery in Early Detroit" (Ph.D. diss., University of Detroit, 1938), 3.

11. Donna Valley Russell, ed., *Michigan Censuses 1710–1830: Under the French, British, and Americans* (Detroit: Detroit Society for Genealogical Research, Inc., 1982), 1762 Census, 19. Karen Marrero, "On the Edge of the West: The Roots and Routes of Detroit's Urban Eighteenth Century," in Jay Gitlin, Barbara Berglund, and Adam Arenson, eds., *Frontier Cities: Encounters at the Crossroads of Empire* (Philadelphia: University of Pennsylvania Press, 2012), 66–86, 76. Early Detroit population numbers are difficult to pin down for several reasons. The size of the settlement was ambiguous because people lived on both sides of the river running for several miles; a ten-mile stretch on either side of the fort and across the river from the fort is assumed in the 1762 French census cited here. Many families had two residences: a home in the fort and a farm in the "country," which meant that people could be counted twice depending on where they were at the time of the name collection. Many individuals were transient, especially hunters and voyageurs, which meant they might not be counted at all. Importantly, the 1762 French census does not include women; an estimated number of women was added in the 1982 publication of Detroit censuses resulting in the number 1,100. Poremba gives the numbers 2,000 for the size of Detroit's population in 1760 and 300 for farms/homes, *Detroit*, 39.

12. Dunnigan, *Frontier*, 50.

13. David M. Katzman, "Black Slavery in Michigan," *American Studies* 11:2 (Fall 1970) 56–66, 60.

14. James Sterling Letter Book, 1761–1765, finding aid, biography, William L. Clements Library, University of Michigan, Ann Arbor, MI.

15. James Sterling to [?], November 22, 1762, Sterling Letter Book; Sterling Letter Book, 1761–1765, finding aid, biography.

16. To James Stirling, Detroit, August 23, 1760, Letterbooks of Phyn and Ellice, quoted in Farmer, *History of Detroit*, 344.

17. Isabella Graham to John Marshal, 1769, Divie Duffield Papers, MS/Duffield (D. B.) Burton Historical Collection, Detroit Public Library, Detroit, MI. Joanna Bethune, *The Life of Mrs. Isabella Graham* (New York: John F. Taylor, 1839), 11–13. Graham is viewed as a philanthropist for her organizing on behalf of poor widows and orphans in New York.

18. James Sterling to Captain Walter Rutherford, October 27, 1761, Sterling Letter Book; James Sterling to Mr. Collbeck, October 27, 1761, Sterling Letter Book, William L. Clements Library, University of Michigan, Ann Arbor, MI.

19. James Sterling to Robert Holmes, April 20, 1762, Sterling Letter Book; James Sterling to John Sterling, June 12, 1762, Sterling Letter Book; James Sterling to Ensign J. Schlosser, June 12, 1762, Sterling Letter Book. Historian Christian Crouch expertly analyzes this escape in her paper: "The Black City: African and Indian Exchange in Pontiac's Detroit," revised version of Christian Crouch, "The Black City: Detroit and the Northeast Borderlands through African Eyes in the Era of 'Pontiac's War,'" The War Called Pontiac's Conference, April 5, 2013, Philadelphia, 20–21.

20. The insight that Sterling might have predicted Pontiac's War comes from Jon William Parmenter, "Pontiac's War: Forging New Links in the Anglo-Iroquois Covenant Chain, 1758–1766," *Ethnohistory* 44:4 (Autumn 1997): 617–54, 626; quoted in Parmenter, "Pontiac's War," 626.

21. Sterling Letter Book, finding aid, biography.

22. The classic treatment of this event is Francis Parkman, *The Conspiracy of Pontiac and the Indian Uprising of 1763* (1851; Boston, 1898). On pageantry in the memory of Pontiac's rebellion, see Kyle Mays, "Pontiac's Ghost in Detroit: Constructing Race and Gender through Indigenous Masculinity at the Turn of the 20th Century Detroit," conference paper, American Society for Ethnohistory Annual Meeting, New Orleans, LA, September 14, 2013.

23. Richard Middleton, *Pontiac's War: Its Causes, Course and Consequences* (New York: Routledge, 2012), 66; Gregory Evans Dowd, *A Spirited Resistance: The North American Indian Struggle for Unity, 1745–1815* (Baltimore: Johns Hopkins University Press, 1992), 36; Andrew Keith Sturtevant, "Jealous Neighbors: Rivalry and Alliance Among the Native Communities of Detroit, 1701–1766" (Ph.D. diss., The College of William and Mary, 2001), 246, 258, 266.

24. Parmenter, "Pontiac's War," 618.

25. Alan Taylor, *American Colonies: The Settling of North America* (New York: Penguin, 2001), 92. McDonnell, *Masters of Empire*, 26. For a clear and succinct breakdown of colonial systems, see Nancy Shoemaker, "A Typology of Colonialism," *Perspectives on History* (October 2015), 29.

26. John Mack Faragher, "'More Motley than Mackinaw': From Ethnic Mixing to Ethnic Cleansing on the Frontier of the Lower Missouri, 1783–1833," in Andrew R. L. Cayton and Fredrika Teute, eds., *Contact Points: American Frontiers from the Mohawk Valley to the Mississippi, 1750–1830* (Chapel Hill: University of North Carolina Press, 1998), 304–326, 305.

27. Middleton, *Pontiac's War*, 65, 68; Dowd, *Spirited*, 35.

28. Middleton, *Pontiac's War*, 65; Sturtevant, *Jealous*, 254.

29. Middleton, *Pontiac's War*, 83.

30. Middleton, *Pontiac's War*, 70.

31. Middleton, *Pontiac's War*, 70, 72.

32. John Porteous Diary, Volume 2: Journal Pontiac's Siege of Detroit, May 7–13, 1763, 17 (Wednesday, May 11, 1763), Burton Historical Collection, DPL. Middleton, *Pontiac's War*, 72.

33. Carl J. Eckberg, *Stealing Indian Women: Native Slavery in Illinois Country* (Urbana: University of Illinois Press, 2010), 14; Trudel, *Canada's Forgotten*, 97.

34. Milo Milton Quaife, ed. *The Siege of Detroit in 1763: The Journal of Pontiac's Conspiracy, and John Rutherford's Narrative of Captivity* (Chicago: R. R. Donnelley, 1958), 43–44, 139.

35. Middleton, *Pontiac's War*, 77.

36. Middleton, *Pontiac's War*, 71; Parmenter, "Pontiac's War," 630.

37. James Sterling to Duncan & Co., July 24, 1763, Sterling Letter Book.

38. Parmenter, "Pontiac's War," 628.

39. James Sterling to John Sterling, October 6, 1763, Sterling Letter Book.

40. Quoted from Parmenter, "Pontiac's War," 628.

41. Dowd, *Spirited*, 35.

42. Parmenter, "Pontiac's War, 630, 631.

43. Andrew J. Blackbird, *History of the Ottawa and Chippewa of Michigan; A Grammar of Their Language, And Personal and Family History of the Author* (Ypsilanti, MI: Ypsilantian Job Printing House, 1887), 7.

44. Parmenter, "Pontiac's War," 636–37; Quoted in Parmenter, "Pontiac's War," 635. After hearing a report about the peace conference that took place at Johnson Hall, the headquarters of Sir William Johnson in New York, Pontiac promised George Croghan, chief deputy to William Johnson, that he would not wage war again. Jon Parmenter argues that even as Pontiac agreed to peace, he did not admit guilt and used the opportunity to skillfully request gunpowder on credit from the British. Decades later, in 1769, Pontiac was killed by an Indian man near Cahokia, Illinois, in an incident unrelated to the war.

45. Katz, "Black Slavery," 60.

46. Emily Macgillivray and Tiya Miles, "'She Has Lived in Fashion': A Native Woman Trader's Household in the Detroit River Region," accepted for Karen Marrero and Andrew Sturtevant, eds., *A Place in Common: Telling Histories of Early Detroit* (Lansing: Michigan State University Press, in progress).

47. Afua Cooper, *The Hanging of Angélique: The Untold Story of Canadian Slavery and the Burning of Old Montréal* (Athens: University of Georgia Press, 2007), 81.

48. The foundational work of carefully recovering the history of slavery in New France was done by French Canadian historian Marcel Trudel in the 1960s, and by Afro-Canadian historian Afua Cooper (focusing on black slavery) and American historian Brett Rushforth (focusing on Indian slavery) in the early 2000s.

49. Trudel, *Canada's Forgotten*, 15; Cooper, *Hanging*, 70.

50. Trudel, *Canada's Forgotten*, 65–70; Brett Rushforth, *Bonds of Alliance: Indigenous and Atlantic Slaveries in New France* (Chapel Hill: University of North Carolina Press, 2012), 169.

51. White, *Wild Frenchmen*, 7, 12.

52. Trudel, *Canada's Forgotten*, 48.

53. Trudel, *Canada's Forgotten*, 37; Cooper, *Hanging*, 72; Quoted in Cooper, *Hanging*, 75.

54. Marcel Trudel and his co-investigator, Micheline D'Allaire, conducted this count as part of a survey of French records. See Trudel, *Canada's Forgotten*, 31, 34, 36, 41, 73, 61, 76, 83; for the research methods that resulted in these numbers, see 58–59.

55. Spear, *Race*, 59–63; While the Code Noir served as a guide for New France residents, it was not legally binding there according to Marcel Trudel, who argues that a new code would have had to be enacted to be legal, as in the case of Louisiana, Trudel, *Canada's Forgotten*, 122; see 119–22 for a full summary of the provisions of the Code Noir.

56. For detailed summaries of the provisions of the two Codes Noir, see Spear, *Race*, 59–68; Rushforth, *Bonds*, 123–31.

57. Spear, *Race*, 72; Ekberg, *Stealing*, 89.

58. Ekberg, *Stealing*, 46.

59. Ekberg, *Stealing*, 13, 21. I am grateful to John Petoskey, the student who introduced me to Blackbird's diary as part of our work on his honors thesis. Petoskey's interpretation of the "Underground" people as Pawnees and as Ottawa captives spurred my use of this example; John Minode'e Petoskey, "Blood Quantum and Twenty-First Century Sovereignty in the Grand Traverse Band of Ottawa and Chippewa Indians," undergraduate honors thesis, University of Michigan, Ann Arbor, 2016, 47–48; Andrew J. Blackbird, *History of the Ottawa and Chippewa of Michigan; A Grammar of Their Language, And Personal and Family History of the Author* (Ypsilanti, MI: Ypsilantian Job Printing House, 1887), 25–26; Martha Royce Blaine, "Pawnee," *Encyclopedia of North American Indians*, Frederick E. Hoxie, ed. (Boston: Houghton-Mifflin, 1996), 472. Rushforth, *Bonds*, 397.

60. This confusion held sway in the colonial period and in modern-day scholarship until Brett Rushforth offered a close examination and detailed explanation in *Bonds*, 169–73. For example, Marcel Trudel wrote in the first history of slavery in New France: "The Panis are the only Amerindian nation to appear each year in slave documents with such astounding regularity. There was a true Panis slave market, just as there was an ebony slave market." Trudel, *Canada's Forgotten*, 65. For another example of "Panis" interpreted as the single nation "Pawnee," see Jorge Castellanos, "Black Slavery in Detroit," in Wilma Wood Henrickson, ed., *Detroit Perspectives: Crossroads and Turning Points* (Detroit: Wayne State University Press, 1991), 85–93, 86.

61. New France records in Canada that mention slaves do sometimes list the captive person's tribe of origin. This difference raises the question of whether French record keepers in the satellite post at Detroit, mainly priests, felt there was a greater need to suppress this information. Trudel, *Canada's Forgotten*, 63–64.

62. Quoted in Rushforth, *Bonds*, 136, 393–95; Cooper, *Hanging*, 76; Trudel, *Canada's Forgotten*, 45–54).

63. Trudel, *Canada's Forgotten*, 46; Rushforth, *Bonds*, 137.

64. Cooper, *Hanging*, 76, 137.

65. Women dressing skins for trade: Karen L. Anderson, *Chain Her by One Foot: The Subjugation of Women in Seventeenth-Century New France* (London: Routledge, 1991), 159. Moccasins: Catherine Cangany, "Fashioning Moccasins: Detroit, the

Manufacturing Frontier, and the Empire of Consumption, 1701–1835," *The William and Mary Quarterly* 69:2 (April 2012): 265–302, 266, 268, 286.

66. Trudel, *Canada's Forgotten*, 121; Jennifer M. Spear, *Race, Sex, and Sexual Order in Early New Orleans* (Baltimore: Johns Hopkins University Press, 2009), 67.

67. Dowd, *Spirited*, 12; Brett Rushforth, "'A Little Flesh We Offer You': The Origins of Indian Slavery in New France," in Alan Gallay, ed., *Indian Slavery in Colonial America* (Lincoln: University of Nebraska, 2009), 353–89, 366.

68. Rushforth, *Bonds*, 68.

69. Rushforth, *Bonds*, 66.

70. For detailed histories and analyses of French-Indian marriages, European-Indian marriages, and metís families, see: Susan Sleeper-Smith, *Indian Women and French Men: Rethinking Cultural Encounter in the Western Great Lakes* (Amherst: University of Massachusetts Press, 2001); Kathleen DuVal, "Indian Intermarriage and Métissage in Colonial Louisiana," *The William and Mary Quarterly*, Third Series, 65:2 (April 2008): 267–304; Anne F. Hyde, *Empires, Nations, and Families: A New History of the North American West, 1800–1860* (Lincoln: University of Nebraska Press, 2011); Lucy Eldersveld Murphy, *Great Lakes Creoles: A French-Indian Community on the Northern Borderlands, Prairie Du Chien, 1750–1860* (New York: Cambridge University Press, 2014); Karen Marrero, "Founding Families: Power and Authority of Mixed French and Native Lineages in Eighteenth Century Detroit" (Ph.D. diss., Yale University, 2011).

71. The French phrase *à la façon du pays* meant "in the custom of the country"; Duval, "Indian Intermarriage," 267. Although many of these relationships are viewed by historians to have been consensual, there were risks involved for indigenous women who entered these cross-cultural marriages. They might gain access to trade goods and improve the status of their families through the creation of ties with influential traders, but they also became subject over time to French-Catholic understandings of hierarchical gender roles that emphasized men's dominance over women and the expectation that a proper woman should serve and obey her husband; Anderson, *Chain Her by One Foot*, 55, 57, 226–27.

72. Catherine J. Denial, *Making Marriage: Husbands, Wives, and the American State in Dakota and Ojibwe Country* (St. Paul: Minnesota Historical Society Press, 2013), 99–100; Sylvia Van Kirk, *Many Tender Ties: Women in Fur-Trade Society, 1670–1870* (Norman: University of Oklahoma Press, 1980) 37–38.

73. Spear, *Race*, 18, 26, 37.

74. For the association of Native women and land, as well as the notion of Native women's "rapeability," see Audra Simpson, "The State Is a Man: Theresa Spence, Loretta Saunders and the Gendered Costs of Settler Sovereignty," *Theory & Event* (forthcoming: spring 2017). Also see Sherene H. Razack, "Gendered Racial Violence and Spacialized Justice: The Murder of Pamela George," *Canadian Journal of Law and Society* 15:2 (2000): 91–130. The historian Margaret Newell has shown through her reading of indirect sources that in seventeenth- and

eighteenth-century New England, indigenous women (and girl) captives were also victims of sexual assault. She notes that women from high-status Native families sometimes received better treatment from their New England owners. Margaret Ellen Newell, *Brethren by Nature: New England Indians, Colonists, and the Origins of American Slavery* (Ithaca, NY: Cornell University Press, 2015), 82, 83, 126, 230, 63.

75. French New Orleans colonist Tivas de Gourville quoted in Spear, *Race*, 29; La Vente quoted in Spear, *Race* 24; Cadillac and La Vente's views described in Spear, *Race*, 23–4.

76. DuVal, "Indian Intermarriage," 269, 271.

77. Trudel, *Canada's Forgotten*, 153; Rushforth, *Bonds*, 265; E. A. S. Demers, "John Askin and Indian Slaves at Michilimackinac," in Alan Gallay, ed., *Indian Slavery in Colonial America* (Lincoln: University of Nebraska, 2009), 392–416, 401. An examination of Ste. Anne's Church records from Detroit between 1760–1815 indicate that one slaveholder, Jean Baptiste, served as godparent to the infant of his Panis slave, Madelaine, and "an unknown father" in 1798. While this fact is not evidence of paternity, it does raise the question of whether a French father might use this religious kinship system to informally claim or create a link with an enslaved child. Ste. Anne Church Records, Bentley Historical Library, 86966mf 534c, 535c, 536c, University of Michigan, Ann Arbor, MI. Used by permission of the Detroit Catholic Diocese.

78. DuVal, "Indian Intermarriage," 279.

79. DuVal, "Indian Intermarriage," 279.

80. Rev. David Bacon, a Protestant missionary from the Congregational Church Association of Connecticut, came to Detroit in 1800. Methodist minister Rev. Nathaniel Bangs came to Detroit in 1804. Poremba, *Detroit*, 71, 89.

81. Burton, *City*, 704; Edward J. Hickey, *Ste. Anne's Parish: One Hundred Years of Detroit History*, ed., Joe L. Norris (Detroit: Wayne State University Press, 1951), 18; Detroit Places Ste. Anne's Church, History, http://historydetroit.com/places/ste_annes.php. Accessed December 9, 2013.

82. This list of tribes comes from a review of the Ste. Anne's Records, BHL, through 1819.

83. The term "Sauteuse" here indicates Ojibwe. For more on the various names and subgroups of Anishinaabe people in the Great Lakes, see Michael Witgen, *An Infinity of Nations: How the Native New World Shaped Early North America* (Philadelphia: University of Pennsylvania Press, 2012), 13.

84. Trudel states that the Campeaus (sometimes spelled Campaus) in Montreal were a tight-knit family with fifty-seven slaves among them although they were only "small-scale fur traders" and not among the ultra-rich; Trudel, *Canada's Forgotten*, 259.

85. Judy Jacobson, *Detroit River Connections: Historiographical and Biographical Sketches of the Eastern Great Lakes Border Region* (Baltimore: Clearfield Company, 1994); Russell, *Michigan Censuses*, 1762 Census, 20. Campau family wealth in the

1800s: Gitlin, *Bourgeois Frontier*, 141–143. The Campau family papers in Detroit do not reveal many details of their slave transactions. Only one document describes the transfer of an enslaved "Negro" woman named Nancy from Jean B. Romain to his daughters on September 4, 1790. A transnational study of this slaveholding family that closely examined records on both sides of the border would be a revealing approach for further research. Campau Family Papers, Burton Historical Collection, Detroit Public Library, Detroit, MI.

86. Russell, *Michigan Censuses*, 1762 Census, 21–25. There are nine head-of-household Campaus listed in the 1762 census. Louis Campau had no accompanying details beside his name in the census and is therefore not listed in my summary. Michel or Alex Campau (first name is uncertain in the record) had no notations for the latter part of the census categories by his name, suggesting either that the information was incomplete or that he had no girls, boys, slaves, or paid workers in his household; he is not listed in my summary.

87. Ste. Anne's Church Records, Reel 1, VII, 1744–1780.

88. James Sterling to Ensign J. S. Schlosser, June 12, 1762, Sterling Letter Book. I am grateful to Jonathan Quint for pointing out the reference to Native women in this letter.

89. Dowry: Crouch, "Black City," 25; James Sterling to [?], February 26, 1765, Sterling Letter Book; quoted in Marrero, "Founding Families," 281; Marrero, "Founding," 282–83.

90. Independent trade routes: Crouch, "Black City," 25.

91. Crouch, "Black City," 1, 4; James Sterling to [?], Sept 29, 1765, Sterling Letter Book. Christian Crouch was the first to analyze Sterling's preference for black male laborers. In her paper, "The Black City," she carefully considers and leaves open the question of why Sterling preferred black male laborers, speculating that black men had a greater facility in travel because of a learned ability to get along with native people lacking in white men like Morrison.

92. Marrero, "Founding Families," 276; quoted in Marrero, 282; quoted in Crouch, "Black City," 25. Karen Marrero first makes this argument that a black slave was a status symbol for Angelique Sterling in "Founding Families," 282.

93. James Sterling to [?], November 12, 1764, Sterling Letter Book.

94. To John Porteous, June 6, 1771, Letterbooks of Phyn and Ellice, merchants, at Schenectady, New York, 1767–1776 (Buffalo Historical Society-BHS Microfilm Publication No. 1), Vol. 1. For several other letters involving slave orders for Detroit, see Farmer, *History of Detroit*, 344.

95. For examples of freedom suits won on the basis of Native American ancestry (especially maternity), see: Lea VanderVelde, *Redemption Songs: Suing for Freedom before Dred Scott* (New York: Oxford University Press, 2014), 7, 39–56; Ariela Julie Gross, *What Blood Won't Tell: A History of Race on Trial in America* (Cambridge, MA: Harvard University Press, 2008), 22–27; Ariela Gross and Alejandro De La Fuente, "Slaves, Free Blacks, and Race in the Legal Regimes of Cuba, Louisiana, and Virginia: A Comparison," *North Carolina Law Review* 91:5

(June 2013): 1699–1756, 1733; Tiya Miles, "The Narrative of Nancy, A Cherokee Woman," *Frontiers, A Journal of Women Studies*, Special Issue: Intermarriage and North American Indians 29:2, 3 (Spring 2008): 59–80; Ekberg, *Stealing*, 91, 93. In Spanish-influenced areas of the Caribbean, Florida, and Southwest, indigenous slavery persisted into the nineteenth century; see Andrés Reséndez, *The Other Slavery: The Uncovered Story of Indian Enslavement in America* (Boston: Houghton Mifflin, 2016).

96. Marrero, "Founding Families," 272.

97. Marrero, "Founding Families," 272, 287, 310; Quaife, *Siege*, 187.

98. Ekberg, *Stealing*, 68; Ste. Anne's Records, May 30, 1764.

99. In his historical study of colonial French Illinois, Carl Ekberg describes this tendency by saying that Indian women were "reserved for white men"; *Stealing*, 76.

100. James Sterling to [?], January 10, 1762, Sterling Letter Book.

101. Ste. Anne's Records, BHL. Our figure does not include enslaved babies listed as "mulatto" or with undesignated racial information, although some of these infants might well have been of indigenous descent. Carl Ekberg gives the number 167 for babies born to enslaved Indian mothers and white fathers in Detroit, citing Marcel Trudel; Ekberg, *Stealing*, 28. Trudel states that 177 "illegitimate children" were born to Indian slaves in Detroit; Trudel, *Canada's Forgotten*, 204. Trudel notes here, too, that Native enslaved women outnumbered men, and he implies that white men's attraction influenced this demographic imbalance.

102. Ekberg, *Stealing*, 75.

103. Jacobson, *Detroit*, 29. Cangany, "Fashioning Moccasins," 285–86.

104. Demers, "John Askin," 397–98. Re: Mannette, Detroit Notorial Register, Vol. A, June 11, 1768, Burton Historical Collection, Detroit Public Library, pp. 68–69.

105. Detroit Notorial Register, Vol. A, June 11, 1768, Burton Historical Collection, Detroit Public Library, pp. 68–69.

106. Armour and Widder, *Crossroads*, 36, 71. Jacobson, *Detroit River*, 36.

107. Detroit can be characterized as a "society with slaves" rather than as a "slave society" because the core feature of the economy (the fur trade) was not produced solely or mainly by slave labor, and other labor systems persisted alongside slavery here. Nevertheless, slavery was important to the stability and economy of the settlement. For a description of this distinction in places where slavery was practiced, see Ira Berlin, *Many Thousands Gone: The First Two Centuries of Slavery in North America* (Cambridge, MA: Harvard University Press, 1998), 8–9.

108. Ekberg discusses this blurred status of Indian slaves in French households; see *Stealing*, 45.

109. Trudel, *Canada's Forgotten*, 140.

2: The War for Liberty (1774–1783)

1. The name of Ann Wyley has been recorded a number of ways in primary and secondary sources. She has been called Ann and Anne, as well as Nancy. Her last name has been spelled Wyley or Wiley. Jean Contencineau's name has likewise been recorded with numerous spellings: Contancinau, Coutencineau. I am using the spelling from the Detroit trial record, March 1776. "Record of criminal trial in 1776, Detroit, ss," reprinted in Charles H. Lanman, *History of Michigan, Civil and Topographical in a Compendious Form: with a View of Surrounding Lakes* (New York: E. French, 1839), 133–35. (Lanman offers as citation: "This record was found in the possession of Judge May. He knew the jury who tried the case.") This trial record is also reprinted in Detroit in the Revolution, File: 2, Box: Works Detroit History 1760, Burton Papers (MS/Burton C.M.), Burton Historical Collection, Detroit Public Library, 61–62.

2. The Detroit River is often described as a "highway" of commerce in the region. See, for instance, Denver Brunsman, "Introduction," in Brunsman and Stone, eds., *Revolutionary Detroit*, 3–22, 5.

3. This by-decade breakdown of the enslaved population is the result of our (Tiya Miles and Michelle Cassidy's) analysis of the Ste. Anne's Church records in which notations about "Panis," "Negro," and "Mulatto" slaves consistently appear. Our numbers are approximate because the Ste. Anne records do not offer a comprehensive count of all slaves in Detroit, some of whom were not involved in the church. In addition, these records include a number of entries about slaves for whom no racial designation is given. We have noted these people in a category labeled "unknown" in our count. The racial "unknowns" for the 1760s totaled thirteen people; the "unknowns" in the 1770s totaled four people. More than likely, the majority of these individuals were "Panis." In the ratio for the 1760s to which this note corresponds, I have combined the number of blacks (three) with the number of "Mulattos" (two) to arrive at the total of five reported, even though the term "mulatto" could be used to designate persons of black and Indian ancestry as well as of black and white ancestry. Michelle Cassidy, a graduate student in the History Department at the University of Michigan, counted the number of entries in the Ste. Anne records and broke them down by decade, race, and gender. St. Anne Records, Bentley Historical Library, 86966mf 534c, 535c, 536c, University of Michigan, Ann Arbor, MI. Used by permission of the Detroit Catholic Diocese.

4. "The Story of Jean Contancinau: Testimony," translated in Detroit in the Revolution, File 2, 57–58, Burton Papers, DPL. (Clarence Burton includes as citation: "The papers here collected are from the Haldimand collection, and Lanman's History of Michigan. The testimony, such as it is, is in French in the old Detroit registry," 56.

5. Burton, "Detroit in the Revolution" (booklet), 25.

6. Lanman, 134. "The Story of Jean Contancinau: Testimony," translated in

Detroit in the Revolution, File 2, 58, Burton Papers, DPL. After the French and Indian War, Detroit operated under British martial law. The Quebec Act, passed in October 7, 1774 (the same year these thefts took place), brought civil rule to Michigan through a hybrid approach of French civil law and British criminal law. William Renwick Riddell, *Michigan Under British Rule: Law and Law Courts, 1760–1796* (Lansing: Michigan Historical Society, 1926), 19–20. The stolen purse was green: "The Story of Jean Contancinau: Testimony," translated in Detroit in the Revolution, File 2, 59, Burton Papers, DPL.

7. For an analysis of the role of clothing in colonial transculturation processes, see Sophie White, *Wild Frenchmen and Frenchified Indians: Material Culture and Race in Colonial Louisiana* (Philadelphia: University of Pennsylvania Press, 2012). For a discussion of the use of clothing to challenge caste and assert creativity and adornment in slave communities, see Stephanie Camp, *Closer to Freedom: Enslaved Women and Everyday Resistance in the Plantation South* (Chapel Hill: University of North Carolina Press, 2004). Barbara Heath describes enslaved people's use of material objects such as buttons and buckles to change the appearance of substandard clothing distributed by owners: Barbara Heath, "Materiality, Race, and Slavery: How Archaeology Contributes to Dialogues at Historic Sites," unpublished paper, National Council on Public History, Nashville, TN, April 2015.

8. "Record of criminal trial in 1776, Detroit, ss," reprinted in Charles H. Lanman, *History of Michigan*, 133.

9. Besides establishing the boundaries of Canada and declaring the application of British law to the former French territory, the Quebec Act of 1774 protected the right of French settlers to maintain their property and the right of Catholics to practice their faith. Lanman, *History of Michigan*, 132–33. The Quebec Act provided for the first civil government in Detroit, with the king slated to appoint "a governor, lieutenant-governor, or commander-in-chief, and a council." Farmer, *History of Detroit*, 84. Of these possibilities, Lieutenant Governor Henry Hamilton, was the only official assigned. He became the supervisor of Philip Dejean, who was already serving as notary and justice of the peace in the town. Dejean had been appointed by military officers Captain Turnbull and Major Bayard, in 1767. In 1768 a public election (the structure of which is unclear) confirmed his role as "judge and justice of the district of Detroit." Burton, "Detroit in the Revolution" (booklet), 20.

10. Detroit in the Revolution, File 2, 108, 48, Burton Papers, DPL; Burton, "Detroit in the Revolution" (booklet), 20.

11. Lanman, *History of Michigan*, 132.

12. Ann is first called "Anne" in this testimony and then "Nancy."

13. Second declaration of Prisoners, Detroit in the Revolution, File 2, 294, Burton Papers, DPL.

14. Cenette, Chatelain and C Enfant did not appear in the 1768 or 1779 Detroit censuses; however, a Mrs. Chatlain is listed for 1779. A Joseph L'Enfant appears

in the 1779 Detroit census as the owner of two slaves. Donna Valley Russell, ed., *Michigan Censuses 1710–1830: Under the French, British, and Americans* (Detroit: Detroit Society for Genealogical Research, Inc., 1982), 42.

15. "Record of criminal trial in 1776, Detroit, ss," reprinted in Charles H. Lanman, *History of Michigan,* 133. "The Story of Jean Contancinau: The Verdict," Detroit in the Revolution, File 2, 60, 61, Burton Papers, DPL.

16. "The Story of Jean Contancinau: The Judgment," Detroit in the Revolution, File 2, 62, Burton Papers, DPL.

17. Presentment against Philip Dejean, Canadian Archives, Series B. Vol. 225, p. 501, reprinted in "Detroit in the Revolution," File 2, 69, Burton Papers, DPL. William Renwick Riddell, *The First Judge of Detroit and His Court* (Ann Arbor: University of Michigan Press, 1915), 9.

18. Secondary sources disagree about Wyley's ultimate fate, and primary sources exist only in piecemeal fashion. The Detroit legal historian and judge William Riddell states that she was not put to death; Riddell, *The First Judge of Detroit,* 9. Detroit historian Clarence Burton also states that she was not executed in a description of the case that includes transcripts of the court record; see Clarence Burton, "Detroit in the Revolution" (booklet), File 2, 69, Burton Papers, DPL. Burton discusses the case similarly in: Clarence Burton "Building of Detroit-People," Works Detroit History 1701, MS/Burton, C.M., Burton Historical Collection, DPL, 10; also see Clarence Burton, "Detroit Under British Rule," Works Detroit History 1760, MS/Burton, C.M. Burton, Historical Collection, DPL, 26. In contrast, Detroit historian Silas Farmer states that Wyley was executed, see: Farmer, *History of Detroit,* 173–174, 957. For other accounts of this case, see: Poremba, *Detroit,* 50 (who calls this the first burglary in Detroit); Kneip, "Slavery in Early Detroit," 27–28; Errin T. Stegich, "Liberty Hangs at Detroit: The Trial and Execution of Jean Contencineau," in Denver Brunsman and Joel Stone, eds., *Revolutionary Detroit*: 67–72.

19. Rashauna Johnson, *Slavery's Metropolis: Unfree Labor in New Orleans During the Age of Revolutions* (New York: Cambridge University Press, 2016), 147.

20. Mr. Thomas William to P. Dejean, August 5, 1778, Detroit, William Papers, Burton Historical Collection, DPL.

21. Tiya Miles, "Taking Leave, Making Lives: Creative Quests for Freedom in Early Black and Native America," in Gabrielle Tayac, ed., *IndiVisible: African-Native American Lives in the Americas* (Washington, D.C.: Smithsonian Institution, 2009), 146–49. Leslie M. Harris, *In the Shadow of Slavery: African Americans in New York City, 1626–1863* (Chicago: University of Chicago Press, 2003), 37.

22. John Bell Moran, *The Moran Family: 200 Years in Detroit* (Detroit: Alved of Detroit, 1949), 28.

23. The Royal Proclamation (October 7, 1763): "established the Allegheny Mountains as a formal boundary line between American colonial settlements and the western Indians' hunting grounds and forbade all future private purchases of

land from the Indians, reserving that privilege to the Crown." However, many settlers ultimately ignored the act, which was difficult to enforce from afar. Quoted from Jon William Parmenter, "Pontiac's War: Forging New Links in the Anglo-Iroquois Covenant Chain, 1758–1766," *Ethnohistory* 44:4 (Autumn 1997): 617–54, 629. Colin G. Calloway, *The American Revolution in Indian Country: Crisis and Diversity in Native American Communities* (New York: Cambridge University Press, 1995), 21.

24. George L. Cornell, "American Indians at Wawiiatanong: An Early American History of Indigenous Peoples at Detroit," in John H. Hartig, *Honoring Our Detroit River: Caring for Our Home* (Bloomfield Hills, MI: Cranbrook Institute of Science, 2003), 20.

25. Ste. Anne's Records, BHL.

26. Quoted in Brian Leigh Dunnigan, *Frontier Metropolis: Picturing Early Detroit, 1701–1838* (Detroit: Wayne State University Press, 2001), 120; Farmer, *History of Detroit*, 472–73.

27. Farmer, *History of Detroit*, 837.

28. Quoted in David McCullough, *1776* (New York: Simon & Schuster, 2005), 135; McCullough, 135–37.

29. To Alex and William Macomb, June 22, 1775, Letterbooks of Phyn and Ellice, merchants, at Schenectady, New York, 1767–76 (Buffalo Historical Society-BHS Microfilm Publication No. 1), Vol. 3. David A. Armour and Keith R. Widder, *At the Crossroads: Michilimackinac During the American Revolution* (Mackinac Island, MI: Mackinac Island State Park Commission, 1978), 1; Peter Silver, *Our Savage Neighbors: How Indian War Transformed Early America* (New York: W. W. Norton & Co., 2008), 229.

30. John H. Hartig, "Introduction," in Hartig, ed., *Honoring Our Detroit River*, 1–8, 6.

31. Quoted in Isabelle E. Swan, *The Deep Roots: A History of Gross Ile, Michigan to July 6, 1876* (Grosse Ile, MI: Grosse Ile Historical Society, 1977), 20, 21.

32. Swan, *Deep Roots*, 14, 23.

33. Harris, *Shadow of Slavery*, 11.

34. Phrasing by Karen Marrero, "On the Edge of the West: The Roots and Routes of Detroit's Urban Eighteenth Century," in Jay Gitlin and Adam Arenson, eds., *Frontier Cities: Encounters at the Crossroads of Empire* (Philadelphia: University of Pennsylvania Press, 2012), 66–86.

35. Catherine Cangany, *Frontier Seaport: Detroit's Transformation into an Atlantic Entrepot* (Chicago: The University of Chicago Press, 2014), 3.

36. Swan, *Deep Roots*, 13–15, 23; Old Deed "Grosse Ile," LMS / Macomb Family Papers, July 6 1776, Detroit Public Library, Detroit, MI; A. Macomb quoted in Swan, *Deep Roots*, 21; Macomb military account: Milo M. Quaife, "When Detroit Invaded Kentucky," *Filson Club History Quarterly* 1:2 (January 1927): 53–67, 55.

37. Swan, *Deep Roots*, 14, 24–26. Size of farm: Record Book of Macomb Estate, Macomb Family Papers, R2:1796, BHC, DPL.

38. Ste. Anne's Records, BHL. James May to Wm Macomb, Jan 12 1790, Alexander Fraser Papers, Detroit Public Library.

39. David M. Katzman, "Black Slavery in Michigan," *American Studies* 11:2 (Fall 1970), 60.

40. Quoted in Swan, *Deep Roots*, 17.

41. Quoted in Armour and Widder, *Crossroads*, 51. De Peyster kinship link: Armour and Widder, *Crossroads*, 51.

42. Calloway, *American Revolution*, 29–32, 36, 39, 43–44, 46; Armour & Widder, *Crossroads*, 51.

43. Donald Lee, "Clark and Lernoult: Reduction by Expansion," in Brunsman and Stone, eds., *Revolutionary Detroit*, 73–77, 75; Quaife, "When Detroit Invaded Kentucky," 1927.

44. Lee, "Clark and Lernoult," in Brunsman and Stone, eds., *Revolutionary Detroit*, 75; Thomas Jefferson to George Rogers Clark, Dec. 25, 1780, *The Papers of Thomas Jefferson*, Julian P. Boyd. ed., Vol. 4 (Princeton, NJ: Princeton University Press, 1951), 234–37.

45. Proclamation by George R. Clark, December 24, 1778, translated in Jerry Lewis, "Red and Black Slaves in the Illinois Territory," in Terry Straus and Grant P. Arndt, eds., *Native Chicago* (Chicago: Albatross Publishers, 1998), 82–86.

46. Americans were not the first to racialize Indians as Clark does in this example. British officers in Pontiac's war also used racial terms, such as "copperheaded" and "black," to indicate Native people.

47. In her illuminating study of the racial term "red," Nancy Shoemaker shows how Native people in the East had their own meanings for color terms (such as red being associated with war) long before "red" came to be associated with Indianness. Both Europeans and American Indians began to adopt the racial term "red," in different ways and for different reasons, in the late 1700s and early 1800s. Clark's negative use of the term in the Illinois document, meant to emphasize slave caste, is not a usage that Native Americans would have willingly adopted. Nancy Shoemaker, "How Indians Got to Be Red," *The American Historical Review* 102 (June 1997): 624–44. Frederick E. Hoxie, "Introduction," in Frederick E. Hoxie, Ronald Hoffman, and Peter J. Albert, eds., *Native Americans and the Early Republic* (Charlottesville: University Press of Virginia, 1999), ix. James Sterling to John Sterling, October 6, 1763, Sterling Letter Book.

48. Clark, Proclamation, in Lewis, trans., "Red and Black Slaves." Slave resistance during the war: Benjamin Quarles, "The Revolutionary War as a Black Declaration of Independence," in Ira Berlin and Ronald Hoffman, eds., *Slavery and Freedom in the Age of the American Revolution* (Urbana: University of Illinois Press, 1983), 283, 290, 291; Manisha Sinha, *The Slave's Cause: A History of Abolition* (New Haven, CT: Yale University Press, 2016), 51–52.

49. Calloway, *American Revolution*, 22.

50. Quaife, "When Detroit Invaded Kentucky," 55.

51. Captain Bird to Major Arent S. De Peyster, June 11, 1780, transcribed in Quaife, "When Detroit Invaded Kentucky," 62–63.

52. Captain Bird to Wm Lee, a Negroe free, 1784, MS Bird Papers, Detroit Public Library.

53. Silver, *Savage Neighbors*, 250–51; Armour & Widder, *Crossroads*, 94; Brunsman, "Introduction," in Brunsman and Stone, eds., *Revolutionary Detroit*, 12. Brett Rushforth notes the importance of slaves as "tokens" of alliance between indigenous groups and the French; Rushforth, *Bonds of Alliance*, 220–21.

54. Judy Jacobson, *Detroit River Connections: Historiographical and Biographical Sketches of the Eastern Great Lakes Border Region* (Baltimore: Clearfield Company, 1994), 17.

55. Statement by Captain John Dunkin, quoted in Maude Ward Lafferty, "Destruction of Ruddle's and Martin's Forts in the Revolutionary War," *Register of the Kentucky Historical Society* 54:189 (October 1956): 15; Lafferty, "Destruction," 26.

56. "Petition of Agnes La Force," Haldimand Papers, MPHC, XIX, 494. Also quoted in Kneip, "Slavery in Early Detroit," 32–33.

57. Quaife, "When Detroit Invaded Kentucky," 3, 4; Lafferty, "Destruction," 26; Kneip, "Slavery in Detroit," 32; "List of Slaves formerly the property of Mrs. Agnes Le Force now in possession of," transcribed in Quaife, 66–67. "Slave Captives at Ruddell's and Martin's Forts," www.frontierfolk.net/ramsha_research/captives3html; Accessed July 28, 2016. Jacques Duperon Baby: Riddell, *Michigan Under British Rule*, 52–53.

58. Calloway, *American Revolution*, 54.

59. Quoted in Clarence Burton, "Detroit in the Revolution" (Booklet—1906 Address to the Sons of the American Revolution) Works Printed Treaty of 1782 Miscellaneous Printed Material, Burton Papers, MS/Burton C. M., Burton Historical Collection, Detroit Public Library, 26; Clarence Burton, Detroit in the Revolution, File: 2, Box: Works Detroit History 1760, Burton Papers, MS/Burton, C. M., Burton Historical Collection, Detroit Public Library, p. 2 typescript/137 handwritten. Riddell, *Michigan Under British Rule*, 50.

60. Burton, Detroit in the Revolution, File 2, p. 3 typescript/ 110 handwritten.

61. "Advertisement," transcribed in Burton, "Detroit in the Revolution," Booklet 22, BHC, DPL.

62. To Sir from Most Humble Servant, Sept. 21, 1777, Quebec, transcribed in John Almon and Thomas Pownall, *The Remembrance of Impartial Repository of Public Events*, Vol. 6 (London: J Almon, 1778), 188–89; also transcribed in Burton, Detroit in the Revolution, File 2, pp. 11–12 handwritten.

63. Stegich, "Liberty Hangs," 68; Burton, Detroit in the Revolution, File 2, p. 1

typescript / 108 handwritten; Clarence Burton, "Building of Detroit-People," Works Detroit History 1701, MS/Burton, C. M., BHC, DPL, 10, 11; Clarence Burton, "Detroit Under British Rule," Works Detroit History 1760, MS/Burton, C. M., BHC, DPL, 26; Armour and Widder, *Crossroads*, 94; William Renwick Riddell, *The First Judge at Detroit and His Court* (Ann Arbor: University of Michigan Press, 1915), 30. Hair buying: Silver, *Savage Neighbors*, 250–51; Burton, Detroit in the Revolution, File 2, p. 1 typescript / 108 handwritten.

64. Gifts: Alan Taylor, *The Divided Ground: Indians, Settlers, and the Northern Borderland of the American Revolution* (New York: Vintage, 2006), 102.

65. Russell, ed., *Michigan Censuses*, 1782 Census, 49–56; Katzman, "Black Slavery in Michigan," 60; Calloway, *American Revolution*, 54, 61.

66. Quoted in Armour and Widder, *Crossroads*, 135, 136, 117, 135.

67. *The John Askin Papers Volume I: 1747–1795*, Milo M. Quaife., ed. (Detroit: Detroit Library Commission, 1928), 68.

68. Askin Papers Vol. I, 94.

69. Detroit move: Cangany, *Frontier Seaport*, 31; Jacobson, *Detroit River*, 32. Barthe lot: "Actual Survey of the Narrows betwixt the Lake Erie and Sinclair," by P. McNiff, reproduced in Dunnigan, *Frontier Metropolis*, 62; Jacobson, *Detroit River*, 34. Sterling as representative: Armour and Widder, *Crossroads*, 75. Askin's setbacks: Jacobson, *Detroit River*, 32.

70. Charlotte: Armour & Widder, *Crossroads*, 37. Pompey and Jupiter: "Sale of Negro Slaves," Askin Papers, Vol. I, 58–59. Toon: Askin Papers, Vol I, 55.

71. John Askin to Jean Baptiste Barthe, June 8, 1778, Askin Papers, Vol. I, 118. Pomp and crew: John Askin to Jean Baptiste Barthe, May 18, 1778, Askin Papers, Vol. I, 91–94. Askin says about this crew, "I have given all three their provisions, and rum, up to June 1, and have paid them their wages for the same time." This line may indicate that Pomp received some pay for his work, although Askin owned him and any pay would have been less than what the others received. More likely, as the sentence syntactically separates "provisions, and rum" from "wages," it can be read as differentiating these categories in a way that would not include Pompey as a recipient of wages.

72. Sale of Indian: John Askin to Jean Baptiste Barthe, June 8, 1778, Askin Papers, Vol. I, 119. Pretty Panis: John Askin to Mr. Beausoleil, May 18, 1778, Askin Papers, Vol. I, 97–98. Shoes and gown: John Askin to Todd and McGill at Montreal, May 28, 1778, Askin Papers, Vol. I, 101–102; Jacobson, *Detroit River*, 31–32. Fancy girls: Edward E. Baptist, "'Cuffy,' 'Fancy Maids,' and 'One-Eyed Men': Rape, Commodification, and the Domestic Slave Trade in the United States," *American Historical Review* 106:5 (December 2001): 1619–50. For more on fancy girls, see also Sharony Green, *Remember Me to Miss Louisa: Hidden Black-White Intimacies in Antebellum America* (DeKalb: Northern Illinois University Press, 2015); Sharony Green, "'Mr. Ballard, I Am Compelled to Write Again': Beyond Bedrooms and Brothels, a Fancy Girl Speaks," *Black Women, Gender & Families* 5:1 (Spring 2011): 17–40.

73. Askin Papers, Vol. I, 135. Sherene H. Razack, "Gendered Racial Violence and Spatialized Justice: The Murder of Pamela George," *Canadian Journal of Law and Society* 15:2 (2000): 91–130, 93.

74. Melissa R. Luberti, "Caught in the Revolution: The Moravians in Detroit," in Brunsman and Stone, eds., *Revolutionary Detroit*, 102–105, 102. Sympathy and complicity: Henry A. Ford, "History of the Moravian Settlement," also titled "The Old Moravian Mission at Mt. Clemens," Michigan Historical Collections, Vol. 10, 107–115, 110. Spies: Greg Dowd writes that the Moravians passed along information about an intended attack on Fort Laurens, Dowd, *Spirited*, 84–85. Taciturn: quoted in Ford, "Moravian Settlement," 1. Flames: quoted in Dowd, *Spirited*, 84. This insight about Zeisberger's reasoning comes from Greg Dowd's analysis. For more on the Moravians in the Midwest, see John Heckewelder, *A Narrative of the Mission of the United Brethren among the Delaware and Mohegan Indians* (Philadelphia, PA: McCarty & Davis, 1820).

75. Luberti, "Caught," 102–103. Mulatto: Moravian Diary, Oct 18, 1776, translation by Del Moyer.

76. Rev. David Zeisberger quoted in Ford, "Moravian Settlement," 110.

77. The attack took place in March of 1782: Luberti, "Caught," 103; Calloway, *American Revolution*, 39; Dowd, *Spirited*, 86; Silver, *Savage Neighbors*, 265–67. Treatment at Detroit: David Zeisberger, *Diary of David Zeisberger: A Moravian Missionary among the Indians of Ohio*, Vol. I, Eugene F. Bliss, ed. (Cincinnati: Robert Clark & Co., 1885), 111–12.

78. *Diary of Zeisberger*, Vol. 1, May, June 1783, 146, 154.

3: The Wild Northwest (1783–1803)

1. Benjamin Quarles, "The Revolutionary War as a Black Declaration of Independence," in Ira Berlin and Ronald Hoffman, eds., *Slavery and Freedom in the Age of the American Revolution* (Urbana: University of Illinois Press, 1983), 283. Manisha Sinha, *The Slave's Cause: A History of Abolition* (New Haven, CT: Yale University Press, 2016), 42–44, 51.

2. Edward Countryman, *The American Revolution* (1985; Revised Edition, New York: Hill and Wang, 2003), 228.

3. Report, Mr. Jefferson, Mr. Chafe, Mr. Howell, Temporary Government of Western Country Delivered March [ ]1784, MS/Jefferson Papers, BHC, DPL. The ordinance of 1784, drafted by a committee led by Jefferson, was viewed to be inadequate in part because it gave too much political authority to settlers in the territorial period. Jefferson was out of the country in 1787 when the new ordinance was written. Denis Duffey, "The Northwest Ordinance as a Constitutional Document," *Columbia Law Review* 95:4 (May 1995): 929–68, 935–37. Other members of Jefferson's 1784 committee included Samuel Chase and David Howell. In 1787, Peter Dane, a delegate from Massachusetts, introduced the slavery article for inclusion in the final text. Peter Onuf has argued that southerners could accept the slavery exception in the Northwest because they expected to benefit

economically through commercial exchange with the region as it grew. Peter S. Onuf, *Statehood and Union: A History of the Northwest Ordinance* (Bloomington: Indiana University Press, 1987), 46–49, 110–11.

4. Northwest Ordinance (1787), www.ourdocuments.gov. Accessed May 5, 2015.

5. Heather Ann Thompson, "Why Mass Incarceration Matters: Rethinking Crisis, Decline, and Transformation in Postwar American History," *Journal of American History* (December 2010): 703–734, on prison labor see 717–23.

6. David G. Chardavoyne, "The Northwest Ordinance and Michigan's Territorial Heritage," in Paul Finkelman and Martin J. Hershock, eds., *The History of Michigan Law* (Athens: Ohio University Press, 2006), 20.

7. Allison Mileo Gorsuch, "Midwest Territorial Courts and the Development of American Citizenship, 1810–1840" (Ph.D. diss., 2013), 40. Duffey, "Northwest Ordinance," 933–34.

8. "Foundational document": Duffey, "Northwest Ordinance," 949. I am borrowing language from Lisa Lowe when I describe slavery and colonialism as "braided." Lowe points to "settler colonialism as the condition for African slavery in the Americas." Lisa Lowe, *The Intimacies of Four Continents* (Durham, NC: Duke University Press, 2015), 37–38.

9. Paul Finkelman, "Evading the Ordinance: The Persistence of Bondage in Indiana and Illinois," *Journal of the Early Republic* 9:1 (Spring 1989): 21–51, 22.

10. Jefferson to Clark, Dec. 25, 1780, Jefferson Papers, Vol. 4, 237.

11. Proclamation by George R. Clark, December 24, 1778, translated in Jerry Lewis, "Red and Black Slaves in the Illinois Territory," in Terry Straus and Grant P. Arndt, eds., *Native Chicago* (Chicago: Albatross Publishers, 1998), 82–86. The Paris Peace Treaty of September 30, 1783, The Avalon Project, Yale Law School, avalon.law.yale.edu. Accessed May 5, 2015. William Renwick Riddell, "Notes on Great Britain and Canada with Respect to the Negro," *Journal of Negro History* 13:2 (April 1928): 185–98, 186.

12. Russell, ed., *Michigan Censuses*, 1782 Census, 49–56; Katzman, "Black Slavery in Michigan," 60. William Macomb re Sale of Two Negro Slaves, Macomb Family Papers, BHC, DPL.

13. Heidi Bohaker, "Reading Anishinaabe Identities: Meaning and Metaphor in Nindoodem Pictographs," *Ethnohistory* 57:1 (Winter 2010): 11–33, 18.

14. Sale of Negro Man Pompey, Copy of Deed Furnished by W.W. Backus of Detroit, "Reports of Counties, Etc.," MPHC, Vol. VI, 417.

15. James Mackelm to John Askin, September 4, 1801, Askin Correspondence, John Askin Papers, Folder 1800, BHC, DPL; James Mackelm to John Askin, September 20, 1801, Askin Correspondence, John Askin Papers, Folder 1800, BHC, DPL. Campau Family Papers, MS/Campau, 1715–1928 (delivery orders: Oct. 1791, Sept. 1792, Jan. 1796, Dec. 1797, Jan. 1804) BHC, DPL.

16. Calloway, *American Revolution*, 23.

17. It can be convincingly argued that these lands were not Great Britain's to cede. For a critical discussion of British claims to possessing Native lands in the Canadian borderland region dating back to 1668, see Adam Gaudry, "Fantasies of Sovereignty: Deconstructing British and Canadian Claims to Ownership of the Historic-Northwest," *NAIS: Journal of the Native American and Indigenous Studies Association* 3:1 (2016): 46–74. Gov. Arthur St. Clair as slaveholder: Lehman, *Slavery in the Upper Mississippi Valley*, 12.

18. David R. Farrell, "Askin (Erskine), John," *Dictionary of Canadian Biography Online*, 2, http://www.biographi.ca/009004-11901-ephp?id_nbr=2242. Accessed Oct. 12, 2012. For more on Belle Isle see Janet Anderson, *Island in the City: Belle Isle, Detroit's Beautiful Island*, Companion Book to an Exhibit at the Detroit Historical Museum, 2001, Bentley Historical Library, University of Michigan, Ann Arbor, MI; Michael Rodriguez and Thomas Featherstone, Detroit's Belle Isle: Island Park Gem (Chicago: Arcadia Publishing, 2003). Taylor, *Divided Ground*, 10.

19. Riddell, *Michigan Under British Rule*, 22, 26.

20. Farmer, *History of Detroit*, 84; David Lee Poremba, ed., *Detroit in Its World Setting: A Three Hundred Year Chronology, 1701–2001* (Detroit: Wayne State University Press, 2001), 61, 62, 63, 346. D W Smith to John Askin, June 25, 1793, Askin Papers, Vol. II, 476–77.

21. Ste. Anne's Records. This marriage also linked Grant to John Askin, as it was Askin's sister-in-law who became Grant's wife. Farrell, "Askin," *Dictionary of Canadian Biography*, 3.

22. Bill of Sale Josiah Cutten, Askin Papers, Vol. I, 284–87, 410–411.

23. Harrow Family File, "The King's Vessels," 29, 36 (1786), BHC, DPL.

24. Alexander Harrow Papers, Journal and Letter Book, typescript, D5 1791–1800, MS/Harrow, BHC, DPL. Stinson argues astutely that slave labor shored up white masculinity and class status in westward settlements where the idealized gentility of white life was difficult to reproduce and maintain. Stinson, "Black Bondspeople," 17, 18 (unpublished version, cited by permission).

25. John Askin Estate Inventory - Detroit 1787, Jan. 1, 1787, John Askin Papers, BHC, DPL. Pompey does not appear in this inventory.

26. Ste. Anne's Records, 1785, BHL, UM.

27. Alexander Coventry, *Memoirs of an Emigrant The Journal of Alexander Coventry, M.D.; in Scotland, the United States and Canada during the period 1783–1831*, Vol. I (Albany: The Albany Institute of Art and History, 1978), 1797, p. 859; quoted in Emily Macgillivray and Tiya Miles, "'She Has Lived in Fashion': A Native Woman Trader's Household in the Detroit River Region," accepted for eds., Karen Marrero and Andrew Sturtevant, *A Place in Common: Telling Histories of Early Detroit* (Lansing: Michigan State University Press, in progress); Ainse's household: Macgillivray and Miles, "'She Has Lived in Fashion.'" Ainse's spouse Montour and relocation to Detroit: Taylor, *Divided Ground*, 397, 399. Emily Macgil-

livray, "Indigenous Trading Women of the Borderland Great Lakes, 1740–1845" (Ph.D. diss., University of Michigan, Ann Arbor, 2017).

28. Askin Papers, Vol. I, 193.

29. Margaret Paulee, captured by the Shawnee warrior White Bark, described Blue Jacket's Detroit home and slaves in two accounts; quoted in John Sugden, *Blue Jacket: Warrior of the Shawnees* (Lincoln: University of Nebraska Press, 2003), 5; Blue Jacket's father-in-law was Jacques Baby, p. 53. For more on Paulee, see John H. Moore, "A Captive of the Shawnees, 1779–1784," *West Virginia History* 23:4 (July 1962): 287–96.

30. Excerpts from Fragments of an Account Book at the Fort Malden Museum Amherstburg, Ontario, May 27, 1784, cited in Macgillivray and Miles, "'She Has Lived in Fashion.'" Ainse's business in Detroit: Taylor, *Divided Ground*, 399. Ainse's male partner in Detroit: Macgillivray, "Indigenous Trading Women."

31. Macgillivray, "Indigenous Trading Women." Macgillivray and Miles, "'She Has Lived in Fashion'"; Emily Macgillivray generously shared her findings about Ainse's familial ties to Moravians in the Detroit area.

32. Zeisberger Diary, Vol. 1, Sept. 1782, p. 111; Oct. 5, 1783, 166; Zeisberger Diary, Vol. 2, Sept. 27, 1796, p. 458; Zeisberger Diary, Vol. 1, June 14, 1784, pp. 194–95; 1782, p.106; 1784, p. 205; Nov. 16, 1785, p. 249.

33. Zeisberger Diary, Vol. 1, 1782, p. 117; Feb. 26, 1784, p. 183; Ford "History of the Moravian Settlement" / "Old Moravian Mission," 110, 113; Zeisberger Diary, Vol. 1, Feb. 22, 1784, p. 183; Feb. 12, 1784, p. 182.

34. Zeisberger Diary, Vol. 1, Feb. 13, 1784, p. 182.

35. Taylor, *Divided Ground,* 136. Harrow Papers, Journal and Letterbook, March 15, 1799, BHC, DPL.

36. "Matthew Elliott Essex County," (Toronto: York University, Harriet Tubman Institute, 2012), 1, 3, 4. For more on Elliott's use of slave and indentured labor, see Reginald Horsman, *Matthew Elliott, British Indian Agent* (Detroit: Wayne State University Press, 1964), 9, 29, 49.

37. Zeisberger Diary, Vol. 2, 1791, p. 232. Diary of the Indian Congregation at Fairfield in Upper Canada, 1801, January 25, 1801, Moravian Archives, Bethlehem, PA, translated for Tiya Miles by Del-Louise Moyer. Diary of the Indian Congregation in Salem, Petquottink in Lake Erie, 1790–91, May 5, 1791, Moravian Archives, Bethlehem, PA, translated for Tiya Miles by Del-Louise Moyer, 2014.

38. Meldrum: Cangany, *Frontier Seaport,* 29. Land: "The Tucker Story," Highlights from the Harrison Township Historical Commission's First Educational Presentation: The Legacy of William Tucker," April 27, 1994. Land and Virginia slaves as the Denisons: Robert F. Eldredge, *Past and Present of Macomb County, Michigan* (Chicago: S. J. Clarke Publishing Co., 1905), 626–27. Location on river: Zeisberger Diary, Vol. 1, Oct. 1, 1784, p. 203. Bride and slaves: "Tucker, William, House," MI State Historic Preservation Objects, www.mcgi.state.mi.us/hso/sites /9541.htm. Accessed January 16, 2013.

39. Zeisberger Diary, Vol. 1, Aug. 9, 1783, p. 160; vol. 2, Sun July 29, 1791, p. 186, Sun Aug. 7, 1791, p. 206.

40. *Denison et al v. Catherine Tucker,* in William Wirt Blume, ed., *Transactions of the Supreme Court of the Territory of Michigan, 1805–1814,* Vol. II (Ann Arbor: University of Michigan Press, 1935), 133–136. Isabella E. Swan, *Lisette* (Grosse Ile, MI: Published by the Author, 1965), 4.

41. Swan, *Lisette,* 3.

42. No record that I was able to identify indicates Hannah Denison's place of birth. Because she was moved through French and Indian circles, it seems likely that she was born in or obtained from Montreal or Quebec, where most slaves in northern New France were held. Within these two cities, Marcel Trudel found a fairly even number of black slaves, who made up 35.9 percent and 39.5 percent of the populations, respectively. Trudel, *Canada's Forgotten,* 257.

43. Swan, *Lisette,* 4 note 6. Mark McPherson, "Lisette's Legacy of Slavery" (second of a five part series), *Michigan Chronicle,* February 3, 1999. File B/Negroes—Forth, Elizabeth Denison, Reading Room, DPL. Elizabeth Denison Forth's Elmwood Cemetery record gives her birth place as Virginia. This is likely an error dating back to county histories that said William Tucker brought a slave family with him from Virginia. This cemetery record also states that Forth died at age 114, another likely error. R. C. Simpson, To Whom It May Concern, Elmwood Cemetery, File B/Negroes—Forth, Elizabeth Denison, Reading Room, DPL.

44. "The Dennison DNA Project," http://www.johnbrobb.com/JBR-DEN-1.htm. Accessed September 13, 2016. "Denniston/Dennison/Denison Homepage," http://freepages.genealogy.rootsweb.ancestry.com/~vadennison. Accessed September 13, 2016.

45. Mark McPherson, "Lisette's Legacy of Slavery," (second of a five part series) *Michigan Chronicle,* February 3, 1999. File B/Negroes—Forth, Elizabeth Denison, Reading Room, DPL.

46. Harrow Papers, Journal and Letter Book, June 24, 1798, BHC, DPL.

47. Chippewa use and defense of land: Zeisberger Diary, Vol. 1, 1782, pp. 91, 122, 184; Nov. 1784, p. 207; Jan. 1785, p. 217; Jan. 1786, p. 256; Ford, "Moravian Settlement," 6.

48. Winter and famine: Zeisberger Diary, Vol. 1, 1784, pp. 183, 203, 211; 1787, p. 353, 1788, p. 451; 1789, p. 47. Pestilence: Zeisberger Diary, Vol. 1, 1789, pp. 57–58.

49. Zeisberger Diary, Vol. 2, 1791, p. 217; Nov. 1793, pp. 329–31.

50. Dowd, *Spirited,* 113.

51. New era and empire creation quotations: Calloway, *American Revolution,* xv.

52. Quoted from title of Karl S. Hele, ed., *Lines Drawn upon the Water: First Nations and the Great Lakes Borders and Borderlands* (Waterloo, Ontario: Wilfrid Laurier University Press, 2008).

53. Zeisberger Diary, Vol. 2, 1796, p. 461.

54. The Jay Treaty, November 19, 1794, The Avalon Project, Avalon.aw.yale.edu, Article 2.

55. The Jay Treaty, November 19, 1794, The Avalon Project, Avalon.aw.yale.edu, Article 2. Gorsuch, "Midwest Territorial Courts," 15, 25, 34.

56. Martha S. Jones, "Time, Space, and Jurisdiction in Atlantic World Slavery: The Volunbrun Household in Gradual Emancipation New York," *Law and History Review* 29:4, Law, Slavery, and Justice: A Special Issue (November 2011): 1031–60, 1034.

57. Christopher Phillips, *The Rivers Ran Backward: The Civil War and the Remaking of the American Middle Border* (New York: Oxford University Press, 2016), 6, 10. Phillips locates his slaveholding ancestors in Kentucky.

58. 1773 Detroit Census, September 22, 1773, *Michigan Pioneer and Historical Collection, 1876–1886*, Vol. 9 (Lansing: Pioneer Society of the State of Michigan), 649; Russell, ed., *Michigan Censuses*, 1782, 49–56, 1796, 59–67; Ste. Anne's Records, BHC.

59. Christian Crouch establishes this point about the racial makeup of slaves changing in Detroit with the influx of Anglo settlers. Christian Crouch, "The Black City: African and Indian Exchange in Pontiac's Detroit," revision of Christian Crouch, "The Black City: Detroit and the Northeast Borderlands through African Eyes in the Era of 'Pontiac's War,'" paper presented at The War Called Pontiac's conference, Philadelphia, April 2013, cited by permission of the author, 2, 29. Marcel Trudel's sums for the number of slaves held in Detroit are larger than mine overall. In a chart that breaks down the number of slaves in the province of Quebec (the borders of which changed over time) by city, he lists for Detroit 523 Indian slaves and 127 black slaves for a total of 650 slaves; Trudel, *Canada's Forgotten*, 83, 75. Unfortunately, his incredibly instructive chart does not indicate exactly which sources he drew from to arrive at these totals for Detroit. My highest total for the enslaved population in Detroit is closer to 300. I attribute this variance to a number of factors. First, Trudel looks at a time span of 1629–1834, Second, he includes a wide range of French Canadian archival documents that I did not review. He counted each mention of a slave in these documents to arrive at a total number of 4,200 slaves in Quebec and the subsequent town breakdown. Third, Detroit's general population numbers shift depending upon what boundaries are drawn (inside the fort walls, or inside as well as outside; on one side of the river, or on both sides), making stable and transparent enumeration a challenge. While I did keep a running count of the number of enslaved people who appeared in Detroit-based slaveholders' manuscript records, I did not add these numbers to my totals. I relied on Ste. Anne's Church records and census records as the main sources for my sums and used them to corroborate each other. The numbers on the Ste. Anne's register ran very close to the census numbers. Adding the church, census, and manuscript record numbers together would have brought me to an overall figure closer to Trudel's at 600, but I strove to avoid double counting in a situation in which many enslaved people went unnamed. Readers may therefore take my figures as conservative estimates. For

additional sources that offer population figures for Detroit's enslaved, see David M. Katzman, "Black Slavery in Michigan," *Midcontinent American Studies Journal* 11: 2 (fall 1970): 56–66, 62, 65. William Renwick Riddell, "The Slave in Upper Canada," *Journal of the American Institute of Criminal Law and Criminology* 14:2 (August 1923): 249–278, 251, note 10.

60. The outcome of Francois's case is not recorded. Askin Papers, Vol. I, 399–401. Ford, "Moravian Settlement" / "Old Moravian Mission," 114–15.

61. Zeisberger Diary, Vol. 2, 1794, p. 380.

62. Madelaine Askin to John Askin, March 4, 1798, Askin Papers, Vol. II, 132–33. Alexander Harrow Papers, Feb. 13, 1797, Feb. 14, 1797, Feb. 28, 1797, March 27, 1797, July 22, 1797, June 1, 1798, March 25, 1799, BHC, DPL.

63. Kenneth W. Porter, "Negroes and the Fur Trade," *Minnesota History* 15:4 (Dec. 1934) 421–33, 424. John Askin Estate Inventory - Detroit 1787, Jan. 1, 1787, "Debts due Me taken from . . . Book No. 11," John Askin Papers, Burton Historical Collection, DPL.

64. Record Book of Macomb Estate, Macomb Family Papers, R2:1796, BHC, DPL. Bet and her sons do not seem to have ended up with Captain Harrow, who tried to buy them in the same year. F. Clever Bald, *Detroit's First American Decade, 1796 to 1805* (Ann Arbor: University of Michigan Press, 1948), 31.

65. Robert B. Ross, *The Early Bench and Bar of Detroit from 1805 to the End of 1850* (Detroit: Published by Richard P. Joy and Clarence M. Burton, 1907), 137.

66. As quoted in Ross, *Early Bench*, 139.

67. May ledger book, James May Papers, D3: 1792–98, BHC, DPL; May Daybook, D3: 1798–1804, BHC, DPL. This may have been a different Pompey than the man Askin bought in 1775.

68. As quoted in Ross, *Early Bench*, 139.

69. John Askin Papers, Vol. II, 358.

70. F. Clever Bald, *Detroit's First American Decade, 1796 to 1805* (Ann Arbor: University of Michigan Press, 1948), 187, 134.

71. Askin Papers, Vol. II, 358–59.

72. Foot injury: Letterbooks of Phyn and Ellice, April 19, 1775, BHS. Toon's death: Askin Papers, diary, v. 1, 50–58. Clinging to rock, frozen to death: Moravian Diary, Thames River, Ontario, June 3, 1807, December 1, 1800, translated by Del-Louise Moyer. These last two references are to enslaved men owned by Matthew Elliott.

73. Askin Papers, Vol. II, 563.

74. Bald, *Detroit's First*, 75, 106, 151.

75. John Askin to Jam & McGill, May 15, 1800, Askin Papers, Vol. II, 293. Also quoted in Bald, *Detroit's First*, 165–66.

76. John McCall was the printer in Detroit in 1796. According to Clever Bald,

citing Silas Farmer, McCall was likely using a printing press formerly owned by William Macomb. Bald, *Detroit's First*, 93, fn 6.

77. As quoted in Ross, *Early Bench*, 138.

78. Frederick A. Ogg, *The Old Northwest: A Chronicle of the Ohio Valley and Beyond* (Toronto: Glasgow, Brook & Co.; Textbook Edition, Yale University Press, 1919), 99, 134–35. Brian Leigh Dunnigan, "The War of 1812 in The Old Northwest: An Introduction to the Bicentennial Edition, in Alec R. Gilpin, ed., *The War of 1812 in The Old Northwest* (1958; reprint, East Lansing: Michigan State University Press, 2012), viii. Bald, *Detroit's First*, 138, 132. R.W. Dick Phillips, *Arthur St. Clair II: The Invisible Patriot* (Bloomington, IN: iUniverse LLC), 39.

79. As quoted in Bald, *Detroit's First*, 132; Bald, *Detroit's First*, 139.

80. Ogg, *The Old Northwest*, 78.

81. Michigan Censuses, 1796 Wayne County, 74. This figure is an undercount. Hundreds more residents lived in settlements stretching along the river for miles, making a total of 2,053. In addition, one hundred absent men were estimated by the census takers to have been missed.

82. As quoted in Bald, *Detroit's First*, 140.

83. As quoted in Bald, *Detroit's First*, 140. For a detailed account of the tobacco spitting incident and Bates's view of French women, see Gitlin, *Bourgeois Frontier*, 147–148. For more on French elite adaptation to American expansion into former French territories, see Eberhard L. Faber, *Building on the Land of Dreams: New Orleans and the Transformation of Early America* (Princeton, NJ: Princeton University Press, 2016).

84. As quoted in Bald, *Detroit's First*, 141.

85. Bald, Detroit's First, 161, 169. Clarence M. Burton, *History of Detroit, 1780–1850, Financial and Commercial* (Detroit, 1917), 43.

86. Notices in French & English: Corporation of the Town of Detroit: Act of Incorporation and Journal of the Board of Trustees, 1802–1805 (Detroit: Printed under the authority of the Common Council of Detroit with an Introduction by C.M. Burton, Historiographer, Burton Historical Collection, 1922), 44. Mail and news: Bald, *Detroit's First*, 92–93. Mail: Observations relative to Wayne County by Sol. Sibley, for the perusal of Capt W. H. Harrison, 1800, Solomon Sibley Papers, BHC, DPL; Geo Wallace to James Henry, October 1802, Sibley Papers, BHC, DPL. Sibley's views: Observations relative to Wayne County by Sol. Sibley, for the perusal of Capt W. H. Harrison, 1800, Solomon Sibley Papers, BHC, DPL.

87. Bald, *Detroit's First*, 189.

88. Burton, *History of Detroit*, 43.

89. John Askin to Robert Hamilton, April 8, 1802, Askin Papers, vol. II, 372–74.

90. Solomon Sibley to S. C. Vance, Aug. 20, 1803, Sibley Papers, BHC, DPL.

91. Quoted in Finkelman, "Evading the Ordinance," 30. Onuf, *Statehood and Union*, 117.

92. Finkelman, "Evading the Ordinance," 22, 23, 24, 36. M. Scott Heerman, "In a State of Slavery: Black Servitude in Illinois, 1800–1830," *Early American Studies: An Interdisciplinary Journal* 14:1 (Winter 2016): 114–39, 117, 118. Allison Mileo Gorsuch, "To Indent Oneself: Ownership, Contracts, and Consent in Antebellum Illinois," in Jean Allain, ed., *The Legal Understanding of Slavery: From the Historical to the Contemporary* (New York: Oxford University Press, 2012), 134, 137. Kinds of labor: Finkelman, 42; Heerman, 127, 129, 130.

93. Henry Hastings Sibley as slaveholder: Walt Bachman, *Northern Slave, Black Dakota: The Life and Times of Joseph Godfrey* (Bloomington, MN: Pond Dakota Press, Pond Dakota Heritage Society, 2013), 19, 20, 59, 198 n. 41. For more on slavery in Minnesota, see Christopher P. Lehman, *Slavery in the Upper Mississippi Valley, 1787-1865* (Jefferson, NC: McFarland & Company Inc., 2011), 114–141. "Governors of Minnesota," Minnesota Historical Society, http://collections.mnhs.org/governors/index.php/10003986. "House Divided," Dickinson College, http://hd.housedivided.dickinson.edu/node/39873. Both accessed July 29, 2016.

94. Donna Valley Russell, ed., *Michigan Censuses 1710–1830,* 1782 (Detroit: Detroit Society for Genealogical Research, Inc., 1982), 49–57.

95. The Declaration of Independence, The Charters of Freedom, www.archives.gov/exhibits/charters/declaration_transcript.html. Accessed April 7, 2015.

96. Macomb County is formally named for Alexander Macomb, son of Alexander Macomb (William Macomb's brother) and a War of 1812 veteran and Army commander in chief from 1828 to 1841. Macomb was born in 1782 in Detroit at the height of the city's slaveholding period. Like his uncle William, Alexander's father owned slaves and had seven enslaved people in his household the year the younger Alexander was born. Alexander Macomb likely inherited human property. Russell, ed., *Michigan Censuses* (Detroit Census of 1782), 54. Governor Lewis Cass established the name for Michigan's third county in 1818. www.michmarkers.com/startup.asp?startpage=S0418.htm. Accessed May 30, 2016.

4: The Winds of Change (1802–1807)

1. Riddell, *Michigan Under British Rule,* 19–20. Northwest Ordinance, July 13, 1787; (National Archives Microfilm Publication M332, roll 9); Northwest Ordinance (1787), www.ourdocuments.gov. Accessed May 5, 2015. Miscellaneous Papers of the Continental Congress, 1774–89; Records of the Continental and Confederation Congresses and the Constitutional Convention, 1774–89, Record Group 360; National Archives; https://ourdocuments.gov/doc.php?flash=true&doc=8. Accessed June 2, 2016. Duffey, "Northwest Ordinance," 956.

2. Adelaide's elder sisters were Thérèse, Ellen, and Archange. Archange Askin's husband was Captain David Meredith. Askin Papers, Vol. I, 13–16; Fashion: Cangany, *Frontier Seaport,* 49; Education: Jennifer Dionne, "Franco-Ontariens avant la lettre? La correspendence de la famille Askin" (PhD. Diss., University of Ottawa, 2007), 46–47.

3. Solomon Sibley to Samuel Vance October 1, 1802, Samuel C. Vance Papers,

Manuscripts and Visual Collections Department, William Henry Smith Memorial Library, Indiana Historical Society, Indianapolis, IN.

4. Wedding: Bald, *Detroit's First,* 19. China: Elijah Brush to Hugh Martin, February 25, 1802, Sibley Papers, BHC, DPL; also quoted in Bald, *Detroit's First,* 191. Silver: E Brush to Robinson and Martin, July 28, 1803; also quoted in Bald, *Detroit's First,* 215. Elijah Brush to Martin & Robinson, July 11, 1802, Sibley Papers, BHC, DPL. Summer cloak, bonnet, shoes: E. Brush to Robinson & Martin, February 9, 1804, Sibley Papers, BHC, DBL, also quoted in Bald, *Detroit's First,* 225. Men's clothing: Brush to Martin & Robinson, July 11, 1802, Sibley Papers, BHC, DPL; Beaver hat: Elijah Brush to Robinson & Martin, Sibley Papers Aug 7, 1802, BHC, DPL. Catherine Cangany first makes this point that the Brushes ordered items from New York while most Detroiters could not; Cangany, *Frontier Seaport,* 45–46.

5. Bald, *Detroit's First,* 215, 225.

6. John Askin to Alexander Henry, February 27, 1802, Askin Papers, Vol. II, 371.

7. John Askin to Robert Hamilton, April 8, 1802, Askin Papers, Vol. II, 372–74.

8. Askin to Hamilton, April 8, 1802, Askin Papers, Vol. II, 372–74.

9. John Askin to Isaac Todd, April 8, 1802, Askin Papers, BHC, DPL.

10. John Askin to Robert Hamilton, April 8, 1802, Askin Papers, Vol. II, 372–74; Bald, *Detroit's First,* 197.

11. Elijah Brush to John Askin, March 22, 1805, Askin Papers, Vol. II, 459–60.

12. Bald, *Detroit's First,* 197. Askin to James and McGill, April 8, 1802; Taxes in 1802, Bald, *Detroit's First,* 193–94. Brush obtained title to the Askin farm in 1806. Sale of Brush Farm, Askin Papers, Vol. II, pp. 530–32; Jacobson, *Detroit River Connections,* 60–61.

13. John Askin Jr. to John Askin, November 11, 1807, Askin Papers Vol. II, pp. 583–84; Bald, *Detroit's First,* 233.

14. Afua Cooper, "The Fluid Frontier: Blacks and the Detroit River Region. A Focus on Henry Bibb," *Canadian Review of American Studies* 30:2 (2000): 130, 133.

15. As quoted in Reginald Horsman, *Matthew Elliott, British Indian Agent* (Detroit: Wayne State University Press, 1964), 46; Shawnee wife: Horsman, 144; quoted in Horsman, 48.

16. Quoted in "Matthew Elliott Essex County" (Toronto: York University, Harriet Tubman Institute, 2012), 4, 5; whipping and shackles: "Matthew Elliott," 5.

17. William Henry Smith, ed., *The St. Clair Papers. The Life and Public Services of Arthur St. Clair,* Vol. II (Cincinnati: Robert Clarke & Co., 1882), 318–19. For a critique of the Northwest Ordinance's effect on black and Native populations, see Sakina Mariam Hughes, "Under One Big Tent: American Indians, African Americans and the Circus World of Nineteenth-Century America" (Ph.D. diss., Michigan State University, 2012), 52–55.

18. Martha S. Jones, "Time, Space, and Jurisdiction In Atlantic World Slavery: The Volunbrun Household in Gradual Emancipation New York," *Law and History Review* 29:4, Law, Slavery, and Justice: A Special Issue (November 2011): 1031–60, 1034.

19. Askin Papers, Vol. II, 357–58. Simon Campaue Complaint, Sibley Papers, March 25, 1802, BHC, DPL. Jas. Henry to any or either Constables of the County of Wayne, July 3, 1802, Sibley Papers, BHC, DPL. In the Case of Toby, a Panis Man, in William Wirt Blume, ed., *Transactions of the Supreme Court of the Territory of Michigan, 1805–1814* Vol. II (Ann Arbor: The University of Michigan Press, 1935), 404, 405. Mary Abbott, Complaint, June 1802, Sibley Papers, BHC, DPL.

20. Elizabeth Audrain married to Robert Abbott: Burton, *History of Detroit*, 20. Abbot v. Jones, September 28, 1807, in Blume, ed., *Supreme Court of Michigan* Vol. II, 23–28.

21. Abbot v. Jones, September 28, 1807, in Blume, ed., *Supreme Court of Michigan* Vol. II, 23–28.

22. For unfree people's negotiation of indenture contracts, see Heerman, "In a State of Slavery." For enslaved people's and free blacks' use of law, see Laura F. Edwards, "Status without Rights: African Americans and the Tangled History of Law and Governance in the Nineteenth-Century U.S. South," *American Historical Review* 112:2 (2007): 365–93; Ariela Gross and Alejandro De La Fuente, "Slaves, Free Blacks, and Race in the Legal Regimes of Cuba, Louisiana, and Virginia: A Comparison," *North Carolina Law Review* 91:5 (June 2013): 1769–56; Ariela J. Gross, *What Blood Won't Tell: A History of Race on Trial in America* (Cambridge, MA: Harvard University Press, 2008); Martha S. Jones, *Birthright Citizens: A History of Race and Rights in Antebellum America* (New York: Cambridge University Press, 2017).

23. A.J. Hull to Jaques Lassell, June 5, 1805, Sibley Papers, BHC, DPL. Antoine and Anna Smith are also referred to as Anthony and Anne Smith in the records.

24. A.J. Hull to Jaques Lassell, June 5, 1805, Sibley Papers, BHC, DPL.

25. Ste. Anne Records, October 15, 1803, June 22, 1816. The record referencing Angelique's birth says she was born to an "unknown father." This may have been an oversight in the record, or Antoine may no longer have been with his family.

26. Alexander Harrow to Robert Taylor his servant, conditional manumission of said Rob, July 2, 1802, Sibley Papers, BHC, DPL.

27. Ransom to Grant, August 7, 1802, Sibley Papers, BHC, DPL. John Reed: August 13, 1803, August 19, 1803, Sibley Papers, BHC, DPL. James May was appointed U.S. marshal from August to November 1806; Farmer History of Detroit, 176.

28. S. Sibley to Col. Grant, August 19, 1803, Sibley Papers, BHC, DPL.

29. Christian Crouch makes a similar point, arguing that enslaved blacks may have learned the terrain and how to negotiate it politically from the example of native people. Christian Crouch, "The Black City: African and Indian Exchange

in Pontiac's Detroit," revision of Christian Crouch, "The Black City: Detroit and the Northeast Borderlands through African Eyes in the Era of 'Pontiac's War,'" paper presented at The War Called Pontiac's conference, Philadelphia, April 2013, cited by permission of the author.

30. Charles St. Bernard, Indenture, October 4, 1799, Berthelet Papers, Burton Historical Collection, Detroit Public Library.

31. Heerman, "State of Slavery," 117. "Bob's Indenture," 1802, William Woodbridge Papers, 1763–1919, BHC, DPL. Preserved servitude contracts are few and far between in Detroit and most often identify poor whites and free Native American workers, but some of these records might be further evidence of the experience of enslaved people. For another Detroit indentured servant record, see Matt Henry, Justice of the Peace, July 31, 1803, Solomon Sibley Papers, BHC, DPL.

32. David Maney to Eliabeth Burnett, September 17, 1802, Sibley Papers, BHC, DPL. James May Papers, D3, 1792–98, Pomp: September 6, 1795, Black Betty: August 3, 1797, BHC, DPL. May Papers, D3: 1798–1804 Daybook, Burnett: August 27, 1800, La Leavre: December 3, 1800, Black Patty: April 10, 1801, BHC, DPL. Black Betty and Black Patty's names are similar enough that they might have been the same person. May's daybook also includes a payment reference for 1793: "cash lent him to pay Baby's man," Vincent Laframboise: June 1793, May Papers BHC, DPL. Macomb Papers, Ledger, August 27, Sept 3, September 10 1804, January 6, 1805, April 9, 1805.

33. Askin Papers, Vol. II, pp. 388–89.

34. Diary of the Reconnoitering Trip Made by Brothers Luckenbach and Haven, Accompanied by the Indian Brother Andreas, at St. Mary's River, the Southern Arm of Miami, which Empties into Lake Erie, August 29, 1808 (B157F11 08-29-1808), Moravian Archives, Bethlehem, PA, translated for Tiya Miles by Del-Louise Moyer, 2015. Tanner, *Atlas of Great Lakes Indian History*, Maps 17, 18 pp. 85–88. Joseph Badger, A Memoir of Rev. Joseph Badger (Hudson, OH: Sawyer, Ingersoll & Co., 1851; Niles, OH: Niles Historical Society, 1997, 100, 130–31. "The Journal of Benjamin Larkin, 1794–1820," in William Warren Sweet, ed., *Religion on the American Frontier, 1783–1840: The Methodists: A Collection of Source Materials*, Vol. 4 (Chicago: University of Chicago Press, 1946), 241. Historian William Hart places the contemporary location of Negrotown at: "the intersections of County Routes 37, 29, and 40 just west of Belle Vernon, Ohio, and north of Upper Sandusky. Bill Hart, "Sources to 'Negrotown,' Ohio, 1800–1843," unpublished compilation, 2016.

35. Diary of Fairfield Mission, Thames River, Ontario, Canada, 1792–1813, July 4 1797, Moravian Archives, Bethlehem, PA, translated for Tiya Miles by Del-Louise Moyer.

36. Kenneth W. Porter, "Negroes and the Fur Trade," *Minnesota History* 15:4 (Dec. 1934), 421–33, 424. Bill Hart, "Sources to 'Negrotown,' Ohio, 1800–1843," unpublished compilation, 2016.

37. Bill Hart, "Sources to 'Negrotown,' Ohio, 1800–1843," unpublished compilation, 2016.

38. Bill Hart, Conversation with Tiya Miles about Negro Town, June 7, 2016, Middlebury, VT. For more on black-Wyandot relations in Ohio, see Sakina M. Hughes, "The Community Became an Almost Civilized and Christian One: John Stewart's Mission to the Wyandots and Religious Colonialism as African American Racial Uplift," *NAIS: Journal of the Native American and Indigenous Studies Association* 3:1 (2016): 24–45.

39. Askin Papers, Vol. II, 561–63. Nobbin was recaptured and held at the Askin estate on May's behalf. May proclaimed that Nobbin was likely afraid of being whipped as punishment. In 1813, John Askin bemoaned the escape of his enslaved woman, Madelaine; Askin Papers, Vol. II, 772.

40. Escapes seem to increase after 1796; however, record keeping improves as well at this moment due to the activity of the court. It is therefore possible that the number of escapes remained nearly constant but that evidence becomes more plentiful because of court recording.

41. As quoted in Judy Jacobson, *Detroit River Connections: Historiographical and Biographical Sketches of the Eastern Great Lakes Border Region* (Baltimore: Clearfield Company, 1994), 6.1

42. Bald, *Detroit's First*, 190; Bald, *Great Fire*, 4–5.

43. Corporation of the Town of Detroit: Act of Incorporation and Journal of the Board of Trustees, 1802–1805 (Detroit: Printed under the authority of the Common Council of Detroit with an Introduction by C.M. Burton, Historiographer, Burton Historical Collection, 1922), 41.

44. An Act for the Relief and Settlement of the Poor, in *Laws of the Territory of Michigan: Laws Adopted by the Governor and Judges*, Vol. 1 (Lansing: W. S. George & Co Printers to the State, 1871), 4 vols. University of Michigan Law Library, Source library: Yale Law Library, *The Making of Modern Law: Primary Sources*, 602. An Act to Regulate Blacks and Mulattoes, and to Punish the Kidnapping of Such Persons, in *Laws of the Territory of Michigan*, 634. The earliest law addressing indentured servitude in American Detroit was a Michigan Territory law passed in 1809: An Act for Support of the Poor stipulated that servants who had completed their contracts could become lawful settlers but that bringing "paupers" into the territory would be penalized. In 1827, a later territorial law, An Act for the Relief and Settlement of the Poor, stipulated that each town had to maintain its own poor and that individuals who had completed their indentures in the territory were legal settlers. Also in 1827, a more detailed Act Concerning Apprentices and Servants was passed, which assumed voluntary servitude for all servants, required parental or guardian approval for minors, set an age limit at twenty-one years for length of childhood indenture and noted that indentures might have varying specific durations, provided for the jailing of servants who reneged on their duties, and allowed for complaints to be made about mistreatment by masters. *Laws of the Territory of Michigan: Laws Adopted by the Governor and Judges.*

Vol. 2. (Lansing: W. S. George & Co Printers to the State, 1874), pp. 40, 507–508, 595. None of these laws make mention of race. For more on Thornton and Lucie (also Rutha) Blackburn, see: Karolyn Smardz Frost, "Forging Transnational Networks for Freedom: From the War of 1812 to the Blackburn Riots of 1833," in Karolyn Smardz Frost and Veta Smith Tucker, eds., *A Fluid Frontier: Slavery, Resistance, and the Underground Railroad in the Detroit River Borderland* (Detroit: Wayne State University Press, 2016), 43–66; Norman McRae, "Crossing the Detroit River to Find Freedom," *Michigan History* Vol. 67, No. 2 (March/April 1983): 35–39.

45. Bald, *Great Fire*, 10–11. By adopting a comprehensive fire prevention system, Detroit was borrowing from cities like Philadelphia, which began adopting similar codes in the early 1700s. Arwen P. Mohun, *Risk: Negotiating Safety in American Society* (Baltimore: Johns Hopkins University Press, 2013), 12, 17, 24.

46. Bald, *Detroit's First*, 197; Bald, *Great Fire*, 10.

47. Corporation of the Town of Detroit: Act of Incorporation and Journal of the Board of Trustees, 1802–1805 (Detroit: Printed under the authority of the Common Council of Detroit with an Introduction by C.M. Burton, Historiographer, Burton Historical Collection, 1922), 37–38, 59. Henry Berthelet applied for U.S. citizenship and took the oath in Detroit in 1807; In the Matter of the application of Henry Berthelet, in William Wirt Blume, ed., *Transactions of the Supreme Court of the Territory of Michigan, 1805–1814*, Vol. I (Ann Arbor: The University of Michigan Press, 1935), 404.

48. The United States vs. Margaret White, September 4, 1800, Woodbridge Papers, BHC, DPL. White pled not guilty. Rashauna Johnson, *Slavery's Metropolis: Unfree Labor in New Orleans During the Age of Revolutions* (New York: Cambridge University Press, 2016), 115–26.

49. Corporation of the Town of Detroit: Act of Incorporation and Journal of the Board of Trustees, 43.

50. J. May meat and trash: Ross, *Early Bench*, 139. Corporation of the Town of Detroit: Act of Incorporation and Journal of the Board of Trustees, 44.

51. Corporation of the Town of Detroit: Act of Incorporation and Journal of the Board of Trustees, 37.

52. Ste. Anne Church Records, BHL, UM.

53. 1802 taxes: Bald, *Detroit's First*, 194; the highest homes taxed in 1802 were owned by Richard Donovan and John Dodemead. 1805 taxes: Other high taxpayers included Solomon Sibley and father Gabriel Richard. R. N. Drake, "Sketch of Judge May: The Grandfather of Mrs. Seymour," From Drake Scrapbook in Possession of R.N. Drake, R.N. Drake, Seattle, WA, from Scrapbook of Drake loaned to C.M.B., James May Papers, Wallet 1, BHC, DPL. The grandson of an original French Detroit settler and slaveholder, Joseph Campau likely inherited slaves. Certainly, he owned at least two Native slaves, Jacques and Thomas, who both died in 1805. Ste. Anne Church Records, BHL, UM.

54. Macomb Ledger, Macomb Estate Papers, BHC, DPL, 19–20.

55. Bald, *Detroit's First*, 235. Bald notes that the western boundary of Michigan Territory differed slightly from the previous boundary of Wayne County. Instead of extending to the western edge of Lake Michigan, Michigan Territory's border was drawn through the middle of the lake.

56. Elijah Brush and Thomas Jones were appointed fire inspectors by the town trustees in 1805; Bald, *Detroit's First*, 237. Brush was appointed lieutenant colonel of Legionary Corps in the Militia of the Territory of Michigan; William Hull, to all to whom these presents shall come, William Woodbridge Papers, September 12, 1805, BHC, DPL.

57. E. Brush to Robison & Martin, October 6, 1803, Sibley Papers, BHC, DPL.

58. Bald, *Detroit's First*, 240.

59. Robert Munro letter, June 14, 1805, as quoted in Farmer, *History of Detroit*, 490.

60. Robert Munro letter, June 14, 1805, as quoted in Farmer, *History of Detroit*, 490–91.

61. Bald, *Great Fire*, 12–14; Bald, *Detroit's First*, 239–40; Jean Dilhet, *Beginnings of the Catholic Church in the United States*, translated and annotated by Patrick W. Browne (Washington, D.C.: The Salve Regina Press, 1922), 114; Robert Munro letter, June 14, 1805, as quoted in Farmer, *History of Detroit*, 491.

62. Munro to Harrison, June 14, 1805, Logan Esarey, ed., *Governors Messages and Letters: Messages and Letters of William Henry Harrison*, Vol. 1, 1800–1811 (Indianapolis: Indiana Historical Commission, 1922), 136–37; also quoted in Farmer, *History of Detroit*, 490.

63. Bald, *Great Fire*, 13–14.

64. Munro to Harrison, June 14, 1805, Logan Esarey, ed., *Governors Messages*, 136–37; also quoted in Farmer, *History of Detroit*, 490.

65. As quoted in Bald, *Great Fire*, 14.

66. Bald, *Detroit's First*, 242. While Jefferson attempted to appoint three judges as stipulated in the plan for Michigan Territory, two men turned down the third open post, resulting in only Woodward and Bates being present after the fire. Bald, *Detroit's First*, 242, footnote 5.

67. Jefferson to John Woodward, Jefferson Papers, Series 1, Vol. 4, Library of Congress, Washington, D.C.

68. Notes on My Visit to Mr. Jefferson, 1796, Augustus Brevoot Woodward Papers, BHC, DPL.

69. Notes on My Visit to Mr. Jefferson, 1796, Augustus Brevoot Woodward Papers, BHC, DPL.

70. "Essay on Habit," 1794, Box 1 Correspondence 1782–94, Augustus Brevoot Woodward Papers, BHC, DPL. Woodward's notes cite at least two cases involving blacks during his Washington years. In one case he played a role in tak-

ing depositions from a free black woman named Milly Smith who was married to an enslaved man and attempting to free her children; Augustus Woodward Papers, Box 2: 1795–1805, April 8, 1803, BHC, DPL. The other case involved an indentured "mulatto woman" named Celeste about whom Woodward had information requested by her employer; Pollock to Woodward, April 23, 1804, Correspondence with Oliver Pollock Folder, 1780–1813, BHC, DPL. Thomas Jefferson, *Notes on the State of Virginia* (Philadelphia: Prichard and Hall, 1788).

71. A.B. Woodward to Thomas Jefferson, October 20, 1803, Jefferson Papers, Series 2, vol. 88, Woodward Papers, BHC, DPL.

72. Bald, *Detroit's First*, 242. Woodward oath of fidelity, September 12, 1805, Woodward Papers, BHC, DPL.

73. Woodward's was the strongest voice on the Supreme Court by far. Justice Frederick Bates resigned in 1806, leaving his seat vacant until 1808 when he was replaced by Justice James Witherell. Justice John Griffin, the third initial appointee, has been described as a fairly passive supporter of Woodward's leadership. Woodward served as chief justice from 1805 to 1823. Burton, "Augustus Brevoort Woodward," 638, 640, 646. Edward J. Littlejohn, "Slaves, Judge Woodward, and the Supreme Court of the Michigan Territory," *Michigan Bar Journal* (July 2015): 22–25, 22, 23. The Woodward Code of Laws, created in 1805, was republished in *Laws of the Territory of Michigan: Laws Adopted by the Governor and Judges*. Vol. 1. Lansing, 1871. 4 vols. *The Making of Modern Law: Primary Sources*.

74. Littlejohn, "Slaves," 22–25, 23.

75. Bald, *Detroit's First*, 241–42.

76. Farmer, *History of Detroit*, 490; Girardin, baker, as slaveholder: Ste. Anne Church Records, January 1, 1786.

77. Bald, *Great Fire*, 15; Bald, *Detroit's First*, 242.

78. William Hull to James Madison, August 3, 1805, as quoted in Farmer, *History of Detroit*, 490.

79. David Braithwaite, "Brigadier General William Hull: His Military and Political Story," *Hull Family Association Journal* 15:1 (Autumn 2004): 96–99, 97.

80. Mr. Gentle as quoted in Farmer, *History of Detroit*, 491; Bald, *Detroit's First*, 241.

81. Bald, *Detroit's First*, 243.

82. See Naomi Klein, *The Shock Doctrine: The Rise of Disaster Capitalism* (New York: Picador, 2007).

83. Bald, *Great Fire*, 12. Elijah Brush, James May, and John Anderson to the President of the United States, 1806, LMS/ Alexander D. Fraser Papers, 1800–1816, BHC, DPL.

84. Bald, *Great Fire*, 16. Kenneth R. Fletcher, "A Brief History of Pierre L'Enfant and Washington D.C.," Smithsonian.com, April 30, 2008. Accessed May 13, 2016.

85. Topica, August 16 & 17, 1792, Woodward Papers, BHC, DPL.

86. Notes: Burke's Reflections on the French Revolution, May 24, 1794, Woodward Papers, BHC, DPL; To the President of the United States of America, July 4, 1798, Woodward Papers, BHC, DPL.

87. Copy of Philip Freneau, "On the American and French Revolutions," January 1, 1790, Woodward Papers, BHC, DPL.

88. "Between a Patriot & a British," July 29, 1796, Woodward Papers, BHC, DPL.

89. May's home, located on the corner of Jefferson Ave. and Cass St. May's Creek, was later closed off and incorporated into the city's sewer system. Ross, *Early Bench*, 140–42. Farmer, *History of Detroit*, 481.

90. Mr. Gentle, Statements, as quoted in Farmer, *History of Detroit*, 491.

91. William Tucker Probate, reel 1, Wayne County Probates, State Library of Michigan, Lansing, MI. In his decision of the *Denison v. Tucker* case, Judge Woodward says British buying and selling of slaves is to be determined case by case.

92. Tucker Probate, Wayne County Probates, State Library of Michigan.

93. Denison et al v. Catherine Tucker, Writ of Habeas Corpus ad Subjiciendum, in William Wirt Blume, ed., *Transactions of the Supreme Court of the Territory of Michigan, 1805–1814*, Vol. II (Ann Arbor: The University of Michigan Press, 1935), 133–36.

94. *Denison v. Tucker*, Blume, ed., *Supreme Court of Michigan* Vol. II, 133–36.

95. "The Brush Homestead in 1850," reproduced in Farmer, *History of Detroit*, 378.

96. Silas Farmer, *History of Detroit*, 367, 374.

97. Jacobson, *Detroit River*, 60.

98. Brush treasurer: Farmer, *History of Detroit*, 89.

99. Jacobson, *Detroit River*, 60.

100. While seamstresses did "piece work" sewing, dressmakers possessed a higher level of skill, and in a free labor economy, earned more pay; Angela P. Robbins, "Bridging the Old South and the New: Women in the Economic Transformation of the North Carolina Piedmont, 1865–1920" (Ph.D. diss., University of North Carolina Greensboro, 2010), p. 21. As quoted in Jacobson, *Detroit River*, 61.

101. VanderVelde, *Redemption Songs*, 9. The records on this case do not include opinions or dissents by any other judge. The notes of Detroit archivist and historian Clarence Burton also indicate that Woodward was the sole decider in this case; Legal Notes, Clarence Burton Papers, DPL. Affidavit of Elijah Brush, respecting ill treatment of Matthew Elliott, *Supreme Court of Michigan*, ed., Blume, Vol. II, 216. Michigan's Dred Scott case quote: Reginald R. Larrie, *Makin' Free: African Americans in the Northwest Territory* (Detroit: Blaine Ethridge Books, 1981), 6; a like phrase also quoted in Charlie Keller, "Detroit's First Black Militia," in

Denver Brunsman, Joel Stone, and Douglas D. Fisher, eds., *Border Crossings: The Detroit River Region in the War of 1812* (Detroit: Detroit Historical Society, 2012), 89. For more on the Dred and Harriet Scott case and an analysis that includes gender and the family, see Lea VanderVelde, *Mrs. Dred Scott: A Life on Slavery's Frontier* (New York: Oxford University Press, 2009).

102. As quoted in Littlejohn, "Slaves," 23.

103. Littlejohn, "Slaves, 23; Charles Moore, "Augustus Brevoort Woodward—A Citizen of Two Cities," in The Committee on Publication and the Recording Secretary, Records of the Columbia Historical Society, vol. 4 (Washington D.C., 1901): 114–27, 126.

104. Littlejohn, "Slaves," 22, 23; Moore, "Slave Law," 126; Burton, "Augustus Brevoort Woodward," MPHC, Vol. 29, 638–39.

105. Quotations and mottos, Woodward Papers April 10, 1789 BHC, DPL.

106. Woodward Papers April 10, 1789 BHC, DPL; Composition of 1793, On the qualities requisite for greatness, May 2 1793, Woodward Papers, BHC, DPL.

107. *Laws of the Territory of Michigan: Laws Adopted by the Governor and Judges*, Vol. 1. Lansing, 1871. 4 vols. *The Making of Modern Law: Primary Sources*, 10.

108. Paul D. Halliday, *Habeas Corpus: From England to Empire* (Cambridge, MA: Harvard University Press, 2010), 1–2, 101, 120, 174. Anthony Gregory, *The Power of Habeas Corpus in America: From the King's Prerogative to the War on Terror* (Cambridge: Cambridge University Press, 2013), 78–80. As Lea VanderVelde has detailed, the first freedom suit decided in the Northwest Territory was brought by black Revolutionary War veteran, Peter McNelly. McNelly petitioned for the freedom of himself and his wife, Queen, in Vincennes, Indiana, in 1794; their suit also employed the writ of habeas corpus. Although the judge found in their favor, power plays among prominent white men led to Peter McNelly's kidnapping and coerced indenture and to Queen's disappearance. VanderVelde, *Redemption Songs*, 24–37.

109. Wilbert E. Moore, "Slave Law and the Social Structure," *Journal of Negro History* 26:2 (April 1941): 171–202, 188.

110. *Denison v. Tucker*, in Blume, ed., *Supreme Court of Michigan*, Vol. II, 133–36.

111. Journal, in Blume, ed., *Supreme Court of Michigan*, Vol. I, 381.

112. Journal, in Blume, ed., *Supreme Court of Michigan*, Vol. I, 381. Woodward decision: Journal, in Blume, ed., *Supreme Court of Michigan*, Vol. I, 387.

113. In the Matter of Elizabeth Denison, James Denison, Scipio Denison, and Peter Denison junior, detained by Catherine Tucker, August–October 14, 1807, Oct. 1, 1807, Woodward Papers, BHC, DPL.

114. Reading List, Sept 6, 1792, Woodward Papers, BHC, DPL.

115. James Wood to Augustus Woodward, Aug. 18, 1807, Sandwich, Harris Hickman Papers, BHC, DPL. "An ACT to enable persons held in slavery, to sue for their freedom," June 27, 1807, Laws of the Territory of Louisiana, Missouri Digital

Heritage, Missouri State Archives. Petitioners held the burden of proof in demonstrating that they were actually free and being held by force. https://www.sos.mo.gov/archives/education/aahi/beforedredscott/1807FreedomStatute. https://www.sos.mo.gov/archives/education/aahi/beforedredscott/history_freedomsuits. Accessed March 30, 2017.

116. Woodward decision: Journal, in Blume, ed., *Supreme Court of Michigan*, Vol. I, 386. As quoted in Littlejohn, "Slaves," 25.

117. Syllabi of Decisions and Opinions, In the Matter of Elizabeth Denison, Et Al, September 26, 1807, in Blume, ed., *Supreme Court of Michigan*, Vol. I, 319.

118. McRae, "Crossing," 36.

119. Pattinson Petition for return of slave Jenney, Woodward Papers, F: 1805–1807, BHC, DPL; Case 76, Pattinson's Affidavit, in Blume, ed., *Supreme Court of Michigan*, Vol. II, 156. Littlejohn, "Slaves," 24; Norman McRae, "Crossing the River to Find Freedom," *Michigan History* 67:2 (March/April 1983): 35–39, 36. In the Case of Toby, a Panis Man, in *Supreme Court of Michigan*, Vol. II, 404, 405.

120. Calendar of Cases, Case 76 In the Matter of Richard Pattinson, in Blume, ed., *Supreme Court of Michigan*, Vol. I, 99–100; Syllabi of Decisions and Opinions, No. 76 In the Matter of Richard Pattinson, October 23, 1807, in Blume, ed., *Supreme Court of Michigan*, Vol. I, 321–22. Journal, in Blume, ed., *Supreme Court of Michigan*, Vol. I, 414.

121. Case 76, Pattinson's Affidavit, in Blume, ed., *Supreme Court of Michigan*, Vol. II, 156; Case 76 In the Matter of Richard Pattinson, in Blume, ed., *Supreme Court of Michigan*, Vol. I, 99. Pattinson Petition for return of slave Jenney, Oct. 19, 1807 Woodward Papers, June 14, 1811 F: 1805–1807 BHC, DPL.

122. James Heward vs. Charles Curry, Affidavit In the Case of Matthew Elliott Esq., October 21, 1807, Selected Papers SC of Michigan, 155–56; James Heward Papers, File 29 (new No. 49), BHC, DPL. "Matthew Elliott Essex County," (Toronto: York University, Harriet Tubman Institute, 2012), 7.

123. Calendar of Cases, Case 60 In the Matter of Elizabeth Denison, James Denison, Scipio Denison and Peter Denison, Jr., 1807, Habeas corpus, in Blume, ed., *Supreme Court of Michigan* Vol. II, 86–87. Brush representing Elliott: Selected Papers, Case 90, Affidavit of Elijah Brush, 1807, in Blume, ed., *Supreme Court of Michigan*, Vol. II, 215–16.

124. Affidavit of Elijah Brush, respecting ill treatment of Matthew Elliott, *Supreme Court of Michigan*, ed., Blume, Vol. II, 216.

125. As quoted in Littlejohn, "Slaves," 24.

126. Veta Smith Tucker, "Uncertain Freedom in Frontier Detroit," in Karolyn Smardz Frost and Veta Smith Tucker, eds., *A Fluid Frontier: Slavery, Resistance, and the Underground Railroad in the Detroit River Borderland* (Detroit: Wayne State University Press, 2016), 27–42. Veta Tucker gives a detailed account of the Denisons' time in Canada; see Tucker, "Uncertain Freedom," 35. Sandwich is now a historic neighborhood in the city of Windsor, Ontario.

5: The Rise of the Renegades (1807–1815)

1. According to David Poremba, the Smyth tavern was located on present-day Woodward Ave., near the Woodbridge intersection. David Lee Poremba, *Detroit in Its World Setting*, 90. Smyth as hatter: Affidavit of Elijah Brush, respecting ill treatment of Matthew Elliott, *Supreme Court of Michigan*, ed., Blume, Vol. II, 216.

2. Augustus B. Woodward to James Madison, March 17, 1808, Ms/Woodward A. B., BHC, DPL. Translation by Michelle Cassidy, November 2016.

3. Duffey, "Northwest Ordinance," 953–54.

4. Braithwaite, "Military Record," 96–98, 97; quote from Braithwaite, 96. Anthony J. Yanik, *The Fall and Recapture of Detroit in the War of 1812* (Detroit: Wayne State University Press, 2011), 13, 14. Hull children, Lake Erie winds, vanished town: "Introduction," MHPC Vol. XL, 30, 31.

5. SH (Sarah Hull) to William Hull, April 10, 1809, William Hull Papers, BHC, DPL. Donna Valley Russell, ed., *Michigan Censuses 1710–1830: Under the French, British, and Americans* (Detroit: Detroit Society for Genealogical Research, 1982), 1805 Lists, 82–86. Catherine Cangany captures this aspect of Detroit's insularity: Detroit's "insularity, its dogged preservation of social and political localisms, its disdain for things unwanted and external, and its refusal to stand on ceremony"; Cangany, *Frontier Seaport*, 167–68. Quote about French residents: Augustus B. Woodward to James Madison, March 17, 1808, Ms/Woodward A. B., BHC, DPL. Quoted description of Detroit: Alec R. Gilpin, *The War of 1812 in The Old Northwest* (2012; reprint, East Lansing: Michigan State University Press, 1958), 24–25. Braithwaite, "Military Record," 96–98, 96. Sarah and William married in 1781; Braithwaite, "Military Record," 96. Sarah Hull at Saratoga: "Biographical Sketch: Sarah Fuller Hull, Wife of General William Hull," *Hull Family Association Journal* 15:3 (Autumn 2004): 99; reprint of Elizabeth F. Ellet, *The Eminent and Heroic Women of America* (New York: Arno Press, 1974, repr. of 1783 ed.), 95–96.

6. Alan Taylor, *The Civil War of 1812: American Citizens, British Subjects, Irish Rebels, & Indian Allies* (New York: Vintage Books, 2010), 102–105. Hull route by boat: Yanik, *Fall and Recapture*, 14.

7. Impressment numbers: James Miller and John Thompson, *National Geographic Almanac of American History* (Washington, D.C.: National Geographic, 2007), 124; ten thousand American men had been captured, with thousands gaining release and six thousand remaining in British custody by 1807; Taylor, *Civil War of 1812*, 105. Jenkin Ratford: Taylor, *Civil War of 1812*, 102.

8. Embargo: Miller and Thompson, *Almanac of American History*, 125. Indian fears and Fort Mackinac Letter: Yanik, *Fall and Recapture*, 16–17.

9. Yanik, *Fall and Recapture*, 16. "Introduction," MPHC Vol. XL, 34–35.

10. Lieutenant Colonel E. Brush Commission by William Hull, Sept. 12, 1805, William Woodbridge Papers, DPL. Brush resigned from this post in 1809.

11. James Askin to Charles Askin, August 18, 1807, Askin Papers, Vol. II, 566.

John Askin to Isaac Todd, September 4, 1807, *Askin Papers*, Vol. II, 570; quoted in Keller, "Detroit's First Black Militia," 85.

12. Lieut. Colonel Grant to Secretary Green, August 17, 1807, MPHC Vol. VI, 41–43.

13. Case 60, In the Matter of Elizabeth Denison, James Denison, Scipio Denison and Peter Denison, Jr., Calender of Cases, Papers in File, *Supreme Court of Michigan*, ed., Blume, Vol. I, 87. Examination of James Dodemead respecting the ill treatment said to have been received by James Heward, a subject of his Britannic Majesty, October 27, 1807, Heward Papers, DPL.

14. Examination of James Dodemead respecting the ill treatment said to have been received by James Heward.

15. Examination of James Dodemead respecting the ill treatment said to have been received by James Heward. Affidavit of Elijah Brush, respecting ill treatment of Matthew Elliott, *Supreme Court of Michigan*, ed., Blume, Vol. II, 216. Case 91, Affidavit of Harris H. Hickman, 218–19.

16. Affidavit of Elijah Brush, respecting ill treatment of Matthew Elliott, 217.

17. Examination of James Dodemead respecting the ill treatment said to have been received by James Heward, a subject of his Britannic Majesty, October 27, 1807, Heward Papers, DPL. Affidavit of Elijah Brush, respecting ill treatment of Matthew Elliott, *Supreme Court of Michigan*, ed., Blume, Vol. II, 216. Augustus B. Woodward to James Madison, March 17, 1808, Ms/Woodward A. B., BHC, DPL.

18. Lieut. Colonel Grant to Secretary Green, August 17, 1807, MPHC Vol. VI, 41–43. Quarles, *The Negro in the American Revolution*, 8, 68, 83. Blacks boarding ships: Taylor, *Civil War of 1812*, 113. Starting with Virginia in 1639, American colonial governments banned the arming of people of African descent, but they rolled back these prohibitions at times when officials felt the need for extra military manpower, such as in the Yamasee War of 1715, during which South Carolina approved of arming Africans, including those who were enslaved, to fight Native combatants. This process did not include training or a formalization of black men's leadership or authority. Charles Johnson, Jr., *African American Soldiers in the National Guard: Recruitment and Deployment during Peacetime and War* (Westport, CT: Greenwood Press, 1992), 1–2. The African American military historian Charles Johnson dates the formal beginning of African American militia groups to the late nineteenth century (1877) and notes that territorial policy sometimes deviated from national policy. This was, he states, the case with William Hull, who "formed a company composed entirely of Africans to assist in protecting the frontier against British invasion." Johnson, *African American Soldiers*, 5. The force from Santo Domingo that fought with French troops in support of the American cause in Savannah during the American Revolution in 1779 was not American-born but Haitian; Quarles, *The Negro in the American Revolution*, 82. In Massachusetts, an all-black company was led by Col. George Middleton during the Revolutionary War; Middleton was African American; Manisha Sinha,

The Slave's Cause: A History of Abolition (New Haven: Yale University Press, 2016), 49. Monuments to black soldiers in the Revolutionary War exist in Savannah as well as Washington, D.C.

19. A.B. Woodward to William Eustis, Secretary of War, July 28, 1812, Clarence Edwin Carter, *Territorial Papers,* Volume 10, 389–92.

20. William Hull to Jaspar Grant, September 3, 1807, MPHC, Vol. 31, 600, quoted in Keller, "Detroit's First Black Militia," 91.

21. "Black History Month: Remembering the First Black Militia," [no date listed], MonroeNews.com, Accessed March 19, 2012. Reconstructing the formation and engagements of the black militia of Detroit is a difficult task due to the piecemeal nature of the written record. Only a handful of primary sources have been found to date about the militia. Two of those sources, a journalistic report on the war from July 2012 and a letter by Augustus Woodward in June of 1811, are, to my knowledge, noted first here. A search for Peter Denison in the War of 1812 pension files achieved no new results. It is my hope that future historians of early Detroit will keep digging for records about this occurrence. Secondary accounts of the development of the militia have been offered in the black history month article cited above as well as by the following scholars. In some details of chronology and interpretation the descriptions by these scholars differ from my own. The lack of plentiful source material means that each scholar working on this topic has had to connect the dots, and they have done so in varying ways at the level of detail. I am indebted to all of the following individuals and projects for their published reconstructions of these events. Veta Tucker, "Uncertain Freedom," in Frost and Tucker, eds., *A Fluid Frontier.* Charlie Keller, "Detroit's First Black Militia," in Brunsman, Stone, and Fisher, eds., *Border Crossings,* 85–100. Gene Allen Smith, *The Slaves' Gamble: Choosing Sides in the War of 1812* (New York: Palgrave Macmillan, 2013), 33–34. Donald R. Hickey, *Don't Give Up the Ship: Myths of the War of 1812* (Urbana: University of Illinois Press, 2006), 191. Johnson, Jr., *African American Soldiers in the National Guard,* 5. "Peter Denison," Detroit African-American History Project, Wayne State University, www.daahp.wayne.edu/biographies. Accessed August 16, 2012. Veta Tucker's chapter, in particular, helped me to see that Peter Denison may have given up freedom to flee with his family. Charlie Keller's chapter is the most precise and best cited account in print.

22. The 1805 law establishing the Michigan militia directed that each "company" should be assigned a captain, lieutenant, and ensign and should wear uniforms. *Laws of the Territory of Michigan,* Vol. I, *The Making of Modern Law,* Yale Law Library, 47, 48.

23. Augustus B. Woodward to James Madison, July 18, 1807, Folder January–July, 1807, Box 1806–1808, Augustus Brevoort Woodward Papers, BHC; also transcribed in MPHC, 12: 511–18. Quoted in Charlie Keller, "Detroit's First Black Militia," in Brunsman, Stone, and Fisher, eds., *Border Crossings,* 89.

24. Judge Woodward's Resolution on Sundry Subjects, and the Report of the

Committee on the Same, Dec. 31, 1806, MHPC, V. 12, 462–65, 463. Only the transcription has been found of this document, and the 1806 date appears to be an error. All other primary sources indicate that the black militia was formed in 1807, after the *Chesapeake* incident. The introduction to the Michigan Historical Collections series that includes the transcription in question notes that Woodward delivered his document to the committee in the fall of 1808. "Introduction," MHPC Vol. XL, 41.

25. Judge Woodward's Resolution on Sundry Subjects, and the Report of the Committee on the Same, Dec. 31, 1806, MHPC, V. 12, 462–65, 463.

26. There was no independent or elected legislature in territorial Michigan. The governor and three judges governed the territory, with Hull and Woodward being the most prominent voices. Hull likely dictated or wrote much of the committee's response to Woodward's Resolutions, which was signed by Judge John Griffin; "Introduction," MPHC Vol. XL, 44. Charlie Keller also points out that Governor Hull probably steered the findings of this committee; Keller, "Detroit's First Black Militia," 91. Judge Woodward's Resolution, MHPC, V. 12, 462–65, 470, 472. Woodward to Leib, [Gesurel?], June 14, 1811 Woodward Papers, BHC, DPL.

27. Indenture of Charlotte Moses, Askin Papers, Vol. II: 607–608.

28. Case 432, Box 9, Supreme Court, Michigan Territorial Records, Archives of Michigan, Michigan Historical Center, Lansing, MI. Laura Edwards presents an illuminating analysis of why textiles were so sought after in the nineteenth century for both their use value and exchange value; she also shows the importance of enslaved women's assumed ability to own textiles as possessions. Laura F. Edwards, "Textiles, Popular Culture and the Law," *Buffalo Law Review* 64 (2016): 193–214.

29. Lieut. Colonel Grant to Secretary Green, August 17, 1807, MPHC Vol. VI, 41–43.

30. Case 60, In the Matter of Elizabeth Denison, James Denison, Scipio Denison and Peter Denison, Jr., Calender of Cases, Papers in File, *Supreme Court of Michigan*, ed., Blume, Vol. I, 87.

31. Cangany, *Frontier Seaport*, 139–40, 154–55.

32. Treaty of Detroit and Related Treaties, *American State Papers: Documents, Legislative and Executive of the Congress of the United States*, Part 2, Volume 1 (Gales and Seaton: 1832), digitized Pennsylvania State University, 745–48.

33. Treaty of Detroit and Related Treaties, *American State Papers: Documents, Legislative and Executive of the Congress of the United States*, Part 2, Volume 1 (Gales and Seaton: 1832), digitized Pennsylvania State University, 745–48.

34. William Hull to Dearborn, February 20, 1807, MPHC Vol. XL, 1805–1813, 100–102.

35. Treaty of Detroit and Related Treaties, *American State Papers: Documents, Legislative and Executive of the Congress of the United States*, Part 2, Volume 1 (Gales and Seaton: 1832), digitized Pennsylvania State University, 745–48. Treaty of Detroit,

1807. http://clarke.cimich.edu/resource_tab/native_americans_in_michigan/treaty_rights/text_of_michigan-related_treaties/detroit1807.html. Accessed March 15, 2012. Poremba, *Detroit*, 91. For an analysis of native political leadership in the region, see: Cary Miller, *Ogimaag: Anishinaabeg Leadership, 1760–1845* (Lincoln: University of Nebraska Press, 2010).

36. Treaty of Detroit and Related Treaties, *American State Papers: Documents, Legislative and Executive of the Congress of the United States*, Part 2, Volume 1 (Gales and Seaton: 1832), digitized Pennsylvania State University, 745–48.

37. Charles E. Cleland, *Rites of Conquest: The History and Culture of Michigan's Native Americans* (Ann Arbor: University of Michigan Press, 1992), 218, 229. Poremba, *Detroit*, 91.

38. Walter Johnson makes the similar and instructive point that the development of lands for plantation enterprises in Louisiana reduced enslaved people's means of hiding and escaping in forested landscapes. Walter Johnson, *River of Dark Dreams: Slavery and Empire in the Cotton Kingdom* (Cambridge, MA: Harvard University Press, 2013), 220–21.

39. Cangany, *Frontier Seaport*, 157, 158. Arthur Mullen, "Detroit through 300 Years—Physical Clues to Our Long History," www.cityscapedetroit.org/articles/Physical _clues.html. Accessed November 18, 2013.

40. Cangany, *Frontier Seaport*, 150, 152, 154, 155; Poremba, *Detroit*, 90.

41. Farmer, *History of Detroit*, 24–25; Quoted in Farmer, *History of Detroit*, 24; quoted in Farmer, *History of Detroit*, 25; quoted in Farmer, *History of Detroit*, 27–28. "Introduction," MHPC Vol. XL, 33.

42. M. Agnes Burton., ed., *Governor and Judges Journal: Proceedings of the Land Board of Detroit* (Detroit: 1915), 20, 44, 47, 116, 207, 230, 231. In the Matter of Hannah, A Negro Woman, *Supreme Court of Michigan*, Vol. I, ed., Blume, 163, 486–87.

43. Taylor, *Divided Ground*, 399. Ainse encountered her own problems with land boards, finding that the Canadian government refused to fully recognize her land claims that were based on previous Indian deeds.

44. Hull to Dearborn, February 20, 1807, MPHC Vol. XL, 96–97; "Introduction," MHPC Vol. XL, 39.

45. Russell, ed., *Michigan Censuses*, 87–91.

46. Cangany, *Frontier Seaport*, 152; Ste. Anne's Church Records.

47. For a discussion of the flexibility and changeability of racial and color terms such as "mulatto" and "mustee," see Jack D. Forbes, *Africans and Native Americans: The Language of Race and the Evolution of Red-Black Peoples* (Urbana: University of Illinois Press, 1993).

48. Poremba, *Detroit*, 91. Deed of Bargain and Sale from Elijah Brush, and wife; Deed of Mortgage from Governor Hull to Elijah Brush; deed Joseph Watts sells land to William Hull; Sarah, Alexander and Angus Makintosh lease land to William Hull; Indenture of lease between Pierre Toussaint Chesne and William

Hull; Deed Joseph Mini and Javotte Mini to William Hull; Deed of Pierre Rivier, Relinquishment of dower Archange Rivard to William Hull; Deed, Pierre Toussaint *Cécile Thérèse Chêne* to William Hull; Incomplete deed between Hull and Daniel Robinson; Watson of New York to William Hull mortgage 1¾ acres lots in Detroit, William Hull Papers, Folder L2: 1808–1810, Folder L2: 1811–25, BHC, DPL.

49. SH (Sarah Hull) to William Hull, April 10, 1809, William Hull Papers, BHC, DPL.

50. Gilpin, *War of 1812 in the Old Northwest*, 66. "St. John's Anglican Church, Sandwich, Ontario, http://essexanglican.awardspace.com. Accessed June 25, 2016.

51. Peter and Hannah baptism: quoted in Tucker, "Uncertain Freedom," 37. Family baptisms: Swan, *Lisette*, 8; the church register includes several individual Denison names in baptism, birth and burial notes (such as James, Hannah, Scipio, Lisette/Elizabeth, Phoebe, Juliet, and Charlotte) between 1811 and 1819. Juliet is listed as a fourteen-year-old daughter of Peter and Hannah in 1816; Phoebe is listed as the daughter of Scipio and Charlotte Denison, so a grandchild of Peter and Hannah; St. John's, Anglican, 1802–1827, Register of baptisms, marriages and burials, 1802–1827, Sandwich, Ontario, Archives of Ontario, Toronto. A third generation was born, raised, and baptized in Canada, and some of these descendants stayed there. Slaveholders in the church: Tucker, "Uncertain Freedom," 35.

52. Peter as "Negro Servt [servant] of Angus McIntosh [Mackintosh]" is noted upon Peter's death: St. John's Register, August 28, 1812. Also quoted in Tucker, "Uncertain Freedom, 37.

53. Rebecca J. Scott, "Social Facts, Legal Fictions, and the Attribution of Slave Status: The Puzzle of Prescription," *Law and History Review* (2017): 1–22, 10.

54. Anonymous Ledger, MS/Anonymous, L4: 1806–15, BHC, DPL. Hum-Hum, a cotton fabric from India, was most popular in the mid- to late eighteenth century; Elisabeth McClellan, *Historic Dress in America, 1607–1800* (Philadelphia: George W. Jacobs & Co, 1904), 388.

55. The Askin Ledger, part of the John Askin Papers at the Detroit Public Library, is a lengthy fifty-page account in the original cursive script that employs financial shorthand. I was very fortunate to have the assistance of an undergraduate student, Paul Rodriguez, aided by a graduate student, Michelle Cassidy, who worked on an initial transcription of this ledger as well as the Macomb ledger over the course of two academic years. Even with this remarkable effort, the ledger is challenging to work with. I have summarized all references to the Denisons here and quoted only when I could be quite sure of my transcription, which drew from the original text and the students' transcription. The Askin ledger has its own page numbers in the top right hand corner, but these are difficult to read and not always present. We therefore renumbered the pages from 1 to 50. When possible, I give two page numbers for references to indicate our numbering and the original numbering. References to the Denisons appear on

pp: 35/180, 36, 37, 38, 39/222, 41/235, 42, 43, 44, 47, and 50. Lisette working winter nights: 36. Many other early Detroiters also appear in this ledger, including Elijah and "Mrs." Brush. MS Askin, J. L4, 1806–1812, BHC, DPL.

56. Askin Ledger, Askin Papers, BHC, DPL.

57. Mary, Tom, George: 35, 33, 34, 37/205. Jim: 29. Jobs performed by people of color: 13, 24, 33/177. Askin Papers, BHC, DPL.

58. Anonymous Ledger, MS/Anonymous, L4: 1806–15, BHC, DPL. Adelaide Brush to Charles Askin, July 27, 1810; Elijah Brush to John Askin, February 13, 1810 Askin family fonds [textual record], Correspondence with the Brush family, 1801-1850, MG 19 A 3 Volume 37, Library and Archives Canada, Ottawa, ON. These letters do not make clear who Peter Denison was buying himself from. The money may have gone to Catherine Tucker, who had indentured Peter and Hannah to Brush, or to William Hull or the town of Detroit due to Peter's abandonment of the black militia in 1807 to flee with his family to Canada. It is possible, but unlikely, that Elijah Brush paid himself to free Peter, since he promises to "furnish the money." I am grateful to Rachel Whitehead for leading me to these letters.

59. Gilpin, *War of 1812 in the Old Northwest*, 27, 28, 29; Yanik, *Fall and Recapture*, 23.

60. Gregory Evans Dowd, *A Spirited Resistance: The North American Indian Struggle for Unity, 1745–1815* (Baltimore: Johns Hopkins University Press, 1993), 142, 144.

61. Gilpin, *War of 1812 in the Old Northwest*, 4, 6, 13, 16; Yanik, *Fall and Recapture*, 20–21. For a detailed study of Tecumseh's revolution and broader native resistance campaigns, see Dowd, *A Spirited Resistance*.

62. Yanik, *Fall and Recapture*, 21–22. John Tyler was Harrison's vice presidential candidate in the 1840 presidential race.

63. Memorial to Congress by Citizens of Michigan Territory, MHPC Vol. XL, 346–53.

64. Witgen, *Infinity of Nations*, 327.

65. Yanik, *Fall and Recapture*, 17; Gilpin, *War of 1812 in the Old Northwest*, 28, 29; Hull quoted in Yanik, *Fall and Recapture*, 22.

66. The longevity of the black militia is a point of debate among the handful of historians who have written about it. Most state that the company was disbanded by 1811, before the start of the war. This argument is sound and based on the fact that Judge Augustus Woodward's references to the group conclude in this year and no primary sources from Michigan officials note a continuation of the force. One historian states that the militia continued past 1811, and its men served in the War of 1812, but the primary sources he cites do not actually show evidence for this claim. There is logic on the side of the argument for War of 1812 involvement. It seems unreasonable that Hull, having taken the risk to form the black militia and being supported in this by a territorial special committee, would not

use this group during war preparations. My representation of the black militia's involvement in the very first months of the war is based on the uncovering of a new source by a reporter that is not full proof of the group's continuation (as the reporter's source could have passed on dated information) but is certainly evidentiary and highly suggestive. Report to readers on war developments, Zanesville, OH, July 20, 1812, *Document Transcriptions of The War of 1812 in the Northwest*, Vol. IV, Anecdotes of the Lake Erie Area War of 1812, Transcribed from Original Sources by Richard C. Knopf (Columbus: Ohio Historical Society, 1957), 120–21.

67. Letter from Detroit to New York, July 18, 1812, *Document Transcriptions of The War of 1812 in the Northwest*, Knopf, trans., 110.

68. Black Swamp: Harry L. Coles, *The War of 1812* (Chicago: University of Chicago Press, 1965), 45–46; Gilpin, *War of 1812*, 36, 51. Yanik, *Fall and Recapture*, 48.

69. We learn that letters have been received, *Document Transcriptions of The War of 1812 in the Northwest*, July 25, 1812, Knopf, trans., 111.

70. We learn that letters have been received, *Document Transcriptions of The War of 1812 in the Northwest*, July 25, 1812, Knopf, trans., 111.

71. Eustis quoted in Yanik, *Fall and Recapture*, 50–51.

72. Report to readers on war developments, Zanesville, OH, July 20, 1812, *Document Transcriptions of The War of 1812 in the Northwest*, July 20, 1812, Knopf, trans., 120–21. Hull's Proclamation: Yanik, *Fall and Recapture*, 56; Gilpin, *War of 1812 in the Old Northwest*, 73–74.

73. bell hooks, "Revolutionary 'Renegades': Native Americans, African Americans, and Black Indians, " in *Black Looks: Race and Representation* (Boston: South End Press, 1992).

74. Fort Mackinac: Gilpin, *War of 1812 in the Old Northwest*, 89; Yanik, *Fall and Recapture*, 63. A. B. Woodward to William Eustis, Secretary of War, July 28, 1812, Clarence Edwin Carter, Territorial Papers, Volume 10, 389–92. While not conclusive for the argument that the black militia was active at the start of the war, Woodward's complaint does not foreclose this likelihood. He makes no mention of the militia having been disbanded, which would seem relevant in a letter about Hull's misdeeds and the war's development in real time.

75. Yanik *Fall and Recapture*, 91, 92; location of artillery on present-day Jefferson Ave., Yanik 89; Brock quoted in Yanik, 88.

76. Yanik, *Fall and Recapture*, 88, 94.

77. Yanik, *Fall and Recapture*, 94–96, 100.

78. Denison in Quebec quote: Smith, *Slaves' Gamble*, 34. Number of Detroit prisoners: Taylor, *Civil War of 1812*, 175.

79. Hull was released from the British on parole in October of 1812. He returned to Massachusetts before being court-martialed by the U.S. government in 1813 for the charges of treason, cowardice and neglect of duty. Although Hull was found guilty of the second two charges and sentenced to death, Presi-

dent Madison commuted this sentence. Negative representations of Hull both at the time and in histories of the war have led to debate and the historian Anthony Yanik's recent book, subtitled "In Defense of William Hull." Yanik and others argue that Hull was a scapegoat for Madison, Hull's officers, and the Republican Party for larger failures of the war. Gilpin, *War of 1812 in the Old Northwest*, 232. Yanik, *Fall and Recapture*, 125–27. Elijah Brush was apparently released by February of 1813; Jacobson, *Detroit River Connections*, 62. Denison's death: St. John's Register, August 28, 1812. Also quoted in Tucker, "Uncertain Freedom, 37.

80. Treaty of Ghent, Primary Documents in American History, Library of Congress, https://www.loc.gov/rr/program/bib/ourdocs/Ghent.html. Accessed July 29, 2016. For more on the reduction of Native negotiating influence after the War of 1812, see White, *Middle Ground*, 516–17, 523, For more on Native persistence, population, and strength in the Great Lakes beyond the War of 1812, see Witgen, *Infinity of Nations*, 27, 325–27; McDonnell, *Masters of Empire*, 318–19.

81. French Town: Ralph Naveaux, *Invaded on all Sides: The Story of Michigan's Greatest Battlefield, Scene of the Engagements at French Town and the River Raisin in the War of 1812* (Marceline, MO: Walsworth Publishing Co., 2008), 17. For more on the battle at the River Raisin, see Naveaux, *Invaded on All Sides*. Brush's death: Swan, *Lisette*, 8; Jacobson, *Detroit River Connections*, 61–63. Gilpin, *War of 1812 in the Old Northwest*, 126; Yanik, *Fall and Recapture*, 162. Taylor, *Civil War of 1812*, 243. Ominous quote: Taylor, *Civil War of 1812*, 439.

82. "Forgotten war": Donald R. Hickey, *The War of 1812: A Forgotten Conflict* (1989; reprint, Urbana: University of Illinois Press, Bicentennial Edition, 2012); Taylor, *Civil War of 1812*, 10.

83. Coles, *War of 1812*, 255. Taylor, *Civil War of 1812*, 10. Ste. Anne's Church Records: Marie Louise baptism, February 3, 1799; Jean Baptiste Rémond, baptism, July 5, 1812; Julie Ford, baptism, August 11, 1813. Ste. Anne's Church Records; Russell, ed., *Michigan Censuses*, 101–147; Katzman, "Black Slavery in Michigan," 62. R. G. Dunlop, W. L. Mackenzie, John H. Dunn, Adolphus Judah, W. R. Abbott, David Hollin, Malcolm Cameron, and J. Levy, "Records Illustrating the Condition of Refugees from Slavery in Upper Canada before 1860," *Journal of Negro History* 13:2 (April 1928): 199–207, 205.

84. Taylor, *Civil War of 1812*, 327.

85. Fergus Bordewich is the first scholar I know of to offer this supposition that black men's involvement in the War of 1812 informed a larger black population about the liberatory possibilities of Canada. Fergus M. Bordewich, *The Underground Railroad and the War for the Soul of America* (New York: Harper Collins, 2005), 114.

Conclusion: The American City (1817 and Beyond)

1. Swan, *Lisette*, 8. St. John's, Anglican, 1802–1827, Register of baptisms, marriages and burials, 1802–1827, Sandwich, Ontario, Archives of Ontario, Toronto.

Marriage Certificate of Scipio Dennison and Charlotte Paul, Zd4-Denison Family, Solomon Sibley Papers, DPL.

2. George McDougall, attorney for Sarah Macomb, *Detroit Gazette*, September 17, 1817, p. 4; George McDougall, agent for David B. Macomb, *Detroit Gazette*, September 17, 1817, p. 4. Clarence Burton, *History of Detroit, 1780–1850, Financial and Commercial* (Detroit: 1917), 58–61. Jacobson, *Detroit River Connections*, 25, 129.

3. "Notice. A Meeting," *Detroit Gazette*, September 19, 1817, p. 3. "Commission Store," *Detroit Gazette*, September 19, 1817, p. 3. John Williams to Samuel Abbott, May 1817, John R. Williams Papers, BHC, DPL. Monroe: MPHC, Vol. 38, p. 446. John R. Williams was the son of Cecile Campau; his father, Thomas Williams, hailed from Albany, NY; Gitlin, *Bourgeois Frontier*, 144–145.

4. John Williams to Samuel Abbott, May 1817, John R. Williams Papers, BHC, DPL. Williams was elected mayor in 1824; Poremba, *Detroit*, 76, 104. "American city": F. Clever Bald, *Detroit's First American Decade*, 1948; "Subscription List," *Detroit Gazette*, September 19, 1817, p. 1; "Statutes of the University of Michigania," *Detroit Gazette*, September 19, 1817, p. 2; "Subscription List," *Detroit Gazette*, October 10, 1817, p. 3; Poremba, *Detroit*, 98, 99.

5. "Subscription List," *Detroit Gazette*, September 19, 1817, p. 1; "Statutes of the University of Michigania," *Detroit Gazette*, September 19, 1817, p. 2; "Subscription List," *Detroit Gazette*, October 10, 1817, p. 3. The subscription lists printed in the newspaper name thirty-five people but are incomplete. The newspaper does not include some names (such as James May, Augustus Woodward, and Barnabas Campau) that are listed as donors in other sources. Augustus Woodward also kept a subscription list for $150 donors that may have been independent of the university treasurer's list. Woodward's list reference: Campau Papers, MS/Campau Family, 1817 May–December, BHC, DPL. Terrence McDonald, director of the Bentley Library at the University of Michigan, calculated that "the total amount of subscriptions was $5100. The two newspaper lists total $4086 . . . we are missing the names of those who together contributed about $1000. The subscriptions were raised between Sept. 19 and Oct. 10 1817." Terrence McDonald to Tiya Miles, email correspondence, July 31, 2016.

6. C.M. Burton, "Augustus Brevoort Woodward," MPHC Vol. 29, p. 658.

7. Burton, "Augustus Brevoort Woodward," MPHC Vol. 29, pp. 658–659.

8. May donation: R.N. Drake, "Sketch of Judge May: Grandfather of Mrs. Seymour," Drake Scrapbook in Possession of R. N. Drake, Seattle, Washington, From SB of Drake loaned to C.M.B., James May Papers, Wallet 1, BHC, DPL, 8. Silas Farmer, *History of Detroit and Wayne County*, 729. Drake gives a figure of $100 for May's contribution. Farmer gives a figure of $25. Both authors provide transcribed or quoted copies of these pledge documents; however, the originals have not been found in the University of Michigan archives at the Bentley Library or in papers at the Detroit Public Library. Records of other contributions: Barnabas Campau: Campau Papers, MS/Campau, Barnabas, Folder 1819–21, BHC, DPL; "the Lodge": Campau Papers,

MS/Campau Family, 1817 May–December, BHC, DPL; use of city fire fund: Campau Papers, MS/Campau Family, 1817 May–December, BHC, DPL. Woodward's slave: Robert B. Ross and George B. Catlin, *Landmarks of Detroit: A History of the City* (Detroit: Evening News Association, 1898), 416. Burton, *History of Detroit, 1780–1850,* 73. Michelle Cassidy, "The Origins of Article 16 and the University of Michigan," paper written for the University of Michigan Bicentennial Committee, Ann Arbor, MI, 2015. Joseph Campau was a member of the Ancient Free and Accepted Masons, Zion Lodge, Number 10; Gitlin, *Bourgeois Frontier,* 54–55. He reportedly died as the richest man in Michigan; Jacobson, *Detroit River Connections,* 85.

9. Cassidy, "The Origins of Article 16 and the University of Michigan," University of Michigan Bicentennial Committee. *An Act to Establish the Catholepistemiad, or university of Michigania* (August 26, 1817), Frank Egelston Robbins, ed., *University of Michigan Early Records, 1817–1837* (Ann Arbor: The University of Michigan, 1935), 3–5.

10. Quote by John Petoskey, University of Michigan College of Literature, Science & the Arts (2016) and School of Law (currently enrolled); used by permission of John Petoskey, June 21, 2016. To be eligible for the tuition waiver, applicants must be enrolled in a United States federally recognized tribal community, of one-quarter blood quantum, with established Michigan residency of at least twelve months. The waiver is defined as a benefit stemming from political relations between government entities (such as the state of Michigan and tribes) rather than race or ethnicity. Michigan Indian Tuition Waiver Frequently Asked Questions, Michigan.Gov, https://www.michigan.gov/documents/mdcr/faqsmitw_329746_7.pdf. Michigan Indian Tuition Waiver, Michigan Department of Civil Rights, http://www.michigan.gov/mdcr/0,1607,7-138--240889--,00.html. Accessed June 20, 2016.

11. First Minority Graduates and Attendees, Bentley Historical Library, UM, http://bentley.umich.edu/legacy-support/umtimeline/minfirsts.php. Accessed July 1, 2016.

12. Catherine Sibley quoted in Swan, *Lisette,* 9.

13. MPHC, Vol. 38, p. 446.

14. Swan, *Lisette,* 9, 13. Deed, Stephen Mack to Elizabeth Dennison; Lease of lots in Pontiac, Scipio and Elizabeth Forth to Scipio Dennison; Lease of lots in Pontiac, Scipio and Elizabeth to Scipio; Promissory note, Scipio Dennison to Elizabeth; Letter, Scipio Dennison to Solomon Sibley; Zd4-Denison Family, Solomon Sibley Papers, DPL. A Michigan state historical marker in Pontiac recognizes Elizabeth Denison Forth's biography and land purchase. http://www.michmarkers.com/startup.asp?startpage=L1860.htm. Accessed July 23, 2016.

15. Swan, *Lisette,* 10, 14, 16, 17; Visitor Elizabeth Campbell quoted in Swan, *Lisette,* 18. Biddle served as mayor from 1827 to 1828; Poremba, *Detroit,* 106. Sibley family: Sibley House Detroit, http://sibleyhousedetroit.com/the-sibley-family; Accessed July 13, 2016.

16. Maurice M. Manring, *Slave in a Box: The Strange Career of Aunt Jemima* (Charlottesville: University Press of Virginia, 1998), 61–65, 74–75. Eliza Biddle to Aaron Ogden, January 15, 1855, Gershom Mott Williams Papers, BHC, DPL, transcribed in McPherson, *Looking for Lisette*, 440. The set of documents that Mark McPherson calls the "Lisette Letters" in his Appendix B refers to twelve letters in the Biddles' correspondences that mention Elizabeth Denison.

17. Swan, *Lisette*, 8, 9, 14, 21. Eliza Biddle to Susan Biddle, June 28, 1859, transcribed in McPherson, *Looking for Lisette*, 445–46.

18. Elmwood Cemetery interment record, B/Negroes-Forth, Elizabeth Denison, Reading Room, DPL. This record is not wholly accurate. It states that Elizabeth Denison Forth was 114 years old at the time of her death in 1866 and that she was born in Virginia. All other records indicate that she was born a slave in the 1780s in Detroit, which means that she died close to the age of 90. Lisette Denison's grave location is given as Strangers Ground 45–194 in the Elmwood record.

19. Draft of Elizabeth Dennison's Will, Zd4-Denison Family, Solomon Sibley Papers, DPL. Elizabeth Denison Forth Will, Folder B/Negroes-Forth, Elizabeth Denison, Reading Room, DPL.

20. Swan, *Lisette*, 15; Indenture of service between Scipio and Eastman Dennison and Charles E. Brush in Green Bay, 1834, Zd4-Denison Family, Solomon Sibley Papers, DPL.

21. Swan, *Lisette*, 49. Saint James Church has produced a historical pamphlet that covers the history of Elizabeth Denison as its "founder." This pamphlet is informative and engaging, but my account here differs from it in some respects, especially regarding the relationship between Lisette Denison and Eliza Biddle. The pamphlet states that the two women "shared a strong bond" and made a "vow" to found a church together on Grosse Ile. I have not seen evidence for this claim. I am grateful, though, to the church for sharing their version of the history so generously; "Saint James Story of the Chapel," Saint James Church, Grosse Ile, MI.

22. Histories of American Indian enslavement retain the idea that the practice died out by the middle 1700s and that Indian slaves after that time were likely to be mixed Afro-Native or lost to the designation "Negro" in plantation records. Studying slavery in Detroit shows the continuation of a clear practice of Indians being kept as slaves well into the nineteenth century.

23. The novelist Gayl Jones includes a haunting refrain of the call to "make generations" in her classic story of generations of black women sexually abused in slavery; Gayl Jones, *Corregidora* (Boston: Beacon, 1975), 10, 60, 90, 101. The historian Susan Sleeper Smith developed this concept of Midwestern Indians using a hiding-in-plain-sight strategy of survival, with a focus on Indiana. Susan Sleeper Smith, *Indian Women and French Men: Rethinking Cultural Encounter in the Western Great Lakes* (Amherst: University of Massachusetts Press, 2001), 115, 116; see Chapter Seven.

24. Swan, *Lisette*, 49. Sibley House Detroit, http://sibleyhousedetroit.com/the-sibley-family/. The Charles C. Trowbridge House is located at 1380 East Jefferson

in downtown Detroit, Detroit 1701, http://detroit1701.org/Trowbridge_Hist.htm. Accessed July 13, 2016.

25. Frost and Tucker, "Introduction," in Frost and Tucker, eds., *A Fluid Frontier*, 2–4. EdDwight.com, http://www.eddwight.com/memorial-public-art/international-underground-railroad-memorial-detroit-mi-windsor-canada; Accessed July 13, 2016. Detroit 1701, http://detroit1701.org/UndergroundRailroad.htm; Accessed July 13, 2016.

A Note on Historical Conversations and Concepts

1. Charles Bright, "'It Was As If We Were Never There': Recovering Detroit's Past for History and Theater," *Journal of American History* (March 2002).

2. Therese A. Kneip, "Slavery in Early Detroit," MA Thesis, University of Detroit, 1938. David M. Katzman, "Black Slavery in Michigan," *American Studies* 11:2 (fall 1970): 56–66. Cooper, "The Fluid Frontier," 129–49.

3. Bill McGraw, "Slavery Is Detroit's Big, Bad Secret. Why Don't We Know Anything About It?" *Deadline Detroit*, www.deadlinedetroit.com, August 27, 2012. Accessed August 28, 2012. In 2005 a senior honors thesis addressed the topic of Midwestern slavery with particular attention to Michigan: Daniel Rhoades, "There Were No Innocents: Slavery in the Old Northwest 1700–1860," Senior Honors Thesis, Eastern Michigan University, Ypsilanti, 2005. Brunsman and Stone, eds., *Revolutionary Detroit*. Brunsman, Stone, and Fisher, eds., *Border Crossings*. David Lee Poremba, ed., *Detroit in Its World Setting: A Three Hundred Year Chronology, 1701–2001* (Detroit: Wayne State University Press, 2001).

4. David M. Katzman, *Before the Ghetto: Black Detroit in the Nineteenth Century* (Urbana: University of Illinois Press, 1973). Reginald R. Larrie, *Makin' Free: African-Americans in the Northwest Territory* (Detroit: Blaine Ethridge Books, 1981). Norman McRae, "Blacks in Detroit, 1736–1833: The Search for Freedom and Community and Its Implications for Educators" (Ph.D. diss., The University of Michigan, Ann Arbor, 1982). Swan, *Lisette*. Swan is also the author of a lengthy local history of Grosse Ile: Swan, *Deep Roots*. Mark F. McPherson, *Looking for Lisette: In Quest of an American Original* (Dexter, MI: Mage Press, 2001). Christian Crouch, "The Black City: African and Indian Exchange in Pontiac's Detroit," revised version of Christian Crouch, "The Black City: Detroit and the Northeast Borderlands through African Eyes in the Era of 'Pontiac's War,'" The War Called Pontiac's Conference, April 5, 2013, Philadelphia, PA, 1–2.

5. Frost and Tucker, eds., *A Fluid Frontier*. Gregory Wigmore, "Before the Railroad: From Slavery to Freedom in the Canadian-American Borderland," *Journal of American History* 98:2 (2011): 437–54.

6. Eric Foner, *Gateway to Freedom: The Hidden History of the Underground Railroad* (New York: W. W. Norton, 2015). Stephen Kantrowitz, *More Than Freedom: Fighting for Black Citizenship in a White Republic, 1829–1889* (New York: Penguin, 2012). Manisha Sinha, *The Slave's Cause: A History of Abolition* (New Haven: Yale University Press, 2016), 9.

7. Brian Leigh Dunnigan, *Frontier Metropolis: Picturing Early Detroit, 1701–1838* (Detroit: Wayne State University Press, 2001). Cangany, *Frontier Seaport.* The three-hundred-year chronology by David Lee Poremba has also been central to the reimagining of Detroit as a diverse and complex settlement. David Lee Poremba, ed., *Detroit in Its World Setting: A Three Hundred Year Chronology, 1701–2001* (Detroit: Wayne State University Press, 2001). Silas Farmer, *History of Detroit and Wayne County and Early Michigan: A Chronological Cyclopedia of the Past and Present* (1890; reprint, Detroit: Gale Research Company, 1969). Clarence M. Burton, ed., *The City of Detroit Michigan: 1701–1922* (Detroit-Chicago: The S.J. Clarke Publishing Company, 1922).

8. Cooper, "The Fluid Frontier," 130.

9. In my use of the term "refusal" here and elsewhere in this book I am drawing mainly from the theoretical work of anthropologist Audra Simpson, who has interrogated the U.S.-Canada border as it has shaped the political and familial lives of Mohawk people in the community of Kahnawake. A key concept that I draw from Simpson is that even while taking into account the many costs and compromises, indigenous people have refused to be defined in static ways by settler states; therefore, the meaning and future of Euro-American and Euro-Canadian political borders on present and former indigenous lands are far from settled. Simpson calls a stance that rejects state "recognition" a politics of "refusal." Audra Simpson, *Mohawk Interruptus: Political Life Across the Border of Settler States* (Durham, NC: Duke University Press, 2014); see especially pp. 7, 11–12, chapter 4. I am also drawing from the work of Beth Piatote, a literary scholar who examines reactions to forced domesticities and competing nationalisms in the work of Pauline Johnson and others during the "assimilation" policy period. Beth H. Piatote, *Domestic Subjects: Gender, Citizenship, and Law in Native American Literature* (New Haven, CT: Yale University Press, 2013), 17, 26.

10. Visit the Detroit Historical Museum at http://detroithistorical.org/detroit-historical-museum/plan-your-visit/general-information. The Detroit Historical Museum is run by the Detroit Historical Society: http://detroithistorical.org. Shawna Mazur, a ranger at the River Raisin Battlefield, has researched and published on the black militia and shared her work with the public, park staff, and visitors. In 2009, reenactor Xavier Allen portrayed a black militia member at the River Raisin Battlefield Commemoration. His photo is featured and captioned in Shawna Mazur's essays. Shawna Mazur, "In Support of America and Freedom: The Establishment of the First Black Militia," *Monroe Evening News* (February 2010); Shawna Mazur, "Slavery and the Black Militia," *River Raisin News & Dispatch,* Newsletter of the Monroe County Historical Museum, Monroe County Historical Commission & Monroe County Historical Society (July/August/September 2009). Visit the River Raisin Battlefield at: https://www.nps.gov/rira/index.htm.

11. Richard White, *The Middle Ground: Indians, Empires, and Republics in the Great Lakes Region, 1650–1815* (New York: Cambridge University Press, 1991), x. For more studies that focus on Native history in the Great Lakes and Midwest as a

borderland, see Michael Witgen, *An Infinity of Nations: How the Native New World Shaped Modern North America* (Philadelphia: University of Pennsylvania Press, 2013); John P. Bowes, *Exiles and Pioneers: Eastern Indians in the Trans-Mississippi West* (Cambridge: Cambridge University Press, 2007); Alan Taylor, *The Divided Ground: Indians, Settlers, and the Northern Borderland of the American Revolution* (New York: Vintage, 2006); Daniel P. Barr, ed. *The Boundaries Between Us: Natives and Newcomers along the Frontiers of the Old Northwest Territory, 1750–1850* (Kent, OH: Kent State University Press, 2006); Karl S. Hele, ed., *Lines Drawn Upon the Water: First Nations and The Great Lakes Borders and Borderlands* (Waterloo, Ontario: Wilfrid Laurier University Press, 2008). For work that treats the Detroit River as a borderland region, see Wigmore, "Before the Railroad," 437–54; Lisa Philips Valentine and Allan K. McDougall, "Imposing the Border: The Detroit River from 1786 to 1807," *Journal of Borderlands Studies*, Special Issue: The Canadian-American Border: Toward a Transparent Border? 19:1 (2004): 13–22. For work that sees the Midwest as a borderland for African American history, see Matthew Salafia, "Searching for Slavery: Fugitive Slaves in the Ohio River Valley Borderland, 1830–1860," *Ohio Valley History* 8:4 (Winter 2008): 38–63; Gary Knepp's *Freedom's Struggle: A Response to Slavery from Ohio's Borderlands* (Milford, OH: Little Miami Publishing Co., 2008). For treatments of social exchange and development in the Midwest borderlands, also see Elizabeth A. Perkins, *Border Life: Experience and Memory in the Revolutionary Ohio Valley* (Chapel Hill: University of North Carolina Press, 1998); James Z. Schwartz's, *Conflict on the Michigan Frontier: Yankee and Borderland Cultures, 1815–1840* (DeKalb, IL: Northern Illinois University Press, 2009).

12. White raises and then critiques an aquatic metaphor in his introduction to *The Middle Ground*. He suggests that the story of white-Indian relations has often been told as a story of the sea (representative of Europeans) repeatedly smashing into a rock (representative of American Indians) like a relentless, inevitable storm. White explains that this is a simplistic metaphor of European advancement and Native assimilation (or, in more progressive histories, Native persistence) that he will strive to avoid; White, *Middle Ground*, ix.

13. Heidi Bohaker closely examines pictographs representing Anishinaabe clans (often used as signatures on treaties) to build an argument that troubles Richard White's representation of the Great Lakes. Bohaker shows that Native people were accustomed to a mobile lifestyle and maintained a clan system and out-marriage structure that meant they had relatives across the region. These groups, she argues, could therefore not be "refugees" with nowhere to go after conflicts and wars. In addition, she asserts that a focus on the "middle ground" fixes our attention on cultural exchange rather than on indigenous cultural formations and practices; Heidi Bohaker, "'Nindoodemag': The Significance of Algonquian Kinship Networks in the Eastern Great Lakes Region, 1600–1701," *The William and Mary Quarterly*, Third Series, 63:1 (January 2006): 23–52. In his broad study of Ottawa influence in and on the Great Lakes, Michael McDonnell chooses to limit his use of the middle ground frame to military forts, making

the point that beyond these dispersed spaces of European or American influence, Native people controlled the terms of interaction. McDonnell also offers a strong overarching dissent from Richard White's characterization of the Great Lakes region, taking issue with White's assessment that the inhabitants were "shattered" groupings of indigenous people in the aftermath of trade wars. McDonnell, *Masters of Empire*, 14, 333, note 6. Andrew Lipman takes a humorous approach to situating and unseating White's argument through a review of several works; Andrew Lipman, "No More Middle Grounds?" *Reviews in American History* 44:1 (March 2016): 24–30.

14. In the use of the term "groundless," I have borrowed from my colleague Greg Dowd, who plays rhetorically with the slate of Native American history text titles that implicitly reflect on Richard White's phrase, "middle ground." Gregory Evans Dowd, *Groundless: Rumors, Legends and Hoaxes on the Early American Frontier* (Baltimore: Johns Hopkins University Press, 2015).

15. White, *Middle Ground*, ix. In her sweeping study of French and Indian families engaged in the western fur trade, Anne Hyde captures the influence and longevity of mixed-race networks. She describes these mixed-race families as making up one of "three worlds" or "three streams" next to the white and Native worlds identified by Richard White. Although she does illuminate people often rendered invisible, like White, Hyde does not explore a black world, or even a world of enslaved Indians. Elite mixed-race families make for compelling objects of study, but, as Hyde notes, they were also people of privilege who owned others as slaves. Her work is an indication that even when we turn to the rubric of "family" as a means of powerfully illuminating the histories of marginalized people—particularly women—we can miss other groups who were oppressed by the very subpopulations that our work unearths. Building on White's and Hyde's formulation of European, Native, and mixed-race Euro-Indian worlds, I point to a world of the unfree on which these other worlds relied for strength and standing. Hyde, *Empires*, 1, 3. Brett Rushforth's broad and insightful study of slavery in New France focuses almost wholly on Native American slaves. Brett Rushforth, *Bonds of Alliance: Indigenous and Atlantic Slaveries in New France* (Chapel Hill: University of North Carolina Press, 2012). As I worked toward this picture of the shared world of bondspeople, I found conversation partners in studies on New England slavery; see, Daniel R. Mandell, "The Saga of Sarah Muckamugg: Indian and African American Intermarriage in Colonial New England," in Martha Hodes, ed., *Sex, Love, Race: Crossing Boundaries in North American History* (New York: New York University Press, 1999), 72–90; Margaret Newell, *Brethren by Nature: New England Indians, Colonists, and the Origins of American Slavery* (Ithaca: Cornell University Press, 2015); Wendy Warren, *New England Bound: Slavery and Colonization in Early America* (New York: W. W. Norton, 2016).

16. Jennifer Kirsten Stinson, "Black Bondspeople, White Masters and Mistresses, and the Americanization of the Upper Mississippi River Valley Lead District," *Journal of Global Slavery* 1:2 (October 2016), pp. 165–195. Christian Crouch, "The Black City: African and Indian Exchange in Pontiac's Detroit," revised version

of Christian Crouch, "The Black City: Detroit and the Northeast Borderlands through African Eyes in the Era of 'Pontiac's War,'" The War Called Pontiac's Conference, April 5, 2013, Philadelphia, PA, 20–21. Michael Witgen, book manuscript in progress, "Native Sons: Indigenous Land, Black Lives, and the Political Economy of Plunder in North America."

17. Frederick Jackson Turner, *The Significance of the Frontier in American History* (Madison: State Historical Society of Wisconsin, 1894).

18. Ira Berlin, *Generations of Captivity: A History of African American Slaves* (Cambridge, MA: Harvard University Press, 2003), 153, 154, 182, 188, 192, 198.

19. Lea VanderVelde, *Redemption Songs: Suing for Freedom before Dred Scott* (New York: Oxford University Press, 2014), 16.

20. William Cronon, *Nature's Metropolis: Chicago and the Great West* (New York: W.W. Norton, 1991), xviii–xix.

21. John Mack Faragher, "'More Motley than Mackinaw': From Ethnic Mixing to Ethnic Cleansing on the Frontier of the Lower Missouri, 1783–1833, in Andrew R. L. Cayton and Fredrika Teute, eds., *Contact Points: American Frontiers from the Mohawk Valley to the Mississippi, 1750–1830* (Chapel Hill: University of North Carolina Press, 1998), 304–326, 305. Faragher borrows the notion of "frontiers of inclusion" from geographer Marvin W. Mikesell. For more on cross-cultural relations in the Old Northwest, see Daniel P. Barr, ed., *The Boundaries Between Us: Natives and Newcomers along the Frontiers of the Old Northwest Territory, 1750–1850* (Kent, OH: Kent State University Press, 2006).

22. A slate of field-changing twenty-first century works that can be categorized as a new incarnation of the "New Indian History," or, as the University of Michigan doctoral student Harold Walker Elliott has termed it, the "Power School" of Indian history, has explored Native empire, power, and influence in the seventeenth, eighteenth, and nineteenth centuries. See, for instance, McDonnell, *Masters of Empire*; Kathleen DuVal, *The Native Ground: Indians and Colonists at the Heart of the Continent* (Philadelphia: University of Pennsylvania Press, 2006); Pekka Hämäläinen, *The Comanche Empire* (New Haven, CT: Yale University Press, 2008); Witgen, *Infinity of Nations*.

23. Max L. Grivno, "'Black Frenchmen' and 'White Settlers': Race, Slavery, and the Creation of African-American Identities along the Northwest Frontier, 1790–1840," *Slavery and Abolition* 21:3 (December 2000): 75–93, 76, 78, 85. Grivno cites examples from Minnesota and Wisconsin where black men claimed a "white" self-identification and were defined as white for a time by territorial organizers, "Black Frenchmen," 85, 89; Michael Witgen explores this dynamic in Minnesota at length in his manuscript in progress, *Native Sons*. In Detroit over the time period of my study, I found no examples of black residents stating that they were "white" or wishing to be seen as such. Zainab Amadahy and Bonita Lawrence, "Indigenous Peoples and Black People in Canada: Settlers or Allies?" In Arlo Kempf, ed., *Breaching the Colonial Contract: Anti-Colonialism in the US and Canada* (New York: Springer, 2009), 121, 120. Jodi A. Byrd, *The Transit of Empire:*

Indigenous Critiques of Colonialism (Minneapolis, MN: University of Minnesota Press, 2011), xxx. Byrd credits the Caribbean (Barbadian) poet Kamau Brathwaite with the origination of this term, xix.

24. Tiya Miles, email correspondence with Jill Mackin (doctoral candidate, Montana State University) and Crystal Alegria (co-director, The Extreme History Project), March 17 and 18, 2017. Quoted material is taken from Alegria's email, March 18, 2017. Prominent historian of the Black West Quintard Taylor also uses the term "refugee," but more often attached to wartime experience and without an explicit critique of Native land dispossession. Taylor frequently uses "pioneers" and "settlers" to describe black migrants. It is important to note that his work predates the currently common critical discussions of settler colonialism in Native American and indigenous studies. Quintard Taylor, *In Search of the Racial Frontier: African Americans in the American West, 1528–1990* (New York: W.W. Norton, 1998). For an illuminating analysis of comparative racialization and settler colonialism, see Patrick Wolfe, "Land, Labor, and Difference: Elementary Structures of Race," *The American Historical Review* 106:3 (June 2001): 866–905. For an innovative use of "refugee" reflective of current events, see David Blight, "Frederick Douglass, Refugee," *The Atlantic*, February 7, 2017.

25. Amadahy and Lawrence, "Indigenous Peoples and Black People in Canada," 120.

26. The historian Roy Finkenbine of the University of Detroit Mercy has compiled a three-page list of primary and secondary sources related to Indians and the Underground Railroad in the Midwest. He is working on a chapter based on his findings, which will appear in the edited collection-in-progress: Damian Pargas, ed., *Fugitive Slaves in North America* (University Press of Florida). For a slave narrative that features Native collaboration, see especially Josiah Henson, *The Life of Josiah Henson, Formerly a Slave* (Boston: Arthur D. Phelps, 1849). Manuscripts and dissertations related to this topic are underway by Natalie Joy, at Northern Illinois University, who is working on a book titled "Abolitionists and Indians in the Antebellum Era," and by Darryl Omar Freeman at Washington State University, who is working on a dissertation titled "The First Freedom Line." I have made short forays into this area; see Tiya Miles, "Of Waterways and Runaways: Reflections on the Great Lakes in Underground Railroad History," *Michigan Quarterly Review* (Summer 2011); Tiya Miles, "'Shall Woman's Voice Be Hushed?' Laura Smith Haviland in Abolitionist Women's History," *Michigan Historical Review* (Winter 2013). Bohaker, "'Nindoodemag,'" 52.

Index